JOHN W. WHI

THE CHANGE
MANIFESTO

JOIN THE BLOCK BY BLOCK MOVEMENT
★ ★ ★ TO REMAKE AMERICA ★ ★ ★

SOURCEBOOKS, INC.
NAPERVILLE, ILLINOIS

© 2008 by John W. Whitehead
Cover and internal design © 2008 by Sourcebooks, Inc.
Cover Design by The DesignWorks Group, Tim Green
Author photo © Jen Fariello

Sourcebooks and the colophon are registered trademarks of Sourcebooks, Inc.

Published by Sourcebooks, Inc.
P.O. Box 4410, Naperville, Illinois 60567-4410
(630) 961-3900
Fax: (630) 961-2168
www.sourcebooks.com

Library of Congress Cataloging-in-Publication Data
Whitehead, John W.
 The change manifesto : join the block by block movement to remake
America / John W. Whitehead.
     p. cm.
 Includes bibliographical references and index.
 1. Civil rights--United States. 2. United States--Politics and govern-
ment. I. Title.
 JC599.U5W524 2008
 323.0973--dc22
                                    2008015075

              Printed and bound in the United States of America.
                   BG 10 9 8 7 6 5 4 3 2 1

To
Carol Whitehead
and
Nisha Mohammed

The following people assisted me in one way or another in putting this book together. Carol Whitehead, my wife, typed my words and offered numerous suggestions. Nisha Mohammed, my assistant, provided valuable insight and offered many ways to sharpen the message of this book. Dave Caddell's research assistance was appreciated. Hillel Black's guidance and editorial suggestions made this a better book. Carol Mann, my agent, was instrumental in getting this book published.

Also assisting were Joe Kasl, Peggy Grimm, Rachel Saunders, Christopher Moriarty, Rob Luther, Christina Arenas, Margaret Hettinger, Tanvi Parmar, Andrea Niculescu, Elijah Haahr, Christopher Thompson, Matt Anderson, Adam Jantzi, Joel Whitehead, Garrett Sawyer, Eleanor Porter, Danielle Kim, and Difie Osborne.

Last, but not least, thanks to Nat Hentoff for his encouragement over the years.

Contents

We Are Not What
We Set Out to Be

As nightfall does not come all at once, neither does op-pression. In both instances, there is a twilight when everything remains seemingly unchanged. And it is in such twilight that we all must be most aware of change in the air—however slight—lest we become unwitting victims of the darkness.

—William O. Douglas, U.S. Supreme Court Justice

The year was 1961, and I was fourteen years old, the only child of blue-collar workers living in Peoria, Illinois. I was young, poor, and lacking any great understanding of the winds of change that were blowing through our nation and the world. Even so, I found myself transfixed as I huddled in front of our small black-and-white television to watch John F. Kennedy deliver his inaugural address as the nation's 35th president. The sound might have crackled and the picture wavered, but Kennedy's message came through loud and clear. It was a message of hope, challenge, and faith in an America that could be a beacon of freedom to the rest of the world.

Kennedy called us the "heirs of that first revolution" and spoke of rights that come not from the state but from God. "Let the word go forth," he said, "that the torch has been passed to a new generation of Americans—born in this century, tempered by war, disciplined by a hard and bitter peace, proud of our ancient heritage—and unwilling to witness or permit the slow undoing of those human rights to which this Nation has always been committed, and to which we are committed today at home and around the world."[1]

Suddenly I realized that he was not talking to my parents or my teachers or the cop on the beat: he was talking to me. Everything in me wanted to be part of an America that was a champion of justice and a model of virtue. I longed to be part of making that dream a reality. It was a pivotal moment in my life, one that eventually led me to seek out a career in constitutional law.

When Kennedy called on Americans to "bear the burden of a long twilight struggle" to defend freedom in its hour of maximum danger, I never would have guessed how long that twilight would last—or that almost half a century later, we, the American people, would come to represent the gravest threat to our freedoms through our apathy, ignorance, and indifference.

The world is a very different place from when I was a teenager. We undeniably live in perilous, uncertain times. Our nation is plagued by perpetual war. An erratic economy. Shadowy enemies bent on terrorizing us. Increasingly aggressive government agencies. An appalling literacy rate. A populace with little understanding of history or the United States Constitution. Porous borders with countless illegal immigrants flowing over them. Ravaging natural disasters. A monstrous financial deficit. Armed forces pushed to their limit, spread around the globe.

We are embroiled in wars in Afghanistan and Iraq against a rebel enemy that seems to attack from nowhere. Our country is both ideologically and politically fractured. America's credibility around the world is at an all-time low. And I am not alone in believing that we may be only one terrorist attack away from becoming a military state.

All of this has contributed to a general air of cynicism, pessimism, and despair. According to a *Time/CNN* poll, 59 percent of Americans believe that the end-times prophecies found in the Book of Revelation—all of which end in massive violence and mayhem—are going to come true.[2] This negative view of the future was magnified by the terrorist attacks of September 11, 2001, when the unthinkable became our worst nightmare and our way of thinking about our freedoms and way of life was forever altered.

Since then, the rights enshrined in the Constitution, particularly those in the Bill of Rights, have come under constant attack. Governmental tentacles now invade virtually every facet of our lives, with agents of the government listening in on our telephone calls and reading our emails. Technology, which has developed at a rapid pace, offers those in power more invasive, awesome tools than ever before. The groundwork has been laid for a new kind of government where it will no longer matter if you're innocent or guilty, whether you're a threat to the nation or even if you're a citizen. What will matter is what the president—or whoever happens to be in power at the time—thinks. And if you're considered a threat to the nation, you'll be locked up with no access to the protections our Constitution provides. You will, in effect, disappear. Some already have.

Sadly, few Americans seem worried. More than once I've heard it said, "I'm a law-abiding citizen. I have nothing to worry about." While that statement might have been true at one time, we are now operating under a system of government where everyone is suspect. No longer do Americans have a clear sense of what it means to be a free people. Nor does it seem as if many of us even care.

BOBBLEHEADS IN BUBBLELAND

We have changed.

Consequently, the light of that once bright and shining city on a hill has dimmed. Americans, says journalist and author Nicholas von Hoffman, are living in a glass dome, a kind of terrarium, cut off from both reality and the outside world. In his words, they are "bobbleheads in Bubbleland....They shop in bubbled malls, they live in gated communities, and they move from place to place breathing their own, private air in the bubble-mobiles known as SUVs."[3]

We are besieged by technological gadgets, which, while they have succeeded in creating numerous conveniences for our already busy lives, have also managed to fully occupy our attention, distracting us from meaningful discourse about issues of national and international significance.

America currently spends in excess of $40 billion annually on public education.[4] Yet the numbers are undeniable: in comparing the literacy level of adults in seventeen industrialized countries, America was number ten on the list. And sixteen- to twenty-five-year-olds under-perform their foreign counterparts as well. Moreover, they do so to a greater degree than do Americans over forty.[5]

The number of Americans who read books has also steadily declined. As a recent National Endowment for the Arts report titled "Reading at Risk" found, many Americans do not ordinarily read voluntarily (that is, matter not required for work or school), and only 57 percent of American adults read a book in 2002.[6] When they do read, it is often fiction or books that focus on narcissistic themes such as diet and self-help.

Millions of adults are lacking the most rudimentary knowledge about history and world geography, such as the identity of America's enemy in World War II. In fact,

> *one reads that 11 percent of young adults can't find the United States on a world map, and that only 13 percent of them can locate Iraq. It turns out that only 12 percent of Americans own a passport, that more than 50 percent were (prior to the fall of the Berlin Wall) unaware that Germany had been split into eastern and western sectors in the aftermath of World War II, and that 45 percent believe that space aliens have visited the earth. As in the Middle Ages, when most individuals got their "understanding" of the world from a mass source—i.e., the Church—most Americans get their 'understanding' from another mass source: television.[7]*

Television, however, has been a poor teacher. Television news has become a function of entertainment to such an extent that political and historical analysis typically amounts to two- to three-minute sound bites. With such shallow content, it is easy to see why, on the eve of the 2004 presidential election and despite overwhelming evidence to the contrary, 42 percent of Americans believed Saddam Hussein was involved in the September 11 attacks and 32 percent believed he had personally planned them.[8] No wonder the average American's understanding of politics is generally reduced to a few slogans picked up the day before from broadcast news or late-night comedy shows.

There is truth in the adage that civilizations do not die from being attacked or invaded. They do themselves in. Americans today have come to embody what the renowned eighteenth-century philosopher Friedrich Nietzsche termed "stupidity." Nietzsche was not referring to an intelligent quotient or ignorance, per se; rather, he meant stupidity as in mentally clogged, anesthetized, numb. As author and professor Thomas de Zengotita recognizes: "He thought people at the end of the nineteenth century were suffocating in a vast goo of meaningless stimulation."[9]

The same could be said of Americans at the dawn of the twenty-first century. We, too, are mentally clogged, anesthetized, numb. Connected to our cell phones, computers, and television sets, we are increasingly disconnected from each other. Even when physically crowded together at concerts and sports spectacles, we fail to truly communicate with one another. According to author Alex Marshall, Americans live "in one of the loneliest societies on the earth."[10]

THE LOSS OF COMMUNITY

To a large degree, we have lost our sense of community.

This precipitous decline in community, as documented in Harvard University professor Robert Putnam's appropriately titled book *Bowling Alone*, began in the last quarter of the twentieth century.[11] As community groups started to disappear, Americans became drastically disconnected from family, friends, neighbors, and social structures. "Church groups, union membership, dinners at home with friends, bridge clubs—all have been decimated. By 1993, the number of Americans who attended one public meeting on town or school affairs during the previous year was down 40 percent from what it had been twenty years before that time."[12] In the mid-1970s, Americans entertained friends at home an average of fourteen to fifteen times per year. By the late 1990s, that figure had dropped 45 percent.[13]

This loss of community has given rise to a "bystander effect" that allows us to view the world around us from a distance, no longer compelled to get involved in matters that do not directly impact us, even when someone is in peril. An incident that occurred in July 2007 illustrates the gravity of the problem. According to police, as a stabbing victim lay dying on the floor of a Kansas convenience store, five shoppers, including one who stopped to take a picture of the victim with a cell phone, stepped over the woman. "It was tragic to watch," said a police spokesman. "The fact that people were more interested in taking a picture with a cell phone and shopping for snacks rather than helping this innocent young woman is, frankly, revolting." The victim, only twenty-seven years old, later died at the hospital from her injuries. "The lack of concern for humanity over this young woman's life is deeply troubling," a policeman noted. [14]

Moreover, the rise of corporatism has negatively impacted community life. Corner groceries and drug stores, owned by people who actually work and live in the community, have all but disappeared. In their place, huge commercial chain stores and multinational outlets have not only eradicated mom-and-pop businesses, they have created a cultural landscape of blandness where, no matter in what city or state you happen to find yourself, everything is the same. Shopping malls are now America's most distinctive public space. But mall culture is not community.

Rejecting community in favor of self-gratification and isolation, we have in essence become an atomistic society, a characteristic of emerging totalitarian societies. Atomistic societies form pseudo-communities in times of perceived crisis, which we briefly saw in the wake of 9/11. But as Michigan State University professor Darren W. Davis recognizes, that did not last long: "People stopped giving to charities and volunteering. American flags displayed in front of homes and patriotic bumper stickers disappeared. Church attendance returned to pre-September 11 numbers, and old animosities resurfaced." [15]

The illusion of community faded. What did not fade, however, was our tendency to be easily led by our fears, especially in times of real or perceived crisis.

ACCOMPLICES IN TERROR

Just before his historic broadcast on McCarthyism, which ravaged 1950s' American culture, the renowned television journalist Edward R. Murrow remarked to his staff, "No one can terrorize a whole nation, unless we are all his accomplices." [16]

Unfortunately, the American people have, for all intents and purposes, become accomplices in constructing their own prison. We have become a culture of fear—a nation divided. Heavily armed and barricaded in our homes, we fear our surroundings, our neighbors, and the encroaching world of terrorism. This is somewhat understandable because the government's system of alarms and alerts keeps the population in tension. All it takes is a color-coded alarm from the government to start the masses clamoring for greater security measures, even if it means relinquishing more of our freedoms.

Murrow's reminder to his viewers at the end of that unforgettable March 9, 1954, broadcast is appropriate for our fearful populace today:

> *We will not walk in fear, one of another. We will not be driven by fear into an age of unreason, if we dig deep in our history and our doctrine; and remember that we are not descended from fearful men. Not from men who feared to write, to speak, to associate, and to defend causes that were for the moment unpopular. This is no time for men...to keep silent, or for those who approve. We can deny our heritage and our history, but we cannot escape responsibility for the result. There is no way for a citizen of a republic to abdicate his responsibilities.*[17]

Despite this timeless warning, we have largely abdicated our responsibilities and allowed our fears to rule us, helped along in no small measure by the events of 9/11.

After the 9/11 attacks, government leaders and politicians naturally focused their efforts on shoring up the nation's security. A mere month and a half after 9/11, the structure for a new governmental scheme was in place. The initial phase included the passage of the massive 342-page USA Patriot Act, which most constitutional scholars consider one of the greatest assaults ever on civil liberties. Ramrodded through Congress by the Bush administration, the bill was passed in the U.S. House of Representatives a day after being introduced (with remarkably little debate and discussion) and in the U.S. Senate. Incredibly, few of the representatives had even read the legislation they were passing. Senator Russ Feingold (D-Wis.) cast the lone dissenting vote on October 25, 2001. President Bush then signed the bill into law on October 26.

New security proposals embodied by legislation such as the PATRIOT Act quickly transformed American society. Americans were warned that they would have to adjust to a new way of life—a new normal—and adjust they did. But the "new normal" came with a price. The adjustments initially took the form of excruciatingly long waits, pat-downs, and heightened security at airports, sporting events, and concerts. These necessary precautions, however, soon gave way to greater encroachments on our rights, some of which went unnoticed by the public at large. As Professor Davis writes, "American citizens would have to adjust to greater limitations on their civil liberties and freedoms through greater surveillance and monitoring of communications, racial and ethnic profiling, stricter immigration rules, and greater scrutiny of reading habits and financial records."[18] Moreover, "[t]he public would have to stomach violations of international laws protecting prisoners from abuse and torture."[19]

A number of Americans did stomach such violations, and some even justified the military actions that resulted in the horrific photographs that surfaced in April 2004 at Abu Ghraib prison. In one picture, a hooded man is standing on a box with electrical wires attached to various parts of his body ("the Statue of Liberty," as the Iraqis sardonically called it), which seemed to indicate that American troops had actually participated in the torture of Iraqi prisoners. As we later learned, the man, Satar Jabar, was nothing more than an accused car thief.

Despite no further attacks on American soil, the nation remained in a heightened state of alert. And soon the new normal—with its loss of freedom, heightened surveillance, and increased sense of vulnerability—began to feel more and more like life as usual, but with a new paradigm in place. As journalist Lisa Anderson observed: "Of all the changes in all the 9/11-related statistics amassing day by day, one of the greatest, and perhaps most lasting, is the abrupt introduction of Americans to feelings of insecurity, fear, and vulnerability to terrorism on their soil. In a space of hours, Americans learned for themselves what people in so many countries have known for years: No one truly is safe from terrorism."[20]

DANGER SIGNS

Many Americans have come to blindly believe that the government will ensure our safety (or at least provide the illusion of safety). But such gullibility comes at a steep price—the devaluation of our freedoms.

What we are presently grappling with is nothing new. The history of governments is that they inevitably overreach. And, if not deterred, they will impinge or eradicate freedom. That is not to say that those who run the government are necessarily evil. Their actions to the contrary, government officials are not malevolent people. They often operate from a misguided sense that whatever they do is for the greater good. Whether the motives were initially benevolent or otherwise, however, the point is that in the process of seeking perhaps even worthy goals, the foundational principles of freedom are being undermined in America.

None of this is a secret. The danger signs are all around us. Although some may heed the warnings, many more choose to look the other way. Indeed, how many of us take our freedoms for granted? How many, in moments of perceived peril or stress, would allow their rights to be taken away? How many have already decided that a temporary security is more important than freedom? How many dare speak up for those brave enough to voice their opposition to government policies? How many, when the basic principles of the Constitution and Bill of Rights are criticized as being too cumbersome or outdated, fail to speak up in their defense? How many Americans have even read the Constitution?

Americans have become much too complacent. A 2007 Pew Research Center survey found that although 65 percent of Americans are satisfied with their private lives, they are overwhelmingly pessimistic about their public institutions—only 25 percent indicated satisfaction with the state of the nation. Two-thirds believe the country is on the wrong track, and 60 percent think the next generation will be worse off than the current one.[21] Yet not much is being done to remedy the problems. As the Pew study indicates, Americans feel helpless to do anything about it. Worse, "[t]hey don't want a change that will upset the lives they have built for themselves." [22] They prefer to preserve their personal peace and affluence—two preeminent American values.

Even given their dissatisfaction with Congress and the president, many Americans continue to place their hopes in politics. There are those who naïvely believe that somehow the next president is going to alter the course of events. But seldom has that happened.

As government invariably oversteps its authority, Americans are faced with the pressing need to maintain the Constitution's checks against governmental power and abuse. After all, it was not idle rhetoric that prompted the framers of the Constitution to begin with the words "We the people."

We must remember that our freedoms were created with extraordinary care and foresight, but they were not meant simply for the moment. Our precious liberties were to be passed on to our descendants indefinitely. As the Preamble to the Constitution declares, the Constitution was drafted to "secure the blessings of liberty to ourselves and our posterity." Formally adopted on September 17, 1787, it has long served as the bulwark of American freedom. And we the citizens are entrusted as guardians of those freedoms. When we shirk that duty, we leave ourselves wide open for an authoritarian regime to rise to power, place restrictions on our freedoms, and usurp our right to govern ourselves.

Lest We Forget Ourselves

William Harlem Hale was a journalist, a broadcaster for Voice of America, and a trusted advisor to President Harry Truman. Writing in 1947, when America first emerged as the most powerful nation in the world, Hale saw the looming forces of "greed, bigotry, and inertia." He saw a country that could annihilate large portions of the world with a single bomb. He saw a world "accused of being overbearing and imperialistic" and a country where communities were feeling the divisiveness of modernity.[23] But Hale had a vision of the role that America should play in the world. This was a vision born out of his experiences in World War II.

Hale tells of entering the German concentration camp at Dachau in 1945, on the heels of a battalion of American liberators. He describes emaciated prisoners scouring the campgrounds for rags and bits of colored cloth to make crude national flags, even before they searched for food. Standing in the drizzling rain, these prisoners in the thousands listened to speeches from various national leaders in a ceremony of liberation. And then came the Americans:

> *An alley was made for the American commanding officer—a tall, gray-haired colonel who now climbed the platform, helmet in hand, and spoke a few words of greeting and fraternity. When he had finished, the great iron gate that the Nazis had built was swung open and three American soldiers marched in—a guard bearing the United States colors. They advanced toward the platform, and I thought they would climb up and mount our colors on it, impressively high. But at the last moment, upon the colonel's signal, they wheeled toward the assembled thousands, carried our flag into their midst, and placed it there with the banners borne by men in convict stripes from a dozen victim peoples. And at this there arose a shout—a general shout of brotherhood and joy that echoed around the sodden walls.*[24]

That moment, for Hale, captured the soul of America. "I thought as I came away: This is what we mean, this is what we are. Should we seem to be less than this—should we stand apart from the lowly, from the people oppressed for faith, from those who will not be bound—then, in spite of all our riches and our power, we are not what we set out to be. We were these people, we have led, and we can again lead, their common aspirations. If we forget this, we forget ourselves." [25]

When I first set out to write this book, I did so grimly, resolutely, and with a deep sadness at the ravages time and circumstances had wrought upon my beloved country. Though a few others and I remained determined to fight the growing authoritarianism, most Americans seemed to have forgotten what it once meant to be American. Few seemed to give a damn about our freedoms. My hope that we could turn things around had been all but extinguished. Thus, this book was to be a roadmap, an autopsy of sorts, of where we as a nation—and a people—had gone wrong.

But this is no longer the book I set out to write.

Change is in the air. Over time, I have begun to catch fleeting glimpses of America's once intrepid spirit among ragtag groups of dissenters scattered across the country, and I have found myself strangely buoyed. More and more Americans seem to be waking from a self-imposed sleep. If they do, and if they can be convinced to hope and care once again, then maybe—just maybe—we can remember what it is to be an American. And in remembering, perhaps we can preserve our own freedoms while once again being an example of freedom to the world. Thus, this book is intended as a freedom manual for those who are willing to ask what they can do for their country.

It feels good to be hopeful again. However, hope is not enough. We must face up to the grim realities of the day, realizing that reclaiming our liberties will entail sacrifice and hard work. There is no easy fix or magic formula. We can make significant progress in protecting our freedoms only if we are realistic. There can be no room for false optimism. Hoping that things will get better will only add fuel to the already raging fire. Doing something about it is our only recourse. We must get organized. We must use the valuable operatives given to us by the architects of the American republic: the Constitution.

There is work to be done. Let us begin.

CHAPTER ONE

A Government of Wolves

A nation of sheep will beget a government of wolves.

—Edward R. Murrow

America is a fundamentally different country than it was before 9/11. Many Americans now view their country with suspicion, and the way in which the government views them, its public institutions, and the Constitution has drastically changed. While most of us were busy attending to the daily routines of life, the government was transformed in such a way as to concentrate power in the executive branch and undermine our system of checks and balances.

Such escalating governmental power poses a clear and present danger to our civil liberties. "What is left that distinguishes us if not our constitutional values?" asked Nadine Strossen, president of the American Civil Liberties Union. "These values—freedom, liberty, equality and tolerance—are the very source of our strength as a nation and the bulwark of our democracy. They are what have permitted us to grow abundantly, and to absorb wave after wave of immigrants to our shores, reaping the benefits of their industrious energy. Now, we are in danger of allowing ourselves to be governed by our fears, rather than our values."[1] As constitutional attorney Bruce Fein, who served as associate deputy attorney general under President Ronald Reagan, recognizes, "The Founding Fathers understood that freedom was the rule, and government intervention to protect security and safety was the exception. There had to be a standard of need or urgency required in order to encroach on freedoms. The United States, post-9/11, has flipped that customary burden of proof. The greatest danger to our civil liberties is the argument that we do not have to think about whether the customary processes work and we can assume 9/11 created a brave new world."[2]

Empowered by such fears, the government continues to undermine our freedoms. What began with the passage of the USA PATRIOT Act in the fall of 2001 has snowballed into a massive assault on our constitutional freedoms, our system of government, and our fundamental philosophies and way of life. Enabled by a paper-tiger Congress, the federal government has repeatedly laid claim to a host of powers, among them the ability to use the military as a police force, spy on Americans, and detain individuals without granting them access to an attorney or the courts.

Many Americans, however, are unaware that the basic foundations of freedom are being systematically undermined. "The United States today is like a cruise ship on the Niagara River upstream of the most spectacular falls in North America," writes historian and best-selling author Chalmers Johnson. "A few people on board have begun to pick up a slight hiss in the background, to observe a faint haze of mist in the air or on their glasses, to note that the river current seems to be running slightly faster. But no one yet seems to have realized that it is almost too late to head for shore."[3]

Without realizing it, American citizens are constantly being watched. Surveillance cameras in schools, on street corners, and perched atop stoplights and in stores and malls are filming our every move. In 2006, Bellows Falls, Vermont, decided to place sixteen surveillance cameras—only three fewer than Washington DC—throughout their town. The stated purpose for the cameras was "crime prevention." This small community, which has only eight full-time police officers, used federal grant money to purchase and place the twenty-four-hour surveillance cameras at street intersections, a sewage plant, and in the town square.[4]

Political correctness now dominates the American psyche to the extent that people self-censor their thoughts—in the workplace, in public areas, and even in their homes. The logic seems to be that if someone is offended, we have no right to speak. Some librarians at Florida Gulf Coast University learned this when they were told not to wear stickers reading, "I'm proud to be an American." Their supervisor informed them that wearing the stickers while working might be offensive to the two hundred foreign students at the university in the aftermath of 9/11. Although the supervisor didn't object to the librarians wearing ribbons or flags, she stated that they should not wear things with words on them, insisting, "As a librarian, I want the highest respect for everyone coming to the desk."[5]

We tend to be suspicious of almost everyone, including our fellow citizens. People have reported their neighbors to government agencies, such as the FBI, simply for criticizing the government—a right guaranteed in the First Amendment. Investigations have followed, as was the case with sixty-year-old Barry Reingold. Shortly after 9/11, while at the gym one afternoon, Reingold expressed a negative view of the U.S. government's handling of the war in Afghanistan. Other gym members, overhearing Reingold's remarks, notified the FBI. A few days later, FBI agents knocking on the door awakened this Oakland, California, resident from his afternoon nap, wanting to know more about his locker room chat. Although the FBI insists that it does not investigate people for their political views, Reingold recalls the agents stating, "Someone's reported to us that you've been talking about what happened on 9/11 and terrorism and oil and Afghanistan."[6]

Derek Kjar found himself under investigation after he mentioned that he did not intend to harm President Bush with anything more than a vote for John Kerry in the November 2004 presidential election. Agents from the Secret Service paid Kjar a visit, telling him that his neighbors had alerted them to a potentially threatening bumper sticker on his car. The sticker, found on a number of websites, features a black-and-white likeness of Bush with a crown tilted slightly on his head. Under the image are the words, "KING GEORGE–OFF WITH HIS HEAD"—a reference to the infamous King George of colonial days. Although the message is protected political speech, Kjar didn't know that. Kjar said the two agents visited him at his job at a dry cleaning service, where they asked him if he had any ties to terrorist groups or enjoyed reading historical accounts of assassinations. They also asked Kjar about his friends and family and wanted to know how he paid his monthly rent. The agents finally left after

Kjar gave them the bumper sticker. Kjar said he feared the agents were going to "take me away."[7]

Under federal legislation passed in the wake of 9/11, businesses, banks, and schools have been harassed by government agents into handing over records of patrons, customers, and students. In the summer of 2005, the FBI demanded that the Library Connection, a group of twenty-six Connecticut libraries, turn over its patrons' library records. The demand was not accompanied with a search warrant, grand jury subpoena, or a court order, as our Constitution requires. The government instead used the USA PATRIOT Act's provision that permits federal agencies to obtain this information through so-called National Security Letters. Such letters are uniformly secret and amount to nonnegotiable demands for personal information—demands that are not reviewed in advance by a judge. In cases such as this, many American citizens under investigation are not even told the government is seeking their records.[8] In June 2007, an FBI audit revealed that FBI agents, under the aegis of National Security Letters, violated federal law over one thousand times while collecting data on such things as the domestic phone calls and emails of American citizens.[9]

American schools have become authoritarian in nature. Draconian zero-tolerance policies have resulted in suspensions and expulsions of children from school for possession of such things as Alka-Seltzer, Midol, and mouthwash and for participating in what used to be considered playtime activities. In March 2000, four kindergarten boys from Wilson Elementary School in Sayreville, New Jersey, were suspended for three days for playing a make-believe game of "cops and robbers" on the school playground, using their fingers as guns. The actions by Sayreville school officials are consistent with those of other school districts that have adopted such rigid policies. Common sense, it seems, has gone the way of the dinosaur.[10]

Even our homes aren't safe anymore. The number of incidents involving police officers crashing through doors to arrest people for minor offenses has grown to epidemic proportions, with countless citizens being injured or killed. Consider Alberta Spruill, who was literally scared to death. On the morning of May 16, 2003, based on a single informant's faulty information, New York City police invaded the Brooklyn home of the 57-year-old, churchgoing woman. Wrongly believing that it was a haven for guns and drugs, police battered down the front door, tossed a stun grenade into the room where Spruill was sitting, and, in the process, destroyed a glass-top table. Police then rushed in and handcuffed the screaming grandmother. After failing to uncover any drugs or weapons, police realized that their invasion had been a mistake, but it was too late for Spruill, who was so frightened that she died of a heart attack moments later.[11]

The threat to our homes isn't limited to the police. Corporations and public officials also pose a threat. Under the guise that private property is needed for public use, city governments—aligned with large corporate interests—are laying claim to private homes and personal property for development purposes. The city of New London, Connecticut, is a prime example of how the Constitution's eminent domain clause is being abused. Deciding that it needed to improve its local economy after a major corporation (Pfizer) moved into the neighborhood, city officials offered to purchase 115 residences in the rundown Fort Trumbull neighborhood in order to develop more attractive amenities, such as a resort hotel, a conference center, and retail complexes. When fifteen homeowners refused to sell, the city resorted to other means to acquire the remaining properties, specifically by calling on its power of eminent domain to force the owners to relinquish their homes. And in a 2005 decision, the U.S. Supreme Court upheld the taking of citizens' property by the city and corporate interests.[12]

Government secrecy has reached such epic proportions that there are secret proceedings and courts. An investigation by the Associated Press revealed that the names of more than 5,000 criminal defendants whose cases occupied our federal courts between 2003 and 2006 remain under wraps. Some cases are even put through the courts on a so-called "secret docket," which means that they are not made public and most are sealed. It is as if the cases and persons held by the police never existed. Most of these unnamed defendants are not suspected terrorists. They were arrested for drug-related or other crimes unrelated to our national security.[13]

Moreover, in clear violation of the Bill of Rights, American citizens have been detained without access to lawyers or to the courts. In May 2002, after stepping off a flight from Pakistan, U.S. citizen Jose Padilla was arrested at Chicago's O'Hare Airport on suspicion of planning to detonate a "dirty bomb." Labeled a so-called "enemy combatant," Padilla spent three years in military detention. Federal prosecutors did not even charge him with a crime until it seemed likely that the U.S. Supreme Court would hear his case and decide whether such detention of a U.S. citizen was lawful. In their indictment, prosecutors made no mention of the prior "dirty bomb" allegation—the initial reason Padilla was retained—and instead charged Padilla with aiding terrorists and conspiring to murder U.S. nationals overseas.[14]

The government has also announced its intentions to erect facilities to "contain" both citizens and noncitizens. In August 2002, then-Attorney General John Ashcroft voiced his desire to build detention camps on American soil. Under Ashcroft's plan, those labeled "enemy combatants" could be imprisoned indefinitely, with no access to the courts or other constitutional guarantees.[15] In January 2006, the federal government awarded a $385 million contract to KBR, a former subsidiary of megacorporation Halliburton, to construct detention centers across the United States. The government has justified the detention camps by stating that they are needed to deal with an emergency influx of immigrants into the United States and to support the rapid development of "new programs."[16] When and where the camps will be built is highly classified information.

The United States is the world's leader in incarceration (recently surpassing Russia), with a prison population exceeding two million inmates—one in every 136 U.S. residents—and prisons and jails locking up more than one thousand inmates each week in 2005.[17] Over the past twenty-five years, this number has quadrupled. Moreover, 13.5 million adults pass through our nation's prisons each year.[18] As a result, the United States spends an estimated $60 billion each year on corrections. There are at least two major factors that have contributed to this drastic rise in the prison population. One is the adoption of "three strikes laws" by politicians attempting to be tough on crime. These laws cause inmates to remain incarcerated for longer periods of time, often for minor felonies.[19] America's "war on drugs" has also caused an increasing number of citizens to serve time for drug offenses, some of which were once considered minor and entailed no jail time.

A CORPORATE STATE

There is a growing sense that our government leaders are not the only ones making the decisions. A July 2002 *New York Times/CBS News* poll revealed that 45 percent of Americans thought "other people are really running the government."[20]

Following World War II, President Dwight Eisenhower expressed concerns about an emerging military-industrial state in his farewell address to the nation. His fear was that powerful industrial and corporate business interests were coalescing into a new form of government, which would eventually become the corporate state. "The corporate state, American style, exemplifies a politico-legal form of syzygy," observed Arthur S. Miller as early as the mid-1970s.[21] Over time, this syzygy—the conjunction of two organisms without either of them losing its identity—has developed beyond what Miller, a constitutional law professor at George Washington University, could have imagined.

With the fusion of Big Business and Big Government into a corporate state, the president has become more powerful than ever. "The Chief Executive would neither ride the tiger nor try to steal its food; rather, he would be part of the tiger from the outset. The White House and the entire Chief Executive network would become the heart (and one of the brain centers) of the new business-government symbiosis," writes Bertram Gross, a presidential advisor to both the Truman and Roosevelt administrations. "Under these circumstances the normal practices of the Ultra-Rich and the Corporate Overlords would be followed: personal participation in high-level business deals and lavish subsidization of political campaigns, both expertly hidden from public view."[22]

Although this could be said of virtually every president since Franklin Delano Roosevelt, to some extent or other, George W. Bush's administration epitomized this corporate-governmental syzygy. Bush, whose career was shaped and fortunes boosted by the oil industry, was "part of the tiger" from the outset, with cabinet members hailing from the highest echelons of America's top automotive, oil, technology, investment, and pharmaceutical industries.[23] Dick Cheney spent five lucrative years as chief executive of Halliburton, the world's largest oil-and-gas services company, immediately before becoming vice president. "The conglomerate, which is based in Houston, is now the biggest private contractor for American forces in Iraq; it has received contracts worth some eleven billion dollars for its work there."[24]

Given the degree to which the corporate state has wedded itself to the military armaments industry, America's motives in carrying out its "war on terror," especially as it is played out in Iraq and Afghanistan, have come under intense scrutiny. "By all appearances, we invaded Iraq for the sake of American business," notes Professor Morris Berman of Catholic University. "Indeed, it would be hard to find a clearer (or more cynical) example of Dwight Eisenhower's military-industrial complex."[25] Alan Greenspan, the former head of the U.S. Federal Reserve, concluded, "I am saddened that it is politically inconvenient to acknowledge what everyone knows: the Iraq war is largely about oil."[26]

Some of our nation's more perceptive founders recognized the danger an inordinate amount of corporate influence can pose to governmental affairs. After the War of Independence, when Thomas Jefferson served as ambassador to France, he reported back on his difficulties with wealthy Americans: "Merchants are the least virtuous of citizens and possess the least amor patriae."[27] After serving two terms as president, Jefferson explained this phenomenon: "Merchants have no country. The mere spot they stand on does not constitute so strong an attachment as that from which they draw their gains."[28]

It is a strange, semantical world where the popular catch phrase "privatization" actually means the "corporatization" of American life. This explains the rapid disappearance of small, independent businesses as they are replaced by large corporate entities. The rise of the corporate state invests a disproportionate amount of power with the president, Congress, and a host of non-elected bureaucrats—all in contravention of the original vision for republican government. In its place is a ruling synchronistic oligarchy with a tendency to view the Constitution as something of an impediment to their increase in profits and power.

This rise in presidential power, and subsequent undermining of our constitutional freedoms, owes much to the government's mastery of propaganda and the people's willingness to believe unquestioningly whatever they are told by the government, especially in regard to clear and present dangers such as terrorist attacks. As Bertram Gross points out, only by wrapping himself around the trappings of the same imminent danger—the war on terrorism—and constitutionality could "the President succeed in subverting the spirit of the Constitution and the Bill of Rights."[29]

EXPERIMENTS ON OUR LIBERTIES

Appropriately dubbed the "father of the Constitution," James Madison warned that "it is proper to take alarm at the first experiment on our liberties. We hold this prudent jealousy to be the first duty of citizens, and one of [the] noblest characteristics of the late Revolution."[30] The American people have failed to heed this warning. We have fallen short in attending to our first duty as citizens to guard our freedoms jealously, thereby subjecting ourselves to untold experiments on our liberties. The amassing of presidential powers, especially so-called wartime powers, provides a perfect case study for how to gradually transform a republic such as ours into an authoritarian state.

Sworn into office as the 43rd president of the United States in January 2001, George W. Bush anointed himself as a wartime president in a struggle for civilization, fighting for "a free way of life against a new barbarism."[31] This perpetual war, such as it is, provided Bush with a convenient rationale for expanding presidential wartime powers. These powers permit the president to assume complete control over any and all aspects of an international war on terrorism, including torture of terrorist suspects who, if labeled as "enemy combatants," can be denied the right to have an attorney and appear in a court of law.

This increase in presidential power has largely been carried forward by way of presidential directives, executive orders, and stealth provisions, used as a means to lay claim to a host of unprecedented powers. Executive orders, which are treated as laws passed by Congress, remain on the books and can be used by future presidents. While executive orders can be challenged by lawsuits, repealed or modified by Congress, or repealed by a new executive order, seldom has this been done.

In the Bush presidency, executive orders have conferred on the president new and vast powers. A "presidential directive" issued in May 2007, for example, allows the president to assume control of the federal government following a "catastrophic event," such as an earthquake, hurricane, or another 9/11. In July 2007, Bush issued an executive order that authorized the government to freeze the financial assets of anyone who directly or indirectly aids someone who has committed or "poses a significant risk of committing" violent acts "threatening the peace or stability of Iraq."[32]

Yet as journalist Walter Pincus pointed out in the *Washington Post*, the text of the order, entitled "Blocking Property of Certain Persons Who Threaten Stabilization Efforts in Iraq," if interpreted broadly, "could cast a far bigger net to include not just those who commit violent acts or pose the risk of doing so in Iraq but also third parties—such as U.S. citizens in this country—who knowingly or unknowingly aid or encourage such people."[33] Furthermore, the language is so broad that ordinary Americans who oppose the Iraq war could find their names on the list of persons who are perceived to be undermining "efforts to promote economic reconstruction and political reform" in Iraq. When public support for a particular war plummets and the citizenry engages in more energetic and active protests, this could mean almost anyone.

Signing statements, used by presidents for decades as a way to thank supporters, provide reasons for signing a bill or express dissatisfaction or pleasure with Congress, have also been used as a way to sidestep the law. George W. Bush used these statements as a way of disregarding laws that he believed interfered with national security or limited the power of the president, essentially doing an end-run around congressionally enacted laws. In his first six years in office, President Bush issued at least 151 signing statements, challenging 1,149 provisions of laws. Over the history of the American republic, from 1789 to 2000, fewer than 600 signing statements that took issue with the bills were issued.[34] Among recent presidents, Ronald Reagan issued 71 statements challenging provisions of laws before him, George H. W. Bush issued 146, and Bill Clinton issued 105.[35] The most notorious of Bush's signing statements related to the so-called McCain Amendment to a 2005 defense authorization bill that barred the "cruel, inhuman, or degrading treatment or punishment" of detainees. The presidential statement raised serious questions about whether Bush intended to obey this new law.

Unfortunately, Congress has done little to prevent the executive branch's amassing of power. In the fall of 2006, prior to the elections that transformed the makeup of the formerly Republican Congress, the Bush administration advocated the inclusion of two stealth provisions into a mammoth 591-page defense budget bill. Congress passed the Defense Appropriations Act with little, if any, awareness of the impact the seemingly insignificant rider would have on American freedoms. Whether or not it was intended, these provisions succeeded in weakening what the *New York Times* refers to as "two obscure but important bulwarks of liberty,"[36] posse comitatus and the Insurrection Act of 1807, making it infinitely easier for the federal government to declare martial law and establish a dictatorship. As *Huffington Post* journalist Jane Smiley noted, "The introduction of these changes amounts, not to an attack on the Congress and the balance of power, but to a particular and concerted attack on the citizens of the nation. Bush is laying the legal groundwork to repeal even the appearance of democracy."[37]

The American people have long mistrusted the use of a national military force to intervene in civilian affairs except in instances of extreme emergency and for limited duration. This dates back to the founding of the country, when King George III used his armies to terrorize and tyrannize the colonies. Hence, as a sign of the founders' concern that the people not be under the power of a military government, control of the military was vested in a civilian government, with a civilian commander-in-chief. The Insurrection Act of 1807 limited a president's domestic use of the military to putting down lawlessness, insurrection, and rebellion where a state is violating federal law or depriving the people of their constitutional rights. (For a state to even consider staging a rebellion against the gargantuan federal bureaucracy would be unthinkable today.) And the Posse Comitatus Act of 1878 furthered the Constitution's safeguards against military law, making it a crime for the government to use the military to carry out arrests, searches, seizure of evidence, and other activities normally handled by a civilian police force.

More than a century later, these two protective acts were eviscerated with one sweep of the pen. Under the 2007 provisions to the defense budget approved by Congress, any president can use the military as a domestic police force in response to a natural disaster, disease outbreak, terrorist attack, or, in a catch-all, nebulous phrase, to any "other condition."[38] According to this law, the president doesn't even have to notify Congress of his intent to use military force against the American people—he just has to notify them once he has done so. At that point, a military takeover would be a fait accompli. The defense budget provision's vague language raises the dire possibility of governmental abuse.

What this means is that if martial law is declared and the military patrols the streets, the Constitution and freedoms guaranteed in the Bill of Rights will be suspended. They become null and void. A standing (or permanent) army—something that propelled the early colonists into revolution—strips the American people of any vestiges of freedom. Thus, if we were subject to martial law, there would be no rules, no protections, and no judicial oversight. "Justice" would be dispensed at the end of the barrel of a gun. Unless these provisions are repealed—which seems unlikely—this presidential power is set in stone for future administrations to use, and potentially abuse.

Yet all the blame cannot be ascribed to George W. Bush for pushing through this legislation. Congress also failed to uphold the Constitution. This failing has become a hallmark of too many of our elected representatives. As Jonathan Alter noted in *Newsweek*, right before leaving for their 2007 summer recess, Congress "sold out the

Constitution to cover their political rears while keeping the rest of us mostly in the dark."[39] Relenting to pressure from the White House, Congress passed the Protect America Act of 2007 (the title alone should be a warning), which authorizes open-ended surveillance of Americans' overseas phone calls and emails without the need for a warrant or security justification, thus bypassing the Fourth Amendment's provisions. As Aziz Huq writes in the *Nation*, it is "power without responsibility."[40]

Such power is rarely paraded before the public. It relies on subterfuge, secrecy, and propaganda for its strength. This explains President Bush's tendency to keep the public in the dark about federal policies and decisions and to suppress discussion of those policies, their underpinnings, and their implications. The Bush administration was one of the most secretive presidential administrations since that of Richard Nixon. This was the conclusion reached in the 2007 annual "report card" on government secrecy compiled by OpenThe-Government.org, a coalition of consumer groups, librarians, environmentalists, labor leaders, journalists, and others who seek to promote greater transparency in public institutions. The report card noted, "Government secrecy, particularly in the executive branch, continues to expand across a broad array of agencies and actions, including military procurement, new private inventions, and the scientific and technical advice that the government receives."[41]

In one example among many, the Bush administration on numerous occasions invoked the so-called "state secrets" privilege, which allows the president to withhold documents from the courts, Congress, and the public. At the height of the Cold War, presidents used the privilege only six times between 1953 and 1976. Since 2001, it has been used a reported thirty-nine times—an average of six times a year in six and a half years, or more than double the average (2.46) over the previous twenty-four years. As the report concludes, the Bush administration "increasingly refused to be held accountable to the public through the oversight responsibilities of Congress. These practices inhibit democracy and our representative government; neither the public nor Congress can make informed decisions in these circumstances. Our open society is undermined and made insecure."[42]

Such arbitrary, limitless, and worrisome power centralized in the executive branch raises many legitimate concerns, chief among them being the establishment of a historical precedent for presidential powers, Congress's weakened ability to influence wartime decisions, the loss of an independent judiciary able to protect fundamental rights, and, from a purely philosophical perspective, the undermining of sound public policy and logic. As Yale Law School Dean Harold Koh states, "The notion that the president has the constitutional power to permit torture is like saying he has the constitutional power to commit genocide."[43]

At the heart of these concerns is a grave sense of disquiet over the dissolution of the "rule of law." If any president has carte blanche to chart his course and set his own rules, not being bound by the legislative or judicial branches of government, that president is effectively "above the law"—in fact, he or she is the law. Although one would hope that political pressures would prevent a president from carrying this rationale to its extremes, history shows that it has happened before. And, at the very least, even slight encroachments on our commitment to abiding by the rule of law would, over time, place us on a slippery slope toward justifying such an action.

We would do well to remember that presidents do not relinquish power; nor is George W. Bush the only president to assume powers never contemplated by the framers. Yet President Bush must be credited with outfitting a toolbox of power for future presidents, which some will likely use, the Constitution be damned. As constitutional historian W. Taylor Reveley III wrote, "If we could find a man in the state of nature and have him first scan the war-power provisions of the Constitution and then look at war-power practice since 1789, he would marvel at how much Presidents have spun out of so little."[44]

LAYING THE GROUNDWORK

While governmental assaults on our freedoms have become much more invidious and overt in the years following the 2001 terrorist attacks, what James Madison termed as "experiments on our liberties" began long before that, as early as the embryonic American republic. The American government has been at war with the Bill of Rights virtually since its conception. Several examples stand out.

A few years after the Constitution was ratified, Congress passed the Alien and Sedition Acts. These four laws were aimed at suppressing political opposition. Under the presidency of John Adams, this resulted in the prosecution and conviction of various newspaper editors and printers. Thomas Jefferson opposed these laws as contradicting the Constitution and, upon becoming president, pardoned all those convicted under them.[45]

The Constitution endured, however, and even survived a civil war that nearly split the nation asunder. But more ominous threats to freedom emerged in the twentieth century when the country entered a near-constant state of war. As recently as the mid-twentieth century, a government at war—especially an all-encompassing war—had trouble relinquishing its war power.

During the McCarthy era of the 1950s, the government began rounding up Americans who were suspected of being Communists. The rise of intelligence and surveillance agencies such as the Central Intelligence Agency and the National Security Agency during the Cold War ensured that not only would external enemies be watched, but American citizens domestically would fall under the purview of government eyes. This period swept over into the 1960s, as the civil rights movement was gaining momentum. The FBI, it must be remembered, severely violated Martin Luther King Jr.'s personal privacy with invasive surveillance. King even received letters written by government agents suggesting that either he commit suicide or the details of his private life would be revealed to the public.[46]

During the Nixon administration, there was massive surveillance of American citizens. It persists today, given credence by President George W. Bush's authorization of the National Security Agency to spy on Americans by listening in on their telephone calls. Furthermore, we continue to see a massive buildup of the war power, which shows little sign of abating now that the United States has committed itself to a war that began with al-Qaeda and "will not end until every terrorist group of global reach has been found, stopped and defeated."[47] As President Bush stated in a speech in September 2001:

> *On September the 11th, enemies of freedom committed an act of war against our country. Americans have known wars—but for the past 136 years, they have been wars on foreign soil, except for one Sunday in 1941. Americans have known the casualties of war—but not at the center of a great city on a peaceful morning. Americans have known surprise attacks—but never before on thousands of civilians. All of this was brought upon us in a single day—and night fell on a different world, a world where freedom itself is under attack.*[48]

A different world, indeed. Little did we know that in the years to follow, our freedoms would come under repeated attack. And the absence of any further terrorist attacks may be the only thing keeping a possible military state at bay. Yet this is small consolation. As General Tommy Franks, commander of the American assault on Baghdad, predicted, another serious terrorist attack on the United States would "begin to unravel the fabric of our Constitution." Franks proclaimed that under such circumstances, "the Constitution could be scrapped in favor of a military form of government."[49]

Historian Kevin Baker fears that we are not far from the day when, like the Roman Senate in 27 BC, the United States Congress will take its last meaningful vote and turn over all power to a military dictator. "In the end, we'll beg for the coup," he wrote in 2003.[50]

WHAT IT MEANS TO BE AMERICAN

The issue is freedom. Freedom internally. Freedom domestically. As the paranoia and fear generated by the government in its ongoing war on terrorism continue, Americans are becoming more accustomed to, indeed conditioned to, the loss of more and more of their rights. Supreme Court Justice Thurgood Marshall spoke with great foresight about this crisis: "History teaches that grave threats to liberty often come in times of urgency, when constitutional rights seem too extravagant to endure. The World War II relocation cases, and the Red Scare and McCarthy-era internal subversion cases, are only the most extreme reminders that when we allow fundamental freedoms to be sacrificed in the name of real or perceived exigency, we invariably come to regret it."[51]

Much like animals in a zoo, many Americans have come to believe that the zookeeper is friendly. The greatest threat to our freedoms is not lurking outside our borders in the guise of foreign terrorists or some purported country in an "axis of evil." The real menace comes from within. The enemy is us—our government of wolves and we the sheep. And there is a lesson here. "Rome did not fall because her armies weakened," writes author Salman Rushdie, "but because Romans forgot what being a Roman meant."[52]

If America falls, it will be largely because many Americans have forgotten what it means to be American. Since our country's inception, America has been synonymous with the concept that there are certain individual rights and freedoms that no one, not even government agents, can violate. The foundational idea that individuals have an inherent right to "Life, Liberty, and the pursuit of Happiness" served as the springboard for the Bill of Rights as they were appended to the Constitution. If not for the freedoms enshrined in the first ten amendments to the Constitution—including the freedoms of speech, press, religion, and association, the right to assemble and petition the government for a redress of grievances, the right of one accused of a crime to a public jury trial, the right to an attorney and to be confronted by witnesses who have accused him, as well as the essential freedom from unreasonable search and seizure—the Constitution would indeed be a rather sterile document.

Absolute rights so precious that no government can violate them? What revolutionary thinking! And yet the early American colonists believed these particular principles were not only worth fighting for, they were worth dying for.

Thomas Jefferson, the author of the Declaration of Independence, said he intended the Declaration "to be an expression of the American mind."[53] But over the generations, it has become an expression of the ideals of all who seek fundamental human rights, which accompany human dignity. As the Declaration boldly proclaims: "We hold these truths to be self-evident, that all men are created equal, that they are endowed by their Creator with certain unalienable Rights, that among these are Life, Liberty, and the pursuit of Happiness." These were revolutionary ideas in an age of kings and serfdoms.

What are these self-evident, or universal, truths? All people must be treated equally before the law. No one, as Jefferson was later to say, is inferior to another. Shortly before his death in 1826, in the last letter he wrote, Jefferson said, "The mass of mankind has not been born with saddles on their backs, nor a favored few booted and spurred, ready to ride them legitimately, by the grace of God."[54]

All human beings are "endowed by the Creator with certain unalienable rights." People are entitled to such rights by "the laws of Nature and of Nature's God." A natural right is a claim to what one owns by birth or by way of one's nature as a human being. Natural rights are "unalienable" because they cannot be alienated or given away to someone else.

In order for a governmental power to be legitimate, it has to be conferred by the consent of the people. As the Declaration states, "That to secure these rights, Governments are instituted among Men, deriving their just powers from the consent of the governed." The presumption is that such consent is enlightened. As University of Dallas professor Thomas G. West and Hillsdale College professor Douglas A. Jeffrey recognize, "But while consent is necessary for government power to be legitimate, consent in itself is not the sole standard of legitimacy or goodness. That is, the people do not have the right to consent to unjust powers. Put another way: Just because the people have consented to something does not make it right. We may only rightly or justly consent to those powers of government that do not violate the unalienable rights of individuals."[55] And logically, consent has two aspects: consent in establishing government and a continuing consent in operating government.

Finally, the right to change or do away with a government that attempts to undermine these rights rests with the people. As the Declaration's statement of principles concludes, "Whenever any form of

Government becomes destructive of these ends, it is the Right of the People to alter or abolish it, and to institute new Government, laying its foundation on such principles and organizing its powers in such form, as to them shall seem most likely to effect their Safety and Happiness." The right to revolution, therefore, follows logically from these principles. Those who gave us the Declaration, however, knew that the "right to revolution does not mean that it is right or good to overthrow a government that is misbehaving in some ways but which is doing a tolerably decent job in most."[56] As the Declaration says, "Prudence, indeed, will dictate that Governments long established should not be changed for light and transient causes." "Prudence" is practical wisdom or good sense.

Jefferson and those who followed took it as a rule of thumb that political progress stems from dissent. Under the First Amendment, the people have a right to dissent and to participate in civil disobedience if necessary. Activists such as Martin Luther King Jr., who forged the civil rights of African Americans, put Jefferson's revolutionary thinking into action nearly two hundred years later. King understood that in order to protect our rights, the people have a right to dissent and, if necessary, to participate in civil disobedience.

U.S. Supreme Court Justice Earl Warren once wrote that dissent, as such, "should be an honored word, and all citizens should be encouraged to engage in it. The opposite of dissent is conformity, and nothing could be more deadly than to have conformity for the sake of conformity."[57] These words are particularly relevant today.

Nevertheless, Jefferson understood that there are times when even dissent is not enough. Governments are brought into being to protect our inherent rights. When they systematically violate such liberties, however, the people have a right—nay, a duty—to revolt. This was the true spirit of 1776 that moved the American colonists to rebel against a government that was violating their rights. This willingness to stand and fight was what it meant to be an American in our nation's early years.

Fast-forward two hundred years, and we seem to have lost sight of that spirit of 1776. Case in point: In Indianapolis, a group of students showed copies of the Declaration of Independence to several hundred people and asked them to sign it. Most refused, stating that it sounded rather "dangerous."[58] In July 1975, the People's Bicentennial Commission passed out copies of the Declaration of Independence in downtown Denver without identifying it. Only one in five persons recognized the document. One man remarked, "There is so much of this revolutionary stuff going on now. I can't stand it."[59]

CONSTITUTIONAL ILLITERACY

Americans once had their heads full of "this revolutionary stuff." They believed they had rights that no government could violate. They believed they had the authority to resist government encroachment on their rights. Abraham Lincoln's famous declaration in the Emancipation Proclamation that we are a "government of the people, by the people, for the people" means exactly what it says. The government exists at the behest of its citizens. It is there to protect, defend, and even enhance our freedoms, not violate them.

It was with those ideas in mind that our forefathers gave us the Constitution. As the Preamble proclaims: "We, the People of the United States, in Order to form a more perfect Union, establish Justice, insure domestic Tranquility, provide for the common defense, promote the general Welfare, and secure the Blessings of Liberty to ourselves and our Posterity, do ordain and establish this Constitution for the United States of America."

It was no idle happenstance that the Constitution opens with these three powerful words: "We the people..." This, in effect, makes "the people" the guardians of America's future.

Thomas Jefferson recognized that an educated citizenry is the only real assurance that freedom will survive—a citizenry educated on the basic freedoms. Jefferson wrote: "I know of no safe repository of the ultimate powers of our society but the people themselves; and if we think them not enlightened enough to exercise their control with a wholesome discretion, the remedy is not to take it from them, but to inform their discretion by education."[60] Jefferson wrote that pre-university education was to "instruct the mass of our citizens in...their rights, interests, and duties as men and citizens."[61] As for university education, Jefferson said it was "to form the statesmen, legislators and judges on whom public prosperity and individual happiness are so much to depend."[62] Furthermore, "The People are the only sure reliance for the preservation of our liberty."[63] But that's where the problem arises for us today. Most citizens have little, if any, knowledge about their basic rights. And our educational system does a poor job of teaching the basic freedoms guaranteed in the Constitution and the Bill of Rights.

A summary released by the McCormick Tribune Freedom Museum in March 2006 shows the gravity of the problem. It found in a national poll that less than 1 percent of adults could identify the five rights protected by the First Amendment—freedom of religion, speech, the press, assembly, and the right to petition the government for a redress of grievances. On the other hand, more than half (52 percent) of the respondents could name at least two of the characters in the animated *Simpsons* television family, and 20 percent could name all five. A majority (54 percent) could name at least one of the three judges on the TV program *American Idol*, 41 percent could name two, and one-fourth could name all three; compare that to the half of those polled who could not name any of the freedoms in the First Amendment.

In a culture infatuated with celebrities and consumed with entertainment, it should come as no surprise that Americans are constitutionally illiterate. "There was a depth of confusion that we weren't expecting," noted Dave Anderson, executive director of the museum. "I think people take their freedoms for granted. Bottom line."[64]

But it gets worse. Many who responded to the survey had a strange conception of what was in the First Amendment. For example, 21 percent said the "right to own a pet" was listed someplace between "Congress shall make no law" and "redress of grievances." Some 17 percent said that the First Amendment contained the "right to drive a car," and 38 percent believed that "taking the Fifth" was part of the First Amendment. Think about this for a moment. How could James Madison, the author of the First Amendment who depended on horses for transportation in his day, have placed the "right to drive a car" in the Bill of Rights?[65]

Another national poll released in August 2006 revealed that Americans are more familiar with the Seven Dwarfs, Three Stooges, Harry

Potter, Homer Simpson, and Superman than the news of the day, world leaders, or classic literature.[66] When asked to name two of Snow White's Seven Dwarfs and two of the nine U.S. Supreme Court Justices, 77 percent of Americans polled were able to identify two dwarfs, while only 24 percent could name two Supreme Court Justices.[67]

Knowledge of government did not fare much better, with 74 percent of those polled able to name all three of the Stooges, while only 42 percent could name the three branches of the government—the legislative, executive, and judicial. "These results are not about how 'dumb' Americans are, but about how much more effectively popular culture information is communicated and retained by citizens than many of the messages that come from government, educational institutions and the media," Syracuse University professor Robert Thompson noted. "There are important lessons to be learned here."[68]

A citizenry can only hold its government accountable if it knows when the government is overstepping its bounds. If the people have little or no knowledge of the basics of government and their rights, then those who wield power, as history teaches, inevitably wield it more excessively. The maxim that power corrupts is an absolute truth. Realizing this, those who drafted the Constitution and the Bill of Rights held one principle, among others, in common: a distrust of all who hold governmental power.

Our problems are further exacerbated by an educational system that is not effectively teaching our young people the essentials for leadership. One study indicates that out of more than one hundred thousand high school students surveyed, 73 percent either did not know how they felt about the First Amendment or took it for granted.[69] The same study showed that 75 percent of those students thought the Constitution banned flag burning, which it does not. It is clear that high school civics classes are failing to teach the importance of our constitutional liberties.

And because post-secondary education tends to be more specialized, the vast majority of students make it through both high school and college totally ignorant of the Constitution—which guarantees our basic freedoms. When these freedoms and rights are threatened, even the "educated" among us may miss the importance of what is at stake and often acquiesce without a fight. Ignorance about the constitutional provisions that protect our basic freedoms—and a lack of awareness of the reality that these affect our daily lives—is one of the major reasons why our freedoms are continuously and uncontestedly eroded. This ignorance about the fundamentals of liberty cuts across the entire American population, both young and old, and includes those who serve in government and law enforcement.

FUNDAMENTAL PRINCIPLES

Such ignorance serves a grievous blow to those who have gone before us, the brave men and women who struggled and fought to secure and preserve the freedoms that were so hard-won. These freedoms were based on certain fundamental principles. Thus, I shall pause for a brief review of the six vital principles that undergird our system of government.

The first principle (one that has largely been turned on its head over the past several decades) is that *governments primarily exist to secure rights*, an idea that is central to constitutionalism. In appointing the government as the guardian of the people's rights, the people give it only certain, enumerated powers, which are laid out in a written constitution. The idea of a written constitution actualizes the two great themes of the Declaration: consent and protection of equal rights. "The people's own law—the Constitution—governs the government even after the government is established," Professors West and Jeffrey write. "And the fact that it is a written document, changeable only in rare circumstances, reflects the conviction that government's duties are guided and limited by a permanent standard of natural right."[70] Thus, the purpose of constitutionalism is to limit governmental power and ensure that the government performs its basic function: preserve and protect our rights, especially our unalienable rights to life, liberty, and the pursuit of happiness, and our civil liberties.

The second principle revolves around the belief that no one is above the law, not even those who make the law. This is termed *rule of law*. Richard Nixon's statement, "When the president does it, that means that it is not illegal," would have been an anathema to the framers of the Constitution.[71] If all people possess equal rights, the people who live under the laws must be allowed to participate in making those laws, and those who make the laws must live under the laws they make.

Separation of powers ensures that no single authority is entrusted with all the powers of government. People are not perfect, whether they are in government or out of it. As history teaches us, those in power tend to abuse it. The government is thus divided into three co-equal branches: legislative, executive, and judicial. Placing all three powers in the same branch of government was considered the very definition of tyranny.

A system of *checks and balances*, essential if a constitutional government is to succeed, strengthens the separation of powers and prevents legislative despotism. Such checks and balances include dividing Congress into two houses, with different constituencies, term lengths, sizes, and functions; granting the president a limited veto power over congressional legislation; and appointing an independent judiciary capable of reviewing ordinary legislation in light of the written Constitution, which is referred to as "judicial review." The framers feared that Congress could abuse its powers and potentially emerge as the tyrannous branch because it had the power to tax. But they did not anticipate the emergence of presidential powers as they have come to dominate modern government or the inordinate influence of corporate powers on governmental decision-making.

Representation "allows the people to have a voice in government by sending elected representatives to do their bidding, while avoiding the need of each and every citizen to vote on every issue considered by government."[72] In a country as large as the United States, it is not feasible to have direct participation in governmental affairs. Hence, we have a representative government. And if the people don't agree with how their representatives are conducting themselves, they can vote them out. At its best, government should filter the public's reason from its irrational passions, which are usually adverse to the rights of others.

Federalism is yet another constitutional device to limit the power of government by dividing power and, thus, preventing tyranny. In America, the levels of government generally break out into federal, state, and local (which further divides into counties and towns or cities). Because local and particular interests differ from place to place, such interests are better handled at a more intimate level by local governments, not a bureaucratic national government. Remarking on the benefits of the American tradition of local self-government in the 1830s, the French historian Alexis de Tocqueville observed, "Local institutions are to liberty what primary schools are to science; they put it within the people's reach; they teach people to appreciate its peaceful enjoyment and accustom them to make use of it. Without local institutions a nation may give itself a free government, but it has not got the spirit of liberty."[73]

TAKING RESPONSIBILITY

"How lucky it is for rulers," Adolf Hitler once said, "that men cannot think."[74] The horrors that followed in Nazi Germany would have been much easier to explain if Hitler had been right. But he wasn't.

Hitler came to power because people did think. For example, on January 30, 1933, in full accordance with the country's legal and constitutional principles, Hitler was appointed chancellor. When German president Hindenburg died in August 1934, Hitler assumed the office of president, as well as that of chancellor. But he preferred to use the title Der Füehrer (the leader) to describe himself. This new move was approved in a general election in which Hitler garnered 88 percent of the votes cast.[75]

The German people were clearly not ignorant of Hitler's goals when they voted for him. The voters were very aware of the Nazi ideology. Nazi literature, including statements of the Nazi plans for the future, had papered the country for a decade before Hitler came to power. In fact, Hitler's book Mein Kampf, which was his blueprint for totalitarianism, sold more than two hundred thousand copies between 1925 and 1932.

Clearly, then, the German people did think, but their thinking was unclear, and it was poisoned by the enveloping climate of ideas that they came to accept as important. At a certain point, the trivial became important, and obedience to the state in pursuit of security over freedom became predominant.

We in the United States are not immune from this kind of unclear thinking, avoidance, and escapism. A series of in-depth interviews conducted by political scientist Kenneth Dolbeare in the mid-1970s revealed that most of the respondents, even at that time, were deeply afraid of some future statist authoritarianism in the United States. "The most striking thing about inquiring into expectations for the future," Dolbeare reported, "is the rapidity with which the concept of fascism (with or without the label) enters the conversation." Even more startling, Dolbeare found that people tend to suppress their fears instead of searching for ways to combat what they perceive as a possible attack on their democracy. As he noted, there is an "air-raid shelter mentality, in which people go underground rather than deal directly with threatening prospects."[76]

There is a constant struggle in modern America with this air-raid mentality, coupled with a population that is ignorant of the basic doctrines—freedom, individuality, and dissent—upon which our society was founded. Many even sacrifice the right to vote on the altar of apathy. During presidential elections, only 50-plus percent of the voting-age population casts a ballot. And during off-year federal elections, the percentage is much lower. Consequently, governmental powers have continued to expand as the freedoms of the average citizen have diminished, if for no other reason than that those in authority have been more vigilant in taking what is not theirs.

Overwhelmed by the informational glut of modernity, it is little wonder that many, ostrich-like, avoid truth. Yet while they may feel snug and secure in their technological wombs, they are only temporarily keeping the wolf at bay. Hiding from reality is not the solution. In fact, nonparticipation by the citizenry only makes matters worse. "Bad officials are elected by good citizens who do not vote," the drama critic George Jean Nathan once remarked.[77]

Thus, for whom does the bell toll? It tolls for us. Everything America was founded upon is in some way being challenged. At stake is the very foundation of the American democratic system. And while it may be easy to fault a particular politician, event, or the media— in particular, television—for the state of our nation, the blame, as the renowned CBS newscaster Edward R. Murrow once noted, rests with us. Amid the Red Scare of the 1950s and the Joseph McCarthy era, people were often afraid to speak out against the paranoia being propagated through the media and the government. Fear and paranoia had come to grip much of the American population, and there was a horrible chill in the air. But with great courage, Murrow spoke up. On March 9, 1954, on his CBS television show *See It Now*, Murrow said the following—a statement very apropos for today:

> *We cannot defend freedom abroad by deserting it at home. The actions of the junior senator from Wisconsin have caused alarm and dismay amongst our allies abroad and given considerable comfort to our enemies, and whose fault is that? Not really his. He didn't create the situation of fear; he merely exploited it, and rather successfully. Cassius was right: "The fault, dear Brutus, is not in our stars but in ourselves."*[78]

It was not idle rhetoric that prompted the framers of the Constitution to begin with the words "We the people." In the words of former Supreme Court Chief Justice Earl Warren, throughout the extraordinary document that is the Constitution and Bill of Rights, "there is an implicit assumption that we, the people, will preserve our democratic rights by acting responsibly in our enjoyment of them."[79] This ultimate responsibility for maintaining our freedoms rests with the people.

The framers of the Constitution knew very well that whenever and wherever democratic governments had failed, it was because the people had abdicated their responsibility as guardians of freedom. They also knew that whenever in history the people denied this responsibility, an authoritarian regime arose which eventually denied the people the right to govern themselves. All governments fall into two classifications: those with a democratic form and those that are authoritarian, ruled by an individual or some oligarchic elite.

Acting responsibly, however, means that there are certain responsibilities and duties without which our rights would become meaningless. Duties of citizenship extend beyond the act of voting, which is only the first step in acting responsibly. Citizens must be willing to stand and fight to protect their freedoms. This is patriotism in action.

What this means is that we can still be patriotic and love our country while disagreeing with the government or going to court to fight for freedom. Responsible citizenship means being outraged at the loss of others' freedoms, even when our own are not directly threatened. It also means remembering that the prime function of any free government is to protect the weak against the strong.

Love of country will sometimes entail carrying a picket sign or going to jail, if necessary, to preserve liberty. And it will mean speaking up for those with whom you might disagree. Tolerance for dissent, we must remember, is a vital characteristic of the citizens of a democratic society. As Supreme Court Justice Oliver Wendell Holmes said, "If there is any principle of the Constitution that more imperatively calls for attachment than any other, it is the principle of free thought—not free thought for those who agree with us but freedom for the thought that we hate."[80]

Loving your country does not mean being satisfied with the status quo or the way government is being administered. Government invariably, possibly inevitably, oversteps its authority. As human beings are not perfect, governments, because they are constructs of human beings, will necessarily be imperfect as well.

Love of country, it must be emphasized, is always strengthened by both a knowledge of history and of the Constitution. "If we have no appreciation of the past," Justice Warren recognized, "we can have little understanding of the present or vision for the future."[81]

The problems facing our generation are numerous and are becoming incredibly complex. Technology, which has developed at a rapid pace, offers those in power more invasive and awesome possibilities than ever before. Never in American history has there been a more pressing need to maintain the barriers in the Constitution erected by our founders to check governmental power and abuse. We need to seek solutions to these pressing needs, some of which are found in our history.

As the delegates to the Constitutional Convention trudged out of Independence Hall on September 17, 1787, an anxious woman in the crowd waiting at the entrance inquired of Benjamin Franklin, "Well, Doctor, what have we got, a republic or a monarchy?"

"A republic," Franklin replied, "if you can keep it."[82]

CHAPTER TWO

Police Overkill

Power makes men wanton. It intoxicates the mind.

—Samuel Adams

A sixty-year-old grandmother sent me this email during the writing of this book:

We live in a small rural town. Moved here in 1961. I don't remember what year the State Troopers moved a headquarters into our town. Our young people were plagued with tickets for even the smallest offense. Troopers had to get their limits for the month. People make jokes about that but it has been true. Every kid I knew was getting ticketed for something.

But now it is so much worse. I raised my kids to respect police. If they did something wrong and got caught they deserved it and should take their punishment. But now I have no respect for the police. I feel threatened and fearful of them. They are aggressive and intimidating. They lie and are abusive and we do not know how to fight them. I am not a minority here but people are afraid if they speak out they will be targeted.

We are just a small town. I just don't care anymore if they do target me. I am afraid they are going to kill someone.

In the not-too-distant past, this grandmother's fears would have seemed totally out of place, but not today. In a 2004 article entitled "It Can't Happen Here," Congressman Ron Paul (R-Tex.) cautioned, "We are not yet living in a total police state, but it is fast approaching."[1]

A lot can happen in a matter of years. A lot, in fact, has happened in the past few years, most of it aimed at amassing greater power for the government while undermining the rights of American citizens. The increasing militarization of the police has become an inescapable and ominous reality. The role of law enforcement, especially local police officers, has drastically changed from when I was a child in the 1950s. The friendly local sheriff in *The Andy Griffith Show* has been shelved for the federal gun-toting terrorist killers in popular television shows such as *24*. Some might insist that the new face of law enforcement is warranted as a sign of the times in which we live. Whereas we once feared nuclear attack by Communist Russia, we now fear each other and the predators that lurk in our midst—serial killers, drug pushers, home-grown and imported terrorists, sexual perverts who prey on small children, the list goes on. One thing is undeniable: armed police officers have become a force to be reckoned with. And it's not just local law enforcement. As the federalization of law enforcement continues to grow, more and more federal agents are armed. As of September 2004, federal agencies employed about 106,000 full-time personnel authorized to make arrests and carry firearms.[2]

FBI agents are only a small portion of the armed federal personnel. It seems as if almost everyone—from postal agents, the Internal Revenue Service, the National Park Service, and the Environmental Protection Agency to agents of the U.S. Fish and Wildlife Service and the Army Corps of Engineers—is now carrying deadly weapons. For instance, in Virginia, game wardens have been renamed "conservation police officers" in an effort to clarify their role as sworn law enforcement officers who are armed and able to make arrests.[3]

"What we've witnessed," says Joseph Farah, editor of *World Net Daily*, "is the biggest arms buildup in the history of the federal government—and it's not taking place in the Defense Department. The kind of arms that are proliferating in Washington these days are the kind pointed at our own civilian population and carried by a growing number of federal police forces with ever-larger budgets and ever-deadlier arsenals."[4]

At all levels—federal, local, and state—the government and the police have merged. In the process, they have become a "standing" or permanent army, one composed of full-time professional soldiers who do not disband, which is exactly what the founders feared. Those who drafted the U.S. Constitution and Bill of Rights had an enormous distrust of permanent armies. They knew that despotic governments have used standing armies to control the people and impose tyranny. James Madison, in a speech before the Constitutional Convention in the summer of 1789, proclaimed: "A standing military force, with an overgrown Executive will not long be safe companions to liberty. The means of defense against foreign danger, have been always the instruments of tyranny at home."[5] As predicted, these very same "instruments of tyranny" are now being used to wage war against the American people. Thus, it would seem that we have become the enemy.

A NATION AT WAR WITH ITSELF

The violent aftershocks of the 1995 Oklahoma City bombing and the 1999 Columbine school shooting, coupled with the events of 9/11, exposed our vulnerability to the dangers of domestic terrorists. Suddenly, the enemy became the quiet man on the street, the technician in the company van, the nonviolent protester at a peace rally.

America had lost its innocence, and in its place was a terror seemingly so vast that Americans found themselves willing to pay almost any price just to feel safe again. To that end, we soon found ourselves welcoming armed SWAT teams to patrol the streets, applauding zero-tolerance policies in the schools, and tolerating a government that regularly violates its citizens' privacy and First Amendment rights. When done in the name of national security, virtually anything seems to be allowed.

Failing to ensure any greater safety, however, we have succeeded in forfeiting one of the principles that has been a hallmark of American democracy—the idea that every person is innocent until proven guilty. This is such a simple concept, yet it undergirds some of our

Constitution's greatest protections, such as the right to an attorney and a fair hearing, protection from unreasonable searches and seizures, and the right to privacy, among others. We have also witnessed a sea change in the way law enforcement views its role, from one that considered itself a servant to the people to one that sees itself as the long arm of an increasingly authoritarian government.

With the end of the Cold War, the nation gained a strange new sense of security. No longer did a Red Scare strike fear in our hearts. No more did we seek refuge in bomb shelters. Lacking an external enemy, we began to see our prime enemies as "internal."[6] In search of ways to combat more pressing dangers, the nation began promoting more prisons, more police, less welfare, and decaying public schools.

By the 1990s, a culture of meanness had taken root. "Meanness today is a state of mind," writes Nicolaus Mills in *The Triumph of Meanness*, "the product of a culture of spite and cruelty that has had an enormous impact on us."[7] Neighborhoods gave way to gated communities, and the nosy neighbor down the street had been transformed into an official neighborhood watch. Surveillance cameras were mounted on sidewalks, in office buildings, schools, and other public places. And we have now come that much closer to embodying George Orwell's futuristic vision of a totalitarian society where privacy is nonexistent and everyone is a suspect. As Mills, a professor at Sarah Lawrence College, notes in his book, the country is now "fortress America with gated suburbs and guarded apartment houses and private schools and private security forces."[8]

Guarding a fortress requires military might, a job for which local police officers were not prepared. So they, too, had to be transformed from benign "officers of the peace" to intimidating paramilitary units with black military-style uniforms displaying a host of weapons. The typical uniform worn by today's SWAT teams bears little resemblance to police apparel of the past: laced-up, combat-style boots; black, camouflage, or olive-colored pants and shirts, sometimes with "ninja-style" or balaclava hoods; Kevlar helmets and vests; gas masks, knee pads, gloves, communication devices, and boot knives; and military-grade weapons such as the Heckler and Koch MP5 submachine gun, which is the preferred model of the U.S. Navy Seals.

A CHANGE OF ATTITUDE AND ARMS

There are undeniably many honorable law enforcement officials who strive to abide by their oath to uphold the Constitution and serve and protect the citizens of their communities. However, when police officers take advantage of their broad discretion and repeatedly step beyond the bounds of the law, ignoring their responsibility to respect the Bill of Rights, they become nothing more than vigilantes—albeit vigilantes with a badge.

An incident in Miami, Florida, during the 2003 Free Trade Area of the Americas summit illustrates the shift in how police view their role in maintaining the peace, especially as it relates to the rights of American citizens. Hundreds of demonstrators had gathered to voice their concerns about the detrimental effects of a trade pact on developing countries. Coral Gables attorney Elizabeth Ritter joined the throngs of protesters on one of the summit's final days. But it wasn't trade issues that prompted her to pick up a protest sign. She was upset because the police had in effect shut down the city that week, including the courthouse. The police had also equipped themselves with riot gear and guns designed to fire rubber bullets in anticipation of protests. "My city, my hometown, was becoming a police state," said Ritter.

Video footage from that day shows Ritter walking alone, wearing a red suit jacket and waving a hastily drawn sign that proclaimed "Fear Totalitarianism." When approached by a squad of law enforcement officials in riot gear, Ritter turned to face them and raised her sign. The police began firing rubber bullets, which often leave welts and bruises and at close range can even break the skin. As the bullets began hitting her, Ritter knelt down, using her sign as a shield. She was shot a total of five times in the legs, upper body, and shoulders. One of the rubber bullets tore through the sign and hit her directly on the head. Stunned, she stood up, faced the police and asked, "Why did you hit me? Is a woman in a business suit a threat?"[9]

In a police training video that was recorded the following day, police officers are shown praising each other for shooting the summit protesters with rubber bullets. One policeman refers to the protesters as "scurrying cockroaches." Another jokes about a protester who was hit in the head with a rubber bullet, saying, "And the lady in the red dress…I don't know who got her, but it went right through the sign and hit her smack dab in the middle of the head!" The police officers then erupt into laughter.[10]

If the laughing response of the police officers in the training video doesn't raise a red flag, the riot gear, stun guns, rubber bullets, and indiscriminate use of force to quell the peaceful dissent at the summit certainly should. A civilian panel that investigated charges of excessive police force employed at the 2003 summit concluded that police indiscriminately used weapons such as stun guns and conducted unlawful searches and arrests during the event. A number of lawsuits claiming that police officers used excessive force and made false arrests while attempting to control the crowds were filed against various law enforcement agencies, including the Broward County Sheriff's Office, Miami Police, and Miami-Dade Police.

NON-LETHAL WEAPONS

In appearance, weapons, and attitude, local law enforcement agencies are increasingly being transformed into civilian branches of the military. One clear distinction between local police and military forces used to be the kinds of weapons at their disposal. With the advent of modern police weaponry, that is no longer the case. Americans would do well to remember that modern police weaponry was introduced with a government guarantee of safety for the citizens. Police tasers, stun guns, and rubber pellets were brought into use by police departments across America supposedly because these "nonlethal" weapons would be safe. But the "nonlethal" label seems to have caused police to feel justified in using these dangerous instruments much more often and with less restraint—with some even causing death.

Tasers are now used by more than 11,000 law enforcement agencies in the United States. Tasers are electro-shock weapons, handheld electronic stun guns that fire two barbed darts designed to cause instant incapacitation by delivering a 50,000-volt shock. The darts, which usually remain attached to the gun by wires, deliver the high voltage shock and can penetrate up to two inches of clothing or skin. The darts can strike the subject from a distance of up to 20 feet, or the taser can be applied directly to the skin. Although a taser shot is capable of jamming the central nervous system for up to 30 seconds, it can disable the subject for even longer. And because tasers can be aimed anywhere on the body, they can immobilize someone more easily than pepper spray, which must be sprayed in the face.

Taser manufacturers and law enforcement agencies argue that tasers are a safer alternative to many conventional weapons typically used to restrain dangerous individuals. This may be true in situations where tasers are used as an alternative to other impact weapons that can cause serious injury, such as batons or even lethal force. However, the potential for government abuse of this so-called "nonlethal" weapon is great, especially in the hands of domestic law enforcement.

Research shows that in many police departments, officers routinely use tasers primarily as a substitute for low-level force weapons such as pepper spray or chemical spray. They have become a prevalent force tool, most often employed against individuals who do not pose a serious danger to themselves, the officers, or others. A 2005 study compiled by Amnesty International reports that in instances where tasers are used, 80 percent of the time they are fired at unarmed suspects. In 36 percent of the cases, they are employed for verbal noncompliance, but only 3 percent of the time for cases involving "deadly assault."[11]

Incredibly, tasers have been fired at children as well as unarmed individuals who fail to immediately comply with officers' commands. Since 2001, more than seventy people are reported to have died in the United States and Canada after being struck by a taser. Most of them were unarmed men who, while displaying disturbed or combative behavior, did not present a serious threat to the lives or safety of others. They were subjected to extreme levels of force, including repeated taser discharges, even when handcuffed or hog-tied on the ground.

In Florida, a fourteen-year-old schoolgirl was tasered for arguing with police officers after she and other students were put off a bus during a disturbance. She was stunned directly to the chest and then stunned twice from a distance before she was handcuffed. In Oregon, a newspaper reported that officers used tasers on noncompliant people "after stopping them for nonviolent offenses, such as littering and jaywalking."[12] In Arizona, a thirteen-year-old girl was tasered in a public library after she threw a book.[13] In Missouri, an unarmed sixty-six-year-old woman was tasered twice as she resisted being issued a ticket for honking her horn at a police car.[14] In another instance, an officer used a taser on a nine-year-old girl who had run away from a residential home for severely emotionally disturbed children. The child, who was already handcuffed and sitting in the back of a police car, was tasered for struggling as the officer attempted to put leg restraints on her.[15]

Malaika Brooks was eight months pregnant when she was pulled over by Seattle police officers for speeding. What began as a routine traffic stop quickly escalated to a nightmarish display of unnecessary police hostility when Malaika refused to sign the ticket. Treating her as a belligerent criminal, the officers used a taser gun to send a 50,000-volt shock of electricity through her pregnant body.[16]

Margaret Kimbrell, a seventy-five-year-old woman who suffers from arthritis and had six broken ribs, was given a 50,000-volt shock from a police taser gun and was forced to spend three hours behind bars. Her crime? Margaret had refused to leave a nursing home before she had the opportunity to visit a friend whose well-being she was concerned about. According to the police, Margaret posed a threat because she was waving her arms and threatening the staff. This was news to Margaret. "As weak as I am, how could I do that?" she asked.[17] Describing the pain of being tasered, this resident of Rock Hill, South Carolina, responded, "It was the worst pain. It felt like something going through my body. I thought I was dying. I said, 'Lord, let it be over.'"

Common sense and good judgment certainly seemed to be in short supply when a police run-in with seventy-one-year-old Eunice Crowder resulted in the blind woman being pepper-sprayed and tasered. City employees had shown up at Crowder's home to remove unsightly shrubs and trash from the handicapped woman's yard. Shortly after city workers began taking her belongings from her yard, however, Crowder became concerned that a ninety-year-old wagon had been placed in the truck to be hauled away with her other belongings. After voicing her concern about the wagon, which was a family heirloom, Crowder asked to be allowed to enter the truck to search for it. Despite the workers' refusal, the elderly woman insisted on searching the truck. The situation worsened when the police showed up to find Crowder with one foot on the curb and the other on the bumper of the trailer. When one of the officers stepped on her foot, Crowder, being blind, asked who it was. Moments later, one of the officers struck her on the head—which dislodged her prosthetic eye—kicked her in the back, and pepper-sprayed her in the face.[18]

In September 2007, a University of Florida student was tasered and arrested after trying to question U.S. Senator John Kerry during a campus forum. Officers pulled twenty-one-year-old Andrew Meyer from the microphone after he asked Kerry about impeaching President Bush and whether he and Bush were both members of Yale's secret Skull and Bones society. "He apparently asked several questions, he went on for quite awhile, then he was asked to stop," a university spokesman said. "He had used his allotted time. His microphone was cut off, then he became upset." Meyer struggled to escape when several officers tried to remove him from the room. Forced to the ground and ordered to stop resisting, Meyer said he would walk out if the officers would let him go. Yet even as Kerry told the audience that he would answer the student's "very important question," Meyer was tasered and then led from the room, screaming, "What did I do?"[19]

Amnesty International has expressed concern that despite the far-reaching use of tasers, there has been no independent and impartial study of their use and effects. The growing employment of these weapons, as well as the number of deaths of individuals struck by them, presents serious questions. Furthermore, the use of tasers in law enforcement raises a number of concerns for the protection of human rights. Portable, easy to use, and with the capacity to inflict severe pain at the push of a button without leaving substantial marks, tasers are open to even more abuse. Their use often violates standards set out under the United Nations Code of Conduct for Law Enforcement Officials, which requires that force be utilized as a last resort and that only the minimum amount necessary be used.[20]

THE RISE OF PARAMILITARY POLICE

Tasers, stun guns, and rubber bullets might very well seem relatively harmless in comparison to the arsenal of weapons now available to local law enforcement, especially paramilitary units like Special Weapons and Tactics, or SWAT, teams. Standard SWAT team weaponry includes battering rams, ballistic shields, "flashbang" grenades, smoke grenades, pepper spray, and tear gas. Many squads are also ferried to raid sites by military-issue armored personnel carriers. Some units even have helicopters, while others boast grenade launchers, tanks (with and without gun turrets), rappelling equipment, and bayonets.[21]

The rise of paramilitary police began in Los Angeles in the 1960s, but until at least the 1980s, SWAT teams and other paramilitary units were used sparingly and only in volatile, high-risk situations such as bank robberies or hostage situations. "No-knock" raids were generally employed only in situations where innocent lives were determined to be at imminent risk. That changed in the early 1980s, when a dramatic and unsettling rise in the use of these paramilitary units in routine police work resulted in a militarization of American civilian law enforcement. The government's so-called "war on drugs" also spurred a significant rise in the use of SWAT teams for raids. In some jurisdictions, drug warrants are only served by SWAT teams or similar paramilitary units and oftentimes are executed with forced, unannounced entry into the home.

Approximately forty thousand no-knock raids are carried out each year, usually conducted by teams of heavily armed paramilitary units dressed not as police officers but as soldiers prepared for war. But as one retired police officer warns: "One tends to throw caution to the wind when wearing 'commando-chic' regalia, a bulletproof vest with the word 'POLICE' emblazoned on both sides, and when one is armed with high tech weaponry. We have not yet seen a situation like [the British police occupation of] Belfast. But some police chiefs are determined to move in that direction."[22]

Paramilitary raids are typically conducted covertly, often late at night or just before dawn when people are asleep, in order to be effective. When conducting such raids, the police are technically bound by law to "knock and announce" themselves and give occupants time to answer the door before forcing entry. This constitutes a minimal compliance with the U.S. Constitution's Fourth Amendment prohibition against unreasonable search and seizure by the police. However, even that minimal requirement is often circumvented through court-sanctioned loopholes, ignored completely with little consequence or only ceremoniously observed with a quick knock and announcement unlikely to be noticed by anyone inside—especially if the raid happens at night when people are sleeping.

During such raids, police can break open doors with a battering ram or blow them off their hinges with explosives. Absent either, police have pried doors open with sledgehammers or screwdrivers, ripped them off by attaching them to the back ends of trucks, or have entered by crashing through windows or balconies. After an entryway is cleared, police sometimes detonate a flashbang grenade or a similar device designed to disorient the occupants in the targeted house and then enter the home under its cover. SWAT teams have entered homes through fire escapes, by rappelling down from police helicopters, and by crashing through second-story windows. Once police are inside, the occupants are quickly and forcefully incapacitated and instructed to remain in the prone position, generally at gunpoint, while police carry out the search warrant. Any perceived noncompliance is typically met with force, which can potentially be lethal, depending on the nature of the noncompliance.

These raids leave a very small margin for error. A wrong address, bad timing, or incorrect information (often from unreliable informants) can, and frequently does, lead to tragedy. In a March 2005 drug raid in Hawaii, police broke into the residence of Sharon and William McCulley, who were at home with their grandchildren. The police were supposedly looking for a box that contained marijuana and believed it to be in the McCulleys' possession. After breaking down the elderly McCulleys' door, police threw the couple to the ground, handcuffed Sharon, whose grandchild was lying next to her, and held a gun to Sharon's head. William—who uses a walker and has an implanted device that delivers electrical shocks to his spine to relieve pain—began flopping around on the floor when the device malfunctioned from the trauma of being violently thrown to the ground.[23] It turned out that the police had the wrong address. Unfortunately, they conducted a second "wrong door" raid before finally tracking down the package.

Such a search-and-destroy mind-set—which is characteristic of armed military actions—has been used in a number of incidents in which police or drug agents have invaded entire streets, city blocks, and towns in drug interdiction efforts, which commonly include no-knock raids. In 1998, more than ninety police officers in full SWAT attire raided thirteen apartments in San Francisco's Martin Luther King-Marcus Garvey housing co-op. Police blew doors off their hinges, deployed flashbang grenades, and, according to residents, slapped, beat, and stepped on the necks of the people inside. Police put gun muzzles against the heads of some occupants. One family's pet dog was shot in front of its owners, then dragged outside and shot again. Children as young as six were handcuffed, which Police Chief Fred Lau said was done to prevent them from "running around." The raid was apparently conducted to scare and intimidate a local gang.[24]

The inherent danger in these no-knock and quick-knock raids exemplifies the troubling characteristics of such paramilitary policing. As Radley Balko, senior editor of *Reason* magazine, details in his insightful study of the problem, these characteristics include:

+ The militarization of domestic policing, not just in big cities but in small towns and suburbs.
+ The increasingly frequent use of heavily armed SWAT teams for proactive policing and the routine execution of drug warrants, even for simple marijuana possession.
+ The use of anonymous tips and reliance on dubious informants to obtain no-knock search warrants.
+ Executing warrants with "dynamic entry," diversionary grenades and similarly militaristic tactics once reserved for urban warfare.
+ A tragic outcome resulting from these circumstances.[25]

Tragic outcomes frequently involve people completely innocent of any crime. Take, for example, a case detailed in Balko's study. On September 4, 1998, police in Charlotte, North Carolina, deployed a flashbang grenade and carried out a no-knock raid based on a tip that someone in the targeted home was distributing cocaine. When police got inside, they found a group of men playing cards, who probably thought they were under attack by criminals. "Only thing I heard was a big boom," one man said. "The lights went off and then they came back on...everybody reacted. We thought the house was being robbed."[26] One of the men, 56-year-old Charles Irwin Potts, who was not the target of the raid, possessed a handgun that he owned and carried legally. Police testified that Potts drew his gun and pointed it at them as they entered. That is when police say they opened fire, killing Potts with four shots to the chest. The three remaining men in the house who witnessed the raid, however, testified that the gun never left Potts's holster. Police found no cocaine in the home and made no arrests.

Needless police violence is bad enough when used against criminals, but it becomes particularly disturbing when innocent people are terrorized or die, as happened with Alberta Spruill. On May 16, 2003, a dozen New York City police officers, acting on a tip from a confidential informant, stormed an apartment building in Harlem on a no-knock warrant. They had been told that a convicted felon was dealing drugs and guns from the sixth floor, but no such felon was to be found. The only resident in the building was Alberta Spruill, described by friends as a "devout churchgoer." Before entering the apartment, police deployed a flashbang grenade. The blinding, deafening explosion stunned the fifty-seven-year-old city worker. As the officers realized their mistake and helped Spruill to her feet, the woman slipped into cardiac arrest. She died two hours later. A police investigation later found that the drug dealer the raid team sought had been arrested days earlier and was still in police custody. The officers who conducted the raid had failed to corroborate the informant's tip.[27]

These are but a few of the epidemic number of SWAT team raids that have resulted in terror and tragedy. "Terrorizing" is a mild term to describe the effect on those who survive such vigilante tactics. "It was terrible. It was the most frightening experience of my life. I thought it was a terrorist attack," said eighty-four-year-old Leona Goldberg, a victim of such a raid.[28]

Yet this type of "terrorizing" activity is characteristic of the culture that we have created. As author Eugene V. Walker, a former Boston University professor, wrote some years ago, "A society in which people are already isolated and atomized, divided by suspicious and destructive rivalry, would support a system of terror better than a society without much chronic antagonism."[29]

AN END-RUN AROUND POSSE COMITATUS

American society has changed. And with that change, the way in which the government views us, the way we view one another, and the way we view and are viewed by law enforcement have undergone dramatic transformations. Where law enforcement officials once looked to us as their employers, we now too often look to them as our wardens and jailers, as something to fear. And where once there was a decided difference between the police and the military and their uses domestically, that line continues to be blurred. Under the Posse Comitatus Act, the federal government is prohibited from deploying the military on U.S. soil as local law enforcement. But what is to stop the local police from becoming the military? Not much, it seems.

The seeds for such a turn of events were planted with the 1981 Military Cooperation with Law Enforcement Act. Arriving on the heels of Ronald Reagan's presidential election, which marked an aggressive posture toward the "war on drugs," this federal law encouraged the military to give local, state, and federal police access to military bases, research, and equipment for drug enforcement. It also authorized them to train civilian police officers to use the newly available equipment. In addition to encouraging the military to share drug war-related information with civilian police, however, this law also authorized the military to take an active role in preventing drugs from entering the country.

By the late 1990s, various laws, orders, and directives had softened the Posse Comitatus Act, which, as noted in Chapter One, was passed in 1878 following the American Civil War. It prohibits federal military personnel and units from acting in a law enforcement capacity. This law is aimed at preventing America from becoming a military state, but as local police departments across the country help themselves to newly available equipment, training, and funding, that is exactly what we are being subjected to. For instance, between 1995 and 1997, the Pentagon distributed 3,800 M-16 rifles, 2,185 M-14 rifles, 73 grenade launchers, and 112 armored personnel carriers to civilian police agencies across the country.[30] In 1997 alone, the Pentagon handed over more than 1.2 million pieces of military equipment to local police departments. That same year, Congress made it even easier for local police departments to acquire military hardware from the Pentagon by creating the Law Enforcement Support Program, an agency headquartered at Ft. Belvoir, Virginia. This new agency was charged with streamlining the transfer of military equipment to civilian police departments.

Since then, transfers of equipment have taken off at an even greater clip. Between January 1997 and October 1999, the Law Enforcement Support agency handled 3.4 million orders of Pentagon equipment from over eleven thousand domestic police agencies in all fifty states. By December 2005, the number had grown to seventeen thousand agencies. The purchase value of the equipment came to more than $727 million. It included 253 aircraft (including six- and seven-passenger airplanes and UH-60 Blackhawk and UH-1 Huey helicopters), 7,856 M-16 rifles, 181 grenade launchers, 8,131 bulletproof helmets, and 1,161 pairs of night-vision goggles.[31]

Keep in mind that these grandiose armaments are for local police. One particular weapon, designed for use by the military and nicknamed Rumsfeld's Ray Gun, has been heavily promoted for use domestically in crowd-control situations. This weapon uses the Active Denial System (ADS), which dispenses brief, high-energy waves at a target, resulting in a sensation of severe burning pain. As one reporter explained, the $51 million crowd-control device "rides atop a Humvee, looks like a TV dish, and shoots energy waves 1/64 of an inch deep into the human skin."[32]

The ADS weapon directs electromagnetic radiation toward its

targets at a frequency of 95 GHz. Upon contact with the skin, the energy in the waves turns to heat, causing the water molecules in the skin to heat to around 130 degrees Fahrenheit. The intent of the weapon is to inflict pain severe enough to cause a person to flee. Experiments were conducted on volunteer test subjects in 2003 and 2004 at Kirtland Air Force Base in Albuquerque, New Mexico. The results indicated that ADS causes pain within two to three seconds and becomes intolerable within five seconds. As a test volunteer explained, "For the first millisecond, it just felt like the skin was warming up. Then it got warmer and warmer and felt like it was on fire....As soon as you're away from that beam your skin returns to normal and there is no pain."[33]

The Air Force also explored the weapon's ability to control riots and unruly crowds by firing the ADS beam at volunteers acting as rioters or intruders. When the beam zapped the volunteers, they held their hands up and were given fifteen seconds to cool down before being targeted again. Most of the volunteers experienced severe pain but were otherwise unharmed. It should be noted that volunteers were required to remove eye glasses, buttons, zippers, and watches for fear that exposure to the beam could cause "hot spots" or severe burns. However, actual targets—such as average, ordinary American citizens—would certainly not be given the opportunity to remove such objects before being fired upon.

Although the military has been guarded about the radiation weapon's effect on humans, several medical professionals insist that ADS beams could cause severe long-term health problems, including corneal damage, cancer, cataracts, and, as Dominique Loye of the International Committee of the Red Cross put it, "new types of injuries we're not aware of and may not be capable of taking care of."[34] And as *AlterNet* reporter Kelly Hearn points out, there are more questions than answers right now about how the weapon works, "what it does to the body and how it will be used in the streets of Basra and Baghdad or, one day, Boston."[35]

The prospect of nonlethal weapons being used on Americans, as we have seen with tasers and the like, is not so far-fetched. Reportedly on orders from the U.S. Justice Department, the Raytheon

Corporation is developing a version of ADS for use by local police departments. Someday, according to a Raytheon spokesperson, ADS may be "miniaturized down to a hand-held device that could be carried in a purse or pocket and used for personal protection instead of something like Mace."[36]

Civilian police departments are finding themselves awash with military arms. As a result of the Pentagon's giveaway program, more and more small towns have SWAT teams, all loaded with warfaring equipment. As of 1997, 90 percent of cities with populations of fifty thousand or more had at least one paramilitary SWAT team. And the number of SWAT teams serving smaller towns with populations between twenty-five thousand and fifty thousand increased 157 percent between 1985 and 1996.[37] With all this funding, equipment, and training from the federal military, police departments are well-equipped to wage war, and that is exactly what has come to pass. Unfortunately, the American people are on the receiving end of such heavy-handed tactics. In January 1999, a SWAT team in Chester, Pennsylvania, outraged the local community when it raided Chester High School in full tactical gear to break up a half-dozen students who had been loitering outside the school in the early afternoon.[38]

Using heavily armed SWAT teams in response to nonviolent offenses has often had tragic results, as was seen in January 2006 when police in Fairfax, Virginia, employed a SWAT team to serve a search warrant on Salvatore Culosi Jr., whom they suspected of gambling on sporting events. When the SWAT team confronted Culosi as he came out of his home, one officer's gun discharged, striking Culosi in the chest and killing him. Police concede that Culosi had no weapon and made no menacing gestures as police prepared to arrest him. Fairfax County conducts nearly all of its search warrants with a SWAT team, including those involving white-collar and nonviolent crime.[39]

Private suppliers of military equipment to local police departments exacerbate the problem. Weapons companies aggressively market to local police departments. This ranges from selling weapons to holding seminars that tend to promote the win-at-all-costs mentality of a

military soldier. Such militaristic marketing has real-world consequences. As David Kopel of the Independence Institute points out,
"When a weapon's advertising and styling deliberately blur the line between warfare and law enforcement, it is not unreasonable to expect
that some officers—especially when under stress—will start behaving
as if they were in the military. That is precisely what happened at
Waco when BATF agents began firing indiscriminately into the building, rather than firing at particular targets."[40]

This mind-set has been displayed at SWAT team conventions held
across the country. As one former police chief said about a convention he attended: "Officers at the conference were wearing these very
disturbing shirts. On the front, there were pictures of SWAT officers
dressed in dark uniforms, wearing helmets, and holding submachine
guns. Below was written: 'We don't do drive-by shootings.' On the
back, there was a picture of a demolished house. Below was written:
'We stop.'"[41] SWAT magazine also abounds in ads featuring soldiers
in full military garb and features articles such as "Polite, Professional,
and Prepared to Kill."[42]

As we have seen, innocent Americans are increasingly finding
themselves in the crosshairs—people like Estelle Newcomb, whose
otherwise quiet evening was interrupted by the unexpected crash of
her door being kicked in. Local drug investigators stormed into her
Virginia home at 9:40 one night while Estelle was busy working on
her computer. They drew their weapons and began screaming at the
fifty-year-old to get down on her hands and knees. Not knowing who
had just barged into her home or why they were there, Estelle was
frightened into compliance. It was only after one of the officers recognized Estelle as a member of the community that the raid unit realized they had mistaken her house for that of a drug smuggler. And
while it is fortunate that Estelle was not physically harmed, her sense
of security and privacy was completely shattered.[43]

CORPORATE SOLDIERS

Like Estelle, more and more Americans are finding their sense of security and privacy under constant siege. We are becoming accustomed to looking over our shoulders and censoring our speech and

actions from intrusive government surveillance and aggressive law enforcement officials. Virtually every area of American life is being infused with some type of militant police presence. And as if that weren't bad enough, we are increasingly finding ourselves forced to deal with modern-day mercenaries.

Although mercenaries have been in existence for centuries, today's mercenaries have evolved into corporate soldiers who are employed by private companies that contract their security services to the government. Thus, they are being paid with American taxpayer dollars. Since the use of private military contractors turned into a profitable industry in the 1990s, the industry has grown in size to about $100 billion in revenue per year.[44]

Many of today's corporate soldiers (who work for private military contractors) are former members of the military, particularly former special operations personnel and law enforcement officers. Unlike the military, private companies often offer their private security force employees yearly salaries of $100,000 to $200,000— two to four times that of their special forces counterparts in the U.S. military—again, paid for by the American taxpayer.[45] Not surprisingly, this disparity in income has led some special forces soldiers to leave the military in order to join the ranks of private military contractors.[46]

Another significant difference between U.S. soldiers and private security forces is accountability. If a member of the military acts inappropriately or fails to obey orders, that person can face a court martial. But if corporate soldiers dislike an assignment, they can breach their contract and leave. And, vigilante style, they can also disobey a military request without having to worry about the threat of a court martial or jail time.

What is especially of concern is the government's growing reliance on private contractors to fill domestic law enforcement responsibilities. In the aftermath of Hurricane Katrina, armed private military contractors were seen patrolling the streets of New Orleans. As Peter W. Singer of the Brookings Institution recognized, "Katrina broke all of the rules. It was the first time you had the deployment of armed private security contractors in the U.S."[47] Ann Duke, a spokesperson for Blackwater, one of the largest suppliers of private mercenaries hired by the U.S. government, confirmed that the private security contracting company had at least two hundred personnel in New Orleans, 164 of whom were working under contract with the Federal Protective Service, a division of the Department of Homeland Security.[48] According to Duke, the Blackwater personnel sent to New Orleans "were not deputized." As she insisted, "They are not law enforcement," and "They were hired much like any other security guard is hired, to protect a place or people."[49] Despite her insistence that Blackwater personnel were not deputized, Duke stated that Blackwater had a letter from Louisiana authorities authorizing their personnel to carry loaded weapons.[50]

Some Blackwater employees have also disabused the notion that they were more akin to security guards after Hurricane Katrina. According to two Blackwater employees, they were actually engaged in law enforcement activities, including "securing neighborhoods" and "confronting criminals."[51] These men said they were on contract with the Department of Homeland Security and the Louisiana governor's office, adding that they not only had the power to make arrests but also to use lethal force.[52] One of them even wore a gold Louisiana state law enforcement badge, saying he had been "deputized" by the governor.[53] Blackwater employees also patrolled the streets openly wielding M-16s and other assault weapons.[54]

Placing trained mercenaries in delicate law enforcement situations during a national disaster is not only foolhardy but dangerous. Consider the fallout that arose in the aftermath of Katrina after an employee of a private security company allegedly opened fire in New Orleans. According to one report, heavily armed Michael Montgomery, employed by Bodyguard and Tactical Security (BATS), was en route to pick up and escort someone through the chaotic city. While traveling under an overpass near the poor Ninth Ward neighborhood, he came under fire from "black gangbangers."[55] Montgomery recalled, "At the time, I was on the phone with my business partner. I dropped the phone and returned fire." Armed with AR-15s and other armaments, Montgomery explained that he and his men unleashed a barrage of bullets in the general direction of the alleged shooters. "After that," Montgomery remembered, "all I heard was moaning and screaming, and the shooting stopped." At that point, Montgomery claimed an Army unit showed up, yelling at them, thinking they were the enemy. "We explained to them that we were security. I told them what had happened and they didn't even care. They just left." According to Montgomery, no government authority figures asked him for any details of the incident, and no report was made.

Accounts similar to Montgomery's contribute to fears that such "vigilantism demonstrates the utter breakdown of the government." Expressing his concern about the deployment of forces like Blackwater on U.S. soil, Michael Ratner, president of the Center for Constitutional Rights, explained, "These private security forces have behaved brutally, with impunity, in Iraq. To have them now on the streets of New Orleans is frightening and possibly illegal."[56]

Unfortunately, this is what happens when individuals trained to deal with brutal situations in war zones are used in domestic situations. In 2007, Blackwater, responsible for providing security to some of the top American officials in Iraq, was faced with being banned from the country by the Iraqi government after a shooting that left eight Iraqi civilians dead. "The deaths struck a nerve with Iraqis," writes *New York Times* journalist Sabrina Tavernise, "who say that private security firms are often quick to shoot and are rarely held responsible for their actions."[57]

Such behavior is, indeed, worrisome, especially when one considers the lack of guidelines that exist governing the quality of individuals hired by these companies and the training they provide. For example, there are no federal regulations providing for consistency of standards among the various private military contractors, nor are companies required to run background checks on those they hire[58] or required to provide a certain level of training.[59]

The law is even vaguer when it comes to how private mercenaries are classified and what protections American citizens are afforded from them. The Fourth Amendment to the Constitution protects Americans from unreasonable searches and seizures by government agents. Although courts have determined that it also protects us against the same intrusions by a private individual acting as an agent of the government, there remains a great deal of debate about whether private military contractors fit this designation. Furthermore, does the federal government violate the Posse Comitatus Act when it uses these private mercenaries to conduct domestic law enforcement missions? The answer remains unsettled since it is difficult to establish whether private mercenaries are under the direction and control of the federal government, local officials, or companies like Blackwater.

CULTURE OF VIOLENCE, A DOMAIN OF TERROR

The militarization of the police, the use of sophisticated weaponry against Americans, and the government's increasing tendency to employ corporate soldiers domestically have taken a toll on more than just our freedoms. They have seeped into our subconscious awareness of life as we know it and colored our very understanding of freedom, justice, and democracy.

Even young people have not been spared. As I discuss in more detail in Chapter Five, young people are also being subjected to life in a police state, complete with police interrogations and SWAT team raids. School districts are increasingly teaming with law enforcement to create what some are calling the "schoolhouse to jailhouse track" by imposing a "double dose" of punishment: suspension or expulsion from school, accompanied by an arrest by the police and a trip to juvenile court. This double dose is often for one relatively minor act of childish misconduct. As an eleventh grader in Denver, Colorado, remarked, unknowingly echoing the anguish of students across the country, "Make our high school more like a school and less like a prison. They have us on lockdown."[60]

Thus, on virtually every front, American culture has been submerged in a violent aura that creates a domain of terror. Primarily, it is "symbolic violence." While the myths and fantasies of popular culture bombard us with opiate-like images and pie-in-the-sky promises that we can get rich, we can all be like the celebrities, and that life is wonderful, the world outside our doors is becoming more and more chaotic. Then there is the horrific side of life that is often portrayed in movies and books. "We make up horrors," writes Stephen King, "to help us cope with the real ones."[61] That may help explain the symbolic violence of television, which gets and keeps our attention. The world of television drama is, above all, a violent one. As some media analysts have recognized, "More than half of all characters are involved in some violence, at least one tenth in some killing, and three fourths of prime hours contain some violence."[62] Add to this mix the spate of former or current police reality shows such as *Cops*, *America's Dumbest Criminals*, *America's Most Wanted*, and *S.W.A.T. USA*. All of these shows foment the power and authority of the police in pursuit of the criminal mind.

American culture is, and always has been, somewhat violent. In recent years, this so-called "culture of meanness" has contributed to a bureaucratic meanness that has come to characterize many aspects of the nation's governmental and social policies. Yet until we have a personal encounter with this governmental "meanness," until we become its unfortunate victims, it is all too easy to close our eyes to what is happening around us and go on with our everyday lives.

THE FOURTH AMENDMENT

Although legal phrases such as "unreasonable search and seizure" continue to be bandied about, the Fourth Amendment's protection from unreasonable search or seizure by the government has diminished over time. It almost seems as if there are two very different versions of the Fourth Amendment: the original, which guaranteed personal privacy and freedom, and today's abused rule of law, which has been littered with countless judicial exceptions.

Those who drafted the Bill of Rights were deeply concerned about preserving personal liberty and property rights. Many of them considered freedom in one's home the most essential liberty. After all, they believed that a man's home is his castle. The framers of the Constitution believed that property and privacy rights were paramount—even over public safety.

In early America, citizens were considered equals with law enforcement officials. Authorities were rarely permitted to enter one's home without permission or in a deceitful manner. And it was not uncommon for police officers to be held personally liable for trespass when they wrongfully invaded a citizen's home. Unlike today, early Americans could resist arrest when a police officer tried to restrain them without proper justification or a warrant—which the police had to allow citizens to read before arresting them. (Daring to dispute a warrant with a police official today who is armed with high-tech military weapons and tasers would be nothing short of suicidal.) This clear demand for a right to privacy was not a by-product of simpler times. Much like today, early Americans dealt with problems such as petty thievery, murder, and attacks by foreign enemies. Rather, the demand for privacy stemmed from a harbored suspicion of law enforcement officials and the unbridled discretion they could abuse.

While many law enforcement agents strive to honor and respect the Constitution, a number of today's police tactics and equipment are in clear conflict with the "freedom" vision of the framers. Equipment utilized by police, such as sophisticated flashlights containing super-sensitive detectors that sense the contents of your breath and computer taps that detect the information you read and write on your computer, undermines the foundation of our liberties. Despite our privacy rights, police conspicuously situate these invasive devices in front of our faces and into our personal space. In the same manner, they frequently use minor breaches of the law—such as failing to fully stop at a stop sign—to justify a complete, but often unnecessary, search and seizure of our persons and belongings. Most disturbing of all, some even resort to using lies and deceit to gain access to our homes, cars, and other private possessions.

The U.S. Supreme Court has also been a willing accomplice in this depreciation of our essential freedoms. Supreme Court opinions are plagued with countless exceptions that pervert the letter and spirit of the Fourth Amendment. Such cases include language the framers never foresaw or intended such as protective sweep exception, hot pursuit exception, inevitable discovery exception, and good faith exception, to name just a few. Even worse, the courts often use rationales such as police safety, national security, and citizen protection to justify these intrusive and corruptive interpretations.

Responsibility and Freedom

The end result is a people cowed into submission by an atmosphere of violence and intimidation. Just the whispered threat of violence can be a powerfully motivating force. An ounce of actual violence can yield a pound of terror—especially in America. This may explain why some people who are tyrannized by violent regimes languish under oppression with little resistance. As early as 1776, Thomas Jefferson noted in the Declaration of Independence that "all experience has shown that mankind are more disposed to suffer, while evils are sufferable, than to right themselves by abolishing the forms to which they are accustomed."

The Soviet dissident Aleksandr Solzhenitsyn noted how the Russian people would kneel inside the door of their apartments, pressing their ears to listen when the KGB (the secret police) came at midnight to arrest a neighbor. He commented that if all the people had come out and driven off the officers, sheer public opinion would have demoralized the effort to subdue what should have been a free people. But the people hid and trembled.

The answer to this dilemma lies in the nature of freedom. *True freedom imposes a corresponding responsibility to remain free.* Freedom is a gift. And on those to whom it is bestowed, a price is exacted. That price is vigilance and involvement. It also means not falling prey to the temptation to allow fear to override common sense or to prefer security over liberty. Such will lead to the death of freedom.

CHAPTER THREE

No Place to Hide

There was of course no way of knowing whether you were being watched at any given moment. How often, or on what system, the Thought Police plugged in on any individual wire was guesswork. It was even conceivable that they watched everybody all the time. But at any rate they could plug in your wire whenever they wanted to. You had to live—did live, from habit that became instinct—in the assumption that every sound you made was overheard, and, except in darkness, every movement scrutinized.

—George Orwell, *1984*

What could be compelling enough to cause a nation of people who claim to value their privacy to relinquish it without a fight? Is it because the so-called security measures trumpeted by the government as necessary are really effective at fighting terrorism and crime? Or is it because they make us feel safer?

Bruce Schneier, founder and chief technology officer of Counterpane Internet Security, seems to think it's the latter. As he remarked in an interview with *Business Week*, "A lot of security measures are very much of a feel-good nature. They're not effective but are meant to look effective. We demand our public officials do something, even if it does no good."[1]

Determined to feel good, we have turned a blind eye to the lessons of history. Whereas our nation's founders fiercely guarded their privacy from intrusion by the government, we, their distant heirs, have become accustomed to life under the watchful eyes of cameras mounted on streets, sidewalks, and ATMs, and in shops, offices, schools, and parks. To younger generations being raised on a diet of twenty-four-hour webcams, paparazzi-fed news coverage, and reality TV shows, the idea of fiercely guarding one's privacy must seem rather foreign.

It is not only that Americans have become culturally acclimated to a loss of privacy. Many have also neglected to heed the lessons of our forefathers and failed to acquire more than a rudimentary and mechanical understanding of our rights. When confronted with a government and society that seem to have gone surveillance crazy, an increasing number of Americans shrug their shoulders and ask, "What's the big deal?" Their logic: If government agents want to eavesdrop on our phone calls, open our letters, read our emails, track our movements with spy satellites, and enlist Mother Nature in their surveillance schemes, well, we have nothing to hide.

Surprising numbers of Americans have bought into the government's sales pitch that relinquishing a little personal privacy and allowing yourself to be tracked, monitored, and spied upon will improve national security. Reassuring ourselves that we have nothing to hide, Americans have grown inured to an increasing lack of privacy and ramped-up surveillance by our own government. What's more, since 9/11, we rarely even question the need for increased government surveillance of ordinary American citizens. Yet necessary or not, it has increased.

ROBOFLY

With one supposed goal in mind—to catch the enemy hiding among us—the U.S. government has subjected Americans to all manners of surveillance that test the limits of technology, science, and the imagination. The robofly is one such example.

Insect-like drones, these mechanized creatures were seen in 2007 hovering over political rallies in New York and Washington DC, seemingly spying on protesters. An eyewitness reported that the drones "looked kind of like dragonflies or little helicopters." Bernard Crane, a Washington lawyer who noticed the strange, machine-like dragonflies, observed, "They were large for dragonflies. I thought,

'Is that mechanical, or is that alive?'"[2] Or could it be some sort of new spy gadget? According to Rick Weiss of the *Washington Post*, some suspect that the insect-like drones are high-tech surveillance tools, perhaps deployed by the Department of Homeland Security.[3]

Such a thing would not be unheard of. After all, the government has been involved in this sort of chicanery for some time now. In the 1970s, for example, the CIA began flirting with the idea of using insect-like robots to survey our "enemies." After determining that a man-made bumblebee was too erratic in flight, the CIA settled on a robotic dragonfly. A laser beam guided this first insect-sized machine, while a miniature oscillating engine propelled its wings. But such technology failed when scientists couldn't maintain control over the device in a gentle wind.[4] Technology has evolved dramatically since that time, making it highly probable that the government has now perfected its spy bugs. As Rick Weiss writes, "Some federally funded teams are even growing live insects with computer chips in them with the goal of mounting spyware on their bodies and controlling their flight muscles remotely."[5]

In 1999, the U.S. government funded a $2.5 million study by researchers at the University of California, Berkeley. The goal was to "see robofly airborne by 2004." With nearly one hundred different model robots in use today, ranging in size from small birds to small planes, many with the capacity to snap pictures as they navigate through the air, that goal has surely been met. Similar efforts have led the Defense Advanced Research Projects Agency (DARPA) to insert computer chips into growing moths, "hatching them into healthy 'cyborg moths.'" DARPA is also working on creating cyborg beetles and literal shutterbugs. In July 2007, a team of scientists from Harvard University successfully put in flight a "fly-like robot" whose synthetic wings buzzed at 120 beats per second.[6]

These attempts to make the government's spy operations more effective by using devices that blend in with Mother Nature haven't been limited to flying insects. The CIA has also tested a 24-inch-long rubber robotic catfish that is capable of swimming among other fish. Virtually impossible to distinguish from real fish, "Charlie," as it has been named, is a secret work in progress. According to Toni Hiley, curator of the CIA museum, "Charlie's mission is still classified, we can't talk about it."[7]

As Donald Kerr, CIA deputy director for science and technology, has noted, "You look at just the number of things we're doing, a week, a year, it's really quite astounding." Kerr admits that CIA scientists spend a lot of time on "so-called tagging and tracking"—government-speak for spying.[8]

Surveillance has become an industry in itself, with huge sectors devoted to developing increasingly sophisticated gadgets to monitor American citizens, with or without their cooperation.[9] The science behind the gadgetry is particularly brilliant. Human motion analysis, a pet project of researchers at the University of Maryland, aims to create an individual "code" for the way people walk—researchers refer to it as "finding DNA in human motion." Dubbed Gait DNA, this surveillance system works by matching a person's facial image to his gait, height, weight, and other elements—all captured through remote observation, thereby allowing the computer to identify someone instantly and track them, even in a crowd.[10]

Soon there really will be no place to hide. Oceanit, a Hawaii-based company that worked with the Hawaiian National Guard in Iraq, rolled out Sense-Through-the-Wall (STTW) technology that supposedly "sees" through walls by picking up on sensitive radio signals the human body emits to determine vital signs such as breathing and heart rates. As Ian Kitajima, the marketing manager for Oceanit, pointed out, in addition to telling users whether someone is dead or alive on the battlefield, the technology also shows "whether someone inside a house is looking to harm you, because if they are, their heart rate will be raised. And 10 years from now, the technology will be much smarter. We'll scan a person with one of these things and tell what they're actually thinking."[11]

DARPA, the central research and development agency for the Department of Defense, is credited with ensuring that the United States keeps pace with other countries when it comes to such far-reaching technology. According to a BBC news report, "Back in the '70s, while we were working with typewriters and carbon paper, DARPA was developing the Internet. In the '90s, while we pored over maps,

DARPA invented satellite navigation that many of us now have in our cars." DARPA is also developing technology that will enable users to understand any language spoken to them, as well as fine-tuning the prototype for an unmanned airplane with surveillance cameras that will be able to stay airborne for up to five years.[12]

One thing is clear: Such surveillance technology provides the government with increasingly sophisticated intelligence tools that are being used domestically, as well as internationally. A large cross-section of the American people have unfortunately been lulled into believing that it is their patriotic duty to grant the government carte blanche power for the sake of waging the war on terror. The result is that they have unwittingly become the government's prime suspects—and convenient guinea pigs on which to test technologies like Charlie the catfish and Robofly.

Since 9/11, the U.S. government has been building an arsenal of surveillance tools aimed directly at American citizens, largely paid for by American taxpayers and fueled by our fears. Such incursions on our privacy rights constitute yet another link in the electronic concentration camp being erected around us.

A LITTLE TEMPORARY SAFETY?

Long before the smoke had cleared from the September 11, 2001, attacks, U.S. government leaders at all levels had succumbed to the idea that surveillance and information technology would make us safe—or so we were told. Computers, surveillance gear, and the ever-increasing information collected on Americans were to be the government's newest tools in its war on terror.

With Americans still reeling in shock and terror, Congress, with most of its members not even reading it, passed—and President George W. Bush signed into law—a mammoth piece of legislation that in the years to follow would undermine the fundamental principles of the Bill of Rights and sweep innocent Americans up in a dragnet of surveillance and detention. A politician's dream and a civil libertarian's nightmare, the USA PATRIOT Act of 2001 broadened the powers of the federal government, not only in regard to investigations relating to terrorism but also to criminal investigations in general. At some 342 pages, this law is both a marvel of political maneuvering and a monstrosity. Hidden within this tome are provisions that in effect turn the FBI, CIA, the Immigration and Naturalization Service, the Department of Homeland Security, and others into secret police; allow the government to access an individual's personal records; and prevent a permanent resident from returning to the United States after expressing views abroad that those in government perceive to be supportive of terrorism.

By expanding the definition of terrorism, the law could be used by the government to harass a broad range of political dissenters, ranging from Greenpeace to anti-abortion protesters to environmental activists to the National Rifle Association. And for the first time in the history of the nation, federal agents and police officers are authorized to conduct black-bag "sneak-and-peak" searches of homes and offices without first notifying an occupant of their intent or allowing anyone even to be present. Government officials can now detain permanent residents indefinitely without charging them with a crime. Law enforcement investigators were also given the authority to use roving wiretaps to listen in on conversations. This law also made it easier for the FBI—using powerful Internet spying technology called Carnivore—to monitor computers, read emails, and track which web pages American citizens visit with merely the say-so of an employer or university.[13]

Caught up in the 9/11 hysteria, few Americans objected to these infringements on their freedoms and even seemed to welcome them. Afraid to open their mail, travel, or voice their opinions publicly, many Americans felt threatened and wanted the government to do whatever was necessary to make them feel safe once again. A *Washington Post/ABC News* poll conducted shortly after the attacks reported that 66 percent of the people surveyed said they "would be willing to give up some of the liberties we have in this country in order for the government to crack down on terrorism."[14] And an *NBC News/Wall Street Journal* poll revealed that 78 percent of those polled would sacrifice some privacy for new security laws. No doubt such widespread approval gave the Bush administration sufficient support to move forward on the Patriot Act.[15]

CONSTANT SURVEILLANCE

The PATRIOT Act justified broader domestic surveillance, the logic being that if government agents knew more about each individual, they could distinguish the terrorists from law-abiding Americans— no doubt an earnest impulse shared by small-town police and federal agents alike. According to *Washington Post* reporter Robert O'Harrow Jr., this was a fantasy that had "been brewing in the law enforcement world for a long time."[16] Suddenly, with 9/11, the government had a perfect excuse to justify conducting far-reaching surveillance and collecting mountains of information on even the most law-abiding citizens.

Surveillance cameras, an increasingly popular tool used by law enforcement in the name of crime prevention, have led the way in transforming the United States into an even more powerful, yet seemingly benign, police state. Big cities, small towns, and everything in between have succumbed to the siren-song promise that surveillance cameras will not only stop crime, they will actually make us safer— a scenario first played out in Great Britain. There are as many as 4.2 million surveillance cameras in Britain. This roughly translates to one for every fourteen people, and a person can be captured on over 300 cameras each day.[17] A similar pattern of surveillance is developing in the United States. New York City is estimated to have over four thousand surveillance cameras.[18] Other big cities using these cameras include the District of Columbia, Boston, Baltimore, and Chicago.

Peering at passersby from their mounted positions on street poles, closed-circuit television systems (CCTVs) are the most common type of surveillance camera. These pole cameras are usually monitored by current and retired police officers and, sometimes, private citizens. Although less common, Portable Overt Digital Surveillance Systems (PODSS) are much more mobile and recognizable by their flashing blue lights. Often referred to as "footballs" for their easy mobility, PODSS are monitored via transportable devices that look like briefcases.

The presence of surveillance cameras on public streets may not seem like much of an intrusion. It might even seem unreasonable to expect any degree of privacy in public. Constant surveillance, some argue, shouldn't make a difference to a law-abiding citizen with nothing to hide. Yet whether or not you've done anything wrong, when you're the one being watched, life suddenly feels more oppressive. And it won't stop with surveillance cameras on the streets. As Rob Selevitch, president of the security company CEI Management Corp., predicts, "Cradle to grave, you're going to be on camera all the time."[19]

Congressman Ron Paul (R-Tex.) echoed this concern with his remarks on the floor of the House of Representatives in June 2002:

> *To prevent crimes in our homes or businesses—to check for illegal drug use, wife beating, child abuse, or tax evasion—government would need cameras to spy on our every move. They would not only need cameras on our streets and in our homes, but would need to constantly monitor our phones, Internet, and travels— just to make sure we are not terrorists, drug dealers, or tax evaders.*[20]

These fears/predictions are not so far from our present reality. Roaming digital eyes are already watching every move students make. Through the use of surveillance cameras, schools are able to monitor students from the moment they step foot on a bus until they arrive home. And schools both small and large are beginning to populate their hallways, classrooms, and buses with observation devices.[21] Viewmont High School in Utah installed thirty-six cameras to provide school officials a bird's-eye view of every square inch of the school's hallways and common areas.[22] "I can just simply scan through the school in less than a minute," boasts the school's principal. Schools in Little Rock, Arkansas, have installed seven hundred cameras, valued at around half a million dollars, in buildings throughout the school district in order to capitalize on "a high-tech ground-breaking surveillance method"[23] that links in real-time to school administrators, as well as to the local police department.

BIG BROTHER IN THE SKY

Many fear that we are on a road leading toward a "total surveillance society" in which the government will know who you are and what you are doing at all times. As one report observes, "From the moment you step out of your house until the time you return, the government will be able to track your every move, read what you're reading, know what you're eating, who you're spending time with, making each person more conscious of their surroundings and less likely to feel free."[24]

Whether we're crossing the street, queuing up at the ATM, or picnicking in the park, we're already under constant scrutiny—our movements monitored by cameras, tracked by satellites, and catalogued by a host of increasingly attentive government agencies. No longer does the idea of an omnipresent, omniscient government seem so far-fetched. As technology becomes more sophisticated, the idea of a total surveillance society moves further from the realm of George Orwell's science fiction fantasy into an accepted way of life.

Few would argue that we do not need a better system of internal security, especially in the wake of 9/11 and school shootings such as that at Columbine High School. The crucial question is whether Americans will be able to limit the government's use of such surveillance tools or whether we will be caught in an electronic nightmare from which there is no escape. That was the question raised by the announcement of a new government spy program in September 2007. A unique combination of George Orwell's *1984*, George Lucas's *Star Wars*, and the 1998 film *Enemy of the State*, the program involves the use of spy satellites in space to peer down on American citizens. Born out of an agreement between Homeland Security Secretary Michael Chertoff and Director of National Intelligence Mike McConnell, the government's host of satellites, which have historically been used to track climate changes and foreign military movements, would for the first time be turned toward the American homeland.

These satellites, which orbit the earth twenty-four hours a day and provide high-resolution photographs, will now be used to seek out and reveal terrorist activity and drug smuggling, among other things. Yet they are a far cry from the satellite imagery many Americans have become acquainted with since the arrival of easy-to-access online maps and photos from Google Earth and MapQuest.

These spy satellites not only take color photos, they also use more advanced technology to track heat generated by people in buildings. This is what we do know of these satellites' capabilities—the rest is top secret. As Robert Block of the *Wall Street Journal* points out, "The full capabilities of these systems are unknown outside the intelligence community, because they are among the most closely held secrets in government."[25] The technology, which is also available to state and local law enforcement agencies, raises serious concerns about the deepening ties between domestic law enforcement agencies and the military.

This citizen surveillance program also comes draped in the familiar government mantra that it will keep us safe from terrorists. As Charles Allen, the chief intelligence officer for the Department of Homeland Security, explained to the *Washington Post*, "These systems are already used to help us respond to crises. We anticipate that we can also use it to protect Americans by preventing the entry of dangerous people and goods into the country, and by helping us examine critical infrastructure for vulnerabilities."[26]

Despite the government's best efforts to sell the program, it is nothing less than "Big Brother in the sky," as Kate Martin, director of the Center for National Security Studies, aptly termed it.[27] Serious concerns have been raised about whether the program would cross a well-established line against the use of military assets in domestic law enforcement in violation of the Posse Comitatus Act of 1878.[28] The law, as previously discussed, in effect protects the American people from a military takeover during times of perceived emergency. But as Robert Block points out, the satellites intended for use under the program were "predominantly built for and owned by the Defense Department."[29] Granting civilian agencies access to this type of military equipment puts America's law enforcement agencies and the military into too cozy of a relationship.

The program also raises serious concerns about Congress's continued lack of oversight of government programs aimed at American citizens. The sole responsibility for overseeing this program rests in the hands of the Homeland Security Department and the Office of the Director of National Intelligence. Instead of using critical review by the courts and Congress to protect Americans' civil liberties, this grave responsibility is handled by officers of the government agencies using the technology. If history has taught us anything, however, it is that the government cannot be trusted to oversee its own surveillance programs. A recent internal FBI audit revealed, "The bureau potentially violated the law or agency rules more than 1,000 times while collecting data about domestic phone calls, emails, and financial transactions in recent years."[30] Given that the audit only covered 10 percent of the FBI's national security investigations since 2002, it is estimated that the number is realistically closer to several thousand.

BIG BROTHER IS TRACKING YOUR BODY

Police departments across the country are using modern technology in a way that relies more on computers and software and less on traditional community-oriented police tactics. For instance, the government already possesses the ability to access information right out of your car; it won't be much longer before it is aware of every time you drive down the road. Unknown to most Americans, nearly one-third of all vehicles on the road today (and 64 percent of the 2005 models) contain small chips and sensors known as event-data recorders (EDRs) that can retain up to 20 seconds of data prior to an accident. This information includes speed, braking, acceleration, and seat belt usage in cars.[31]

These "black boxes," which are similar to devices found in airplanes, are being used by car rental companies, transport companies, and even parents alongside other technology such as global positioning systems (GPS) to determine how fast their employees or children are driving, the number of hours behind the wheel, and general driving patterns. Newer technology makes it possible to capture up to three hundred hours of driving data, which is then easily downloaded onto a personal computer.[32] Black boxes are also being used in the nation's courtrooms to determine the outcome of criminal trials involving vehicular accidents, but their use doesn't stop there. Insurance companies are interested in using the technology to track their customers' driving habits, which, while not a true indicator of a driver's overall driving record, could lead to higher insurance rates. Some insurance companies have begun offering their customers discounts for voluntarily providing them with the information captured by the recorders.

This new technology, and its use by the government (in conjunction with the automobile corporations), concerns many privacy experts. Barry Steinhardt, director of the ACLU's Program on Technology and Liberty, observed, "We have a surveillance monster growing in our midst. These black boxes are going to get more sophisticated and take on new capabilities."[33] An increasing concern that this technology will chip away at citizens' privacy rights has prompted several states to pass laws regulating their use and accessibility. In 2004, California was the first state to pass legislation that requires automakers to inform buyers if their vehicle has a black box and to restrict anyone from downloading the information from the box without the owner's permission. Other states have since passed similar laws, and more are considering doing so. The issue has also received attention in Congress, with Representatives Mary Bono (R-Calif.) and Michael Capuano (D-Mass.) sponsoring a bill that would allow car owners to turn off their recorders.

Two additional technologies that have been tested by American police forces are license plate recognition cameras and facial recognition software. In the fall of 2006, the Los Angeles Police Department unveiled a police cruiser outfitted with $25,000 worth of this type of modern technology. "Patrolling the streets and highways of L.A., this smart car uses infrared technology to scan the license plates of cars it passes on both the left and right," noted one report. "A computer in the trunk immediately runs the collected information against a database that is updated daily with plate numbers associated with stolen vehicles, felony wanted suspects and Amber Alerts." This particular cruiser's identification system has the remarkable capability to automatically scan between five thousand and eight thousand cars each day. This includes the license plates of all citizens—not simply so-called criminals.[34]

Gregg Easterbrook, a writer for the *New Republic*, is one of the most outspoken critics of the new police devices. He explains that a machine that issues tickets today could easily become a "machine that classifies a person as an offender." Unfortunately, says

Easterbrook, "you can't confront your accuser because there is no accuser." He continues, "Can it be wise to establish a principle that when a machine says you did something illegal, you are presumed guilty?"[35]

In addition to the license plate recognition system, the LAPD equips its officers with a modern portable facial recognition device. Called a Mobile Identifier, this software is essentially a "traveling mug book." The Mobile Identifier is a handheld device that provides police officers on a street-beat with instant access to a database of thousands of facial images. Using this device, they practically become gang experts. With the ability to access the faces of all the known gang members in the community, any police officer can make visual recognitions.[36] Similar facial imaging technology has been tested in other police departments. During Super Bowl XXXV, the Tampa Bay Police Department used facial recognition software called FaceIt to search the entire crowd of football fans for potential criminals and terrorists. People at the game, of course, had no idea their faces were being scanned by the police.[37]

Facial imaging technology creates a so-called "faceprint" by graphing "nodal points," which are the peaks and valleys unique to each person's face. These nodal points include things such as the distance between the eyes, width of nose, depth of eye sockets, cheekbones, jaw line, and chin. There are about eighty nodal points the software can use to distinguish one face from another. The software then uses biometrics (also used in fingerprint and retina scanning) to chart and detect the similarities of one face to thousands of faces previously stored in a database.

Government agents at airport security checkpoints are using a new technique called "behavior detection." The program, which the U.S. government borrowed from Israeli airport security agencies, trains a small group of agents from the Transportation Security Administration on how to identify people with "evil intent." Formerly routine security screeners, these agents receive only four days of classroom training and three days of practice before they are sent off to focus in on passengers' facial expressions, body and eye movements, changes in vocal pitch, and other indicators of stress.[38]

While many Americans are concerned with the privacy issues relating to this program, even those who are close to the project recognize its flaws. Paul Ekman, a retired psychology professor from the University of California and the developer of some of the facial analysis tools used by the U.S. government in this program, admits, "We have no basis other than the seat of our pants to know how many points should be given to any one thing."[39] In other words, the government has no idea if the program will have even a modicum of success at identifying those with "evil intent." How could they, based on such subjective and unreliable indicators? People at airports are often in a hurry, under stress, and agitated—all of which is expressed in their facial expressions and mannerisms.

Very little, it seems, is going to be beyond the scope of government eyes. In December 2007, the FBI announced that it was building the world's largest computer database of people's physical characteristics. This $1 billion project gives the government unprecedented abilities to identify individuals in the United States and abroad and significantly expands the amount and kinds of biometric information stored on American citizens.

Law enforcement authorities around the world will be able to rely on iris patterns, face-shape data, scars, and perhaps even the unique ways people walk and talk to solve crimes and identify criminals and terrorists.[40] Called Next Generation Identification, the FBI system will collect a wide variety of biometric information in one place for identification and forensic purposes. This means that a police officer making a traffic stop or a border agent at an airport can run a ten-fingerprint check on a suspect and within seconds know if the person is on a database of the most wanted criminals and terrorists. An analyst can take palm prints lifted from a crime scene and run them against the expanded database. Intelligence agents will be able to exchange biometric information worldwide. The FBI intends to make both criminal and civilian data available to authorized users—that is, government agents and the police. And, in fact, there are over nine hundred thousand federal, state, and local law enforcement officers who can query the fingerprint database today.[41]

This technology is already being used in the government's "war on terror." For some time, the U.S. Defense Department has been storing in a database the images of fingerprints, irises, and faces of more than 1.5 million Iraqi and Afghan detainees, Iraqi citizens and foreigners who need access to U.S. military bases. The Pentagon also collects DNA samples from some Iraqi detainees, which are stored separately.

While biometric data clearly has its uses in crime-fighting, civil libertarians have voiced their concerns about it being used to track law-abiding citizens. As Barry Steinhardt of the ACLU states, "It's enabling the Always On Surveillance Society."[42] Marc Rotenberg, executive director of the Electronic Privacy Information Center, sees the ability to share data across systems as problematic. "You're giving the federal government access to an extraordinary amount of information linked to biometric identifiers that is becoming increasingly inaccurate."[43]

Privacy advocates are concerned about the ability of people to correct false information. "Unlike say, a credit card number, biometric data is forever," notes Paul Saffo, a Silicon Valley technology forecaster. He fears that the FBI, whose computer technology record has been marred by expensive failures, could not guarantee the data's security. "If someone steals and spoofs your iris image, you can't just get a new eyeball," Saffo said.[44]

From Orwell's Telescreen to Your TV

In their pursuit of increased ad revenue, some private corporations seem to be mirroring George Orwell's vision of the future where Big Brother was always watching and the Thought Police were always listening. As Orwell writes in his novel *1984*: "The telescreen received and transmitted simultaneously. Any sound that Winston made, above the level of a very low whisper, would be picked up by it."[45]

When his futuristic book was published in 1949, little did Orwell realize that his concept of an eavesdropping technology would one day become reality. Yet if Google succeeds in its pursuit of an Internet technology that would enable your computer to "listen" to what's being watched on your TV, that reality may happen sooner than you think.

According to *Technology Review*, the technology "uses a computer's built-in microphone to listen to the sounds in a room. It then filters each five-second snippet of sound to pick out audio from a TV, reduces the snippet to a digital 'fingerprint,' searches an Internet server for a matching fingerprint from a pre-recorded show, and, if it finds a match, displays ads, chat rooms, or other information related to that snippet on the user's computer."[46] The "fingerprint" is thus used by Google to match Internet advertisements that would appeal to you, the computer user, based on your TV viewing preferences.

The idea is that Google would be able to attract more advertisers by providing them with direct access to consumers' desires. An article in *Technology Review* explains, "Nicole Kidman fans, for instance, might enjoy knowing what dress she's wearing on a broadcast of 'Extra!' or where they can buy a similar outfit. Or ads for Cooper Minis might appear whenever the car showed up in TV rebroadcasts of *The Italian Job*."[47]

While the prospect of having one's entertainment tailored to fit one's viewing preferences may seem appealing, even the best-intentioned plans can be perverted for nefarious purposes. In this case, Google's proposed listening technology poses serious privacy concerns. Google insists that the only information gleaned from a listening computer would be your TV watching preferences, since the "fingerprinting technology" used to monitor your TV viewing makes it impossible to eavesdrop on other sounds in the room such as personal conversations. But when it comes to protecting freedom, Google's track record has not been all that stellar. Lest we forget, it was Google, in an agreement with the authoritarian Chinese government, that was willing to censor its search services in China in order to gain greater access to China's fast-growing market.[48]

Google's listening apparatus is just the tip of the iceberg, the latest in a series of yet-to-be-unveiled surveillance devices that herald a privacy nightmare. Using a personal computer to listen in on your TV habits is only a small step away from audio software that can record your living room small talk or, even worse, webcams that would videotape everything that goes on in the comfort of your own home.

It is widely believed that existing Internet software already puts Google and other search engines in your living room today. As *Technology Review* points out, "Google probably already knows what search terms you use, what Web pages you're viewing, and what you write about in your email."[49] Danny Sullivan, the editor of *Search Engine Watch*, an observer of the various search engine providers, notes that search engines retain records detailing all the websites people visit, along with the search terms they use to find the websites.[50] Even more troubling, these search terms and websites are directly traceable to the user. This is particularly concerning in light of America Online's security breakdown in 2006 that resulted in the accidental release of more than six hundred thousand of its members' search records.

Despite the modern capabilities of search engines to delve into Americans' psyches by monitoring their Internet search habits, actually recording sounds from one's home raises the bar—and increases the opportunities for foul play. "Pretty soon the security industry is going to find a way to hijack the Google feed and use it for full on espionage," a report from the *Register* recognizes. "We should think that 'spyware' might take on an extra meaning if someone less scrupulous decided on a similar piece of software."[51]

The government, as we shall see, is already collecting customer data (phone and email) from private telecommunications companies. Once the technology is perfected, it won't be long before the government targets search engines like Google.

LIFE IN A TECHNOCRACY

We have moved into a new paradigm from that of the military-industrial complex President Dwight D. Eisenhower warned of in his 1961 farewell address. As the military-industrial complex has morphed into a security-industrial complex, the forecast becomes clear. Eisenhower warned about unaccountable power, and that's what we are really dealing with in the surveillance state.

Yet it would be wrong to lay the blame for the government's amassing of power solely on the politicians. The combination of advanced technology with a concentration of power in the centralized federal government has resulted in a technocratic elite directing government activity. Thus, while the politicians may seem to run the show, behind the scenes, an elite of intellectuals—composed of academic, scientific and government leaders, and bureaucrats—are pushing the buttons and calling the shots. "These men are close to the seat of modern governmental power," writes law professor Jacques Ellul of Bordeaux University. "The state is no longer founded on the 'average citizen' but on the ability and knowledge of this elite. The average man is altogether unable to penetrate technical secrets or governmental organization and consequently can exert no influence at all on the state."[52]

Presidents may come and go, but non-elected bureaucrats remain. Too often, we fail to recognize that the massive computerized and electronically interconnected bureaucracies that administer governmental policy are a permanent form of government. Non-elected technicians, therefore, often make the basic decisions of the American government. This includes presidential advisors who work for subsequent administrations and ubiquitous bureaucracies such as the Department of Homeland Security and the various intelligence gathering agencies, among many others. This means that the corporate state—its business, its education, its government, even the daily pattern of the average citizen's life—under the control of a technocratic elite, constitutes a form of government diametrically opposed to that which the American founders envisioned and largely outside the boundaries of the Constitution.

As a non-elected bureaucracy increasingly administers the government, we are now operating for all intents and purposes in a technocracy. As a result, we frequently find our lives shaped by the edicts of the courts and technicians who attempt to impose a national bureaucracy from a centralized state, rather than the dictates of the Constitution. This is illustrated very clearly in the numerous regulations passed by bureaucratic agencies such as the U.S. Department of Homeland Security, the Department of Education, the Environmental Protection Agency, the Internal Revenue Service, and so on. Although these regulations are seldom put to a vote by the electorate, they operate as laws.

The framers of the Constitution intended Article I of the Constitution, which requires that all laws be passed by Congress, to maintain the power of the people. In this way, the people can unseat their congressional representatives if they disagree with their performance. Without this safeguard, there is no representative government and we are left with a governmental system that has expanded beyond the borders of its governing document.

"Democracy in such a society," Ellul writes, "can only be a mere appearance."[53]

SOLD A BILL OF GOODS

As a society, we have become experts at comforting ourselves with illusions rather than facing up to the grim reality of a world in which freedom is fast disappearing. Americans have become easy targets for almost any scheme that promises them increased safety. Kept in a state of constant unease by color-coded terror alerts and vague government reports of foiled terror plots, we have been primed to meekly accept that government officials have our best interests at heart and are doing their best to keep us safe.

The debate over installing surveillance cameras on public streets, in parks, and at other venues is a prime example. Repeatedly, we have been assured that giving government agents access to our every move on the streets will reduce crime and prevent terrorism. We have been sold a bill of goods.

A 2005 study by the British government, which boasts the most extensive surveillance camera coverage in the world at approximately 4 million cameras (one for every fourteen people), found that of all the areas studied, surveillance cameras generally failed to achieve a reduction in crime. While these snooping devices tended to reduce premeditated or planned crimes such as burglary, vehicle crime, criminal damage, and theft, they failed to have an impact on more spontaneous crimes, violence against a person, and public order offenses like public drunkenness. Surveillance cameras have also been found to have a "displacement" effect on crime. Rather than getting rid of crime, surveillance cameras force criminal activity to move from the area being watched to other surrounding areas.[54]

While a surveillance camera might help law enforcement identify a suicide bomber after the fact, as Marc Rotenberg of the Electronic Privacy Information Center notes, "Cameras are not an effective way to stop a person that is prepared to commit that kind of act." Rotenberg points to the 2005 terrorist subway bombings in London as an example. He explained that surveillance cameras "did help determine the identity of the suicide bombers and aided the police in subsequent investigations, but obviously they had no deterrent effect in preventing the act, because suicide bombers are not particularly concerned about being caught in the act."[55]

Human nature being what it is, no amount of technology will completely prevent people, especially terrorists, from committing evil. And, in the end, it's the law-abiding citizens who will suffer. Imagine every conversation you've had or every place you've visited being tracked by someone behind a camera. It's a chilling thought—or at least it should be to anyone who values privacy. Under such constant surveillance, you will eventually become conscious of being observed, recorded, and judged. And without realizing it, you will naturally begin to censor your own actions—in regard to even the most innocuous things. In a society where there is no right to privacy and surveillance cameras are the eyes and ears of government, we are all suspects.

DATA SURVEILLANCE IN A TECHNOLOGICAL AGE

The advent of computers and the Internet has taken surveillance and the amassing of personal information on American citizens to new heights. The credit bureaus and data centers that now proliferate are good examples. These "private" firms, which exist by selling credit information, collect an incredible amount of information on average Americans. When you use your cell phone, you leave a record of when the call was placed, whom you called, how long it lasted, and even where you were at the time. When you use your ATM card, you leave a record of where and when you used the card. There is even a video camera at most locations watching you.

Under the USA PATRIOT Act, your bank is required to analyze your transactions for any patterns that raise suspicion and to see if you are connected to any objectionable people—ostensibly in the hunt for terrorists. If there are questions, your bank alerts the government, which shares such information with intelligence and law enforcement agencies across the country (local, county, state, and federal).

When you buy food at the supermarket or purchase merchandise online or through a toll-free number, these transactions are recorded by data collection and information companies. In this way, private companies specifically target you, a victim of "dataveillance," as a particular type of consumer. Government intelligence agencies routinely collect these records—billions of them—on what you've done and where you've lived your entire life. This includes every house or apartment in which you resided, all your telephone numbers, the cars you've owned, and more.

The trade-off is that this dataveillance can make one's life easier and more convenient. Yet record keeping of this kind is also ripe for abuse and fraught with the potential for errors—some of which are not so easy to correct—that can brand you for life. Take what happened to Matthew Frost of Tampa, Alabama, a businessman and father of two who was a victim of identity theft. Frost simply wanted to vote in the 2000 presidential election. But when he attempted to cast a ballot, the election worker told him, "Sorry, sir, you have a felony. You can't vote."

A credit card fraudster, convicted of a felony in 1995, used Frost's name while he was living abroad. When government officials attempted to use a private data contractor to help purge the electoral votes of felons and other ineligible people, that fraud apparently provided a tenuous link in the data between Frost and a felony. Although it was clearly a mistake because Frost had never been convicted of a felony, he still was not allowed to vote.[56] This was "a glaring demonstration of what can happen when the government and private data services team up to target individuals," notes *Washington Post* journalist Robert O'Harrow. "The use of computerized personal information can—and often does—spin out of control."[57]

The company responsible for Frost's exclusion was ChoicePoint, a Georgia-based organization that acts as a database of personal information. Commonly referred to as a commercial data-broker,

ChoicePoint is a private intelligence agency. Several years ago, thieves gained access to ChoicePoint's databases by using stolen identities to create seemingly legitimate businesses. They were able to gain access to individuals' names, addresses, Social Security numbers, and credit reports.

While ChoicePoint's security breach raises serious concerns regarding identity theft, even more alarming is the relationship between commercial data brokers such as ChoicePoint and the U.S. government. The federal government has increasingly turned to commercial databases for information to aid criminal investigations and homeland security in cases where they are not allowed to collect the data themselves. And a large portion of the commercial data broker's business comes from government contracts—at taxpayer expense, of course. ChoicePoint even has websites for federal agencies, such as www.choicepoint.com/government, where only government officials can access information.

No matter what arguments are made to the contrary, the federal government should not be probing into the lives of Americans whenever it wants. Various laws have been enacted over time to guard against unreasonable intrusions by the government into our private lives. One such law is the Privacy Act, which was passed by Congress in 1974 and prohibits the government from forming a database. Although the fear was that such a database could constitute an invasion of privacy, the law only prevents the government from creating a database.

At the time the law was passed, Congress had no reason to suspect that private corporations would ever have the desire or means to create such databases. The emergence of corporations such as ChoicePoint, LexisNexis, and others, however, has enabled government intelligence and police agencies to circumvent the law and gain information on private citizens with the click of a button. Although such tactics clearly contradict the spirit of privacy laws intended to guard against government abuse, it is technically legal for the government to gain access to these databases. Government officials have taken full advantage of this loophole. Due to the fact that these databases are owned and operated by private corporations, they are relatively unregulated and fall outside the scrutiny of privacy watch-dog groups. Reports of security breaches at numerous data broker-age companies only serve to fan concerns about the lack of oversight and regulation.

The American founders would be aghast at the extent to which the government is involved in citizen data gathering. A quick read of the First Amendment provides a stark reminder of this. It says: "Congress shall make no law respecting an establishment of religion, or prohibiting the free exercise thereof; or abridging freedom of speech or of the press; or of the right of the people peaceably to assemble, and to petition the government for a redress of grievances." In these forty-five words are found the fundamental values of republican democracy: a belief in privacy, individuality, intellectual freedom, open criticism, and community action.

Equally important, the words of the First Amendment assume, and even insist on, a citizenry that not only has access to whatever information the government may have on them but control over the information as well. They also presume a people who know how to use information to further their own interests. "There is not a single line written by Jefferson, Adams, Paine, Hamilton, or Franklin," writes New York University professor Neil Postman, "that does not take for granted that when information is made available to citizens they are capable of managing it."[58]

SPYING ON AMERICANS

While corporations such as ChoicePoint enable the government to take advantage of loopholes in laws protecting our privacy rights, the government has devised other ways to spy on Americans. When it was revealed in December 2005 that President Bush had authorized the National Security Agency (NSA) to listen in on the domestic phone calls of American citizens, the spotlight focused for a brief time on the NSA, which is among the least known and most influential organizations within the U.S. government.

With its massive bank of computers, the intelligence organization breaks codes, directs spy satellites, intercepts millions of electronic messages transmitted by friends and enemies from every corner of the globe, and recognizes certain target words in spoken communications. The NSA, however, is more than a computerized collection agency. This virtually unknown government agency has also sought to influence the operation and development of communication networks widely used by the American public.

Created in absolute secrecy in 1952 by President Harry S Truman's Executive Order 12333, the NSA is a component of the Department of Defense that oversees the country's military and nonmilitary cryptology, surveillance, intelligence, and security operations. The charter establishing the agency authorizes it to collect information that constitutes "foreign intelligence or counterintelligence" pertaining to national security or ongoing military operations, but it prohibits acquisition of "information concerning the domestic activities of United States persons." The NSA's mission, therefore, is legally confined to obtaining intelligence of adversaries' communications and securing sensitive governmental and military communications.[59] Its two main undertakings are codemaking (under the encryption division, Information Assurance) and codebreaking (under the signals intelligence division, SIGINT).[60] The agency maintains listening posts around the world and also operates communications interception bases in both West Virginia and the state of Washington, allowing it to detect, decipher, and overhear the verbal and written communications of foreign governments, diplomats, trade negotiators, drug lords, and terrorists, among others.[61]

A tight screen of secrecy and uncertainty surrounds the size and scope of the mission of the NSA. Because Congress has never passed a law defining its responsibilities and obligations, the NSA is able to operate outside the constitutional system of checks and balances. Agencies such as the NSA that operate with "black ops" (or secret) budgets are not truly accountable to Congress—our elected representatives.

Article 1, Section 9, Clause 7 of the Constitution empowers Congress and makes the United States a democracy by guaranteeing that the people's representatives will know what governmental agencies are actually doing and also requiring full disclosure of their activities: "No money shall be drawn from the Treasury, but in Consequence of Appropriations made by law; and a regular Statement and Account of the Receipts and Expenditures of all public Money shall be published from time to time." But this constitutional accountability clause has not been applied to the CIA or NSA since their creation. These agencies, thus, do not function within the bounds of the Constitution or, as the Declaration of Independence so famously put it, by "a decent respect for the opinions of mankind." And nothing short of a revolution could abolish agencies such as the NSA and the CIA or at least bring them under democratic control.

In his book *Body of Secrets*, the second installment of the most extensively researched inquiry into the NSA, author James Bamford describes the NSA as "a strange and invisible city unlike any on earth" that lies beyond a specially constructed and perpetually guarded exit ramp off the Baltimore–Washington Parkway. "It contains what is probably the largest body of secrets ever created."[62]

Bamford's use of the word "probably" is significant because the size of the NSA's staff, budget, and buildings is kept secret from the public. Intelligence experts estimate that the agency employs around 38,000 people, with a starting salary of $50,000 for its entry-level mathematicians, computer scientists, and engineers.[63] Its role in the intelligence enterprise and its massive budget dwarf those of its better-known counterpart, the Central Intelligence Agency (CIA). The NSA's website provides its own benchmarks:

> *Neither the number of employees nor the size of the Agency's budget can be publicly disclosed. However, if the NSA were considered a corporation in terms of dollars spent, floor space occupied, and personnel employed, it would rank in the top 10 percent of the Fortune 500 companies.*[64]

If the NSA's size seems daunting, its scope is both disconcerting and relatively unknown. Yet media investigations in recent years have revealed that the agency has engaged in highly suspect activities domestically. In December 2005, the *New York Times* reported that President Bush had secretly authorized the NSA to monitor international phone calls and email messages initiated by individuals (including American citizens) in the United States.[65] Bush signed the executive order in 2002, under the pretext of needing to act quickly and secretly to detect communication among terrorists and their contacts and to quell future attacks in the aftermath of September 11, 2001.[66]

In doing so, Bush and the NSA circumvented the Foreign Intelligence Surveillance Court, which reviews requests to target any domestic communications it deems a potential threat. The ten-member court was established by Congress's 1978 Foreign Intelligence Surveillance Act (FISA), which also delineates requirements for domestic surveillance.[67] FISA declares itself the "exclusive means" for authorizing foreign intelligence surveillance and obliges the NSA to appear before the special court, demonstrate probable cause that the target is linked to a terrorist group, and obtain a criminal or intelligence warrant before installing domestic wiretaps.[68]

The *New York Times* story forced President Bush to admit that he had secretly instructed the NSA to wiretap Americans' domestic communications with international parties without seeking a FISA warrant or congressional approval. Bush affirmed that the federal government has "been on the offensive against the terrorist networks plotting within our borders" and acknowledged that he had reauthorized the surveillance program more than thirty times since its inception. The president justified the program as being "a vital tool in our war against the terrorists" that is "critical to saving American lives" and "fully consistent with my constitutional responsibilities and authorities."[69]

"There's no doubt in my mind," declared Bush, "[that] there are safeguards in place to make sure the program focuses on calls coming from the outside of the United States in, with the belief that there's an Al Qaeda person making the calls."[70] Bush also warned that "disclosure of this effort damages our national security and puts our citizens at risk. Revealing classified information is illegal, alerts our enemies, and endangers our country."[71]

The *New York Times* had already sat on its story for a full year due to White House pressure not to publish its findings. It would be another six months before *USA Today* delivered the second and most significant piece of the puzzle. In May 2006, *USA Today* divulged that the NSA had been secretly collecting the phone records of tens of millions of Americans who used the national "private" networks AT&T, Verizon, and BellSouth. Failing to differentiate between citizens suspected of terrorist affiliation and those simply making international calls, the NSA has been amassing detailed records of private phone conversations between friends, relatives, co-workers, and business contacts practically since 9/11. This arrangement between the NSA and the three largest national phone companies violates Section 222 of the U.S. Communications Act, first passed in 1934, which prohibits such companies from revealing their customers' calling habits. But to an even greater extent, this arrangement abrogates the NSA's obligation to obtain a warrant before engaging in domestic eavesdropping.[72]

In March 2006, the ACLU filed a lawsuit on behalf of scholars, attorneys, and journalists who regularly communicate with contacts in the Middle East and who argued that the surveillance hinders their communications and relationships. U.S. District Judge Anna Diggs Taylor's August 2006 ruling declared the domestic spying program unconstitutional for violating both free speech and privacy rights and the principle of the separation of powers. Subsequently, a unanimous ruling by a three-judge Sixth Circuit Court of Appeals panel granted the government's request for a stay of the lower court ruling, thereby allowing the NSA to continue its eavesdropping while an expedited appeal was processed.[73]

Yet it's not as if the NSA had no alternatives other than its warrantless surveillance system. The NSA had already pretested a technology that would have safeguarded Americans from excessive privacy encroachment. ThinThread, a pilot program developed by the NSA in the late 1990s, would have enabled the NSA to collect, analyze, and secure massive quantities of communications data while protecting personal privacy in the process. ThinThread combined four advanced surveillance tools: the most sophisticated method of sorting through phone and email data to identify suspicious communications; identification and encryption of domestic phone numbers to ensure their holders' privacy; an automated auditing system to monitor how security analysts process communications data and improve their efficiency; and a feature which detected and chronicled relationships between callers so that only when evidence of a potential threat had been developed could analysts request decryption of the records.[74] This last component, in effect, would have enabled the NSA to identify suspicious targets and take their case of probable cause to the Foreign Intelligence Surveillance Court for authorization of domestic surveillance.

The information-sorting system could have provided a simple solution to the vexing conflict between national security and personal privacy interests but was discarded following the September 11 attacks. In the swift expansion of executive authority claimed by the president after 9/11, ThinThread's innovative safeguards became as inconsequential as the privacy it was designed to protect.

So long as it remains invisible to the scrutiny of legislative and judicial overseers and the eyes of common Americans, the NSA will, in all probability, continue to violate constitutional provisions and civil liberties. Once referred to by insiders and informants as "No Such Agency" and "Never Say Anything," the organization seems to be living up to its alternative acronyms. This is much to the dismay and detriment of Americans everywhere, or at least to those of us who have communicated by phone or email since 2002.

ECHELON

The NSA also developed Echelon, a global electronic surveillance network that allows security agencies of Great Britain and the United States, as well as Canada, Australia, and New Zealand, to collect and exploit intelligence collected worldwide. Created in the heat of the Cold War, Echelon intercepts and analyzes virtually every phone call, fax, and email message sent anywhere in the world. It does so by positioning "listening stations" (including land bases, satellites, and ships sailing the seven seas) all over the globe to capture data, satellite, microwave, cellular, and fiber-optic communications traffic.

Although Echelon was originally established as an international spy system, suspicions arose at the dawn of the new millennium that its intelligence ambitions might have turned inward. In 1999, the House Intelligence Committee proposed an amendment to the

Intelligence Reauthorization Act requesting that the NSA and the CIA provide a report to Congress detailing the privacy precautions taken while monitoring the communications and activities of American citizens.[75]

It became evident that Echelon had not only turned inward, targeting such peaceful political groups as Amnesty International, Greenpeace, and several Christian groups,[76] but had actually broadened the scope of its mission to include both political and commercial espionage. It also became a means of benefiting big business and advancing personal political agendas. During the Reagan Administration, the NSA targeted Maryland Congressman Michael Barnes, intercepting and recording his telephone conversations with Nicaraguan officials. In March 2003, the British *Observer* asserted that the Bush administration had used its Echelon satellite station in New Zealand to spy on council members from Angola, Bulgaria, Cameroon, Chile, Guinea, and Pakistan in its effort to garner support for the impending war against Iraq.[77]

A somewhat incestuous relationship had also developed between the government and defense and private intelligence contractors, which had helped to devise and power the Echelon effort. In 1993, President Bill Clinton directed the NSA to use Echelon facilities to spy on Japanese car manufacturers developing zero-emission cars and to pass on critical information to the three largest American car manufacturers, Ford, General Motors, and Chrysler.[78]

Echelon remains an active monitoring mechanism for legitimate security purposes, as well as political and economic ends. Patrick S. Poole, a writer for *FrontPage* magazine, notes, "What is most frightening is the targeting of such 'subversives' as those who expose corrupt government activity, protect human rights from government encroachments, challenge corporate polluters, or promote the gospel of Christ. That the vast intelligence powers of the United States should be arrayed against legitimate and peaceful organizations is demonstrative not of the desire to monitor, but of the desire to control."[79]

Almost since its conception, the NSA has secretly targeted the communications of American citizens while claiming to confine its scope to foreign intelligence collection. From the early 1960s to 1973, the agency compiled "watch lists" containing names of U.S. residents whose activities "may result in civil disturbances or otherwise subvert the national security of the U.S."

Operation SHAMROCK constituted the largest governmental interception program affecting Americans and involved the NSA's interception of millions of international telegrams leaving or transiting the United States. Eerily reminiscent of the NSA's phone and email eavesdropping program, SHAMROCK was in operation through 1975 and was made possible by the cooperation of three private international telegraph companies. As long as three decades ago, a U.S. Senate intelligence committee recognized the agency's "vast technological capability" and noted that "if not properly controlled," this lurking giant "could be turned against the American people, at great cost to liberty."[80]

Indeed, there has been an alarming rise in the number of reports that federal intelligence agencies have been spying on domestic antiwar groups. Religious groups all across the United States have come under particular scrutiny by federal agencies, especially antiwar groups with ties to the Quakers.

Paranoia and Political Intimidation

The Iraq Pledge of Resistance–Baltimore, a nonviolent Quaker-linked peace group, is "a nationwide network of activists and organizations committed to ending the war in Iraq through nonviolent" civil resistance in the spirit of Martin Luther King Jr. and Mahatma Gandhi.[81] The group requires any individual who participates in direct action or civil disobedience to take nonviolence training before doing so.[82] The Pledge of Resistance also "lobbies Maryland congressmembers via letters, phone calls, faxes, emails, and face-to-face meetings," in addition to its periodic acts of civil disobedience.

Given that the Quakers tend to inform authorities ahead of time when they will be protesting and even whether those protests will include acts of peaceful civil disobedience, they hardly seem to warrant the attention of the intelligence community. Even so, reports show that the NSA has been keeping a close watch on the Iraq Pledge of Resistance since shortly after 9/11. According to one NSA document, "[i]n one instance, the agency filed reports approximately every 15 minutes from 9:30 AM to 3:18 PM on the day of a demonstration at the National Vigilance Airplane Memorial on the NSA Campus in Maryland."[83] The NSA collected extensive information on Pledge of Resistance members, including "license numbers and descriptions and the number of people in each car," and then filed a report about them gathering in a church parking lot for the demonstration. NSA agents also logged their travel to the demonstration, including stopping at a gas station along the way. A canine dog unit was used to search a minivan when it was stopped on the way to the demonstration, but nothing was found.[84]

The NSA increased its security measures for a demonstration on October 4, 2003, evidently expecting trouble from the pacifist organization. An NSA letter even showed that the agency planned to have its Weapons of Mass Destruction Rapid Response Team on site. The team would include an officer with a shotgun, an increase in the number of officers, mobile units monitoring the highway and parking lot, roving patrols on bicycles in various areas, four K9 handlers, agents to provide countersurveillance, aerial observations by the Anne Arundel police, and photography/video surveillance of the activities.[85]

Agents have reportedly attempted to infiltrate the pacifist group. During a demonstration on March 20, 2003, a provocateur, whom none of the Pledge members could identify, began "taunting the police in a violent manner."[86] But when the police finally arrested the Pledge members, he was nowhere to be found. Despite the harassment, the NSA failed to demonstrate any tangible evidence that the Pledge of Resistance poses a threat to national security. With their extensive nonviolence training and commitment to peaceful action, it is unlikely that the Pledge members posed a threat of disruption to any functions. Evidence suggests that the government's motives are tied to a growing paranoia and the political intimidation of peace organizations.

The U.S. Defense Department is even getting involved in domestic surveillance activities. The Department of Defense had largely cut off its domestic spying programs after it was revealed that it had infiltrated antiwar groups and conducted investigations on at least one hundred thousand American citizens during the Vietnam era.[87] The public outcry that followed prompted Congress to strictly limit military spying. The Department of Defense appears to once again be pushing its boundaries, presumably under the authority of its "Counterintelligence Field Activity (CIFA) office, which was founded in 2002" and "now employs more than 1,000 people."[88] Reports reveal that the U.S. military spied on the meetings of the Truth Project, an antiwar group that meets in a Quaker Meeting House in Lake Worth, Florida.[89] In a Department of Defense database acquired by NBC News, nearly four-dozen antiwar meetings or protests were monitored over a ten-month period.[90]

The Truth Project was one of many groups whose activities were listed as a "threat" in the Department of Defense database.[91] Records obtained by the ACLU in a Freedom of Information Act lawsuit confirm that the Defense Department had been collecting information on antiwar groups and keeping the information "in an internal database past the 90 days its guidelines allowed, and even after it was determined there was no threat."[92] This information evidently contained detailed information, and "[t]he document indicated that intelligence reports and tips about antiwar protests, including mundane details like the schedule for weekly planning meetings, were widely shared among analysts from the military, the Federal Bureau of Investigation and the Department of Homeland Security."[93]

A close examination of the FBI's surveillance of various religious groups involved in antiwar protest activities reveals a rather troubling qualitative shift in recent years from benign intelligence gathering to outright political intimidation. While it is unlikely that the Quakers will be afraid to conduct protests by petty intimidation tactics, this does not mean that less committed activists would not be frightened off. The ultimate victim in this sort of security atmosphere is democratic discourse.

THE ABYSS FROM WHICH THERE IS NO RETURN

Senator Frank Church (D-Ida.) served as the chairman of the Select Committee on Intelligence that investigated the National Security

Agency in the 1970s. Church recognized that such surveillance powers "at any time could be turned around on the American people, and no American would have any privacy left, such is the capability to monitor everything: telephone conversations, telegrams, it doesn't matter. There would be no place to hide." Noting that the NSA could enable a dictator "to impose total tyranny" upon an utterly defenseless American public, Church declared that he did not "want to see this country ever go across the bridge" of constitutional protection, congressional oversight, and popular demand for privacy. He avowed that "we," implicating both Congress and its constituency in this duty, "must see to it that this agency and all agencies that possess this technology operate within the law and under proper supervision, so that we never cross over that abyss. That is the abyss from which there is no return."[94]

Senator Church was not the only official wary of the executive branch's capacity to vastly overstep its authority in the name of national security, nor was he alone in understanding that the other branches are duty bound to check such audacious affirmations of authority. As the late Supreme Court Justice William Brennan cautioned:

> *The concept of military necessity is seductively broad, and has a dangerous plasticity. Because they invariably have the visage of overriding importance, there is always a temptation to invoke security "necessities" to justify an encroachment upon civil liberties. For that reason, the military-security argument must be approached with a healthy skepticism: its very gravity counsels that courts be cautious when military necessity is invoked by the Government to justify a trespass on First Amendment rights.*[95]

A STATE OF FEAR

Trapped by our fears, we have become our own jailers. People are afraid of crime. People are afraid of terrorism. People are even afraid of their neighbors. Added to this, the "war on crime" and "war on terror" propaganda has created a state of fear in people who, in large urban areas, barricade themselves at the first sign of darkness.

Whether these fears are entirely valid, whether these fears are greatly enhanced by the media, and whether other ages have had much more to fear is irrelevant. What is relevant is that our breakdown in social trust and fear creates an open-arms mentality toward police surveillance. It also fosters "crackdowns" by the police, which only serve to heighten tension and fear.

In such an atmosphere of paranoia and fear, people are more willing to give up their rights. History provides a valuable lesson here: most police states, perhaps counterintuitively, came into being through the democratic process with majority support. No military coup was necessary. All that is required is the demand for economic and physical security to prevail over liberty, whether in response to an actual or perceived crisis. People are easily led to believe that security and liberty are mutually exclusive. But, as Benjamin Franklin remarked: "They that can give up essential liberty to obtain a little temporary safety deserve neither liberty nor safety."[96]

SUSPECTS

Many of the effects of surveillance are subtler than ever. The knowledge that one cannot discard one's past, that advancement in society depends heavily on a "good" record, creates considerable pressure on people to conform. Many work hard to keep their records clean, stay out of view, if possible, of surveillance cameras, avoid any controversial or so-called "deviant" actions—whatever their private views and inclinations. People self-censor their thoughts and actions to align them with a politically correct society. We have, in effect, become our own "thought police." Diversity and individuality suffer. In the long run, independent, private thoughts will be greatly reduced.

Every United States citizen has the right to participate in society without the express or implied threat of coercion. That is exactly what constant surveillance is—the ultimate implied threat of coercion. Like driving down the highway with a police officer trailing, constant surveillance causes one to self-censor any activity that might be construed wrongly, no matter how legal or profitable that activity might be. But law-abiding citizens should not fear government officials in a free society. Remember that government officials are supposedly our servants, not the other way around.

The overused rejoinder that "if you're innocent, you shouldn't care" undermines the basis of the rule of law. The idea that you're innocent until proven guilty is a core principle of the Bill of Rights. But if the government is filming you when you drive, listening to your phone calls, using satellites to track your movements and insect drones to further spy on you, you have more to worry about than just a loss of privacy: you'd better believe that you're already a suspect.

CHAPTER FOUR

From Cradle to Grave

First they came for the Socialists, and I did not speak out because I was not a Socialist. Then they came for the Trade Unionists, and I did not speak out because I was not a Trade Unionist. Then they came for the Jews, and I did not speak out because I was not a Jew. Then they came for me, and there was no one left to speak for me.

—Martin Niemöller, Inscription at the U.S. Holocaust Museum

"I am not a number. I am a free man." Number 6 proclaimed this mantra in every episode of *The Prisoner*, the British television series that aired worldwide in the late 1960s and intrigued a generation. The brainchild of British actor Patrick McGoohan, *The Prisoner* is perhaps the best visual debate ever on individuality and freedom and is especially relevant to post-9/11 America.

The plot centers on a high-level government operative who, after having abruptly resigned, is drugged and kidnapped. He wakes up in a mysterious, self-contained, cosmopolitan community called The Village, whose inhabitants are known only by numbers. McGoohan played Number 6, the kidnapped agent. In the opening episode ("The Arrival"), Number 6 meets Number 2, who explains to him that he is now in The Village because the information stored in his head has made him too valuable to remain "outside." Seeking to preserve his individuality as a "free man," Number 6 chooses not to give in to authorities and continually tries to escape from The Village or learn the identity of Number 1, the person presumed to run The Village. Number 6 is under constant surveillance by cameras and other devices, and his escapes are repeatedly thwarted. Although his prison resembles an idyllic resort with parks and green fields, recreational activities, and even a butler, Number 6 remains a prisoner. Even so, he does not give up or give in. "I will not make any deals with you," he pointedly remarks to Number 2. "I will not be pushed, filed, stamped, indexed, debriefed, or numbered. My life is my own."

The Prisoner was clearly ahead of its time in foretelling a surveillance society in which individuals are numbered, tracked, and controlled. From the moment we arrive in this world, we find ourselves pushed, filed, stamped, and indexed. Like cattle, we are branded, assigned a number, and tracked. From cradle to grave, we are prisoners within an invisible cage. There seems to be no escape from this electronic prison.

The battle for each of us, as it was for Number 6, is to maintain our individuality and freedom in the face of humanity's destructive, dehumanizing tendencies. At times, it can seem impossible. We are so bombarded with images, dictates, rules, punishments, and discipline from the day we are born that it is a wonder we ever ponder a concept such as freedom. And as technology becomes more sophisticated and the government and its cohorts further refine their methods of keeping tabs on us, there will be no end to the ways in which we are monitored.

"Not so long ago, our lives were mostly recorded on paper. From the doctor's office to the supermarket, any record of where we had gone or what we had done could only be tracked by looking at paper and ink," ACLU Executive Director Anthony Romero has observed. "Today, however, the most intimate details of our personal habits and behaviors are computerized. On millions of hard drives and microchips, more and more of what we do every day is recorded—not only by the government but by corporations."[1]

We are tracked in a myriad of ways: through our Social Security numbers, bank accounts, purchases, and electronic transactions; by way of our correspondence and communication devices—email, phone calls, and mobile phones; through chips implanted in our vehicles, identification documents, even our clothing. Data companies such as Acxiom are capturing vast caches of personal information to help airports, retailers, police, and other government authorities instantly determine whether someone is the person he or she claims to be.[2] Add to this the fact that businesses, schools, and other facilities are relying more and more on fingerprints and face recognition to identify us. All the while, banks and other financial institutions must verify the identities of new customers and make such records of customer transactions available to the police and government officials upon request. This informational glut is converging into a mandate for a national ID card.

NATIONAL ID CARDS

Government agencies such as the Transportation Security Administration (TSA) already require workers to use hardened IDs. The Pentagon has millions of plastic "smart cards" containing name, rank, photograph, and fingerprint. However, the idea of improved identification for all Americans received a substantial boost from the 9/11 Commission, which recommended that the government combine passports with biometric identifiers in order to "improve terror watch lists and travel checkpoints to find known terrorists, and ease travel for those people who don't appear to pose a risk."[3]

The ultimate human tracking device, the national identification card (dubbed "an internal passport" by its critics) has been hailed by many as a necessity in America's fight against terrorism. What once was seen as a tool for controlling immigration and zeroing in on terrorist activity has become a pivotal part of the government's ability to monitor and track American citizens, especially now that Congress has given its blessing to the sharing of information between major counterintelligence branches of government.

In the wake of 9/11, there was little opposition to the creation of a national tracking device that would include a centralized computer-based registry of all U.S. citizens. In a survey conducted by the prestigious Pew Research Center, when Americans were asked whether, in order to curb terrorism, they would favor requiring that all citizens carry a national identity card at all times to show to a police officer on request, 70 percent said yes.[4] (Of those same individuals surveyed, the majority did not approve of allowing the government to monitor personal telephone calls and emails or credit card purchases—which the USA PATRIOT Act allows and President Bush approved post-9/11.)

Currently, our Social Security system comes closest to resembling a national database. Yet as some states consider linking their computer networks, thus creating a national database by default, state-issued drivers' licenses are quickly becoming the back door to a national ID card. Several states are seriously considering proposals to increase the amount of information provided in drivers' licenses to include fingerprints and retinal patterns. According to Simon Davies, director of the watchdog group Privacy International, in order for a national ID card to play any major role in the war against terrorism, three components are necessary: mandatory biometric information (i.e., finger or retina print or DNA data, along with personal data such as race, age, and residential status); an expansion of police authority to demand the card in a wide range of circumstances; and a greater sharing of information among all government divisions.[5] The national ID card will make accessible information that many would not want anyone, including the government, to know about them. With a mandated national ID card, there would be very little information that could not be tracked, monitored, and cross-referenced.

The term "national identification card" encompasses a broad range of technologies. Most, if not all, of these cards will be "machine readable," allowing government agents to scan them for any information they want to collect—information that can later be accessed by corporate entities as well. These cards (slated to replace traditional drivers' licenses and passports) will eventually contain memory devices able to store information as basic as a person's name, birth date, and place of birth, as well as private information, including a Social Security number, fingerprint, retina scan, and personal, criminal, and financial records. As the technology behind the identification cards becomes more sophisticated, the information contained on the cards, including biometric data, will be voluminous.

Such a card pushes the constitutional limits of privacy. David Banisar, deputy director of Privacy International, claims that in order for "a national ID card to actually do what its proponents claim it would, someone would have to watch every individual's move from when they got into their car and where they drove to what they bought throughout the day."[6]

REAL ID ACT

With little regard to the potential for abuse and the undermining of constitutional principles, the U.S. Congress rapidly moved forward in approving a de facto national ID card in May 2005. The Real ID Act was supposedly an effort to curb the threat posed by terrorists such as the 9/11 hijackers who used phony identifications, Social Security numbers, and birth dates to establish bank accounts and set up lives in the United States. Even though none of the hijackers lived in Virginia, seven of them attained identification cards through the Virginia Department of Motor Vehicles, which allows individuals to meet residency requirements with a simple notarized letter. "The system had long been abused by immigrants seeking to establish themselves in the region—with the help from immigration lawyers and local notaries," writes journalist and author Robert O'Harrow Jr. "But despite warnings from the FBI and DMV investigators, the department maintained the system as a convenience until shortly after September 11."[7]

To remedy this problem, Congress decided to establish a national identification system designed to make all states' IDs uniform. This, they reasoned, would make it more difficult for terrorists to travel in and among the various states and would prevent further terrorist attacks. As former Congressman Tom DeLay (R-Tex.) argued, "If these commonsense reforms had been in place in 2001, they would have hindered the efforts of the 9/11 terrorists, and they will go a long way toward helping us prevent another tragedy like 9/11."[8]

The Real ID Act passed effortlessly in the U.S. House of Representatives and was then attached to an emergency "must-pass" spending bill that provided funds for the troops in Iraq and tsunami relief in Indonesia. In a closed-door meeting with no hearings or debate, it passed unanimously in the U.S. Senate with only a handful of representatives opposing the concept of a national ID card. One of the Act's most vocal opponents, Congressman Ron Paul (R-Tex.), stated, "A national identification card, in whatever form it may take, will allow the federal government to inappropriately monitor the movements and transactions of every American. History shows that governments inevitably use the power to monitor the actions of people in harmful ways." He continued, "Claims that the government will protect the privacy of Americans when implementing a national identification card ring hollow. We would do well to remember what happened with the Social Security number. It was introduced with solemn restrictions on how it could be used, but it has become a de facto national identifier."[9]

On May 11, 2005, President Bush signed the Real ID Act into law, essentially establishing the first national identification system in American history. The law requires that all 245 million license and state ID holders in the United States visit their local DMVs to acquire a special identification card.[10] Citizens who do not have this special identification by a given date will not be able to perform important yet routine tasks such as travel on an airplane, open a bank account, collect Social Security payments, enter federal government buildings, or take advantage of most government services.[11] Under proposed regulations issued in January 2008 by the Department of Homeland Security, by December 1, 2014, all Americans under the age of fifty will be expected to present Real ID-compliant cards in order to board a plane or enter a federal building. Three years later, all Americans, regardless of age, will have to meet these requirements.[12]

The law requires that each person provide a photo ID, birth certificate, proof of their Social Security number, and proof of residence in order to receive the identification. This information will then be stored in massive databases maintained by the states and shared among them.[13] Once the DMV receives all the necessary information, it will issue the applicant a new identification card, which will include the person's name, date of birth, picture, and some form of machine-readable technology.

As many citizens and state legislators quickly realized, the only thing "real" about the Real ID Act is the bureaucratic nightmare it will create for states and taxpayers. The foremost concern among a growing number of state officials is the overwhelming financial and administrative costs they will be forced to shoulder in order to meet the law's requirements. Those close to the issue insist that if states are to collect, scan, and verify the information of every single ID holder, as the law demands, motor vehicle bureaus will need "more staff, computers, and software, and a world-class security system."[14] All of this, according to the Department of Homeland Security, could add up to a massive $23.1 billion over ten years.[15]

Where will this money come from, the states want to know. It's a valid question, considering that the federal government has failed to provide the states with the funding necessary to support the program. On July 26, 2007, the Senate set aside a spending bill that would have spread $300 million across the states to assist their efforts.[16] This lack of financial support has led the National Conference of State Legislatures (NCSL) to label the federal law an "unfunded mandate" and demand that the federal government either provide more of the costs or scrap the law altogether.[17]

Understandably reluctant to shoulder such a bureaucratic and financial burden, many states have rebelled against the Real ID Act. As of the fall of 2007, seventeen states had enacted anti-Real ID bills or resolutions, and twenty-one additional state legislatures had similar bills or resolutions pending before them.[18] Of those seventeen states, seven—Arkansas, Georgia, Maine, Montana, New Hampshire, Oklahoma, and Washington—will never issue a Real ID license as a result of enacting binding laws prohibiting them from participating in the program.

With the federal government shirking the responsibility of paying for this "unfunded mandate," NCSL spokesman Bill Wyatt predicted that whether it is through a new transportation tax, motor vehicle tax, or gasoline tax, the expense will ultimately have to be borne by the American taxpayer. An alternative to a tax would be to raise the cost of purchasing the mandatory identification to as much as $100, but again, the cost would fall on the taxpayer.[19]

No matter how this program is funded, Americans will inevitably have to contend with more red tape, at their local DMVs and elsewhere. "All this is going to do is make life miserable for American citizens," states U.S. Representative James P. Moran Jr. (D-Va.). The lines to get licenses "are going to be several blocks long, 24 hours a day."[20] According to Juliette Kayyem, the homeland security adviser to Massachusetts Governor Deval Patrick, "It's not just computer changes; it's personnel, too. And everything our registrars have been doing in the last 10 years for you and me, making it easier to renew licenses online, it's gone. Now you have to show up in person and wait in line, like before."[21]

While the added expense and inconvenience associated with implementing a national ID is problematic enough, it also poses numerous threats to privacy. For example, the law's requirement that machine-readable technology be incorporated into the card opens the door for radio frequency identification (RFID) tags to be placed in our licenses.[22] RFID, as will be detailed later, is a type of automatic identification system that enables data—in this case the private information of American citizens—to be transmitted by a portable device. This will provide the government with unprecedented access to American citizens' personal information. In addition, RFID tags emit radio frequency signals that allow the government to track the movement of the cards, as well as the cardholders.[23] As Neal Kurk, a Republican state representative from New Hampshire, declared, "This is another effort of the federal government to keep track of all its citizens."[24] The ACLU of Connecticut echoed this point: "The standardized national driver's licenses created by Real ID will become an 'internal passport' that will increasingly be used to track and control United States citizens' movements and activities."[25]

In the long term, Real ID means that government agents will have the ability to scan for any and all personal information stored on the card, advocate for new laws requiring that more information be stored on the license, and track our every move. These are certainly not the hallmarks of a free society. RFID tags could also place our personal information in jeopardy of being accessed by megacorporations and stolen by identity thieves. The ACLU of Connecticut reports, "Private businesses may be able to use remote scanners to read RFID tags too, and add to the digital dossiers they may already be compiling. If different merchants combine their data—you can imagine the sorts of profiles that will develop. And unlike with a grocery store checkout, we may have no idea the scan is even occurring; no telltale beep will alert us."[26]

Coupled with the fact that several states already sell the personal information of identification holders to third parties,[27] massive databases of private information could very well be floating around unsecured. And by linking cardholders' personal information to every state's database, one state's foul-up could lead to disastrous consequences for everyone involved. In March 2005, thieves drove through the back wall of a DMV near Las Vegas and stole computer equipment containing personal information on more than 8,900 people.[28] If the Real ID Act had been in effect, the personal information of millions of Americans would have been stolen. As this example illustrates, linking all states' DMV databases together will, in the words of Ken Ritter of the *Las Vegas Sun*, create a "bonanza for identity thieves."[29]

The government insists these are risks that must be tolerated in order to protect us from the more serious threat of terrorism, but the verdict is still out on whether these national IDs will provide more security for our country. Industry experts suggest that Real IDs will most likely be vulnerable to counterfeiting and tampering.[30] These experts point out that while the new government identification card has placed great emphasis on high-tech security features, they have ignored important low-tech risks. "Give me six minutes with a personal computer, a lamination machine, a digital image and some data," said Jack Kantak, senior vice president of Vanguard Research Inc., who claims he can make a counterfeit identification that meets the standards set forth under the new law.[31]

Questions continue to be raised over whether a national ID system would provide any real safety and security benefits. For instance, developments in late 2007 cast doubt on the government's insistence that a national ID would aid agents in protecting and closing our borders. Critics have speculated that the government's national ID plan could actually be a move toward opening our borders to surrounding countries, a merging of the American, Canadian, and Mexican legal, economic, and physical borders, which I discuss in more detail in Chapter Six. As Missouri State Representative Jim Guest recognizes, "This is part of a plan by bureaucrats and trade groups that act like bureaucrats to little by little transform us into a North American Union without any vote being taken and without explaining to the U.S. public what they are doing."[32]

"The first 'North American Union' driver's license, complete with a hologram of the continent on the reverse, has been created in North Carolina," author Jerome R. Corsi recognizes. According to Marge Howell of the North Carolina DMV, the hologram of all three North American countries is a security element that will eventually be on the back of every driver's license in North America.[33] Jason King of the American Association of Motor Vehicle Administrators (AAMVA), which is responsible for creating the North American logo for driver's licenses, confirmed Ms. Howell's claim. King explained that the goal is to create a continental security device that could be used by police and motor vehicle agencies throughout North America, including the United States, Canada, and Mexico.[34]

TAGGING PEOPLE

While a national ID card provides the government with a method for tracking Americans, technology in the form of a tiny device implanted and used for tracking purposes provides the means. Although the concept may seem to echo the plot of a science-fiction movie, this is all too real. The device is a small wireless gadget that has long been attached to products for the purposes of tracking inventory. Railroads and the U.S. Department of Defense have been using RFID tags for years, and companies such as Wal-Mart, Best Buy, and other megacorporations have adopted the technology as well.

As briefly discussed earlier, ID cards with RFID tags pose the greatest threat to privacy. According to the Electronic Privacy Information Center, "Radio Frequency Identification is a type of automatic identification system. The purpose of an RFID system is to enable data to be transmitted by a portable device, called a tag, which is read by an RFID reader and processed according to the needs of a particular application."[35] RFID is currently used in all kinds of fields and endeavors, but this technology has other potential uses. The most likely scenario is that RFID tags, which use biometric technology, will be employed by the government to track the real-time movements of American citizens.

The Hitachi Corporation has created the world's smallest, thinnest RFID tags. Referred to as the "powder type," these tags are barely detectable to the naked eye. They are so small that they can be easily incorporated into thin paper or a single clothing fiber. These tiny tracking devices contain microchips and radio antennas and can range in size from inches to mere millimeters. The antenna transmits an identifying number known as the Electronic Product Code (EPC) to an electronic reader that is linked to a database which contains information about the specific object, thus allowing it to be tracked. In addition, radio tags, unlike standard bar codes using a Universal Product Code (UPC), can be read from more than a mile away through the use of radio waves, as opposed to lasers.

While the original purpose of RFID tags was supposedly to track inventory for large businesses, they are increasingly becoming a routine part of the average American's daily life. What once cost vast amounts of money to manufacture and distribute now costs only pennies, making it more affordable for government agencies and companies alike to use these tags. Starting in 2007, new and renewed U.S. passports were transformed into e-Passports with the chip implanted in the back cover. And while there is enough memory to include data such as fingerprints and iris patterns, only information already in the passport will be recorded on the chip, at least for now.

There are understandable benefits for big businesses, and even a few for the ordinary consumer. These tags allow companies to keep track of their inventory to know when stock is low or items are missing. It would take a multitude of man-hours and energy to do what these high-tech tags can accomplish quickly and effortlessly. For the consumer, these tags provide convenience and save time. An RFID tag stuck on your windshield allows you to pass quickly through tollbooths without stopping to rummage for spare change. Passing your card by a device at the supermarket checkout saves you the time and hassle of swiping your credit card or scrounging up dollar bills and coins. The touchless payment technology espoused by Chase and MasterCard utilizes these tags to allow the user to simply wave a card near an electronic reader at checkouts. Access passes into office buildings and parking structures also operate on an RFID system. It is likely that those who do not possess a tag will someday find it difficult (if not impossible) to buy, sell, or operate in society.

Some people have even had a chip implanted in their arm to provide personal and medical information to doctors and emergency personnel when needed.[36] Human microchip implantation took a leap forward in July 2007 when the American Medical Association (AMA) announced that such devices "may help to identify patients, thereby improving the safety and efficiency of patient care." Scott Silverman, chief executive officer of VeriChip, a pioneer in human microchips, says the primary aim is to help high-risk medical patients such as those with diabetes, Alzheimer's, cancer, and heart conditions.[37] VeriChip's sister corporation, DigitalAngel, has been implanting chips in animals (including pets) for years. The chip, which uses an RFID tag, is implanted in the upper right arm and allows medical personnel to access a patient's medical history in the event the person is unconscious or otherwise unresponsive. The person's data is stored in VeriChip's database, which is then accessible to government agencies.

The AMA admits that there are questions of patient security with such implants. Silverman recognizes that once you have a chip, it could be used for other "applications."[38] But the program is well on its way to becoming an everyday reality, and many seem oblivious to the chip's implications. As *St. Petersburg Times* reporter Ivan Penn writes, "One company injected two employees with chips for security reasons. In addition, nightclubs in Barcelona, Spain, Rotterdam, Holland, and Edinburgh, Scotland, use them so patrons can access VIP lounges and make purchases."[39]

Katherine Albrecht, co-author of the book *Spychips*, argues that corporations such as VeriChip are taking us down a treacherous road. "You can feel the writing on the wall that this is the direction our society is moving. If everybody had a chip in them we would be blissfully unaware of Big Brother."[40] And with the fact that satellites from outer space now monitor American citizens, RFID technology allows Big Brother to track us even from the heavens.

The dangers posed by RFID tags are evident. They will allow companies and the government to track virtually everything a person does. The windshield sticker that allows you to pass quickly through tollbooths can also record your car's movements on those roads. More and more tollbooths are becoming a matter-of-fact part of a security and law enforcement infrastructure as digital police checkpoints. Cameras are often pointed at drivers' faces and their license plates. And because databases now interface with one another, when "drivers use an electronic transponder such as E-ZPass to automatically pay tolls, they're also handing over information about themselves."[41] The technology in the tollbooth, accessible to government agents and the police, records the identification number on the E-ZPass, along with the exact time and location of the car as it passes through the booth, making it an effective system for tracking citizen movement.

RFID tags are quickly moving beyond the realm of security and becoming an integral part of Americans' daily routines and everyday purchases such as food, shoes, and hardware. Potentially everything you buy will eventually have a tiny microchip hidden in the label or between layers of fabric, conceivably undetectable. Personal information such as credit card data could be linked to devices that use this technology, and that personal information would be accessible to any radio-frequency eavesdropper. Records could be made of exactly what products you buy, when you buy them, and where you take them. If an RFID chip is imbedded in the sole of your tennis shoe, literally every step you take would be traceable through radio waves.

Pfizer has tagged bottles of prescription Viagra, which is one of the most counterfeited drugs.[42] It will not be long before the U.S. Food and Drug Administration mandates the use of RFID tags on all prescription drugs, which means that personal credit information will be linkable to every prescription you buy. A master profile will be made that contains basic information such as your name and address, in addition to an accounting of every penny you spend and every move you make. As a result, the most private facts about your life can be exposed to government agencies, private corporations, potential employers, or even private investigators, such as your Social Security number, photograph, legal offenses, and details about marriages and divorces, as well as your financial records. It doesn't take a fortune-teller to see the Fourth Amendment's provision against unreasonable searches and your right to privacy being repeatedly violated by government agencies and law enforcement.

Exploitation is a vast area of concern with respect to RFID technology. With radio waves, collecting data from a transmitting tag is possible from great distances, out of the line of sight and even through shielding material. Unlike standard bar codes, machines can read RFID tags through a woman's purse as soon as she steps inside a store. This allows a variety of people, including criminals, easy access to your information without your knowledge. For instance, thieves can stand at a distance with a hand-held RFID reader to surreptitiously monitor the contents of bags and suitcases.

Unaware that products they buy contain RFID tags, many Americans are increasingly susceptible to an invasion or misuse of their personal information. Consumers Against Supermarket Privacy Invasion and Numbering (CASPIAN) has called for initiation of the Right to Know Act, which would require that commodities containing RFID tags bear labels stating that fact in order to protect consumer privacy.

More and more, RFID and other tracking technologies provide an inexpensive and easy surveillance method applicable to every consumer. In "Privacy Lost: These Phones Can Find You," Laura Holson of the *New York Times* reported on the "latest advancement in cellphone technology": the implementation of Global Positioning System (GPS) chips. GPS chips track the cell phone's every movement in real time. Such technology allows parents to track their children, enables employers to know exactly where their employees are and allows people to find out where their late dinner date is. As Holson explains, "If G.P.S. made it harder to get lost, new cellphone services are now making it harder to hide."[43]

Charles S. Golvin, a wireless analyst at Forrester Research, admits that "[t]here is a Big Brother component" to the use of GPS chips in wireless phones.[44] "The thinking goes," he explains, "that if my friends can find me, the telephone company knows my location all the time, too."[45] Of greater concern, if the telephone company knows where you are, government agents, if they so desire, will as well. According to the ACLU, the government has pushed for the authority to "monitor certain Internet content without a warrant, and to collect tracking information about the physical locations of cell phone users—turning cell phones into what, for all practical purposes, are location tracking bugs."[46]

The rate at which companies are already turning over customers' private information to government agents for tracking and spying purposes is staggering. As the ACLU revealed, "Many companies are willing to hand over the details of their customers' purchases or activities based on a simple request from the FBI or other authorities."[47] This includes banks, retail stores, and even phone companies. In 2002, Bell South received sixteen thousand subpoenas from government agents and 636 court orders for customer information.[48] Attorneys representing these companies have reported that in addition to more requests for customer information, the government requests are getting broader,[49] more akin to "shotgun approaches" or "just fishing."[50]

FINGERPRINTING CHILDREN

In a surveillance society, no one is overlooked—not even children. Some schools are now requiring students to drape RFID tags around their necks, thus allowing school officials to literally track every single step the students take.[51] *New Standard News* reporter Catherine Komp explains the eerie scene: "The highly controversial programs, implemented in the name of student protection, see pupils wearing tags around their necks and submitting themselves to electronic scanning as they enter and leave school property."[52] An agitated British parent who belongs to an organization called Leave Them Kids Alone, which is attempting to keep this technology away from the children, noted, "Tagging is what we do to criminals we let out of prison early."[53]

Part of the logic is that students who are monitored and tracked in such a fashion will be deterred from committing violent crimes. The problem is that these devices do not deter teens from acting violently.

While a camera will record crime, it will not stop a troubled teen who plans to wreak havoc or commit suicide. (An armed security guard and twenty-six security cameras placed throughout a Cleveland school didn't stop Asa H. Coon from opening fire on two students and two teachers before killing himself in the fall of 2007.)[54] What these devices will manage to do, however, is "normalize electronic surveillance at an early age, conditioning young people to accept privacy violations while creating a market for companies that develop and sell surveillance systems."[55] According to Annie Cutler writing for *ABC 4 News*, "Some students say they live in an era where cameras are always recording so the idea is not a big deal."[56]

We are in essence laying the groundwork for future generations of automatons, conditioned to accept a way of life in which their movements are always tracked and they have no autonomy. And as is often the case, it begins with the best of intentions—security, convenience, peace of mind.

More and more schools, for example, are using a fingerprint identification program that allows children to purchase lunch without carrying cash.[57] Students place their index fingers on small scanners, and a template matches them with their electronic print. The program plots twenty-seven points on a grid that corresponds with the fingerprint ridges. The fingerprint image is discarded, and the points are assigned numbers. This is the brave new world of biometric devices that identify people by physical characteristics such as eye patterns, voice tones, and handprints—which was once only seen in science fiction films.

Until recently, the economic costs of biometric devices had restricted their use mainly to government offices and military bases. Government benefits such as welfare payments are increasingly being secured with biometrics. The Immigration and Naturalization Service relies on handprint scans to allow thousands of international travelers to reenter the country without a passport. Efficiency is how these devices are being sold to the public. And, of course, who can be against efficiency?

As for the children, we are told that biometrics is a way to trace lost or kidnapped children. And programs such as fingerprint identification for school children are being promoted as a way for parents to watch what their children eat. A student slides a tray toward the cafeteria cash register with a plate of food, for example, but then adds a piece of chocolate cake. When he punches in his code for the prepaid account his parent set up, a warning sounds: "This student has a restriction."

The obvious concern with all this is that any sense of privacy is being lost. But it is a sign of things to come. The government will be able to identify all of us—even our children—with biometrics in virtually every situation. The use of the digital fingerprint is just one example of that. As an ACLU attorney recognizes: "Fingerprinting is for felons not for 5-year-olds. We're setting up our children that surrendering your fingerprints or other parts of your identity for school lunches is a good idea."[58] We are also teaching children that the government has a right to track us from cradle to grave. This used to be considered a bad lesson in political science.

The government is not the only entity that will have access to this information. "Right now you have databases full of information that can be hacked," Richard Norton, executive director of the International Biometrics Association has said.[59]

SURROUNDED DAY AND NIGHT

There is a permanent government in Washington DC that consists of people whose power does not depend on election results. The largest part of the permanent government is the bureaucracy, which has approximately three million federal civilian employees. Ten times that number are funded by American taxpayers through government contracts and other venues. With one in ten of our citizens working for the government, it is not surprising that the bureaucratic presence is increasingly dominant in our lives.

Everywhere we look these days, we are either being watched, taxed, or some bureaucrat is placing another bit of information in our government electronic files. And with the American Community Survey, the census form that reports on various households on a continuous basis—about three million households are surveyed each year—the federal bureaucracy is further thrusting its expansive tentacles toward us. Unlike the traditional census, which collects data every ten years, the American Community Survey is taken yearly at a cost of between $120 and $150 million per year.[60]

Article I, Section 2, of the Constitution provides for a census every ten years. The intention of the founders was for a simple head count, so as to ensure fair representation among the states in the House of Representatives. In contrast, at twenty-four pages and sixty to seventy questions, the American Community Survey contains some of the most detailed, intrusive questions ever put forth in a census questionnaire. These questions concern matters that the government has no business knowing, including a person's job, income, physical and emotional health, family status, place of residence, and intimate personal and private habits.

The survey asks how many persons live in your home, along with their names and detailed information about them such as their relationship to you; marital status; race; their physical, mental, and emotional problems; and so on. The survey also asks how many bedrooms and bathrooms are in your house, along with the fuel used to heat your home, the cost of electricity, what type of mortgage you have and monthly mortgage payments, property taxes, and the like. Personal questions, such as whether any householders receive food stamps, require answers. This questionnaire also demands to know how many days you were sick last year, how many automobiles you own, and the number of miles driven. Also on the questionnaire are intimate questions of privacy such as whether you have trouble getting up the stairs, difficulty dressing and bathing, and whether a physical, mental, or emotional condition makes concentrating, remembering, or making decisions difficult. The government seems to think it necessary to know what time you leave for work every morning, as well as how you get to work and how long it takes to get there. This information has revealed such statistics as the respective average travel times to work for African Americans and non-Hispanic whites. For African American workers, it was twenty-seven minutes, while the average travel time for non-Hispanic white workers was twenty-four minutes.[61] As minor as this detail might seem, it takes on a more ominous quality in a post-9/11 America where government agents can come into your home secretly and go through your personal belongings while you are away, often without a search warrant.

That's not all. The survey also includes highly detailed inquiries about your financial affairs—something that could be passed on to the Internal Revenue Service (IRS) and result in numerous inconveniences and problems for respondents. It has happened before. In 1983, the IRS attempted to use computer matching of census data and private mailing lists to track down people who didn't file income tax returns.

The survey demands that you violate the privacy of others by supplying the names and addresses of your friends, relatives, and employer. The questionnaire also demands information on the people in your home such as their ethnic origin, educational levels, how many years of school were completed, what languages they speak, and when they last worked at a job, among other items.

You are now in effect being told by the government to inform on your family and friends—much like that described by George Orwell in *1984*. "The family," writes Orwell, "had become in effect an extension of the Thought Police. It was a device by means of which everyone could be surrounded night and day by informers who knew him intimately."[62]

While some of the questions may seem fairly routine, the real danger is in not knowing why the information is needed or how the government will use it. There are also other worries specific to minorities and immigrants. Information received from the census will not only be implanted on your ID card, it will also be passed to the Immigration and Naturalization Service. Thus, there is the very real possibility that the information could be collected and used against certain groups in society.

The American Community Survey for 2008, available on the Census Bureau's website,[63] illustrates this in a fairly unsubtle way. Question five asks, "Is Person 1 of Hispanic, Latino, or Spanish origin?" and is the first question about ethnic origin to appear on the census. It is only at the next question that the survey asks, "What is Person 1's race?" This order of questioning suggests that those of Hispanic origin are of more interest to the government than those of other origins. There are no specific questions that deal solely with whether a person has another ethnic origin other than for Hispanics. The categories "White" and "Black" under question six are simple homogenous categories—people from these categories are by no means so—but this seems of little interest to the government.

In addition to the risk to Hispanics, there are ominous lessons from history that should concern the Arab American and Muslim communities. In 1940, American citizens of Japanese origin supplied their race and national origin on census forms. Two years later, after the bombing of Pearl Harbor, the government started placing American citizens of Japanese descent into internment camps. Federal agents used the 1940 census data to locate which areas of California, Oregon, and Washington had high percentages of Japanese Americans. In 1943, the Census Bureau revealed every Japanese citizen or alien in Washington DC to the U.S. Secret Service.[64] The information provided by the Census Bureau helped the War Department round up more than 120,000 Japanese Americans and confine them to internment camps.[65] This information, just like the information that is provided in the American Community Survey, was supposedly private.

The Census Bureau has continued this policy of disclosure to government agencies, but the new victims are those of Arab ancestry. On July 23, 2004, the Electronic Privacy Information Center obtained documents revealing that the Census Bureau provided the Department of Homeland Security with statistical data on people who identified themselves on the 2000 census as being of Arab ancestry. The special tabulations were prepared specifically for the law enforcement agency. There is no indication that the Department of Homeland Security requested similar information about any other ethnic groups.[66] One table shows cities with populations of 10,000 or more and with 1,000 or more people who indicated they were of Arab ancestry. For each city, the tabulation provides total population, population of Arab ancestry, and percent of the total that is of Arab ancestry.[67] Another table shows the number of census responses indicating Arab ancestry in certain zip codes throughout the country. Those of Arab ancestry are subdivided into Egyptian, Iraqi, Jordanian, Lebanese, Moroccan, Palestinian, Syrian, Arab/Arabic, and Other Arab.[68] With the ongoing "war on terror," the parallels with the 1940s must be of concern to those respondents who identified themselves as being of Arab ancestry.

The American Community Survey is not voluntary. You are legally obligated to answer the questions, and if you refuse, the fines are staggering. For every question not answered, there is a $100 fine. For every intentionally false response to a question, the fine is $500. Therefore, if a person representing a two-person household refused to fill out any questions or simply answered nonsensically, the total fines could range upwards of $10,000 to $50,000 for noncompliance.

Representative Ron Paul (R-Tex.) introduced into a spending bill an amendment that would have eliminated funds for this intrusive survey. He explained on the House floor that such information gathering went much too far in violating the privacy of American citizens. The amendment was met by either indifference or hostility, and in the end, Congress did nothing.

When examining massive bureaucratic programs such as the American Community Survey, it's important to look at who else stands to benefit. In this particular case, there are clear advantages for the corporate sector. The personal data collected by the government provides private entities with a treasure trove of market research on the American consumer. And there's also money to be made in spearheading the census efforts. Lockheed Martin, the world's largest defense contractor and a major player in previous census efforts in the United States, Canada, and the United Kingdom, was awarded a $500 million contract by the U.S. government to conduct the 2010 census—that is, the American Community Survey or a facsimile thereof—in the United States.[69] With 95.8 percent of its revenues coming from the U.S. Department of Defense, other federal government agencies, and foreign military customers, Lockheed clearly has a vested interest in maintaining a demand for its services.[70]

Yet Article I of the U. S. Constitution makes it clear that the census should be taken for the sole purpose of congressional redistricting. Remember: what the founders intended was a simple head count of the number of people living in a given area so that numerically equal congressional districts could be maintained. The founders never envisioned or authorized the federal government to continuously demand, under penalty of law, detailed information from the American people. Neither did the founders anticipate a massive and meddlesome federal bureaucracy or the growth in power and influence of the corporate sector.

SECURITY-INDUSTRIAL COMPLEX

The increasingly complex security needs of our massive federal government, especially in the areas of defense, surveillance, and data management, have been met within the corporate sector, which has shown itself to be a powerful ally that both depends on and feeds the growth of governmental bureaucracy, particularly in a post-9/11 America. Peter Swire, the nation's first privacy counselor in the Clinton administration, warned that we are creating a "security-industrial complex."[71] Swire intentionally echoed a famous phrase from President Eisenhower's 1961 farewell address:

In the councils of government, we must guard against the acquisition of unwarranted influence, whether sought or unsought, by the military-industrial complex. The potential for the disastrous rise of misplaced power exists and will persist. We must never let the weight of this combination endanger our liberties or democratic processes. We should take nothing for granted. Only an alert and knowledgeable citizenry can compel the proper meshing of the huge industrial and military machinery of defense with our peaceful methods and goals, so that security and liberty may prosper together.[72]

Swire, now a law professor at Moritz College of Law, voices some legitimate concerns about the emergence of a security-industrial complex. Five years after the terrorist attacks, reports *USA Today*, the homeland security business is booming to such an extent that it now eclipses mature enterprises like moviemaking and the music industry in annual revenue. This security spending is forecast to exceed $1 trillion in the near future.[73] "The business has moved from a frantic and often inefficient scramble in the wake of 9/11 to shore up security at airports to a much broader effort," Gary Stoller writes for *USA Today*. "The scope of security-related spending has expanded to include more sophisticated information technology and the protection of other vulnerable terrorist targets such as ports and nuclear reactors."[74]

As Mark P. Mills, writing for *Forbes* magazine, notes, "A security-industrial complex is rapidly emerging, echoing its military kissing cousin, visible in conference exhibitions across the country. More than 800 companies packed exhibit aisles at the American Society for Industrial Security exhibition in Dallas in late September. A few weeks later many of the same companies were at the massive annual Army tech expo in Washington DC."[75]

Given the government's constant reminder that we live under imminent threat of another terrorist attack, the close ties between security companies and the government won't be ending anytime soon, much to the dismay of civil liberties advocates. ACLU Executive Director Anthony Romero warns, "Americans from across the political spectrum understand that 'the right to be left alone' is central to our constitutional democracy—that a secure sense of personal privacy is vital to preserving the openness of American life, and to protecting the boundless creativity, innovation and prosperity for which we are known. If we allow the fear of terrorism to create a new industrial base for surveillance technology, unfettered by reasonable and effective privacy constraints, these special characteristics of the American way of life will wither on the vine."[76]

Technophiles such as Mills, a founding partner of Digital Power Capital, which invests in securities technologies, insist that while we all value our privacy, "the worriers have no imagination. As just one example, emerging technology to find weapons or explosives hidden beneath clothes is devilishly challenging. The American Civil Liberties Union protested in 2002 that using such tools would be like 'a virtual strip search.' But the ACLU has this backwards. This kind of technology will make true privacy invasions, like real strip searches, less necessary. It will be a cinch to use software to modify scanning images so that they show contraband but nothing more."[77]

Despite Mills's assertions to the contrary, one does not have to be a worrier with no imagination to see that the national security threat is being used to justify measures that seriously undermine individual privacy and autonomy, as well as constitutional and civil liberties. According to Mills:

> *The military, for instance, needs sophisticated devices to protect its bases in the Middle East. The danger is not from planes dropping bombs, but, for example, from vehicles or people hiding explosives. The same dangers are now faced by military and civilian sites back home, including airports, nuclear plants, ports and banks. Technology that protects soldiers—that can, for example, detect whether something approaching a perimeter at night, in fog or dust, is a person or a dog— is eagerly sought in the private sector, too. All of it inevitably becomes more affordable as deployment spreads from the military to airports and then on down to commercial industries and buildings. A pleasant side effect of all the spending on antiterror technology will be a reduction in crime.*
>
> *The enabling technologies for terror-sensing tools will rapidly migrate to applications in medicine, industry, transportation, telecom and even entertainment, driving a tech boom. Examples: Sensors to sniff potential chemical weapons will improve industrial processes and environmental monitoring. Scanners to see through packages will advance medical imaging. Infrared vision to keep a 24/7 all-weather eye out will land in automotive dashboards. Radar to monitor perimeters and borders will be seen in safety enhancements in trucks.*[78]

Behind these measures is an entire litany of governmental-corporate agencies. Included in the mix are the increasingly powerful private contractors to which the government is outsourcing many of the exigencies of surveillance and security. As Mills points out,

"There's plenty of money flowing into this new sector. The Pentagon is spending $100 million a year just to help coordinate civilian tech transfer for security. Plus, the Department of Defense is spending $60 billion a year for new technologies—$15 billion for advanced research and development—with security-related technology an important part of the total. Much of the R&D money is flowing to university researchers and startups. Venture capital is targeting this sector, too. Many defense companies, like L-3, GE, and Northrop Grumman have security divisions to advance these technologies."[79]

Money, power, control. There is no shortage of motives fueling the convergence of megacorporations and government, but who will pay the price? The American people, of course, and you can be sure that it will take a toll on more than our pocketbooks. "You have government on a holy mission to ramp up information gathering and you have an information technology industry desperate for new markets," said Swire. "Once this is done, you will have unprecedented snooping abilities. What will happen to our private lives if we're under constant surveillance?"[80]

What will happen, indeed? Are Americans really prepared to have their every move monitored? And are they willing to give up their right to anonymity, if such a right even exists?

THE LOSS OF ANONYMITY

Throughout history, anonymous expression has been a critical vehicle for political dissent. The ratification of the United States Constitution would likely have taken much longer without the vital discourse stirred up by the *Federalist Papers*, which were penned collectively and anonymously by Alexander Hamilton, James Madison, and John Jay writing under the pseudonym Publius.

With its broad guarantee of rights, the Bill of Rights inherently supports the right to be anonymous. The First Amendment guarantees the right to free speech and the right to peaceably assemble. Without the right to do so anonymously, exercising these rights would be meaningless. After all, if the government could record every word you spoke or note every organization you associated with, your right to freely speak out and associate with whomever you please would be significantly hampered. In such cases, people would be afraid to speak up for fear of being implicated by government authorities.

The Fourth Amendment provides us with the right to keep our "persons, houses, papers, and effects" secure against "unreasonable searches and seizures" by the government. In essence, as the U.S. Supreme Court noted in 1965, these collective protections seem to guarantee a right to privacy.[81] Even so, our judicial system has not always been the best champion of our right to privacy and, in fact, has often aided the government in its quest to know who we are, where we go, what we say, and with whom we associate.

For example, although the U.S. Supreme Court has long held that "people are not shorn of all Fourth Amendment protection when they step from their homes onto the public sidewalks,"[82] the courts have not yet recognized that a pervasive system of public surveillance cameras infringes upon Fourth Amendment rights.[83] And in 2004, the U.S. Supreme Court ruled that the police can arrest someone for failing to identify him/herself if the police have "reasonable suspicion" to believe the person is engaged in criminal activity.[84] "Reasonable" suspicion in such cases can mean almost anything. While these court rulings do not seem to completely disregard the privacy rights of Americans, when coupled with today's increasing technological advancements, they do represent a dangerous trend that jeopardizes our right to blend in with the rest of society.

Whatever the law says, American society today is vastly different from the days when Hamilton, Madison, and Jay presumed their right to not be known. Government today has the tools and resources to keep an eye on everyone all the time, with surveillance cameras that scan our surroundings 24/7 and high-tech computers that can track everything from phone calls and emails to facial characteristics and body mannerisms. And if the government isn't doing the watching, chances are that your neighbors, acquaintances, teachers, co-workers, bank tellers, and so on will be.

Government agents are even tracking the travel habits of Americans. The government has a massive database on Americans who fly, drive, or take cruises abroad.[85] The stored data also includes information on the persons with whom they traveled or planned to stay and the personal items they carried during their journeys, including books.[86] What's more, the government is being fed this data directly from commercial reservation systems.[87] These records are stored for as long as fifteen years so the Department of Homeland Security can assess the security threat posed by all travelers entering the country.

With all this surveillance, how can Americans expect to be anonymous? As we walk down the street, we are videotaped. When we use our credit card at the store, the government likely knows where we are and what we buy. Anytime we board a plane, all our travel habits are stored in a government database. Even before we board the plane, a computer analyzes our face. On our way to work, government spy satellites can zoom in on our drive. And with a national ID card on its way to becoming a permanent fixture, we can no longer escape.

ENOUGH IS ENOUGH

Browbeaten into compliance and conditioned to accept routine incursions on their privacy rights, many Americans have adopted an attitude of blind obedience to executive authority figures. But others, such as Deb Davis, are still attuned to the fact that measures implemented under the guise of security are often nothing more than "a lesson in compliance—the big guys pushing the little guys around."[88]

On the morning of September 26, 2005, Davis decided she would no longer submit to identification checkpoints on her daily bus route. Several weeks earlier, Davis had boarded Regional Transportation District Bus No. 100 for the first time. Over the course of its route, the bus traveled through the Denver Federal Center, a ninety-building facility occupied by federal agencies, including the U.S. Geological Survey, the Interior Department, General Services Administration, and the Bureau of Land Management. The office complex "is not high security," recalls Davis. "It's not Area 51 or NORAD or the Rocky Mountain Arsenal."[89] Upon its entry into the federal district, officers from the Federal Protective Services, a branch of the Department of Homeland Security, repeated their regular morning routine. They boarded Davis's bus and approached each passenger individually, requesting to see personal identification. Startled by the unexpected order, Davis produced her ID for the officers' approval.

That morning, Davis became one among many Denver area passengers to be subjected to identification checkpoints since the Federal Center began implementing them shortly after the April 1995 bombing of a federal building in Oklahoma City. The measure has since been justified in the context of post-9/11 increased security. Carl Rusnok, Homeland Security spokesperson, rationalized the ID check as "one of the multiple forms of security" implemented at the Federal Center: "The identification is one means of making sure that, whoever comes on base, you know that they are who they say they are."[90]

Over the next several weeks, as Davis became familiar with the security checkpoint, she grew skeptical about the ID check, finding it arbitrary and inefficient. When the federal guards demanded to see each passenger's ID, Davis explained, "They kind of glanced at it....They didn't even look at it. It just seemed like anything in your hand, they'd just walk by you. If you didn't have your ID, they'd leave you alone....It seemed kind of subjective."[91] The guards also failed to check the names on the IDs against any sort of list specifying people who were forbidden to ride through or exit at the Federal Center. This lack of consistent enforcement and a prohibited passenger list suggested to Davis that the procedure was more about symbolism than security. And it was more about the federal guards (and government, by extension) demonstrating their authority than ensuring the safety of either the passengers or the Federal Center visitors and employees. So Davis decided to stand and, if need be, fight. She stopped bringing her ID. And when the guards asked why she refused to comply, she told them she had no ID and was not exiting at the Federal Center.

One Friday in late September, a guard informed Davis that she would not be allowed to ride the bus anymore without her ID. By that point, Davis had had enough of what she deemed "faux security. It doesn't aid our security. They didn't take my name and compare it to a no-ride list. It's just a keep-us-scared kind of thing. They're not doing anything with it."[92] So Davis did some basic research, brushing up on the concepts she had first learned in her junior high civics class. "I spent the weekend making sure that the Constitution hadn't changed since I was in the eighth grade, and it hadn't," she declared. "We're not required to carry papers.... We have a right to be anonymous."[93]

The next Monday, upon arrival at the Federal Center, a guard boarded Deb's bus and asked her if she had her ID. She answered in the affirmative. He requested to see it. She flatly replied "No." And this is where the story takes an extreme turn.

Deb Davis remained seated while the guard summoned a Federal Protective Services officer who demanded to see her ID. Deb repeated calmly that she would not comply: she was just riding a public bus and trying to get to work. The officer left, returned with a second policeman, and a third interrogation took place. "Grab her," ordered the second cop, tossing Deb's cell phone to the back of the bus. The guard then jerked her out of her seat and wrenched her arms behind her back, scattering the contents of her purse. Davis was physically forced off the bus, handcuffed, thrown into the backseat of a patrol car, and taken to a police station within the Federal Center.

Once in federal custody, Davis sat waiting for two hours, still handcuffed, while the two policemen rifled through her purse and conferred with each other and their computers. Struggling to find something with which to charge her, the officers finally issued Davis tickets for two petty misdemeanors. Next they took her outside, removed her handcuffs, and returned her belongings. The guards then pointed her toward the same bus stop at which they had accosted her. The police told Davis that if she ever entered the Denver Federal Center again, she would go to jail. Davis stood both dazed and defiant. "I never thought this would happen. I was just trying not to show my ID because I don't have to. That's all."[94]

Facing criminal charges, Davis consulted with the Identity Project, an activist organization opposed to unwarranted federal security matters, and also with the ACLU of Colorado. Both organizations took up her legal case and her principal cause. Publicized by each organization as well as by the national media, Deb's story became a compelling example of one American's battle for privacy, anonymity, and personal integrity. Columnists compared Davis's ordeal to the Nazi regime requirement that citizens carry identification papers at all times.[95] Other editorials referred to her as "the Rosa Parks of the Patriot Act generation."[96]

Some invasions of privacy may be justified by the government's interest in advancing safety. But as Mark Silverstein, legal director of the ACLU of Colorado, recognizes, "The ID check on the bus doesn't do anything to enhance safety. They don't check to make sure it is a valid ID. They don't even check the names against a pre-determined list of suspicious people." Davis herself has acknowledged the competing interests. "I'm not opposed to security," she affirms. "I'm opposed to being bullied. This is not about security. It's about compliance."[97]

Asked whether she was prepared to spend as much as sixty days in jail for her cause, Deb responded, "If that's what it takes, absolutely."[98] She also said that the attention and support garnered by her case "gives me a lot of hope. People have come out of the woodwork. People do care."[99] Two days before her scheduled arraignment, the charges against Davis were dropped due to a "technicality" regarding the official signs notifying passengers of the pending checkpoint. Evidently someone in charge of prosecution at the Colorado U.S. Attorney's Office, perhaps affected by the media attention the Davis debacle had received, realized there was little use in pursuing Davis further.

I AM NOT A NUMBER

We are at a crucial crossroads in American history. It is the Deb Davises of the world, those willing to stand and fight and oppose efforts to brand, track, and dehumanize us—whether through national ID cards, radio tags, or massive databases—who provide a glimmer of hope that maybe, just maybe, we might be able to stem the tide. Should we fail to maintain our individuality and autonomy, however, history and the world around us abound with examples of the grim alternative that awaits us.

The idea of singling out and "identifying" individuals for the sake of national security is nothing new. National identity cards also carry with them a historic risk of oppression and persecution, as they have been used to identify and track ethnic, racial, and religious groups and have facilitated oppression and persecution against these groups. As recently as the 1990s, identity cards played an instrumental role in one of the worst genocides of the twentieth century, second only perhaps to the Holocaust.

The most elaborate identification system used in the abuse of a class of people was the one created by the Nazis. The program started in late 1937, when the German Interior Ministry required all Jews to carry special identification cards for travel within Germany. In July 1938, the infamous "J-stamp" was added to the identity cards, and later to the passports, of Jewish people. These stamped ID cards, a prelude to the yellow Star of David badges, which were usually issued in the months prior to deportation, were instrumental in identifying over 750 Jews, who were subsequently deported to death camps in Poland.[100]

On October 3, 1940, Vichy France issued the first *Statut des Juifs* (Jewish Statute), which was modeled on the Nuremberg laws and required Jews living in Vichy France to have their identity cards stamped with the word *Juif* (Jew). During the Nazi occupation of the Netherlands, the Dutch were required to carry proof of their identity, which the Nazis used as a means to identify Jews, many of whom later ended up in concentration and death camps. Author Raul Hilberg summarizes the impact that such a system had on the Jews:

> *The whole identification system, with its personal documents, specially assigned names, and conspicuous tagging in public, was a powerful weapon in the hands of the police. First, the system was an auxiliary device that facilitated the enforcement of residence and movement restrictions. Second, it was an independent control measure in that it enabled the police to pick up any Jew, anywhere, anytime. Third, and perhaps most important, identification had a paralyzing effect on its victims.*[101]

In South Africa during apartheid, a separate form of identification known as a "pass book" was issued to black citizens in an attempt to regulate the movement of black Africans in urban areas and, as such, segregate the population. The Pass Laws Act of 1952 stipulated where, when, and for how long a black African could remain in certain areas. Any government employee could strike out entries, which cancelled the permission to remain in an area. A pass book that did not have a valid entry resulted in the arrest and imprisonment of the bearer.[102] These pass laws remained in effect until 1986. Such pass books were also used in the same fashion to discriminate against black Africans in Rhodesia (now Zimbabwe and Zambia).[103]

In 1994, identity cards played a crucial role in the genocide of the Tutsis in the central African country of Rwanda. The assault, which extremist Hutu militia groups called the Interahamwe and the Impuzamugambi carried out, was the largest atrocity during the Rwandan Civil War. It lasted around one hundred days and resulted in the deaths of at least 500,000 Tutsis and thousands of moderate Hutus.[104] Other estimates put the figure somewhere between 800,000 and one million killings.[105] While the ID cards were not a precondition to the genocide, they were a facilitating factor. Once the genocide began, the production of an identity card with the designation "Tutsi" spelled a death sentence at any roadblock.[106]

It is not just in such extreme areas that ID cards have helped an oppressive regime achieve its objectives. In other eliminationist policies—mass expulsion, forced relocation, and group denationalization—identity cards played a role in the governmental regime's success. Through the use of identity cards, the Ethiopian authorities were able to identify people with Eritrean affiliation during the mass expulsion of 1998, while the Vietnamese government was able to locate ethnic Chinese more easily during their 1978–79 expulsion. The USSR used identity cards to force the relocation of ethnic Koreans (1937), Volga Germans (1941), Kamyks and Karachai (1943), Crimean Tartars, Meshkhetian Turks, Chechens, Ingush, and Balkars (1944), and ethnic Greeks (1949). Ethnic Vietnamese were identified for group denationalization through identity cards in Cambodia in 1993, as were the Kurds in Syria in 1962.[107]

While more than twenty nations still have a line on their identity cards for some form of ethnic, racial, or religious affiliation, many of these nations are places where intergroup tension or violence is prevalent. Even in countries that do not place such discriminatory information on the cards, problems often still arise. In continental Europe, where ID cards are required in many countries, tensions have risen between ethnic minorities and the police. French police have been accused of overzealous use of the ID card against blacks and, particularly, North Africans. The Institute for Advanced Studies in Internal Security drew attention to the link between the French ID cards and tightening immigration laws, adding that "although the card itself provided no threat to civil liberties, the police powers to check ID provided an ever growing intrusion." Similarly, according to Mouloud Aounit, the secretary general of the French anti-racism group MRAP: "They aren't in themselves a force for repression, but in the current climate of security hysteria they facilitate it.... Young people of Algerian or Moroccan descent are being checked six times a day."[108]

Despite any claims that the United States could never commit such abuses, the worries about how a national ID card could be abused are already apparent. In particular, in the post-9/11 period, Muslim men from Arab or South Asian countries were rounded up on the basis of religion and ethnicity and detained indefinitely in the United States, often without access to an attorney or a judge. With the introduction of an identity card that contains information such as ethnic origin, government agencies will be able to identify people on the basis of race or religion with considerable ease. This, combined with the fact that KBR, a former affiliate of the Halliburton Corporation, is building detention camps in the United States, begs the question: where are people's basic constitutional rights—privacy, habeas corpus, etc.—heading?

PRISONERS OF THE MIND

Whether the means used to corral Americans is a national ID card or something altogether different, in the end, we are prisoners not just of a powerful government entity—we are prisoners of our own minds. No bars can fully contain a people who are truly free in their hearts and minds. It is in the mind that prisons are created for us. Thus, if we condemn ourselves to life under an oppressive, authoritarian regime, we have only ourselves to blame—we have in essence become our own jailers.

Yet we must recognize that we all have the potential to be a Deb Davis with the power to confront and possibly vanquish such oppression. All it takes is one person to decide that "enough is enough."

CHAPTER FIVE

Children under Fire

Unfortunately, children do not organize, have no access to the media, and do not vote. They are relatively powerless to improve their own condition. Children need adults who will advocate for them.

—Professor David Elkind, Tufts University

Paducah. Columbine. Red Lake. These names conjure up images of gunfire, with our young people caught in the crosshairs.

On October 1, 1997, sixteen-year-old Luke Woodham of Pearl, Mississippi, shot and killed two fellow students and left seven others wounded. On December 1, 1997, fourteen-year-old Michael Carneal fatally shot three students as they participated in a prayer circle at a local high school in West Paducah, Kentucky. In 1998, Mitchell Johnson and Andrew Golden (ages thirteen and eleven), shooting from a nearby woods, killed four fellow students and a teacher as the student body evacuated the school building during a false fire alarm. Later that year, fifteen-year-old Kip Kinkel brought several firearms to school and killed two students and wounded twenty-five others. The previous day, he had shot and killed his parents, whose bodies were later found at home.[1]

On April 20, 1999, Eric Harris and Dylan Klebold of Littleton, Colorado, embarked on a violent rampage at Columbine High School that injured twenty-three and left one teacher and fourteen students dead. On February 29, 2000, gun violence in schools claimed its youngest victim when six-year-old Kayla Rolland was shot and killed by a fellow six-year-old in her elementary school classroom in the small town of Flint, Michigan. On March 21, 2005, in

Red Lake, Minnesota, sixteen-year-old Jeff Weise entered his high school and shot and killed one teacher, five students, and a security guard before taking his own life. And on April 16, 2007, third-year Virginia Tech student Cho Seung-Hui went on a shooting rampage that left thirty-three college students and professors dead (including Seung-Hui himself), and fifteen wounded, in what might be the largest school shooting massacre to date in U.S. history.[2]

While grievous, the damage inflicted on our young people by this rash of school violence has not been limited to guns and bullets. Just as the 9/11 terrorist attacks created a watershed between the freedoms we enjoyed and our awareness of America's vulnerability to attack, so the spate of school shootings over ten-plus years has drastically altered the way young people are perceived and treated, transforming them from innocent bystanders into both victims and culprits. Consequently, school officials, attempting to both protect and control young people, have adopted draconian zero-tolerance policies, stringent security measures, and cutting-edge technologies that have all but transformed the schools into quasi prisons. Yet by treating young people as if they have no rights, we are seemingly laying the groundwork for future generations that are altogether ignorant of their rights as citizens and unprepared to defend them.

TROUBLE SIGNS

If children are the living message we send to a time we will not see, what will America's young people say about us, our values, and our freedoms years from now?

Our much-vaunted culture of consumerism and material comforts has resulted in an overall air of cynicism marked by a spiritual vacuum. As German sociologist Georg Simmel recognized a century ago, the more that money moves to the center of our lives, the more cynical we become about higher values.[3] Since the mid-twentieth century, changes in family patterns and childrearing have shifted the responsibility for the upbringing of children from the traditional family to other settings in society. With children spending a majority of their waking hours at school, the parenting task has largely been replaced by public school officials. In its modern context, however, public education cannot inculcate character and teach right and wrong, thus providing the necessary moral limitations on behavior. Still, the state of the family can be found at the heart of many of the problems confronting young people today. As Cornell University professor Urie Bronfenbrenner wrote: "While the family still has the primary moral and legal responsibility for the character development of children, it often lacks the power or opportunity to do the job, primarily because parents and children no longer spend enough time together in those situations in which such training is possible. This is not because parents do not want to spend time with their children. It is simply that conditions have changed."[4]

Conditions have indeed changed. Gone is the innocence of childhood. Today's young people often know more about sex, drugs, and violence than their adult counterparts. By the year 2000, 25 percent of U.S. teens were involved with weapons; 70 percent admitted cheating on tests in school; more than 15 percent had shown up for class drunk; and 5 million children—including three-year-olds—were regularly left home alone to care for themselves.[5]

More so than any previous generation, young people are growing up in an age of overwhelming mass media, mixed messages, and multitasking. The average American child lives in a house with 2.9 TVs, 1.8 VCRs, 3.1 radios, 2.6 tape players, 2.1 CD players, and a computer. Forty-two percent of American homes are "constant TV households," meaning that a set is on most of the time. The average American watches television about four hours per day, and it consumes 40 percent of his or her free time.[6]

Wherever they turn, life is chaotic—wars, violence, environmental crises, oil depletion, and terrorism, to name a few. Children are confronted on a daily basis with issues, images, and material of all sorts—abortion, drugs, alcohol, pornography—and preyed upon by sexual predators, marketing mavens, even the government. Although teenagers can cope with a number of emotional hazards, with each additional hazard introduced, their resilience—like soldiers in combat too long—diminishes to such an extent that breakdowns are imminent. As Cornell University professor James Gabarino recognizes, one of the key factors leading to violence is a "spiritual emptiness" that brings on a feeling of not being connected to anything, of having no limits for behavior and no reverence for life.[7]

Finally, we must consider the impact that our school systems are having on young people and their psyches. Looking at America's public schools today, it may be difficult to imagine that they were once considered the hope of freedom and democracy. According to a report by the Acton Institute, "Ninety-five percent of American 17-year-olds cannot read well enough to understand technical materials and literary essays. This means that only about 5 percent of America's 17-year-olds can read well enough to understand the Bible....Almost one-third of 17-year-olds do not know that Columbus discovered the New World before 1750!"[8] Additionally, we now have school systems that are, for the most part, heavy on curtailing inappropriate behavior and light on common sense and compassion. Nowhere is this more evident than in the over-all lockdown mentality sweeping through our public schools.

PUBLIC SCHOOL LOCKDOWN

On November 5, 2003, a SWAT team conducted a random drug sweep at Stratford High School in Goose Creek, South Carolina. Carrying guns and leading drug dogs, the officers, all in full paramilitary uniform, handcuffed 150 students and forced them to the ground at gunpoint. The mass search was prompted by the principal's suspicion that a student was selling marijuana. The student in question happened to be absent the morning the search was conducted. No guns or drugs were found. In another incident, the entire student body at Mumford High School in Detroit, Michigan, was subjected to mass physical searches, patted down, and held for an hour and a half despite there being no individualized suspicion of criminal activity.

While these may appear to be isolated incidents, students throughout the country in urban, suburban, and rural schools are being subjected to similar searches in the so-called quest to make the schools safer and drug free. Over the past decade, the adoption of disciplinary and security measures has caused the public schools to increasingly resemble penitentiaries, particularly as the employment of fingerprinting, photo identification, metal detectors, security cameras, barbed-wire fencing, drug testing, and random searches has become more common.

In the 2003–2004 school year, 28 percent of primary schools, 42 percent of middle schools, and 60 percent of high schools employed at least one security camera. Thirteen percent of high schools use random metal detecting; 59 percent of schools employ random drug dog sniffing; and 28 percent of schools use random sweeps not involving dogs.[9] Locked and monitored gates or doors limit access to the schools, while metal detectors, security cameras, and drug searches monitor the students. These procedures supposedly serve a dual purpose: protecting schools from intruders, while restricting the students within. The use of ID cards to be swiped when entering and exiting school buildings has also become much more prevalent. Cameras monitor the movements of students throughout the course of the day. And software developed by Raptor Technologies, a Houston-based firm, is commonly used to track school visitors by checking their driver's licenses against a national database of sex offenders.[10]

There has also been an increase in the use of biometrics, or identification taken from records of physiological information such as fingerprinting and retinal scans. In the Freehold Borough School District of New Jersey, retinal scans have been used to identify parents coming to pick up their children from school.[11] In some schools in both Massachusetts and California, fingerprinting has been used to pay for students' lunches, while others use fingerprinting to account for students getting on and off buses.

The prospect of such sensitive information being collected by the state has given rise to serious privacy concerns over how the data is stored, how long the state should retain it, under what circumstances the state can access it, and whether parental consent should be required to even collect such biometric data in the first place. Iowa, for example, has passed a law that effectively bans the use of fingerprinting technologies in schools under most circumstances, while Illinois has put into effect a law that regulates the collection and use of such information, requiring parental consent for the gathering of biometric information.[12]

In a post-Columbine, post-9/11 era, legislators and school administrators are understandably concerned about the safety of students and faculty, their public relations in conjunction with these events, and liability issues in the case of a crisis happening in their schools. Thus, these various technologies and security systems are intended to assuage the fears and anxieties of school officials and parents alike. As Kenneth Trump of the National School Safety and Securities Services, an Ohio-based consulting group that has provided services for schools in thirty states, reminds administrators, changing technologies have altered the school environment, with bombs, anthrax, and concealed weapons now posing a "real" threat.[13]

ZERO TOLERANCE

The current climate of anxiety and fear verging on paranoia in the schools has spawned countless security measures, policies, and procedures aimed at protecting young people—often from themselves. Of these, zero-tolerance policies have proven to be the most ineffective and nearly disastrous.

The concept of zero tolerance—the prescription of full and mandatory punishment for any transgression of the law or rules, regardless of size or magnitude—first appeared in the United States during the 1980s as a safeguard against drug abuse and various other legal infractions, including trespassing and sexual harassment.[14] By the early 1990s, this mandatory punishment policy had been adopted by the nation's school systems in response to the numerous school shootings and student-initiated acts of violence.

Zero-tolerance policies punish all offenses severely, no matter how minor. School systems began adopting these tough codes after Congress passed the 1994 Gun-Free Schools Act, which required a one-year expulsion for any child bringing a firearm or bomb to school. Zero-tolerance rules in many states also cover fighting, drug or alcohol use, and gang activity, as well as relatively minor offenses such as possessing over-the-counter medications and disrespect of authority. Nearly all U.S. public schools have zero-tolerance policies for firearms or other "weapons," and most have such policies for drugs and alcohol.

In the wake of the Columbine school shootings, nervous legislators and school boards further tightened their zero-tolerance policies, creating what some critics call a national intolerance for childish behavior. In some jurisdictions, carrying cough drops, wearing black lipstick, or dying your hair blue are expellable offenses. As *Time* magazine reports, "By definition zero tolerance erases distinctions among student offense. Hence the national crackdown on Alka-Seltzer."[15] At least twenty children in four states have been suspended from school for possession of the fizzy tablets in violation of zero-tolerance drug policies.[16]

Advocates of zero-tolerance policies often cite violence in schools as justification for encroachments upon the constitutional rights of students. But critics say the strict one-strike-and-you're-out policies being imposed to stop school violence and misbehavior sometimes go too far. These policies have also been heavily criticized by such professional organizations as the National Association of School Psychologists: "Research indicates that, as implemented, zero-tolerance policies are ineffective in the long run and are related to a number of negative consequences, including increased rates of school drop out and discriminatory application of school discipline practices."[17]

Furthermore, the imposition of draconian and inflexible zero-tolerance policies teaches Americans that government authorities have total power and can violate constitutional rights as they see fit. They also communicate to young people the idea that their rights may be highly—and often unjustly—restricted on school property. An anti-drug, anti-weapons law that Congress passed in 2006, which requires school districts to develop search policies, including strip searches by teachers and other school staff, illustrates this. Groups such as the American Federation of Teachers and the National Parent Teacher Association have expressed their opposition to the law, insisting that it condones random, unconstitutional searches of students by teachers who are not trained law enforcement officials.[18]

Despite mounting criticism, zero-tolerance policies proliferate, creating a vortex that sucks in otherwise innocent children who make a single mistake. The public-school crime blotter is teeming with examples.

On a school bus in rural Mississippi, five high school students passed the time on their long ride home by tossing peanuts at each other. When one of the nuts hit the bus driver, however, she pulled the bus over, called the police, and had the boys arrested for assault, which is punishable by five years in prison. Although the criminal charges were dropped, the teenagers lost their bus privileges. Unable to make the thirty-mile trip, all five dropped out of school.[19]

In October 1996, Erica Taylor, a thirteen-year-old resident of Fairborn, Ohio, was suspended from school for acquiring Midol tablets from a fellow student. Although Taylor did not consume the pills, she was accused of violating the school's policy concerning drug use. It was only after Taylor agreed to attend extra classes regarding drug abuse that she was allowed to return to school.[20]

In April 1998, Christine Rhodes, a twelve-year-old student at Mount Airy Middle School in Maryland, was charged with violating the school's zero-tolerance policy on "drug use and trafficking" and suspended from taking part in school activities. Rhodes' crime? She had attempted to help a friend who was suffering from an asthma attack by offering her an inhaler. The friend's mother insists that her daughter might have died had Rhodes not come to her aid.[21]

Tawana Dawson, a fifteen-year-old African American student at Pensacola High School in Florida, was expelled for the 1999–2000 school year for possession of a "weapon" in violation of the school's zero-tolerance policy. The weapon in question was a nail clipper with a 2-inch metal nail file.[22] Other examples abound:

- ✦ In York, Pennsylvania, a six-year-old boy was suspended for carrying a pair of nail clippers to school.
- ✦ In Columbus, Ohio, a second-grader was suspended for drawing a paper gun, cutting it out, and pointing it at classmates.
- ✦ A nine-year-old Ohio boy was suspended after writing, "You will die an honorable death" as a fortune cookie prediction for a class assignment.
- ✦ A twelve-year-old Florida boy was handcuffed and jailed after he stomped in a puddle, splashing classmates.
- ✦ A thirteen-year-old boy in Manassas, Virginia, who accepted a

Certs breath mint from a classmate, was suspended and required to attend drug-awareness classes.

+ Jewish youths in several schools were suspended for wearing the Star of David, which was sometimes used as a symbol of gang membership.[23]

Incidents like these have made zero-tolerance policies the subject of great debate. What has become apparent, however, is the fact that zero-tolerance policies are ineffective tools for discouraging school violence. Russell Skiba and Reece Peterson have noted "that the rate of school violence has remained fairly level since the early 1990s."[24] As Skiba, an educational psychology professor at Indiana University, recognizes, studies show that 35 to 45 percent of suspensions are for repeat offenders. "So we end up punishing honor students to send a message to bad kids. But the data indicate that the bad kids are not getting the message."[25] Furthermore, numerous statistics indicate that these stringent security measures fail to decrease the number of students bringing weapons to school, victims of violent crime, and students trying alcohol, cigarettes, and other illegal drugs.

Zero-tolerance policies that create blanket punishments for students regardless of age, maturity, mental and emotional status, or circumstance often lead to the creation of a student-aged population that is woefully ignorant of the rights they intrinsically possess as American citizens. Under such a system of mandatory punishment, one would punish an elementary school student in the same way that one would punish an adult high school senior, or a student who intends to harm others would be treated the same as one who breaks the rules accidentally with no true mens rea, or guilty mind. Students might be labeled as "drug dealers" and "weapon wielders" due to purely accidental circumstances and still be punished for actions that hardly qualify as transgressions of the rules, let alone dangerous crimes. Thus, zero-tolerance policies do not educate and reform America's youth but instead teach them that they possess no true rights.

Some zero-tolerance cases have made their way into the courts, but the judiciary has done little to rectify what most people would consider to be miscarriages of justice. A common pattern that has emerged in many zero-tolerance cases is the judiciary's tendency to allow school bureaucracy to triumph over common sense and the Bill of Rights. Three cases in particular come to mind.

The first involves a young boy who was given a four-month suspension from Blue Ridge Middle School in Virginia after persuading a suicidal friend to relinquish a knife she had brought to school. Although officials for the Loudoun County Public Schools acknowledged that Benjamin Ratner's actions were "noble" and "admirable" and admitted that he posed no threat to himself or others, they nevertheless upheld the suspension. When Ratner's family turned to the courts, they were informed by a three-judge panel of the Fourth Circuit Court of Appeals that the federal courts were not properly called upon to judge the wisdom of school policies and that the implementation of the school's zero-tolerance policy against Ben did not violate his constitutional rights. However, in a separate written opinion that seemed to contradict the court's ruling, Judge Clyde H. Hamilton expressed compassion for Ben, his family, and "common sense," calling each "the victim of good intentions run amuck." Judge Hamilton then went on to say that the four-month suspension was "not justifiable" and called the punishment a "calculated overkill" in light of Ben's good faith intentions.[26] Nevertheless, the suspension was allowed to stand.

In another instance, under a zero-tolerance policy against food consumption in the Washington DC metro system, a teenager was arrested for eating a french fry. The case eventually reached the Court of Appeals for the District of Columbia, where Justice John G. Roberts was presiding prior to his appointment to the U.S. Supreme Court. In handing down a ruling in *Hedgepeth v. Washington Metro*, Judge Roberts stated that "no one is very happy about the events that led to this litigation." Ansche Hedgepeth, he recounted, "was arrested, searched, and handcuffed. Her shoelaces were removed, and she was transported in the windowless rear compartment of a police vehicle to a juvenile processing center, where she was booked, fingerprinted, and detained until released to her mother some three hours later—all for eating a single french fry in a Metrorail station. The child was frightened, embarrassed, and crying throughout the ordeal." Despite his ability to recognize the harshness of her treatment, Roberts ruled that Ansche's constitutional rights had not been violated in any way.[27]

The third case involves a young kindergartner from Sayreville, New Jersey, who was suspended for engaging in a make-believe game of cops and robbers on the school playground (he used his finger as a pretend gun). While the school district claimed to have no official written policy mandating zero tolerance of violent behavior or threats, the actions by the Sayreville school officials were consistent with those of many other school districts that have adopted such blanket policies. A lawsuit seeking to have the suspension expunged from the boy's school record made its way through the courts—all the way to the U.S. Supreme Court, in fact—only to be dismissed at every turn.[28]

FREE SPEECH GRAVEYARD

Whereas the concept of zero tolerance was at one time limited to a set of actions and behaviors that might be construed as violent or drug-related, it has since evolved to encompass a broader range of activities, one of which is expression. That certain forms of expression, including speech, are now being treated with zero tolerance in the schools is also indicative of a national trend toward political correctness that seeks to silence or censor anything that might be considered offensive or disagreeable. The following are just a few examples of how this authoritarian mindset is influencing the manner in which student expression is handled in the schools.

Nicholas Noel was attempting to convey to the more than one thousand people gathered for Grand Rapids Union High School's graduation ceremony his belief that high school paints an incomplete picture of life for students. However, because the 2004 senior class president strayed from his approved commencement speech and referred to Grand Rapids as a "prison," school officials turned the microphone off. Noel insists that he described the school as a "prison" because students were "expected to act alike." Unfortunately, when Noel returned to his seat, school officials initially refused to award him his diploma.

"The colors of life are yet to come," Noel said. "It was really nice, nothing in bad taste. I tried to be different, and I was punished."[29]

Depictions of the Confederate flag have also become a source of contention in the schools and part of a larger debate over what constitutes free expression. Pointing to highly publicized incidents of hate crimes and racist violence, many authorities have opted for acts of censorship in order to avoid conflict. For example, officials at a Kansas middle school suspended one student after he sketched a Confederate flag, familiar to him from the *Dukes of Hazzard* television show, on a sheet of paper at the request of a friend. According to the school's zero-tolerance policy, the Confederate flag is a prohibited symbol of "racial harassment and intimidation." The student sued and lost in court, and the Supreme Court refused to hear his case.[30]

In 1999, Adam Porter, then fourteen years old, drew a picture of his school, East Ascension High School, in a sketchpad in the privacy of his home. The drawing depicted the school under siege by a gasoline tanker truck, a helicopter, and a missile launcher. Two years later, Adam's brother Andrew used the sketchpad for his own drawings, then took the pad to school. After a fellow student saw Adam's old drawing and showed it to school officials, Andrew was questioned about the drawing and suspended for possessing the sketch on school grounds. School officials at East Ascension Parish School then questioned and searched Adam, who had no previous disciplinary record, and found a box cutter that Adam was using in his after-school job at a grocery store. Later that day, Adam was arrested on charges of terrorizing the school and carrying an illegal weapon. He spent four nights in jail for a harmless drawing. While a federal district court supported the school's actions, especially in light of the Columbine school shootings, a panel for the Fifth Circuit Court of Appeals declared that Adam's sketch was entitled to First Amendment protection. "Private writings made and kept in one's home enjoy the protections of the First Amendment, as well as the Fourth," the panel wrote. "For such writings to lose their First Amendment protection, something more than their accidental and unintentional exposure to public scrutiny must take place." Nevertheless, the Fifth Circuit still ruled in favor of the school officials by granting them qualified immunity, a doctrine that protects government officials from liability in civil rights actions when they do not violate clearly established principles of law. The U.S. Supreme Court refused to hear the case.[31]

Religious expression has also come under attack in the schools. A vivid example is Brittany McComb, who was chosen to give the valedictory speech at Foothill High School in Nevada. School officials asked Brittany to speak to her fellow classmates about what was important in her life. To Brittany, her faith as a Christian was paramount. After composing her remarks, she was required to submit them to school administrators, according to standard district policy. However, upon the advice of their district legal counsel, school administrators censored Brittany's speech, deleting all three Bible references, several references to "the Lord," and the only mention of the word "Christ."

When Brittany delivered her graduation address on June 15, 2006, she attempted to deliver the original version of her speech, rather than the edited one, believing that the district's censorship amounted to a violation of her right to free speech. When school officials realized that she was straying from the approved text, they unplugged her microphone. School officials justified their actions by claiming that Brittany's speech amounted to proselytizing, but Brittany was having none of that. Determined to stand and fight, Brittany filed a case in federal court challenging the school's actions in the belief that the First Amendment's protections for freedom of speech should have kept her plugged in. As Brittany remarked, "People aren't stupid. They know we have freedom of speech, and the district wasn't advocating my ideas. Those are my opinions. It's what I believe."[32]

Eleven-year-old Nashala Hearn and her family are followers of Islam, which requires women to wear the hijab (a Muslim head covering) in public places. Nashala, a public middle school student who had never been in any kind of academic trouble, consistently followed this requirement in expressing her commitment to her sincerely held beliefs. On September 11, 2003, Nashala was informed by her school principal at Benjamin Franklin Science Academy in Muskogee,

Oklahoma, that she would no longer be permitted to wear the hijab to school because such attire was prohibited by the school's dress code—in effect, a zero-tolerance policy that prohibited hats, caps, bandannas, plastic caps, and hoods or jackets inside the school building. Supposedly aimed at gang-related wear, the code made no mention of hijabs or any other kind of religious head covering. The sixth grader and her parents were greatly concerned by the school's attempt to force Nashala to violate her religious beliefs. Believing she had to live consistently with her religious beliefs, Nashala refused to remove the hijab. Shortly thereafter, Nashala was suspended from school for three days. Upon returning to school after serving the suspension, Nashala again wore the hijab and this time was suspended for five days.

At that point, Nashala's father contacted The Rutherford Institute, which filed a lawsuit in federal court alleging that school officials had violated Nashala's rights to free speech and the free exercise of religion, among other important guarantees of the U.S. Constitution. The U.S. Department of Justice later intervened on Nashala's behalf, with the attorney general certifying the case as "one of general public importance." He understood the far-reaching ramifications of the case: If these types of dress code policies in American schools are successfully upheld, Jewish students would not be able to wear yarmulkes, and Christians who want to wear symbols such as crucifixes would also be affected. With the case attracting national media attention, the school eventually relented, and it was settled in Nashala's favor.[33]

Whether we're talking about threats of violence and chaos or free speech, it is common sense, compassion, and moral strength—not fear and anxiety—that should shape our policies and guide our reactions. School administrators should understand that there is a difference between child's play and threatening behavior. They would do well to stop acting like prison wardens in a totalitarian state and start acting like role models of a democratic society.

The costs for students and faculty alike go far beyond what can be accounted for on a balance sheet. Zero-tolerance policies dramatically interrupt the learning process, leave kids with a sense of unfair and disproportionate punishment, increase anxiety and promote feelings of distrust among parents, students, and administrators. These measures also habituate young people to meek acceptance of arbitrary punishments, unreasonable searches, constant surveillance, and censorship.

SUICIDE: AMERICA'S SICK SOUL

While draconian zero-tolerance policies and the transformation of public schools into mini-police states can be shown to negatively impact America's youth, they are not the only influences preying on our young people. American society has for decades battled the issue of suicide, striving to adopt various preventative measures which may ultimately restrain this widespread health problem and thwart its citizens from resorting to practices of brutal self-destruction.[34] While the suicide rate for society as a whole has declined slightly over the past twenty years (from approximately 13.2 deaths per 100,000 population in 1980 to 10.8 in 2003),[35] the issue of suicide among American children and adolescents has become more prevalent and problematic. Recent data reported by the Centers for Disease Control and Prevention (CDC) shows a large and distinct increase in the suicide rate among individuals aged ten to twenty-four in the United States.

According to the American Association of Suicidology, "In 2004, suicide ranked as the third leading cause of death for young people (ages 15–19 and 15–24)....Whereas suicides accounted for 1.4 percent of all deaths in the U.S. annually, they comprised 12.9 percent of all deaths among 15–24 year olds."[36] These statistics clearly illustrate that youth suicide is a vast problem in the United States. A 2007 report shows that suicide has grown sharply over the past few years. According to the CDC, the suicide rate among ten- to twenty-four-year-olds in the United States has increased by a staggering 8 percent, the largest one-year increase in nearly fifteen years.[37]

One explanation for this escalation in the suicide rate can be found in the link between antidepressant medication and suicidal thoughts. In May 2007, the U.S. Food and Drug Administration (FDA) proposed that producers of antidepressant medication include a "black box" warning informing the public that an increase in suicidal thoughts or actions may be a potential side effect of such prescription medication. These warnings specify that the use of antidepressant drugs may increase "suicidality" in individuals ages eighteen to twenty-four during the first few months of intake and treatment.[38]

While statistical experiments that identify a causal relationship remain open for future study and speculation, the CDC has created a list of other factors that may have influenced youth suicide rates and presented an extra risk to young people in the United States. Some of these factors (including family history of suicide and previous suicide attempts) remain unchanged and probably have not increased drastically within the past decade. Other factors, such as alcohol or drug abuse, stress or loss, access to lethal methods, exposure to the suicidal behavior of others, family issues, mental disorders and depression, and incarceration, have fluctuated, and could also have contributed to an increase in the overall suicide rate among American children and adolescents.[39] The CDC claims that the increase, which has been seen in young girls ages ten to fourteen and fifteen to twenty-four, may also be attributed to the "greater use of methods (e.g., hanging by rope) that are readily accessible."[40]

Insisting that the American public should focus their energy on the prevention of suicide among the youth population by "addressing the underlying reasons for suicide,"[41] the CDC has suggested that such preventative measures may include educating the school-aged population on the importance of mental health and the value of seeking aid (without shame or stigma) when feelings of depression arise, providing confidential screening "for depression, substance abuse, and suicidal ideation" and limiting access to lethal and dangerous methods of committing suicide.[42]

RITALIN NATION

While "Say No to Drugs" campaigns frequently target teens who abuse drugs, both prescription and illegal, not enough has been said about the toll that overmedicating young people has on their psyches.

Young people have become a prime market for the pharmaceutical industry, as the explosion in the use and abuse of Ritalin illustrates. As of 2004, approximately 6 million children—roughly one out of every eight—were being prescribed Ritalin for what is termed "attention-deficit/hyperactive disorder" (ADHD), a condition once labeled as hyperactivity. Since ADHD became a commonplace term in the 1980s, prescriptions for Ritalin have skyrocketed. Since 2000, there has been a 23 percent increase for all children, including those under five years of age.

The drugs prescribed for ADHD are cocaine-like stimulants. According to the U.S. Drug Enforcement Administration (DEA), the human nervous system cannot differentiate between cocaine, amphetamines, and methylphenidate (Ritalin). As the DEA reports, "Methylphenidate, a schedule 2 substance, has a high potential for abuse and produces the same effects as cocaine or the amphetamines. Binge use, psychotic episodes, cardiovascular complications, and severe psychological addiction have all been associated with methylphenidate."[43] It's little wonder, then, that adolescents are increasingly giving or selling their Ritalin medication to schoolmates and friends who are taking it orally, crushing the tablets, and snorting Ritalin powder like cocaine. Ritalin is often referred to as "Kiddie Cocaine." Ritalin is also closely related to the illegal street drug methamphetamine—or "crystal meth."

According to DEA reports, in addition to being a dangerous narcotic, Ritalin also produces numerous troublesome side effects: difficulty sleeping, loss of appetite, irritability, nervousness, stomach aches, headaches, blurry vision, nausea, dizziness, drowsiness, ticks, hypersensitivity, anorexia, blood pressure and pulse changes, cardiac arrhythmia, anemia, scalp hair loss, and toxic psychosis. Other rare side effects include abnormal liver function, cerebral arteritis, leucopenia, and sometimes death.

Evidence also ties Ritalin and other methylphenidate derivatives to abnormally violent behavior in young people who take them. Kip Kinkel, the fifteen-year-old high school student from Oregon who killed four people, including his parents, and wounded twenty-five others, did so after taking methylphenidate and Prozac. Eric Harris, one of the Columbine High School killers, masterminded the killing of twelve students and a teacher while on similar drugs. He and his partner then shot themselves.

These and other violent killings by young students have been linked to the burgeoning legalized prescription drug market that has invaded America's public schools. Rod Matthews, a fourteen-year-old Massachusetts youth who had no history of violence but was placed on methylphenidate, soon developed extreme psychological problems. In October 1986, Rod wrote: "My problem is I like to do crazy things. I've been lighting fires all over the place. Lately, I've been wanting to kill people I hate, and I've been wanting to light houses on fire. What should I do?" Shortly thereafter, Rod lured a fellow student into a forested area and beat the young man to death with a baseball bat. Tried as an adult and convicted of second-degree murder, Rod became the youngest inmate in the Massachusetts prison system. After he was arrested and taken off methylphenidate, his violent thoughts and behavior ceased.[44]

Ritalin has been shown to cause especially severe reactions in children under six years of age. Despite this finding, the number of stimulants prescribed for children aged two to four increased 200 to 300 percent between 1991 and 1995. This will hopefully change with the release of the first long-term study by the U.S. government in October 2006, which warned about the severe side effects of Ritalin and concluded that it should not be recommended for children under the age of six.[45]

Does Ritalin really help settle down hyperactive children? A comprehensive study at Montreal Children's Hospital reveals that the behavior of hyperactive children did not differ significantly from the behavior of nonhyperactive children after taking Ritalin for five years. "Although it appeared that hyperactive kids treated with Ritalin were initially more manageable," the report stated, "the degree of improvement and emotional adjustment was essentially identical at the end of five years to that seen in a group of kids who had received no medication at all."[46]

Schools bear a large part of the blame for the increased prescription of Ritalin and other mind-altering drugs for young children, especially in light of anecdotal reports of public school officials barring disruptive children from school unless parents agree to use drugs to treat their ADHD or attention deficit disorder. A 2005 bill before the U.S. House of Representatives addressed this very concern by prohibiting schools from requiring students to take Ritalin or other antihyperactivity drugs as a condition of attending class.[47]

Does Ritalin help our children academically? According to Dr. Mary Ann Block, "It may surprise many to know that studies have found that children who take amphetamine-type or other mind-altering drugs do not perform better academically. No studies indicate enhanced academic performance from these drugs."[48] The fact is that academically the schools are getting worse, not better. Despite increased funding for education and drugs for children, the U.S. literacy rate plummeted from fifth in the world among nations in the 1960s to fortieth by 1999, its lowest rating ever.

MENTAL HEALTH TESTS

Schoolchildren across the nation are finding themselves subjected to behavioral exams and mental health tests, often without their parents' knowledge or consent. One such program is the Youth Risk Behavior Surveillance System (YRBSS). Utilized in at least forty-five states, the YRBSS test takes approximately thirty-five minutes to complete, with questions on how much television the student watches to thoughts on suicide, sexual activity, and drug use. The 2007 middle-school questionnaire included such questions as:

+ Have you ever seriously thought about killing yourself?
+ Have you ever made a plan about killing yourself?
+ Have you ever used marijuana?
+ Have you ever used any form of cocaine, including powder, crack, or freebase?
+ Have you ever had sexual intercourse?
+ The last time you had sexual intercourse, did you or your partner use a condom?
+ Have you ever sniffed glue, or breathed the contents of spray cans, or inhaled any paints or sprays to get high?
+ Have you ever taken any diet pills, powders, or liquids without a doctor's advice to lose weight or to keep from gaining weight?

✦ Have you ever vomited or taken laxatives to lose weight or to keep from gaining weight?

Developed in 1990 by the CDC, the test's stated purpose is to track health risk behaviors among America's youth. YRBSS is similar to other mental health screening programs that have crept into the classroom ever since a mental health commission appointed by President George W. Bush recommended mental health screenings for all school-age children. In April 2002, President Bush launched the New Freedom Commission on Mental Health. After supposedly conducting a comprehensive study, the commission recommended mental health screening for "consumers of all ages," including preschool children. Schools, the study concluded, are in a "key position" to screen the 52 million students and 6 million adults who work in the public schools.

The report called for linking the results of the screening to "state-of-the-art treatments."[49] It also mentioned using "specific medications for specific conditions." No mention was made of other forms of treatment such as counseling. The commission report praised a diagnosis manual known as the Texas Medication Algorithm Project (TMAP), which helps define mental disorders and connect diagnoses with treatments.

TMAP, developed in Texas while President Bush was governor, lists psychotropic drugs exclusively as treatments—but only the newest and most expensive ones. The lone exception is TMAP's endorsement of electroshock therapy in cases where drug regimens fail. TMAP has been faulted for liberally defining mental illness and including behaviors that many feel are a matter of will. An example is oppositional defiant disorder, which the TMAP manual defines as being present in any child who "often argues with adults" and "often actively defies or refuses to comply with adults' requests or rules."[50] If such behavior is mental illness, then most if not all teenagers at some point suffer such a crisis.

Given the fact that many of the commissioners who were appointed by President Bush have strong ties to the pharmaceutical industry, questions have been raised regarding the objectivity of the New Freedom Commission and TMAP. The commission's report seems heavily supportive of pharmaceutical solutions to mental health problems. It even mentions one screening program by name, TeenScreen, praising it as a model for nationwide screening.

TeenScreen has found its way into many public schools. The creators of TeenScreen believe that teens answering questions such as those posed in their survey will reveal potential warning signs for mental health issues, especially depression, which can lead to suicide. Both of these claims are heavily contested.

Some states have even begun to implement recommendations by the commission. In Illinois, the legislature passed a plan to screen the mental health of all pregnant women and children up to eighteen years of age. Under such a plan, which also includes the use of anti-depressant drugs, both children and adults will be screened for so-called mental illness during their routine physical exams.

There are serious potential conflict of interest issues raised by the complex interactions among the New Freedom Commission, the pharmaceutical industry, various federal and state agencies involved in implementing the recommendations of the commission, TMAP, and TeenScreen. TeenScreen developer David Shaffer, who is at Columbia University, home of a research program generously funded by pharmaceutical corporations, has served as an expert witness for various drug companies and as a consultant on psychotropic drugs. Shaffer was president of the Foundation for Suicide Prevention in 2000 when the foundation's national survey on suicide was released. A major pharmaceutical company financed the survey, and its results pointed to a suicide crisis among teens.[51]

TeenScreen director Laurie Flynn formerly served as the head of the National Alliance for the Mentally Ill, which received millions of dollars from pharmaceutical companies and was involved in the New Freedom Commission studies. Although TeenScreen officials claim to be entirely funded by private donations, their website indicates that a TeenScreen survey in Tennessee was funded by Eli Lilly, a large pharmaceutical company. And one private donor to TeenScreen who gave $8 million has substantial investments in various pharmaceutical corporations.[52]

In addition to grave concerns about whether programs like Teen-Screen are compromised by their close ties to the pharmaceutical industry, there is doubt concerning psychiatrists' ability to accurately diagnose mental illness at all, let alone TeenScreen's ability to foresee potential suicides from fourteen yes/no questions. The Substance Abuse and Mental Health Services Administration, the federal agency tasked with implementing the recommendations of the New Freedom Commission, cites research by the U.S. Preventative Services Task Force in 2004 indicating that high school screening has correctly identified two-thirds of participants who subsequently attempted suicide or developed serious depression later. Flynn, testifying before the U.S. Senate in 2004, stated that "research has established that...screening programs are one of the most effective means of youth suicide prevention."[53]

However, the same research revealed the tendency of screening programs to generate false positive results. In this case, 84 percent of the participants (some 5,040 out of 6,000) who were initially deemed suicidal were later found to not be at all, meaning that all along they were normal teenagers. Such poor predictive power ultimately renders a program's benefits negligible. The U.S. Preventative Service Task Force report states that there is "no evidence that screening for suicide risk reduces suicide attempts or mortality."[54]

There are also legitimate concerns about how the tests are being administered. Health screening tests such as Teen Screen and YRBSS are often given to students without parental knowledge or consent. While the CDC insists that local parental permission procedures are followed prior to administering the test, many school systems use so-called passive parental notification procedures, which assume that parents have given their consent unless they notify the school of an objection. But passive notification is simply a way to avoid obtaining written parental consent. In the end, whether due to the child losing the notification form or forgetting to give it to the parents, parents are often left in the dark, unaware that their children are being subjected to such invasive tests.

Critics of these risk assessment tests insist they're aimed at pushing antidepressant drugs on teenagers. TeenScreen, which is similar to YRBSS in its stated intent to identify suicidal tendencies and social disorders, has been labeled a "duo-drug promotion scam" that declares "otherwise normal children to be mentally ill" by the Alliance for Human Research Protection. Another vocal critic of the tests, Phyllis Schlafly of Eagle Forum, points out that drug companies are gearing up for bigger sales of antidepressants at the same time that the FDA is issuing warnings about antidepressants increasing the risk of suicidal thinking and behavior in children who take them.[55]

Legitimate questions remain about whether such tests really help students achieve healthier lifestyles. And although the CDC insists that there is no danger in asking students highly suggestive questions about sex, drugs, and suicide, many parents would rightfully prefer to decide the timing and content of such sensitive discussions.

INHUMANE EXPERIMENTS

It has been suggested that America's schools are beginning to resemble laboratories. Whether such programs as Teen Screen prove beneficial or not, the reality is that children have become the guinea pigs of our age.

The U.S. Environmental Protection Agency's (EPA) forays into human experimentation came to light after the *Washington Post* reported that the EPA had approved a two-year study in which families who use pesticides in Duval County, Florida, would be paid to continue using them and to monitor their children's exposure. Each family would receive $970 so that scientists might discover how children's bodies absorb hazardous chemicals. Although scientists may not know the full effects of these poisonous chemicals, they do know that children are at greater risk than adults. Yet rather than advising parents to keep children away from pesticides, the government was paying them to poison their children. U.S. Senators Barbara Boxer (D-Calif.) and Bill Nelson (D-Fla.) threatened to block the full-time confirmation of Stephen Johnson, the EPA's acting administrator, if the experiment was not cancelled. On April 8, 2005, Johnson ended the Florida pesticide program.[56]

The pesticide study is not the only unethical experimentation in U.S. history. From 1945 to 1949, at a prenatal clinic at Vanderbilt

University Hospital, nearly 830 poor, pregnant Caucasian women were given a drink containing radioactive iron. Told the drink would be good for their fetuses, within an hour, the radioactive material was circulating in the blood of the unborn babies.[57]

The list of inhumane experiments does not stop at endangering the unborn. During the 1940s and 1950s, the U.S. government was involved in many radioactivity tests in which humans, especially young children, were used as guinea pigs. Most notable was the MIT and Quaker Oats-sponsored testing at the Fernald School in Waltham, Massachusetts, in which mentally retarded students were fed cereal containing radioactive iron in order to trace iron absorption. Neither the students nor their parents were informed of the use of radioactive materials or the possible health risks.[58]

From 1948 to 1954, Johns Hopkins University conducted an experiment on 582 third graders, testing the effects of Nasal Radium Irradiation. Although it is now known that this procedure places the participant at greater risk for cancer, the government has not contacted the participants to warn them of this risk.[59] During the 1950s and 1960s, mentally retarded children between the ages of three and eleven at Willowbrook State School in New York were intentionally infected with hepatitis. The early test subjects were reportedly infected with strains of the virus obtained from the feces of hepatitis patients in order for researchers to study the hepatitis virus.[60] In the 1960s, the DC Children's Center in Laurel, Maryland, used mentally retarded children as test subjects. They were given a diet pill called NeoBazine, which contains thyroxin, a drug that causes tremors, nervousness, insomnia, and tachycardia. The FDA later found that this drug was not safe for use.[61]

As recently as 1989–1991, Kaiser Permanente of Southern California and the CDC treated 1,500 poor African American and Latino inner-city children in Los Angeles with experimental measles vaccines. The same vaccination, which was given to infants in Mexico, Haiti, and Africa by the World Health Organization, was discontinued after a large number of those tested died.[62]

In a series of articles written for the *New York Press* in July 2004, Liam Scheff reported on experiments at Incarnation Children's Center in New York where AIDS drugs were being tested on HIV-positive children, the majority of them orphans. Although the HIV test is not always accurate, once the children test positive, they are considered terminal patients and are subjected to debilitating experimental drugs. Despite the fact that these drugs can be torturous for the children, those carrying out the experiments seem to feel justified in doing so since the children will most likely die anyway.[63]

PREYED UPON

Our children have become unwitting victims of the predatory tendencies of government bureaucrats, law enforcement officials, and those within the various drug industries. But nowhere is their plight so heartbreaking and disconcerting as it is in relation to sexual predators, especially those who do their hunting online through social networking websites like MySpace.com. (While MySpace requires that users be at least fourteen years old and warns them not to post any "personally identifiable material," that advice is routinely ignored.) The Center for Missing and Exploited Children reported more than 2,600 incidents in 2005 of adults using the Internet to entice children.[64]

Sexual trafficking is yet another way in which young people are preyed upon. The buying and selling of women and children for prostitution and forced labor is one of the fastest growing areas of international criminal activity, second only to drugs and guns. One source estimates that profits from trafficking in sexual slavery alone exceed between $7 and $12 billion annually—and that's just based on the figures that are reported.

News headlines have routinely reported on grown men preying on young children, sometimes even kidnapping them from their homes. But half a world away, it rarely makes headlines when grown men prey on little girls—and boys. In many countries worldwide, the sexual trafficking of children has become a booming tourist industry. Up to 7,000 girls, many as young as nine years old, are sold every year in India's red-light districts. And 10,000 children between the ages of six and fourteen are "employed" in Sri Lankan brothels.[65] UNICEF reports that approximately one million children are taken into forced prostitution each year around the world: 200,000 in Thailand; 400,000 in India; 100,000 in the Philippines, Taiwan, and Brazil; 35,000 in West Africa; and between 244,000 and 325,000 in the United States.[66]

Hunger, poverty, and a lucrative demand by fetishists for young flesh fuel the industry. One investigator who tracks global sex trends attributes the demand to individuals "eager to push the envelope of carnal exploration," as well as pedophiles. In addition, the fear of HIV and AIDS being communicated by older, more experienced prostitutes contributes to the recruitment of younger women and girls, some as young as seven, into the business on the erroneous assumption that they are too young to have been infected.[67]

In impoverished countries, young girls are often sold by their own families to a pimp or brothel for $150 to $200. In the Philippines, India, and Cambodia, among others, families sell their daughters for $350—enough to support the family for one year.[68] The experiences of these young children at the hands of pimps, slave traders, and, tragically, their own families are unforgettable and heartbreaking. When Pia Agustin Corvera from the Philippines was nine, her aunt started selling "encounters" with her for $3 per visit. Three years later, she was sold to a German pedophile.[69] The parents of two sisters in Bangkok, ages six and twelve, sold them to a pimp who "rented" them out to a visiting Australian to abuse and photograph for months on end. Six girls, ages eleven to thirteen, were rescued from a Cambodian brothel that offered only young children.[70]

An Oklahoma City mother was accused of prostituting her two daughters, ages four and seven, on the streets of Las Vegas. Connie Behymer allegedly ordered the little girls to engage in sexual acts with between twenty and fifty men. To those interested in the goods she offered, Behymer's deal, according to media reports, was "$50, no refunds, no money back." After spending a year in jail awaiting trial, Behymer pled guilty to two gross misdemeanor counts of child neglect. She was sentenced to the time she had already served and set free.[71]

Unfortunately, the judicial system offers little justice for those sold for profit in the flesh trade. When compared to the penalties imposed for crimes such as drug and gun trafficking, the penalties for trafficking humans—especially young children—for sexual exploitation are often relatively minor and are frequently seen as merely a nuisance or temporary obstruction. In many instances, the young victims are also treated like criminals, while their abusers walk free. That was the case for two sisters, ten- and eleven-year-old runaways from Atlanta. Forced into prostitution by a relative, they were arrested by police and placed in jail. According to an article in the *Atlanta Journal-Constitution*, "In Georgia, pimps are rarely arrested, even when the prostitute is a child. When pimps are charged, their cases often are dismissed or result in a small fine....Statistics for adults show a clear disparity in the system's treatment of pimps and prostitutes. Since 1972, 401 adults—nearly all women—went to prison in Georgia for prostitution. No one went to prison for just pimping."[72]

The fact that so many women and children continue to be victimized, brutalized, and treated like human cargo can be attributed to three things: a consumer demand that is increasingly lucrative for everyone involved—except the victims; a level of corruption so invasive on both a local and international scale that there is little hope of working through established channels for change; and an eerie silence from individuals who usually speak out against such atrocities.

The effectiveness of legislative attempts to resolve the problem of trafficking women and children remains questionable. In passing the Trafficking Victims Protection Act of 2000, Congress attempted to create a protocol for combating sexual slavery. Despite Congress's attempts to hold countries accountable through a variety of incentive programs and financial penalties, the Office to Combat Trafficking, which was created in the U.S. State Department, has become, in the words of the International Justice Mission, the Office to Obscure Trafficking.

Even the 1989 U.N. Convention on the Rights of the Child has proved weak and ineffective. Promising children around the world the right to life, liberty, education, and health care, the convention provided protection to children in armed conflict, protection from discrimination, protection from torture or cruel, inhuman or degrading treatment or punishment, protection within the justice system, and protection from economic exploitation, in addition to many other fundamental protections. But despite the well-meaning intentions of those who signed and ratified the treaty, more than ten years later, it remains a piece of paper with no real power.

For children to be so used, abused, and deprived of their childhood innocence is nothing less than a crime against humanity. As citizens, we have a moral duty to right the wrongs being done to these children.

THE STRUGGLE

In a multitude of ways, children have been adultified, and their childhood is disappearing. As University of Edinburgh professor Stuart Aitken writes, "In short, the sense of a so-called disappearance of childhood is, in actuality, about the loss of a stable, seemingly natural foundation for social life that is clearly linked not only to laments over the lost innocence of childhood, but also a growing anger at and fear of young people."[73]

This disconnect became clear at the October 2006 White House conference on school violence, where one of the speakers, Craig Scott, was a survivor of the Columbine massacre. Scott said that in his travels for Rachel's Challenge, an organization founded in memory of his slain sister, he frequently meets potential shooters. The group urges students to reach out to loners, victims of bullies, and other vulnerable students. "I see a lot of depression. I see a lot of loneliness and a lot of anger. I've heard all kinds of terrible stories about things they've been through," he said. "Eric Harris and Dylan Klebold were very smart," Scott noted of the two Columbine shooters who killed his sister and twelve others at the Colorado school. "The problem wasn't their education at my school, Columbine. Their problem was their character." Thus, Scott urged educators to "take a look at teaching that doesn't just teach the head, but teaches the heart." He added: "You can help point them to what's right and what's wrong."[74]

What Scott was calling for was a reprioritizing of our lives and our social values to aid in combating the ever-increasing disillusionment and alienation among young people in all segments of American society. Change must start with the family. Parents and children need to spend more time together, preferably in the home and away from the many distractions such as the Internet and television that tend to disrupt quality time together.

Young people at one time had both the cushion of the family and the local community. To begin with, families used to be bigger—not in terms of more children so much as more adults. This included grandparents, uncles, aunts, cousins, etc., and relatives who did not live with the family lived nearby. There were community visits, dinners, and get-togethers. People knew one another. "Besides, everybody minded your business," Cornell University professor Urie Bronfenbrenner writes. "They wanted to know where you had been, where you were going, and why. And if they did not like what they heard, they said so (particularly if you had told the truth)."[75]

But it wasn't simply one's relatives that could be counted on to keep an eye out. Everyone minded each other's business. People in the neighborhood watched the children. If they walked on the railroad trestle, the phone rang at their parents' house. Children also had the run of the neighborhood. Unlike today, youngsters could, without their parents worrying, play in the park and go to the store, the movies, the lumberyard, and so on.

Although these are now distant memories, they still have their present-day vestiges. Research has systematically documented important facets of American neighborhood life. These investigations compared the daily lives of children growing up in a small community with those living in larger towns. The principal difference is that, unlike their urban- and suburban-age mates, children in a small town become well acquainted with a substantially greater number of adults in different walks of life and are more likely to be active participants in adult settings, which they enter.[76]

Unfortunately, the relatively stable world of the small town has been absorbed by an ever-expanding suburbia. As a consequence, children are growing up in a different kind of environment. Urbanization has reduced the extended family to a nuclear, atomistic one with only one or two adults. The functioning neighborhood—where it has not decayed into an urban or rural slum—has withered to a small circle of friends, most of them accessible only by car or cell phone. Paradoxically, although there are more people around, there are fewer opportunities for meaningful human contact.

Whereas previously the world in which a child lived consisted of a diversity of people in a wide array of settings, for millions of American children the neighborhood is now nothing but row upon row of buildings where "other people" live. One house or apartment is much like another—and so are the people. As Bronfenbrenner writes:

> *They all have more or less the same income, and the same way of life. But the child does not see much of that life, for all that people do in the neighborhood is to come home to it, have a drink, eat dinner, mow the lawn, watch television, and sleep. Increasingly often, today's housing projects have no stores, no shops, no services, no adults at work or play. This is the sterile world in which many of our children grow, and this is the "urban renewal" we offer to the families we would rescue from the slums.*[77]

The entire concept of the neighborhood has largely been lost. Rarely can a child see people working at their trades. Everyone is out of sight. Nor can the child listen to the gossip at the post office or on the park bench. There are no abandoned houses, no barns, no attics to explore. It is a pretty bland world for children to grow up in.

Then again, children are rarely at home anymore. They leave early in the morning on the school bus and return around dinnertime—often to an empty home. "If the mother is not working, at least part-time ... she is out a lot because of social obligations—not just to be with friends, but to do things for the community," Professor Bronfenbrenner recognizes. "The men leave in the morning before the children are up. And they do not get back until after the children have eaten supper. Fathers are often away weekends, as well as during the week."[78]

What this means is that American parents do not spend nearly as much time with their children as they used to. In fact, contact between parents and their children has progressively lessened. Consequently, American society affords decreasing prominence and importance to the family as a socializing agent. This is a by-product of a variety of changes, all operating to diminish the prominence and power of the family in the lives of children. These social changes include "urbanization, child labor laws, the abolishment of the apprentice system, commuting, centralized schools, zoning ordinances, the working mother, the experts' advice to be permissive, the seductive power of television for keeping children occupied, the delegation and professionalization of child care."[79] All these manifestations of "progress" have operated to decrease opportunities for contact between children and parents or, for that matter, adults in general.

Yet if parents cannot increase the time they spend with their children, the "alienation gap" is only going to increase, leaving children feeling estranged and seeking attention in more disruptive and, ultimately, violent, ways.

We're Not Listening
Suicide or homicide
Homicide and suicide
Into sleep I'm sinking
Why me I'm thinking
Homicidal and suicidal thoughts, intermixing
My life's not worth fixing.

This poem, written by a young man before he entered a school and began shooting, is not merely a suicide note. It is a cry for help.[80] As the incidents of bomb threats and shootings increase, one thing is clear: something more sinister than disgruntled students is occurring in America's schools. On October 10, 2006, a thirteen-year-old seventh grade boy, apparently fascinated with the 1999 Columbine High School bloodbath, carried an assault rifle into his Joplin, Missouri, middle school. Dressed in a dark green trench coat and wearing a mask, he pointed the rifle at fellow students and fired a shot into the ceiling before the weapon jammed. This was no spur-of-the-moment act. It was a planned attack. The student's backpack contained military manuals, instructions on assembling an improvised explosive device, and detailed drawings of the school. Yet moments before he fired the rifle, the boy said to a school administrator: "Please don't make me do this."[81]

In 2002, after interviewing students who had planned and executed school shootings, the U.S. Secret Service released a report on school violence. Their first crucial finding was that there is no profile for a school shooter. Shooters come from many types of families and from all incomes, races, and academic backgrounds. And there are no easy explanations—such as mental illness, drugs, or video games—for their actions.[82] Since no profile exists, to many school officials, anyone walking the hallways is a potential shooter. Paranoia often saturates the school environment where, through the use of zero-tolerance policies, a child who mistakenly brings her nail clippers to school is treated as harshly as the youngster who brings a gun.

This attitude is one reason that school shooters continue to go undetected. By suspecting everyone and punishing kids for innocent mistakes, the shootings are bound to happen for the simple reason that school officials are focusing on the wrong individuals. Unlike the student who mistakenly brings nail clippers to school, however, the shooters plan their shootings in advance. As the Secret Service report found, the killers "did not snap." According to the report, most shooters told their friends what they were planning. But the friends neither reported what they had been told nor tried to stop the shooters. When the Secret Service asked former school shooters what they would have done if a teacher had asked them what was wrong, the shooters said they would have told the adult the truth, including their plans.[83]

Our young people are trying to tell us something, but they don't believe adults are listening. As one school shooter recalls, "Most of them don't care. I just felt like nobody cared. I just wanted to hurt them."[84]

Before the Columbine shootings, the local sheriff had been given copies of Eric Harris's website, describing his pipe bombs, with page after page of threats: "You all better f...... hide in your houses because im comin for EVERYONE soon, and I WILL be armed to the f...... teeth and I WILL shoot to kill and I WILL f...... KILL EVERY-THING." Shortly thereafter, Harris and Dylan Klebold entered the high school and fulfilled the threat.

There are conditions—such as peer pressure, low self-esteem, childhood abuse, etc.—that can trigger or facilitate violent behavior. These influences speak to the deeper societal and cultural influences that come into play when young people elect violence as their response to the chaotic, stressful conditions surrounding them.

Along with the loss of stable family institutions, we have to take into account the dehumanizing nature of modern society. Graphic and violent images bombard our children on a continual basis—such as the dehumanizing images in the media of photographs showing Iraqi prisoners being subjected to abuse by American military police. Video games increasingly glorify violence as a solution. Lurid pornographic images proliferate on the Internet, as pedophiles stalk the young. The list goes on, and it gets worse.

America's children are the ones paying the heavy price. They have unfortunately become the casualties of our age. Our young people know that something is dreadfully wrong, but many adults, busy trying to make ends meet and keep pace with the demands of work and raising a family, often do not hear when the kids scream for help. If we continue to lead our young people along this path, it certainly does not bode well for the future.

Yet all is not lost. There is still hope. It will, however, mean taking responsibility for our own lives, as well as our children's.

CHAPTER SIX

American Empire

*Overgrown military establishments are under any form
of government inauspicious to liberty, and are to be regarded as particularly hostile to republican liberty.*

—George Washington

On January 1, 1791, the national debt (the amount of money owed
by the U. S. government) totaled $75 million. By December 2007, it
was growing by that same amount every hour or so and, according
to the National Debt Clock, totaled $8.9 trillion. By 2010, the na-
tional debt is estimated to reach an astounding $11.2 trillion.[1]

Since it's difficult to conceive of such an astronomical sum of
money, think of it this way: if the nation's debt as of December 2007
was divvied up among Americans, every man, woman, and child in
the United States would owe approximately $38,000 (that's apart
from any personal debt they might owe). Yet the government continues to spend money it does not have, much of it frittered away on
ill-advised schemes and far-flung wars.

Since 2001, the wars in Afghanistan and Iraq have cost American
taxpayers hundreds of billions of dollars. As of May 2007, Congress
had already approved roughly $610 billion for the three military op-
erations initiated since the 9/11 attacks: Operation Enduring Freedom in Afghanistan and other counter-terror operations; Operation
Noble Eagle, providing enhanced security at military bases; and Operation Iraqi Freedom. The Congressional Budget Office estimates
that total funding for Iraq, Afghanistan, and the "global war on terror" could reach $1.45 trillion by 2017.[2] However, that's not the ex-
tent of our military presence. U.S. military bases and personnel are
spread around the globe—again, at great taxpayer expense.

Much like the Romans who were faced with the challenge of raising sufficient funds to support their overextended military, America is facing the consequences of financing a global military presence. David Walker, comptroller general of the United States, issued a report in 2007 wherein he stated that there are "striking similarities" between America's current situation and the factors that contributed to the fall of the Roman Empire. These include "declining moral values and political civility at home, an over-confident and over-extended military in foreign lands and fiscal irresponsibility by the central government."[3]

ARE WE ROME?

America's ascension to power has long been compared to the rise of the Roman Empire—and its subsequent fall. In recent years, the emphasis has been on the nation's similarities to Rome's imperialist drive, its quest for world domination, the way in which its social integrity and morality was undermined by civil religion, and the impact of an entertainment culture on its people. While we may not have attained the cruelty of the Romans, our failings at Abu Ghraib and Guantanamo do not bode well.

Cullen Murphy, author of *Are We Rome?* and editor-at-large of *Vanity Fair*, suggests that there may have been a time when the comparisons to Rome were more favorable—when Rome represented the ideals of republican governance, the idea of checks and balances, certain notions of Roman virtue, and what it meant to be a citizen and an upright person.[4] Murphy asserts that until the recent past, the comparison with Rome was made in optimistic and assertive ways. "In other words," he remarked, "the Pax Romana lives anew as the Pax Americana, providing worldwide cultural benefits and worldwide security."[5]

That viewpoint has largely given way to the worry that, as Murphy puts it, we no longer live in "Jefferson's America." He cites a number of factors: the hollowing out of government, the mismatch of ambitions and resources, a growing economic inequality, an increasingly dangerous reliance on the military, and a populace that is ignorant of the world beyond its borders and, hence, is apathetic about world affairs—all of which raises serious questions. As Murphy recognizes: "A millennium hence America will be hard to recognize. It may not exist as a nation-state in the form it does now—or even exist at all. Will the transitions ahead be gradual and peaceful or abrupt and catastrophic? Will our descendants be living productive lives in a society better than the one we inhabit now? Whatever happens, will valuable aspects of America's legacy weave through the fabric of civilizations to come? Will historians someday have reason to ask, Did America really fall?"[6]

Clearly, our so-called American empire faces a violent contradiction between its long republican tradition and its more recent imperial ambitions. As historian Chalmers Johnson writes, "The fate of previous democratic empires suggests that such a conflict is unsustainable and will be resolved in one of two ways. Rome attempted to keep its empire and lost its democracy. Britain chose to remain democratic and in the process let go its empire. Intentionally or not, the people of the United States already are well embarked upon the course of nondemocratic empire."[7]

I would suggest that what we have is a confluence of factors and influences that go beyond mere comparisons to Rome. It is a union of Orwell's *1984,* with its shadowy, totalitarian government—i.e., fascism, the union of government and corporate powers—and a total surveillance state with a military empire extended throughout the world.

This is not to say that America should withdraw internationally and become isolationist. The world we live in requires a strong military presence. But as we have seen with the militarizing of the police, the growth of and reliance on militarism as the solution for our problems both domestically and abroad affects the basic principles upon which American society should operate. The military does not view the Constitution in the same way as someone engaged in ensuring that the Bill of Rights and its freedoms are kept intact. Those in the military are primarily trained to conduct warfare, not preserve the peace. We must keep in mind that a military empire will be ruled not by lofty ideals of equality and justice but by the power of the sword.

A MILITARY EMPIRE

Imagine this: the year is 2012, and the president has just died. General E. Thomas U. Brutus has managed to "persuade" the vice president not to take the oath of office and proceeds to declare himself commander-in-chief. Just like that, the American government is placed under martial law and, thus, under military control.

Sound far-fetched? Not according to Air Force Brigadier General Charles Dunlap, whose 1992 article "The Origins of the Military Coup of 2012" provides such a scenario for a military takeover. Written by then-Lieutenant Colonel Dunlap as part of his studies at the National War College in Washington DC, the article paints a chilling picture of our nation being slowly overtaken by military rule. Dunlap warns: "People need to understand that the armed forces exist to support and defend government, not to be the government. Faced with intractable national problems on one hand, and an energetic and capable military on the other, it can be all too seductive to start viewing the military as a cost-effective solution. We made a terrible mistake when we allowed the armed forces to be diverted from its original purpose."[8]

Such a "mistake" is more likely to happen in times of national panic or societal malaise, a state of affairs reflected in the lack of political participation by the citizenry. Voter apathy is such that, as of 2004, barely more than 50 percent of eligible voters even cast a ballot for presidential candidates. With the immense distractions of entertainment and media, the average citizen has no idea what goes on in the halls of government. If martial law were declared, the military would be in power before the citizenry had a clue that anything had happened.

USING THE MILITARY TO FIX CIVIL PROBLEMS

Considering our responses thus far to the fear and trepidation gripping American culture and an economy so unreliable that the stock market dips and swings like an erratic pendulum, I fear that we may already have traveled too far down the road General Dunlap warns against. One thing is certain: the populace's clamor for security, which the military provides, is at an all-time high.

Unlike the rest of the government, the military has enjoyed a remarkably steady climb in popularity since the 1980s. Through their academies, the armed forces are turning out some of the brightest, best-educated, and best-disciplined Americans in history. While polls consistently show that the public invariably gives Congress low marks, confidence in the military is surpassing every other institution in American society. Consequently, in many ways, Dunlap's concerns about the military being used to "fix" civil problems are now being realized.

The increasing use of the military to patrol the borders in the fight against drugs has resulted in the military's assumption of various police functions formerly allotted to civilian law enforcement. This historic change of policy occurred under the presidency of Ronald Reagan and was endorsed by Congress in 1981 with the enactment of the Military Cooperation with Civilian Law Enforcement Act. As a result, the Department of Defense now spends billions of dollars on counternarcotic crusades, and American troops have become an adjunct to many local police forces in the country.

The military is also being called upon to deal with environmental problems and catastrophes. After 9/11, when more commercial airlines were declaring bankruptcy and discontinuing unprofitable air routes, it was speculated that the military could be called on to provide essential air support to various regions of the country. Overseas, humanitarian, and nation-building assignments have proliferated. This was clearly demonstrated in Operation Iraqi Freedom, as newscasts showed American troops distributing aid packages to haggard civilians in Iraq. This practice has been duplicated worldwide.

These new military programs—and the growing dependence on them—have forced a consolidation of power in the military. The Goldwater-Nichols Defense Reorganization Act of 1986 greatly strengthened the office of the Chairman of the Joint Chiefs of Staff. This legislation reversed 200 years of American history by establishing a single uniformed officer as the "Principal Military Advisor" to the president. The chairman is also responsible for furnishing the strategic direction of the armed forces and developing a joint doctrine for all four services.

Unlike its role in the past, the military is now involved in policy-making—a state of affairs that inevitably raises the specter of a figurehead president manipulated by a military elite. Congress specifically and overwhelmingly rejected this concentration of power in one military office in 1947, 1949, and 1958 on the grounds that in a democracy, no single military officer, no matter what his personal qualifications are, should have such power. And with the continuing unification of the four branches of the armed forces, the power of the chairman is staggering.

A SHADOW GOVERNMENT

Unknown to the majority of Americans, we operate a "shadow" government that is referred to internally as "COG" (Continuity of Government).[9] Comprised of roughly 100 to 150 senior civilian managers, this concentration of powers is supposedly intended to prevent the collapse of essential government functions in the event of a disabling blow to Washington. Yet according to the *Washington Post*, "Only the executive branch is represented in the full-time shadow administration."[10]

It doesn't take a great leap of the imagination to envision such a government being activated with the military at the helm. The pieces are already in place. One of these involves the use of the military in disaster relief—but in a very loosely defined way—and fused with other mega-bureaucratic governmental agencies such as FEMA. In 1979, President Jimmy Carter signed an executive order that merged many of the disaster relief agencies into one large conglomerate known as the Federal Emergency Management Agency, or FEMA. After the events of 9/11, FEMA became one of the four major branches of the new Department of Homeland Security. As of 2007, FEMA had 2,500 full-time employees and approximately 5,000 disaster-ready reservists.[11]

FEMA is generally associated with natural disasters. The agency's actual purpose, however, is much broader and includes any national emergency related to terrorism or civil unrest. With broad powers to act in times of "widespread internal dissent," FEMA's job, when it comes right down to it, is to ensure the survivability of the United States government.

Consequently, FEMA has expanded powers, which are given to few government entities. These include the power to develop plans to take control of the mechanisms of production, distribution, energy sources, wages, salaries, and the flow of money during a national emergency.[12] FEMA is also empowered to take over modes of transportation, assume control of the media as well as food resources, take control at airports, and seize and direct citizens.[13] FEMA essentially has the power to put the Constitution and the Bill of Rights on hold while trying to restore order in the wake of a perceived disaster, thereby turning the country into a military state.

No doubt, FEMA needs to be able to draw upon whatever resources are available when aiding in disaster relief. The problem is that all the power given to FEMA has come through presidential executive orders, rather than the legislative process, which has scuttled the representative process. During a time of national emergency, FEMA, which is run by unelected officials, would become the most powerful governmental authority.

Yet very few Americans know much about this powerful entity. FEMA is rarely discussed except on the few occasions when it makes headlines for leading disaster relief efforts following an earthquake or hurricane—or for failing to provide effective support. For example, FEMA was called in to head up the relief effort for Hurricane Andrew in the early 1990s but supposedly lacked the resources to provide the proper level of assistance necessary. The agency came under intense scrutiny, which revealed that FEMA was spending many times more for secret programs labeled "black operations" (or black ops) than for disaster relief—again in conjunction with the military. It was also reported that FEMA had devoted so much of its efforts to creating bunkers and preparing to protect the "chosen few" in case of a national emergency that only about 6 percent of its funding was focused on what it was created for in the first place—actual preparation for a natural disaster. Even more disconcerting is that only a limited number of our representatives in Congress with top security clearance had any idea that FEMA was spending $1.3 billion-plus of taxpayer money on secret black ops projects unrelated to natural disasters.[14]

The following two examples provide a better understanding of FEMA's power and the threat it may pose to civil liberties during a national emergency. The first occurred during Ronald Reagan's first year in office. Having signed a number of directives on civil defense policy and emergency mobilization preparedness intended to strengthen FEMA, President Reagan appointed Louis O. Giuffrida, a former national guard general, to head up the disaster response agency. Giuffrida focused most of his attention on preventing domestic civil unrest. By 1982, this emphasis on civil unrest led to the creation of a joint FEMA-Pentagon paper known as "The Civil/Military Alliance in Emergency Management," which advocated the use of the military in civil law enforcement, thereby disregarding portions of the Posse Comitatus Act. This new civil alliance equipped the military and FEMA with additional emergency powers to prevent domestic civil disturbances.

In the spring of 1984, FEMA and the Department of Defense undertook a secret operation to train thirty-four federal agencies on how to deal with domestic civil unrest. Code-named Rex-84, the operation brought together groups including the CIA and the U.S. Secret Service in anticipation of civil disturbances, demonstrations, and strikes that would hinder continuity of the government. To counter these disturbances and regain continuity of government, the military would be authorized to move groups of people, arrest segments of the population, and impose martial law. The exercise envisioned at least 100,000 U.S. citizens, identified as threats to national security, being rounded up and, for unspecified periods, thrown into "containment" camps—some of which are already in operation, while others are being built by KBR, a former subsidiary of the powerful megacorporation Halliburton.[15]

The second "red flag" example deals with the existence of an underground bunker the size of a small city. Mount Weather, near Bluemont, Virginia, is one of a number of facilities sprinkled around the country that would reportedly be used as a safe haven for high-level government officials in the case of a national emergency. Built into the side of a mountain, the Mount Weather bunker contains a hospital, crematorium, dining and recreation areas, sleeping quarters, reservoirs of drinking and cooling water, an emergency power plant, and a radio/television studio, which is part of the Emergency Broadcasting System.[16]

FEMA's role at the facility is allegedly to establish a "backup government" in the event of a national disaster. There is supposedly also an Office of the Presidency at Mount Weather, which is appointed by FEMA and regularly receives top-secret national security information from all the federal departments and agencies. The facility was largely a secret to everyone, including Congress, until a Senate Subcommittee on Constitutional Rights hearing in 1975. While some minimal information about the various facilities surfaced during this hearing, senators were rebuffed in their quest for specifics about Mount Weather. Testifying before a Senate subcommittee, Air Force General Leslie W. Bray said, "I am not at liberty to describe precisely what is the role and the mission and the capability that we have at Mount Weather, or at any other precise location."[17] Congress still has no oversight, budgetary or otherwise, on Mount Weather, and the specifics of the facility remain top secret.

PUTTING SOLDIERS ON AMERICA'S STREETS

FEMA leadership and the architects of Rex-84 continued to play a significant role in subsequent administrations, including that of George W. Bush. Colonel John R. Brinkerhoff, who was instrumental in martial law planning during Giuffrida's time as head of FEMA, is with the influential Anser Institute for Homeland Security. His paper supporting the legality of using military personnel on American streets is a justification for the use of martial law.[18] Essentially, under this rationale, all it would take for a military takeover of the government is a severe national crisis.

When and if martial law is instituted, it would most likely be conducted under the Defense Department's updated Unified Command Plan, which established the U.S. Northern Command in 2002 (commonly referred to as NORTHCOM). Hidden deep inside Cheyenne Mountain, NORTHCOM is a Pentagon power center located at Peterson Air Force Base in Colorado Springs, Colorado, where more than one hundred analysts collect information from federal and local law enforcement around the United States, as well as Canada and Mexico. If they find something they believe warrants investigation (whatever they decide that may be), they have the Army, Navy, Air Force, Marines, and the Coast Guard to deploy in response.[19]

NORTHCOM is designed to take command of and unify every National Guard in the country, as well as regular troops. With an annual budget of about $70 million, its vaguely stated purpose includes fighting the war on drugs and supporting civilian authorities in case of a natural disaster, civil disorder, or terrorist attack. NORTHCOM is also responsible for locating terrorists before they strike. This wide-reaching function serves as the command's direct link between local law enforcement intelligence, private security and information companies, and military intelligence operations. Partnerships with private information companies such as ChoicePoint and LexisNexis are the military's loophole to get around clearly established federal privacy laws that forbid it from maintaining electronic files on ordinary citizens. As discussed in Chapter Three, companies such as ChoicePoint have been under investigation for the theft of thousands of individuals' identities.

When NORTHCOM's national surveillance system was questioned on *NewsHour with Jim Lehrer*, Air Force General Ralph E. Eberhart defended the command center, stating, "We are not going to be out there spying on people—we get information from people who do."[20] Eberhart's statement refers to NORTHCOM's partnership with private information companies, enabling them to "legally" gather personal data from confidential sources, thereby furthering the secretive domestic surveillance that can be conducted on ordinary citizens.[21]

NORTHCOM, the military's first domestic combatant command center, is a clear mark of the government's daily expansion of military operations into areas of local civilian government and law enforcement. As previously discussed, under the longstanding Posse Comitatus Act of 1878, the U.S. military is explicitly prohibited from using federal troops in civilian law enforcement. The domestic military surveillance conducted at NORTHCOM, however, seems to directly violate this law.

Concern about NORTHCOM's expansive powers is evident among those who are aware of it. "The military can follow you around," remarks Kate Martin, director of the Center for National Security Studies. "It can use giant, secret databases of linked networks to gather a picture of the activities of millions of Americans, mapping all of their associations, and the only restriction is that such surveillance be done for purposes of foreign intelligence, counterterrorism, the drug war, or force protection."[22] Suzanne Spaulding, chair of the American Bar Association's Standing Committee on Law and National Security, warns, "A domestic military operation could look exactly like a law enforcement operation, and yet it wouldn't be constrained by any of the safeguards that might be in place if it were a law enforcement activity."[23]

The increasing military role in law enforcement activities is a major, and dangerous, departure from past policy, and its impact is far-reaching. Mackubin T. Owens, a professor of strategy and force planning at the Naval War College, believes the long-term effect is "a military contemptuous of American society and unresponsive to civilian authorities."[24] And the momentum of recent events has created a military component that, if it should ever decide to take control, will be nearly impossible to stop.

WHAT ABOUT THE CONSTITUTION?

A basic distrust of the military is firmly embedded in American history. This is why the Constitution and the Bill of Rights advocate arms for citizens and civilian control of the military. George Washington warned of the dangers of an overgrown military establishment in his farewell address. Standing armies, as we saw in Chapter Two, were especially to be feared. The fear was, and still is, that a military establishment that was more powerful than a reasonably predictable threat could become a republic within itself.

That is, in fact, what has happened. The United States essentially dominates the world through its military power. As historian Chalmers Johnson writes, "A vast network of American military bases on every continent except Antarctica actually constitutes a new form of empire."[25] And: "Our country deploys well over half a million soldiers, spies, technicians, teachers, dependents, and civilian contractors in other nations and just under a dozen carrier task forces in all the oceans and seas of the world."[26] As of 2003, the total number of American military personnel was approximately 2.7 million servicemen and women.[27] But this figure does not include the myriad civilians employed by the military or those on the government payroll as military contractors.

The American military's reach is indeed global. As of September 2001, the Department of Defense acknowledged that at least 735 American military bases exist outside the U.S. There are actually many more secret bases that exist under various kinds of arrangements.[28]

We are in the process of globalization—with the military as the police—and it is transforming not only the world but America itself. "In my opinion," writes Chalmers Johnson, "the growth of militarism, official secrecy, and a belief that the United States is no longer bound, as the Declaration of Independence so famously puts it, by 'a decent respect for the opinions of mankind,' is probably irreversible."[29] Johnson believes that a "revolution would be required to bring the Pentagon back under democratic control"[30]—or to contemplate enforcing Article I, Section 9, Clause 7 of the U.S. Constitution: "No money shall be drawn from the Treasury, but in Consequence of Appropriations made by Law; and a regular Statement and Account of the Receipts and Expenditures of all public Money shall be published from time to time."

This provision is so important because it maintains the United States as a democratic republic. It guarantees that the people's representatives will know what the government (along with its agencies) is doing, and it requires full disclosure of governmental activities. But it does not allow black ops funding or secret spending by the government. Unfortunately, the provision has not been applied to Department of Defense agencies such as the NSA, CIA, and FEMA since their creation.

With no constitutional oversight, the "militarized empire," as it has been called, has become a physical reality with a distinct way of life. It is a network of economic and political interests that operate in conjunction with other government agencies, American corporations, universities, and communities formerly kept separate from "the homeland." But, as Chalmers Johnson notes, "even that sense of separation is disappearing—for the changing nature of the empire is altering our society as well."[31]

"The growth of the Empire is a very long story that goes back to the 18th century, particularly the latter part of the 19th century," writes Claremont Graduate University professor David Ray Griffin. "It goes as far back as the taking over of Cuba, the Philippines and Hawaii. That is when the American government began taking the Empire beyond the continent. So we have had a period of almost uninterrupted extension of the Empire for the past two centuries. And in many cases, this has involved great evils economically, militarily and in terms of human rights violations. Therefore, we didn't suddenly become an evil Empire under the reign of Bush and Cheney, but it did become exponentially worse under them. It became more explicitly militaristic. But, to a great extent, this was simply a revelation of practices that we have been carrying on for a long time."[32] All that is needed now, says Griffin, is "the support of the American people to use military power to dominate the world in a way that we never had before."[33]

A MILITARY-INDUSTRIAL COMPLEX

With the fusion of the military and worldwide corporate conglomerates, the military has essentially become a global police force. In his often-quoted January 1961 farewell to the nation address, Dwight D. Eisenhower warned against the wedding of such interests:

> *Our military organization today bears little relation to that known by any of my predecessors in peacetime, or indeed by the fighting men of World War II or Korea. Until the latest of our world conflicts, the United States had no armaments industry. American makers of plowshares could, with time and as required, make swords as well. But now we can no longer risk emergency improvisation of national defense; we have been compelled to create a permanent armaments industry of vast proportions.... Yet we must not fail to comprehend its*

grave implications. Our toil, resources and livelihood are all involved; so is the very structure of our society. In the councils of government, we must guard against the acquisition of unwarranted influence, whether sought or unsought, by the military-industrial complex. The potential for the disastrous rise of misplaced power exists and will persist. We must never let the weight of this combination endanger our liberties or democratic processes. We should take nothing for granted. Only an alert and knowledgeable citizenry can compel the proper meshing of the huge industrial and military machinery of defense with our peaceful methods and goals, so that security and liberty may prosper together.[34]

Morris Berman, a professor at Catholic University, seems to think that the power balance has already shifted. As he points out, "After World War II the American republic was essentially replaced by a national security state, largely exempt from congressional oversight and answerable to practically no one."[35]

The military empire is an important element in the American corporate state's continuing globalization efforts. According to Berman, the goal is "to create an integrated international order" that offers "no barriers to the flow of goods, capital, and ideas, and that is administered by the United States"—meaning that the "whole world is to become a free-market economy and the U.S. military is there to remove any opposition to this process."[36] With the military playing a key role in American foreign policy, there is greater need for an expanded military budget and, consequently, more business for American defense industries and weapons manufacturers.

To put this military expansion in context, in the 1920s and 1930s, the United States deployed an army that was roughly the size of Portugal's. In 2007, however, America had a quarter of a million troops and civilians stationed in 130 countries worldwide. America has become the largest military establishment in the world and is the world's largest arms exporter—selling roughly half of all the weapons sold worldwide, some of which routinely falls into enemy hands.[37]

This puts the Pentagon at the center of the American military empire. As Professor Berman notes:

> *By 1990, Pentagon property was valued at nearly $1 trillion, the equivalent of 83 percent of all of the assets of all U.S. manufacturing industries. With an annual budget (during that time) of $310 billion, the Pentagon was (and presumably remains) America's largest company: 5.1 million employees, 600 fixed facilities nationwide, more than 40,000 properties, and 18 million acres of land. Indeed, the Pentagon's economy is twice as large as all of Japan's. In 1997, the government spent $47 billion on military research and development, nearly two-thirds of what the entire world spent on the same. In 1998, while the entire world spent $864 billion on military forces, the American fraction of this was nearly one-third.*[38]

In the wake of September 11, George W. Bush's $2.13 trillion budget (which put the country $80 billion in the red) increased the Pentagon's annual account to $451 billion by 2007. This is more than the budgets of the next fifteen largest militaries combined. As of 2003, the United States was spending more than $400 billion per year on defense and another $100 billion a year for the wars in Iraq and Afghanistan.[39] This in effect means that the Department of Defense is the largest industrial entity in the United States, and the president is its CEO.

These ominous developments cannot be laid at the feet of President Bush alone. Bill Clinton's expansive use of the military during his presidency paved the way. As journalist Dana Priest writes, on President Clinton's watch, "the military slowly, without public scrutiny or debate, came to surpass its civilian leaders in resources and influence around the world."[40]

"Our Congress has been hijacked by corporate America and its enforcer, the imperial military machine," author Gore Vidal writes. "We have allowed our institutions to be taken over in the name of a globalized American empire that is totally alien in concept to anything our Founders had in mind. I suspect it is far too late in the day for us to restore the republic that we lost a half-century ago."[41]

Besides the questionable doctrine of preemptive warfare—which was treated as a war crime at the Nuremberg trials—the nation is now driven irreversibly into perpetual war around the globe. Between 1989 and 1999, the country was engaged in forty-eight open military interventions, as opposed to sixteen during the entire Cold War period.[42]

To some observers, it would seem that the United States is attempting to erect a global police state in an effort to impose a "Pax Americana"—a New Roman Empire. However, the cost of maintaining such an empire is astronomical. In addition to the expense involved in stationing U.S. service personnel throughout the world, billions are spent on luxury military installations. The U.S. Embassy in Iraq, dubbed "Fortress Baghdad," cost $592 million and covers 104 acres. It boasts a "city within a city" that includes six apartment buildings, a Marine barracks, swimming pool, shops, and fifteen-foot-thick walls. And Camp Anaconda in Iraq, like many U.S. military bases scattered across the globe, has been structured to resemble a mini-city with pools, fast-food restaurants, miniature golf courses, and movie theaters.[43]

Of grave concern is the fact that American taxpayer dollars are not being used wisely or well. In early 2007, it was revealed that although the United States had transported nearly $12 billion in shrink-wrapped $100 bills into Iraq, there was no proper accounting of who received it and how it was spent.[44] In August 2007, it was revealed that the Pentagon had paid about $20.5 million over six years to a small South Carolina parts supplier, much of it for fraudulent shipping costs. Included in this exorbitant bill was $998,798 for shipping two nineteen-cent washers to an Army base in Texas. Incredibly, the invoice was paid.[45] Also in the summer of 2007, the Government Accountability Office issued a report indicating that the Pentagon could not track approximately 30 percent of the weapons distributed in Iraq since 2004. These included 110,000 AK-47 rifles and 80,000 pistols, in addition to 135,000 body armor pieces. The concern is that many of these very same weapons are being used against U.S. forces on the ground in Iraq.[46]

In addition to the enormous financial burden laid upon American taxpayers to maintain a colossal military machine, not to mention the enormous strain on the country's economy, there are also moral, political, and social costs, as well as human costs to consider. Besides the disruption of families, which can lead to marital problems and abuse, the impact on the individual soldier has been high, especially in terms of physical and mental health. A report released by the military in August 2007 indicated that 2006 saw the highest suicide rate in twenty-six years. More than a quarter of these suicides involved those serving in Iraq and Afghanistan. Failed personal relationships, legal and financial problems, and the stress of military service were factors motivating the soldiers to kill themselves.[47]

American soldiers who have taken an oath to protect and defend the Constitution are also increasingly finding their own freedoms jeopardized. Such was the case with Martha McSally and Jason Adkins.

MARTHA MCSALLY

Martha McSally's experience, while unique in many ways, is also representative of every enlisted man and woman who has ever been given an unlawful directive and must decide what to do. As we saw with the human rights violations that took place at Abu Ghraib—reportedly at the hands of American service people—not all men and women in uniform have the courage to stand up for what is right. Martha McSally did.

In 1993, when the military opened combat positions to women, McSally, a graduate of the Air Force Academy, was one of seven female officers the Air Force chose to fly combat aircraft. After training as a fighter pilot, McSally became the first woman to fly combat sorties, piloting an A-10 "Warthog" attack plane over Iraq. She then served as a flight commander and trainer of combat pilots deployed to Kosovo and South Korea and did a tour of duty in Kuwait from 1995 to 1996. McSally was promoted to the rank of major two years ahead of her peers and ascended to lieutenant colonel four years in advance, a rare commendation reserved only for the most exceptional officers identified early on as future leaders in the Air Force.

In 2000, McSally was assigned to the Prince Sultan Air Force Base in Saudi Arabia as principal adviser to the commander of the joint task force's search and rescue operation in Southwest Asia, a region whose responsibility included Afghanistan and Iraq. Unfortunately, upon landing at the Saudi Arabian base, McSally's outstanding credentials and service to her country were quickly overshadowed by one undeniable fact: she is a woman. Suddenly, this fierce fighter pilot who ruled the skies was prohibited from driving a car or traveling anywhere without a male escort. In keeping with Department of Defense guidelines governing the operation, when traveling off base, McSally was also required to wear an abaya, a shapeless black garment concealing the body from neck to toe, accompanied by a headscarf and worn by all Saudi women on order of the mutawa, the religious police.

A fighter pilot forbidden to drive and a leader of men forced to portray herself as their inferior, McSally declared the Defense Department's policy "ridiculous and unnecessary."[48] And, "I can fly a single-seat aircraft in enemy territory, but I can't drive a vehicle."[49] The directive contrasted sharply with that pertaining to men in the military, who were not required to trade in their crew cuts and jeans for standard Eastern attire. The men were instructed to wear standard western-style shirts and pants, to escort and account for their female counterparts as their wives, and to relegate these women to the backseat when traveling off base. Also in contrast to the policy affecting military servicewomen were the State Department's guidelines for female embassy employees working in Saudi Arabia. State Department employees were not instructed to wear the abaya when on official calls and were free to dress according to personal judgment off duty, advisedly in a conservative manner so as to avoid harassment by the mutawa. The embassy affirmed that it would "support a woman in whatever personal choice" she made in her attire, an option not extended to military servicewomen.[50]

To McSally, the restrictions impacted more than her mobility and role as an authority figure—they violated her rights under the U.S.

Constitution. She declared, "The women whom this affects—the officers and enlisted personnel serving over there—are putting our lives on the line to serve our nation, and we are over in Saudi Arabia as officials of the United States government and the United States military, doing a mission alongside the men. Wearing the abaya, sitting in the backseat, not being able to drive and having your subordinate have to claim you as his wife, as opposed to his supervisor, is so demeaning and so humiliating. To treat just some of our people in that way ... is unacceptable."[51]

Gender equality was not the only constitutional guarantee violated by the abaya mandate. McSally also objected to the directive because it conflicted with her Christian faith. By labeling (or disguising) her as a Muslim woman, McSally felt that the abaya implied both her acceptance of subordinate social status and her adherence to the doctrines of the Koran and the dictates of the mutawa. "I'm a follower of Christ, and my Christian faith is the centerpiece of who I am," affirmed McSally. "To be forced to put on the garment of a religion that I do not believe in and a faith I do not follow, to me, was unacceptable."[52]

McSally respected the abaya as "a customary Muslim outfit for women" but reiterated, "I'm not Muslim and I'm not Saudi. I am a Christian."[53] Wearing the garment, McSally said, "to me is defying Christ" and accepting treatment as "a Muslim piece of property."[54] By depriving her of the opportunity to express her own faith and imposing upon her the symbolic speech of another religion, the dress code stood in gross violation of the First Amendment principles of free speech and free exercise of religion.

In light of America's ongoing military mission in the Middle East, the sex-specific code not only violated constitutional concepts of religious freedom and gender equality but was also criticized for its sheer hypocrisy. Soon after the American military began bombing Afghanistan in the wake of 9/11, the U.S. government quickly learned that the American public responded most amiably to its antiterrorist agenda when framed as the amelioration of the fundamentalist Taliban government's oppression of Islamic women. The government adjusted its pro-war rhetoric accordingly. "The most powerful images of freedom in Afghanistan," wrote *Washington Post* columnist Ellen Goodman, "have been the faces of its women."[55] Even characteristically apolitical First Lady Laura Bush got on board, denouncing gender oppression and declaring that "the fight against terrorism is also a fight for the rights and dignity of women."[56] Yet there was clearly a double standard at play. "What makes this particularly bizarre," Senator Bob Smith (R-N.H.) remarked, "is that we are waging a war in Afghanistan to remove those abayas, and the very soldiers who are conducting that war have to cover up."[57] In a letter to the secretary of defense, Congresswoman Louise Slaughter (D-N.Y.) declared that in enforcing its "unconscionable" policy, the U.S. government was condoning the "institutionalized disrespect of women by requiring that Americans conform" to the Saudi standards of gender oppression.[58]

Air Force authorities defended the abaya policy as a gesture of sensitivity to Saudi cultural norms where the freedom of religion is prohibited and the freedoms of speech, press, and assembly are greatly restricted, as are women's rights. While McSally affirmed her respect for Muslim culture, she refused to be subjected by her own government to its restrictions: "When those customs and values conflict with ones that our Constitution is based on, and that women and men in uniform died for in the past," she explained, "that is where you draw the line" between cultural sensitivity and constitutional violation.[59]

Believing that the directive "abandons our American values that we all raised our right hand to die for,"[60] McSally prepared to do battle with the U.S. government. Seven years after voicing her initial objections to the government's unconstitutional assault on gender equality and religious freedom, McSally turned to The Rutherford Institute for help. "The last thing I ever wanted to do was make a big deal about being a woman," she said. "As an officer, you need to shut up and follow when an order is lawful." But McSally also recognized that "you need to step out when it's unlawful."[61]

I was personally involved in McSally's case and enlisted a triple threat of media publicity, litigation, and legislation. A team of Rutherford Institute attorneys filed a lawsuit in federal court, charging Secretary of Defense Donald Rumsfeld and the Department of Defense with violating McSally's free speech and equal protection rights. The lawsuit also charged the U.S. government with advancing regulations that "are irrational, promulgated without sufficient governmental justification, and do not evenhandedly regulate dress and conduct."[62] In March 2002, the Defense Department rescinded its policies requiring servicewomen to sit in the back seats of cars and be escorted by men while off base in Saudi Arabia. McSally's legal team also drafted legislation that the Senate passed unanimously in June 2002, prohibiting the Pentagon from requiring or even formally recommending that female officers serving in Saudi Arabia wear the abaya.

It must be acknowledged that in speaking out and challenging the directive, Martha McSally endangered a promising career and was forced to endure disrespect and disdain. But her rigorous air force education, which emphasized the concepts of justice, uniform policies, and purposes and defense of personal honor, had molded McSally into an officer committed to those principles, with the courage to uphold them, even when doing so proved unpopular. "They turned me into a fighter pilot," McSally declared. "This is who I am. When I see something messed up, I'm going to challenge it."[63]

JASON ADKINS

Jason Adkins is another individual who put himself at great risk in order to challenge a military practice that was jeopardizing the constitutional rights of men and women in uniform, as well as their health.

A decorated Air Force sergeant, Adkins's fourteen years of service were marked by numerous special operations missions, including the first flight of a C-5 aircraft into Baghdad during the Iraq War. Sergeant Adkins had established a reputation as a dedicated serviceman and courageous airman, proudly assuming the risks that high-pressure combat situations often compelled him to take. Adkins's exemplary bravery was officially recognized when he was nominated, along with his flight crew, for the Distinguished Flying Cross award for the successful landing of a 374,000-pound missile-ridden aircraft.

Although Adkins was publicly commended for undertaking the risks requisite to national security, he found himself reprimanded professionally for assuming another kind of risk: challenging authority in the name of constitutional freedoms. On October 21, 2004, Adkins reported a crippling headache to the Dover Air Force Base flight surgeon. Military protocol excuses crew members who are experiencing unsafe medical conditions from duties without interrogation or repercussion, and Adkins felt obligated to ground himself from any flight activity that day. The doctor affirmed his judgment and would not allow him to fly in adherence to the Air Force's "safety of flight" principle. Concerned for his own safety as well as that of his fellow service members, Adkins voiced the suspicion that he might be suffering adverse effects of the experimental anthrax vaccine he had been required to receive. Shortly after voicing his concerns about the vaccine and being excused from flight activity, Adkins was given a career-ending written reprimand and was accused of dereliction of duty and faking his medical condition. The unexpected, and unprecedented, reprimand came as a shock.

While stationed at Dover, Adkins had received a series of eight anthrax inoculations since 1998, the same year the Clinton administration mandated the vaccination. Anthrax is a potentially deadly disease caused by the spore-forming bacteria *Bacillus anthracis*, which produces toxins that kill cells and cause fluid to accumulate in bodily tissues.[64] The vaccine for anthrax has been decried for its debilitating side effects, which were largely downplayed, according to those subjected to it. One retired soldier recalls the vaccine briefing he and fellow service members received the day before his first inoculation. "They left out all of the negative things about the vaccine," he explained. "Instead of telling us a whole list of symptoms, they told us the side effects are very minimal and very rare—maybe slight irritation of the skin." This former soldier, who suffers the debilitating effects of the vaccine he was forced to receive, said, "I can't work....I take steps like an old man; I can barely walk. You can draw a line though my life from the day of my anthrax vaccination and boom! There goes my health."[65]

Both before and after the vaccine came to be in high demand in

2001, thousands of soldiers who were aware of its severe side effects willingly faced reprimands, demotions, and discharges rather than submit to inoculation. After the inoculation movement gained momentum in 2001, more than four hundred members of the military refused to be vaccinated. They subsequently left military service voluntarily or were involuntarily dismissed or moved to inactive status.[66] The summer of 2003 marked an outbreak of more than one hundred potentially life-threatening pneumonia cases among GIs that medical experts attribute to the anthrax vaccine. That year, twenty-seven people refused the vaccine and defected from the military; ten did so in 2004.[67] Tragically, allegations of experimental vaccinations being used on U.S. troops are becoming all too common.[68]

Testing by the Food and Drug Administration discovered that six of the doses given to Jason Adkins were tainted with squalene, a fatlike substance linked to autoimmune disorders. Biomedical research has found that trace amounts of squalene can suppress the immune system, causing arthritis, neurological problems, memory loss, and incapacitating migraine headaches.[69] Adkins counts memory loss, muscle and joint pain, an occasional racing heartbeat, weight loss, and severe migraines among his vaccine-induced debilities. Once a competitive power lifter, Adkins weighed 250 pounds and could bench-press 425 pounds at his physical peak. Today, Adkins struggles to bench his own 200-pound frame.

Adkins decided to stand and fight—not only for himself but also for his fellow service members. With the help of The Rutherford Institute, he filed a lawsuit against his Air Force supervisors, Air Force Secretary James Roche, and Defense Secretary Donald Rumsfeld. Adkins argued that for five years, the Defense Department's compulsory vaccination program subjected select military personnel to a dangerous experimental vaccine with life-threatening and debilitating adverse effects. The lawsuit cited the Defense Department for suppressing Adkins's free speech rights by retaliating against him for expressing his concerns about the vaccine.

The real issues in the case are whether the military is above the law in the American system of government and whether those in the military can be stripped of their basic constitutional rights when they relinquish civilian clothing. If left unaddressed, the military's actions could very well give rise to a dangerous chilling free speech effect on our military members. After Adkins filed his lawsuit—which in December 2007 was settled in his favor—Dover personnel were ordered by the military to inform the base's public affairs coordinator before they spoke with the media. They were also ordered to refrain from discussing the vaccination program and were warned that they would be held "accountable" for any comments they made. The Defense Department structurally filtered the soldiers' right to speech following the rise in reports of illnesses attributed to the vaccine that ensued after Adkins's lawsuit broke the silence.

It is true that those in uniform are sometimes more restricted in pressing their freedoms, as opposed to civilians. Although the courts have generally agreed with this proposition, it does not mean that American citizens in uniform do not have constitutional rights. The Constitution, to some degree, travels with those in uniform. It is unfortunate that this important principle is increasingly being challenged on a number of fronts.

MAINTAINING OUR SOVEREIGNTY

One hot topic of debate in recent years involves what constitutional rights American citizens—and noncitizens—should be afforded in situations involving questions of national security. Should an American citizen, captured overseas and accused of plotting against the United States, be treated the same as an American arrested and charged with wrongdoing within our borders? That was at the heart of the legal battle involving Yaser Hamdi, a U.S. citizen who was captured in Afghanistan and detained indefinitely by the U.S. government as an "illegal enemy combatant."[70] While the U.S. Supreme Court ruled that detainees who are U.S. citizens must have the ability to challenge their detention before an impartial judge, the debate is far from over.

Another emerging debate centers on what constitutional protections Americans should be afforded in a nation without borders. In light of concerns about the creation of a North American Union, this is not an untoward question.

In November 2006, Representative Tom Tancredo (R-Colo.)

voiced his concerns over proposals to do away with the United States as a stand-alone entity: "The president of the United States is an internationalist. He is going to do what he can to create a place where the idea of America is just that—it's an idea. It's not an actual place defined by borders. I mean this is where this guy is really going."[71] Tancredo's remarks were made in the context of President Bush's perceived laxity on securing American borders and, most specifically, the efforts to merge the United States with both Mexico and Canada. "I'm telling you the tide is great," Tancredo said. "The tide is moving in their direction."[72]

The idea of a North American Union—a merging of the American, Canadian, and Mexican physical, economic, and legal borders, which was once ruminated on only by conspiracy theorists, no longer seems quite so far-fetched. According to some commentators, academics, and political analysts, the groundwork has already been laid.

In October 2004, the Council on Foreign Relations brought together leaders from the United States, Mexico, and Canada to study how the three countries could better facilitate economic activity across their physical and legal borders. Building on the groundwork established by the North American Free Trade Agreement (NAFTA), this task force published two documents, *Trinational Call for a North American Economic and Security Community by 2010* and *Building a North American Community*, which chart a drastically different course for the United States. A spring 2005 summit in Waco, Texas, attended by President Bush, President Vicente Fox of Mexico, and Canadian Prime Minister Paul Martin Jr., seemingly took one step along this path when the three leaders agreed to establish the Security and Prosperity Partnership of North America (SPP), which could serve as a framework for a North American Union.[73]

So what would a North American Union mean for the United States? Some believe it would completely unify North America—meaning no American currency, no American borders, and, most critically, no sovereign American law. Proposals have already been floated for a North American Court of Justice (with the authority to overrule a decision of the U.S. Supreme Court), a Trade Tribunal, and a Charter of Fundamental Human Rights. Coupled with a national or transnational identity card, this means a definite restructuring of the former American republic.[74] Under such a unified court structure, author Jerome R. Corsi foresees an immediate challenge to First Amendment free speech laws, as well as the Second Amendment's right to bear arms. As he explains in *Human Events*, "Citizens of both Canada and Mexico cannot freely own firearms. Nor can Canadians or Mexicans speak out freely without worrying about 'hate crimes' legislation or other political restrictions on what they may choose to say."[75]

All the measures and laws that flow from such a merger would have to be enforced. The military—in conjunction with an already militarized police—would obviously be called on to be the enforcers. Particularly worrisome is the fact that most of these proposals are being advanced in secret, behind closed doors. "President Bush signed a formal agreement that will end the United States as we know it," CNN correspondent Lou Dobbs proclaimed, "and he took the step without the approval from either the U.S. Congress or the people of the United States."[76] As Corsi has noted, the plan seems to be "to knit together the North American Union completely under the radar through a process of regulations and directives issued by various U.S. government agencies."[77]

Integration of the North American countries would facilitate commerce by making it easier for corporations and immigrants to cross borders. This could drastically alter America's constitutional and legal framework and create a monstrous bureaucracy that would make the Office of Homeland Security look like a well-organized machine—again, with the military as its enforcer.

As with all things, it comes down to the bottom line. For megacorporations, a North American Union may be the gateway to more money. But for Americans, the bottom line must be something more than economic concerns—it must be about maintaining our sovereignty as a nation. That's what the American Revolution was all about. Along with sovereignty come the Bill of Rights and our Constitution. They are what made America unique and a beacon of democracy to the rest of the world.

A WOLF BY THE EAR

In 1820, near the end of his life, Thomas Jefferson wrote a friend to express his dismay at the state of the nation: "I regret that I am now to die in the belief that the useless sacrifice of themselves, by the generation of '76, to acquire self government and happiness to their country, is to be thrown away by the unwise and unworthy passions of their sons, and that my only consolation is to be that I live not to weep over it, if they would but dispassionately weigh the blessings they will throw away against an abstract principle more likely to be effected by union than by scission, they would pause before they would perpetrate this act of suicide on themselves and of treason against the hopes of the world."[78]

It was not pessimism that compelled Jefferson to weep for his country. It was concern. As Jefferson wrote in that same letter, "we have the wolf by the ear, and we can neither hold him, nor safely let him go."[79] The wolf that we wrestle with today is none other than a distorted American empire, complete with megacorporations, a security-industrial complex, and a burgeoning military. And it has its sights set on absolute domination. Yet at the height of its power, even the mighty Roman Empire could not stare down a collapsing economy and a burgeoning military. Prolonged periods of war and false economic prosperity largely led to its demise, and it is feared that America, by repeating Rome's mistakes, is headed toward a similar collapse. As Chalmers Johnson predicts, "The United States will within a very short time face financial or even political collapse at home and a significantly diminished ability to project force abroad."[80]

To sustain their empire, the Romans raped the world and heavily taxed those subject to its power. As Henry Kissinger recognizes, such "empires almost always elicit universal resistance, which is why all such claimants have sooner or later exhausted themselves."[81]

The Romans faced revolt. And the American empire is now facing its own rebellions at home and abroad in the form of terrorist threats, insurgency, financial instability, economic volatility, civil unrest, increased oppression of its citizens, and a military whose power and presence grow more threatening by the day.

Although the United States remains the most powerful nation in history, it certainly seems as if we're moving in the direction of a fall. There are two choices that remain to us: we can continue to pour our resources into building a military empire or we can focus on shoring up our democracy. The Romans chose the military route, and history shows how that ended. Will we make the same mistake? Or will we reject the quest for empire and, as *Vanity Fair* editor-at-large Cullen Murphy suggests, remember who we are and, in so doing, hold fast to our belief "in self-betterment, in the possibility of improvement for everybody"? That ethic, says Murphy, "is our saving grace: It's the empire of possibility."[82]

CHAPTER SEVEN

The Final Frontier

In a word, as a man is said to have a right to his property,
he may be equally said to have a property in his rights.

—James Madison

The American Dream can be summed up in three simple words: life, liberty, and property. As the words of Emma Lazarus's "New Colossus," inscribed at the base of the Statue of Liberty, proclaim, "Give me your tired, your poor, / Your huddled masses yearning to breathe free, / The wretched refuse of your teeming shore. / Send these, the homeless, tempest-tossed to me, / I lift my lamp beside the golden door!"

Lured by the dream of a better, freer life, millions of individuals make their way across the U.S. border every year.[1] They come by plane, train, boat, or on foot, crossing continents, deserts, and oceans in their quest for the land of opportunity where, they are told, a pauper can become a president or the CEO of a multimillion-dollar corporation.

At its core, this quest for the American dream is about gaining sovereignty over one's life and property. Without it, there can be no freedom. As author Ayn Rand observed in *Atlas Shrugged*, "Just as man can't exist without his body, so no rights can exist without the right to translate one's rights into reality, to think, to work and keep the results, which means: the right of property."[2] Referred to as the labor theory of property, this idea holds that you own your life. And it follows that you must own the products of that life and that those products can be traded in free exchange with others. In many ways, the right to property is the first—and last—right, and perhaps the most inherent. Having set the match to the American Revolution, it may well prove to be one of the few things to rouse the American people to action.

As polls show, Americans have been willing to accept limitations on their rights to free speech, privacy, and due process, as well as other important freedoms, in exchange for the phantom promise of security. Yet whether they live in a modest two-bedroom walkup in the Bronx or a mansion in Bel Air, Americans have not been quite as willing to barter away their right to property. No matter how affluent or poor, Americans seem more inclined to fight to protect the things they own. In this way, we are not so far removed from the revolutionary spirit that saw a ragtag assortment of colonists standing up to the military might of Great Britain.

The signing of the Declaration of Independence marked a new beginning for our nation. It signaled a shift in the balance of power from one in which the people served an elite ruling class to one in which government was instituted to serve the people. The government's role would not be to create or define the people's inherent rights but rather to guarantee their protection.

As the Declaration states, "We hold these truths to be self-evident, that all men are created equal, that they are endowed by their Creator with certain unalienable Rights, that among these are Life, Liberty, and the pursuit of Happiness. That to secure these rights, Governments are instituted among Men, deriving their just powers from the consent of the governed."

The Declaration, which embodied all the passion, outrage, and noble ideals of the day, could easily have ended there. But the founders understood that in order for the newly born nation to survive, it would need more than revolutionary sentiment. It would require a government that existed to serve the people, not itself, and a contract to guarantee basic liberties and bind the union together.

Thus was the U.S. Constitution born in the summer of 1787. It sprang forth from the experiences of a revolutionary generation, still wary of the strong arm of government. From that wariness came the Bill of Rights. The first ten amendments to our Constitution are intended as a blueprint to keep the government in its place, off our backs, and away from our property.

For early Americans, the right to own property was fundamental to all other rights. The Fifth Amendment to the United States Constitution states: "No person shall be ... deprived of life, liberty, or property, without due process of law; nor shall private property be taken for public use, without just compensation." Property is grouped in the same category as life and liberty because it is difficult to enjoy life and liberty without the stability, security, and assurances that property provides. Property, at a minimum, checks governmental power for it provides the citizen a right of space where even government agents cannot intrude without proper authority.

However, as our government has utilized its eminent domain privilege to obtain private property for public use under sometimes questionable circumstances, even this most sacred of rights has increasingly come under siege. To many Americans, the battle to protect their private property has become the final constitutional frontier—the last holdout against their freedoms being usurped.

While we have become accustomed to equating property with land ownership, the term is much more fundamental and personal. It refers to a kind of sovereignty over one's life and possessions—especially one's money. Questions about who has ultimate control over our money, how much of it can be claimed by government, and how it gets spent go to the heart of the battle over property rights. It must be pointed out that governments generate no wealth on their own. Any resources that they have at their disposal have been appropriated from the original producers of that wealth, the citizens.[3] This fundamental truth has largely been forgotten over the years. Yet the government's respect for and treatment of the property of its citizens often reflects its attitude regarding its citizens' rights as a whole. Conversely, a government that doesn't respect the rights of its citizens will have even less regard for their property—be it land, money, or personhood.

RIPPING OFF TAXPAYERS IS THE NAME OF THE GAME

Over the years, American taxpayers have been swindled out of billions of dollars. If there is any absolute maxim by which the federal government seems to operate, it is that the taxpayer always gets ripped off.

The complete lack of accountability and disclosure for money being spent in America's "war on terror" is a perfect example of what I'm referring to. For instance, in 2005, auditors determined that $8.8 billion in Iraqi oil revenue money that was disbursed by the United States to Iraqi government agencies could not be accounted for.[4] According to congressional testimony by L. Paul Bremer, the former Iraqi reconstruction administrator, the funds were provided to the Iraqis in cash, often in shrink-wrapped packages of $100 bills that were flown into Baghdad on giant pallets aboard military cargo planes.[5] Representative Henry Waxman (D-Calif.) zeroed in on the absurdity of the government's actions when he asked, "Who in their right mind would send 363 tons of cash into a war zone?"[6]

Who in their right mind, indeed? While the government continues to spend money it does not have on ill-advised schemes and far-flung wars, the national debt keeps skyrocketing. As discussed in the previous chapter, the wars in Afghanistan and Iraq have cost the American taxpayer hundreds of billions of dollars. By May 2007, Congress had approved roughly $610 billion for the three post-9/11 military operations.[7] The Congressional Budget Office estimates that total funding for Iraq, Afghanistan, and the "global war on terror" alone could reach $1.45 trillion by 2017.[8]

This war on terror is providing legislators with new opportunities to spend taxpayer money, especially on pet projects. Indeed, hundreds of millions of dollars are being earmarked annually by members of Congress in return for special favors, frequently eliminating competition for government contracts and depriving taxpayers of competitive pricing. Iraq is a good example. According to the *Boston Globe*, "American contractors swindled hundreds of millions of dollars in Iraqi funds, but so far there is no way for Iraq's government to recoup the money."[9] Millions of dollars of U.S. rebuilding funds have also been wasted. A $43 million government contract to build a residential camp for Iraqi police trainers resulted in a camp that includes an Olympic-size swimming pool, which has never been used.[10] U.S. officials supposedly spent $36.4 million on armored vehicles, body armor, and communications equipment, but it could not be accounted for.[11] And approximately 80 percent of the $21 billion earmarked by the U.S. government for Iraqi reconstruction has already been spent, but very little can be found to show for it.[12] Much of this is due to a lack of congressional oversight. As Representative Waxman noted, "There has been no cop on the beat. And when there is no cop on the beat, criminals are more willing to engage in crimes."[13]

Equally disturbing is the way in which many of these government contracts are issued. Rather than requiring private companies to compete for government projects through the traditional bidding process, many are awarded no-bid contracts, the end result of aggressive lobbying campaigns. The U.S. government sends billions of taxpayer dollars each year to so-called government contractors, much of which is never accounted for, with the remainder often spent on obscure pet projects. Federal spending on government contracts has been on the rise for decades, soaring from $207 billion in 2000 to about $400 billion by 2006.[14] This unprecedented level of government issuance of contracts to private companies is not only fueled by the war in Iraq, domestic security, and Hurricane Katrina, but also by a philosophy that encourages outsourcing almost everything the government does.

Many government officials claim that using private enterprise instills efficiency and savings for the U.S. government and the American taxpayer. To the contrary, the government's dependence on corporate America has bred corruption while undermining basic notions of our representative democracy. As Ron Nixon and Scott Shane observed in the *New York Times*, "The most successful contractors are not necessarily those doing the best work, but those who have mastered the special skill of selling to Uncle Sam. The top 20 service contractors have spent nearly $300 million since 2000 on lobbying and have donated $23 million to political campaigns."[15] The biggest federal contractor in the nation, Lockheed Martin, receives more federal money than either the Departments of Justice or Energy.[16] These contractors, who never have to compete with other companies over who can do the best job for the best price, still get paid with taxpayer funds. It's a win-win situation for them and a huge loss for the taxpayer.

Pork barrel legislation involves the appropriation of government funds for projects primarily intended to benefit particular constituents or campaign contributors. Such government appropriations are yet another way in which taxpayers are bilked of their hard-earned dollars in order to favor a select few. Also referred to as Christmas tree items, pet projects, WAMs (walking around money), and earmarks,[17] pork projects continue to be tacked onto every major appropriations bill that makes its way through Congress.

Earmarking, which is a way a congressional representative can fund specific pet projects without going through the normal debate and budgetary process, is particularly popular. Such projects are "earmarked" (added) to larger bills, such as those aimed at funding the war effort. Among the pork projects highlighted in the *2006 Congressional Pig Book* were $13.5 million for the International Fund for Ireland, which helped finance the World Toilet Summit; $6,435,000 for wood utilization research; $1 million for the Waterfree Urinal Conservation Initiative; and $500,000 for the Sparta Teapot Museum in Sparta, North Carolina.[18] In his book *The Government Racket: Washington Waste From A to Z*, Martin Gross lists a number of self-serving pork projects approved by Congress over the years, as well as the projects that were denied funding.[19]

Congress, for example, approved a $6 million bill to upgrade the two-block-long Senate subway system and $250,000 to study TV lighting in the Senate meeting rooms but rejected a $3 billion bill that would help recruit and train qualified teachers in failing school systems around the nation. Congress approved a $350,000 bill to renovate the House beauty salon and $19 million to examine gas emissions from cow flatulence, but rejected a healthcare reform bill that would offer affordable prescription plans to lower-income families.[20] In 2006, a $3.1 million bill was approved to convert a ferryboat into a crab restaurant in Baltimore, along with a $320,000 bill that would rehabilitate the South Carolina mansion of Charles Pinckney, a signer of the Constitution, even though the house was built after he died.[21]

There was a time in our nation's history, not that long ago in fact, when pork barrel spending was the exception to the rule. Ronald Utt, a senior research fellow at the Heritage Foundation, found only three earmarks for transportation projects in federal budgets between 1970 and 1985. By 2005, the federal budget had grown to roughly 15,000 total earmarks,[22] with an astounding 6,371 of them tacked onto a $286 billion highway bill.[23]

While Congress gives special attention to legislation that can be adorned with Christmas tree items, weightier legislation is often rushed through without careful deliberation, as evidenced by the passage of both the Military Commissions Act of 2006 and the USA PATRIOT Act of 2001. The Military Commissions Act was misunderstood and misinterpreted by many members of Congress who voted for it.[24] In the case of the PATRIOT Act, "many representatives and senators expressed reservations about the Patriot Act but voted for it out of fear that political opponents would label them 'unpatriotic.'"[25] One senator noted, "[Some of] my colleagues on the other side have told me personally that they wished they hadn't [voted for the Patriot Act], that they should have read it a little closer."[26] As Representative Barbara Lee (D-Calif.) conceded, "The Patriot Act was passed in a blind rush, and in that rush to judgment, Congress trampled some important civil liberties."[27]

DO-NOTHING CONGRESS

A blind rush, indeed. A deeply divided, often lethargic Congress has proven to be a constant disappointment to those hoping for viable solutions to the problems facing Americans. A nationwide *NBC* poll showed a 16 percent approval rating of Congress in 2006, its lowest in 16 years.[28] Pork barrel spending, hastily passed legislation, partisan bickering, a skewed work ethic, graft, and moral turpitude have all contributed to the public's increasing dissatisfaction with congressional leadership.

The number of days actually worked by Congress has steadily decreased over the years. In 2006, members of the House and Senate met for a combined total of 218 days. As a *Rolling Stone* article on congressional efficacy noted, "The second session of the 109th Congress will set the all-time record for fewest days worked by a U.S. Congress: ninety-three. That means that House members will collect their $165,000 paychecks for only three months of actual work."[29] As a Pew Research Center study points out, "The polls suggest that the 109th Congress has made its mark on the public mostly for what it hasn't done."[30] Summarizing the so-called work of Congress, one reporter explained: "It failed to enact a host of once top-priority legislation on issues such as overhauling Social Security, immigration and lobbying laws. None of those is expected to be resolved in Congress's brief lame-duck session after the elections."[31]

As a 2006 ABC News report notes, "Congress is on schedule to meet fewer days this year than any Congress since 1948."[32] The House of Representatives was expected to meet seventy-one days, down from Congress's average of 162 days a year during the 1960s and 1970s and 139 days a year during the 1980s and 1990s. Representative Jim Cooper (D-Tenn.) aptly captured Congress's work routine when he observed: "They call it the Tuesday to Thursday Club. That means you get here Tuesday night, you have a few easy votes, you vote on Wednesday, and then you go back home Thursday afternoon."[33]

With most of their time spent fund-raising, members of Congress have rightly earned the moniker of a "Do-Nothing Congress." Paul Herrnson, director of the Center for American Politics and Citizenship at the University of Maryland, has determined that candidates spend unprecedented amounts of time campaigning and fund-raising for upcoming elections. According to a 2000 study, 55 percent of those running for statewide office, 43 percent running for Congress, and 33 percent running for state legislatures spent one-quarter of their campaign time raising money. Nearly one of every five spent as much as half their campaign time fund-raising.[34]

RULE BY THIEVES

Far worse than Congress's appalling work ethic is the rampant corruption that many Americans have come to expect from their government leaders. The abuses of office run the gamut from neglecting their constituencies to engaging in self-serving practices, including the misuse of eminent domain, earmarking hundreds of millions of dollars in federal contracting in return for personal gain and campaign contributions, having inappropriate ties to lobbyist groups, and incorrectly or incompletely disclosing financial information. The following is just a sampling of the kinds of corruption that have become associated with elected officials of all political persuasions.

Randy "Duke" Cunningham (R-Calif.) ran for Congress in 1990 with the slogan "A Congressman we can be proud of." Cunningham has since been accused of accepting bribes and special favors, including prostitution, luxury vacations, and tickets to the Super Bowl. Allegedly in return for such favors, he earmarked tens of millions of dollars in government contracting. These contracts involved defense contractor Brent Wilkes and CIA official Kyle Foggo; one was a $1.7 million deal with a 60 percent markup.[35] As a member of the Defense Appropriations Committee, Cunningham sold his house at a suspiciously inflated price and then lived rent-free in the yacht of MZM, Inc.'s founder Mitchell Wade. Coincidentally or not, since 2003, MZM, a high-tech national security corporation, has reportedly garnered as much as $150 million in prime contracting awards. Cunningham resigned from the U.S. House of Representatives in 2005 after pleading guilty to accepting at least $2.4 million in bribes and underreporting his income for 2004, among other charges.[36]

Representative Jerry Lewis (R-Calif.) allegedly used his position as a ranking member of the Appropriations Committee to secure hundreds of millions of dollars in contracts for family, friends, and clients connected with lobbyists in direct exchange for contributions. Lewis has been investigated by a federal grand jury in connection with close ties to former Congressman Bill Lowery, a lobbyist in the firm known until recently as Copeland Lowery Jacquez Denton & White. Lewis has also been tied to the same contractors as Duke Cunningham and is under FBI investigation.[37]

Representative Ken Calvert (R-Calif.) has also been investigated by a federal grand jury for ties with Lowery, having passed through thirteen earmarks amounting to $91 million in contracting relating to clients of his firm. Calvert has been accused of using his position to increase his personal wealth through land deals, purchasing property with a group of investors at depressed prices and then pushing through earmarks for such things as freeway construction and commercial development that make the land more valuable. The investors gained $435,000 on one deal and $475,000 on another. Calvert is under investigation by the FBI.[38]

Representative John Murtha (D-Pa.) has been investigated for having close ties to a lobbyist firm and its clients. The lobbyist firm PMA and nine of its clients have been among the top twenty contributors to the congressman's campaigns, giving hundreds of thousands of dollars. In the 2006 Defense Appropriations Bill, PMA's clients received at least sixty earmarks amounting to $95.1 million in contracting.[39] In May 2007, Representative Mike Rogers (R-Mich.) proposed a change that would have stripped $23 million of Murtha's earmarks from a bill. In response, Murtha threatened Rogers's own earmarks in a defense appropriations bill. When told that was not the way things were "done" in Congress, Murtha replied, "That's the way I do it."[40]

Representative William Jefferson (D-La.) was indicted on June 4, 2007, on sixteen criminal counts, including soliciting bribes, honest services fraud, Foreign Corrupt Practices Act violations, money laundering, obstruction of justice, and racketeering. He allegedly agreed to perform official acts for eleven different companies in return for bribes, and he was also accused of bribing a Nigerian official with $100,000, of which $90,000 was found in his freezer when criminal investigators raided his home. In June 2007, Jefferson pled not guilty to the indictment.[41]

Representative Gary Miller (R-Calif.) has been investigated for the misuse of eminent domain for personal gain and tax evasion. In three separate real estate sales to the cities of Monrovia and Fontana in California, Miller invoked the Internal Revenue Code, claiming eminent domain. In these sales, Miller realized a profit of over $10 million, which he reinvested in real estate. Miller worked for the Lewis Operating Company real estate firm before entering Congress and retains close ties to the company. The company has made generous donations to his campaign, and Miller has reportedly made between $1 and $6 million in private deals with the company since becoming a representative. Miller's transactions are under investigation by the FBI.[42]

Senator Ted Stevens (R-Alaska) has been investigated by the Justice Department on charges that he accepted bribes or other unreported gifts from VECO, an Alaskan oil field engineering firm. He admitted that the company paid for at least part of the renovations on his home. In the Senate, Stevens supported legislation for the construction of Alaskan oil pipelines, directed federal job training funds to benefit VECO, and advocated for a natural gas pipeline. VECO secured $65 million in federal contracts. The FBI and IRS raided Stevens's Alaskan home in July 2007.[43]

Representative Rick Renzi (R-Ariz.) came under scrutiny for sponsoring legislation in 2003 that, according to environmentalists, directed hundreds of millions of dollars to his father's business, while simultaneously devastating the San Pedro River. The company of Renzi's father, ManTech International Corporation, has secured $467 million in contracts with options for an additional $1.1 billion between the years 2004–2008. ManTech was the largest contributor to Renzi's campaign in 2003 and the second largest in 2004. Renzi is also under federal investigation for his involvement in a land-swap deal. In April 2007, the FBI raided his family business, and he temporarily resigned from the House Intelligence Committee. Thereafter, Renzi denied claims that he was considering resigning from office. However, in August 2007, Renzi announced that he would not be a candidate for reelection in 2008.[44]

Senator Mitch McConnell (R-Ky.), minority leader of the 110th Congress, has significant sway in the rewarding of contracts as a member of the Senate Appropriations Committee. His earmarking of projects involving clients for his former chief-of-staff, lobbyist Gordon Hunter Bates, has come under particular scrutiny.[45] Donations to McConnell's nonprofit organization, the McConnell Center for Political Leadership at the University of Louisville, from businesses that desire McConnell's assistance have also been regarded with some suspicion. The senator has always stressed the importance of fund-raising, having raised over $220 million over his career. What has raised speculation, however, is a report of a nexus between his actions and his donors' agendas. As the *Lexington Herald-Leader* reported in October 2006, "He pushes the government to help cigarette makers, Las Vegas casinos, the pharmaceutical industry, credit card lenders, coal mine owners, and others."[46]

Representative Allan B. Mollohan (D-W.Va.) has engaged in huge amounts of earmarking and has been investigated for inaccurate and incomplete financial disclosures. He directed $369 million in federal grants to his district between the years 1997 and 2006. Of this, $250 million was directed to five nonprofits created by Mollohan and staffed by his friends. Important members and contractors of these organizations in turn have given $397,122 to his campaign. Mollohan also reportedly requested that $1 million be earmarked to expand a wilderness area that abuts his property, which would greatly increase its value. In April 2006, the FBI notified three nonprofit organizations that were created by Mollohan and financed primarily through special federal appropriations that he allegedly steered their way that they would be subpoenaed for financial and other records.[47]

Graft is not limited to politicians. Reports over the past several years indicate that various members of the news media have accepted money from the Bush administration in exchange for promoting certain political agendas. Unfortunately, many of them failed to reveal this important fact to their readers, viewers, and listeners. Maggie Gallagher, a syndicated columnist, had a $21,500 contract with the Department of Health and Human Services to promote President George W. Bush's $300 million initiative to support marriage and abstinence education to youth, especially among the poor. Columnist Armstrong Williams apologized for not disclosing a $240,000 contract to promote the controversial No Child Left Behind legislation of the Bush administration on his cable show, syndicated radio, and other venues. The notion of a public "watchdog" in the media and an informed voter population is compromised when the government cannot expect scrutiny from the news media and the public fails to receive unbiased reporting from journalists.[48]

Despite promises to fight this culture of corruption that has permeated Congress, few meaningful reforms have been put into effect. Members of Congress continue to flout the laws and codes, which are meant to guide their behavior. Observers have noted that over time, especially when there has been a Republican majority in power, key aspects of the system of checks and balances have deteriorated.[49]

In the 108th Congress, only 28 percent of the bills were open to amendment, barely half of what Democrats allowed in 1993–1994, when they controlled Congress. Committee meetings were often conducted secretly, late at night, thereby circumventing established rules and practices. Certain bills were pushed through the House and Senate so quickly that few could make an informed vote, while others languished indefinitely. A record 3,407 pork barrel projects were put into the 2006 federal budget that were never debated or voted on in advance, as compared with the forty-seven in committees in 1994.[50] The ethics committees of both houses have been extremely reticent about investigating their peers and themselves. Despite this, the American people continue to reelect many of these politicians.

Government corruption, pork barrel spending, and a ballooning national debt are not characteristics of a government that is, in Abraham Lincoln's words in the Gettysburg Address, "of the people, by the people, and for the people." Rather, they are symptomatic of a runaway government with little regard for the rights of its citizens or their property. Somewhere along the way, democracy has given way to kleptocracy, and representation by statesmen has been rejected in favor of rule by career politicians, corporations, and thieves. But this, too, was not always the case.

Today's politicians, many of whom are far removed from those they represent, are chauffeured around in limousines, fly in private jets, and eat gourmet meals, all paid for by the American taxpayer. Such luxury can make it difficult to identify with the "little guy"— the roofers, plumbers, and blue-collar workers who live from paycheck to paycheck and keep the country running with their hard-earned dollars and the sweat of their brows. Yet for many of our founders, while administering to the needs of a young government was important, it was not their full-time job. They were statesmen who served out of a love of country and a sense of duty, all the while working for their wages.[51] To them, it was a public service, not a lucrative job. As the National Archives notes, "Many pursued more than one career at the same time and thirty-five were lawyers or had benefited from legal training."[52]

At the Constitutional Convention of 1787, thirteen of the delegates were businessmen, merchants, or shippers, six were major land speculators, and eleven speculated in securities on a large scale. Twelve owned or managed slave-operated plantations or large farms, including George Mason and George Washington, and several were small farmers.[53] Nine of the men received a substantial part of their income from public office. Three had retired from active economic endeavors, including Benjamin Franklin, who was a scientist. Three were physicians, and one was a university president. Another was a minister, and several had studied theology but never been ordained. A few of the delegates were wealthy, while most of the others had financial resources that ranged from good to excellent. Some had modest incomes, and still others were self-made men who rose from humble beginnings.[54]

PHILOSOPHICAL UNDERPINNINGS OF THE FIFTH AMENDMENT

The founders left us with a rich legacy of ideas and principles on which to grow our nation, especially those embodied within the Declaration of Independence and the Constitution. Yet while "Life, Liberty, and the pursuit of Happiness" is possibly the most recognizable phrase in the Declaration of Independence, for all intents and purposes—at least in the Bill of Rights—the pursuit of happiness is tantamount to material success, i.e., the ownership of property and the pursuit of material possessions. While modern Americans may have a love affair with material things, philosophical underpinnings associated with the right to own property can be found in the writings of such European thinkers as John Locke, William Blackstone, and Baron de Montesquieu.

Near the end of the seventeenth century, the British philosopher John Locke published his classic *Second Treatise of Government*,[55] which established the "social contract" theory of government. As historian Carl Becker wrote, Locke, more than anyone else, made it possible for eighteenth-century minds to believe that men could "correspond with the general harmony of Nature"; that since man, and the mind of man, were integral parts of the work of God, it was possible for man, by the use of his mind, to bring his thought and conduct into a perfect harmony with the Universal Natural Order.[56] In the eighteenth century, these truths were widely accepted as self-evident: that a valid morality would be a "natural morality," a valid religion would be a "natural religion," a valid law of politics would be a "natural law."[57]

This was another way of saying that morality, religion, and politics should conform to God's will as revealed in the essential nature of man.[58] Locke extended this principle to mean that the sovereign or government may not violate a person's property rights and that the sovereign's doing so allowed a person to disobey the sovereign (or government).[59] In his seminal work, Locke wrote:

> *Though the Earth, and all inferior Creatures be common to all Men, yet every Man has a Property in his own Person. This no Body has any Right to but himself. The Labour of his Body and the Work of his Hands, we may say, are properly his. Whatsoever then he removes out of the State that Nature hath provided, and left it in, he hath mixed his Labour with, and joyned to it something that is his own, and thereby makes it his Property.*[60]

These views on property were influential in the founding of our government. Pace University School of Law professor Donald L. Doernberg opined that it would be difficult to overstate John Locke's influence on the American Revolution and the people who created the government that followed it.[61]

William Blackstone, an English jurist and professor, penned possibly the most important and influential legal work of the eighteenth century when he wrote *Commentaries on the Laws of England*. Blackstone's defense of property is epitomized in his claim that "so great moreover is the regard of the law for private property that it will not authorize the least violation of it; no, not even for the good of the whole community."[62] Blackstone best articulated the Roman law precept of strict property rights when he wrote of "property as absolute dominion, 'that sole and despotic dominion which one man claims and exercises over the external things of the world, in total exclusion of the right of any other individual in the universe.'"[63] James Madison, in the years after he authored the Fifth Amendment, incorporated Blackstone's definition of property rights into his writings on property.[64]

Baron de Montesquieu was one of the great political philosophers of the Enlightenment. A lawyer by trade, he spent several years of his life visiting the governments of Italy, Germany, Austria, and England.[65] These visits, and his resulting study of their governments, were instrumental in his writing *The Spirit of the Laws*.[66] This work was so important that it has been called "the political Bible" of Thomas Jefferson and a primer to George Washington, James Madison, and Alexander Hamilton.[67]

Montesquieu advocated the right of individuals to own property and to keep it safe from unbridled interference by the government. City College of New York law professor Morris R. Cohen wrote, "Montesquieu's view that political laws must in no way retrench on private property because no public good is greater than the maintenance of private property, became the basis of legal thought in America."[68]

Property rights were of paramount importance to the founders in their quest for sovereignty and independence from Great Britain, as elucidated by the revolutionary firebrand and patriot Samuel Adams in his most famous work, *The Rights of the Colonists*: "Among the natural rights of the colonists are these: first, a right to life; second, to liberty; third, to property."[69] In the same work, Adams elaborated on that principle when he asked, "Now what liberty can there be where property is taken away without consent?"[70]

A few years after the Constitution was ratified, U.S. Supreme Court Justice William Paterson, a member of the Constitutional Convention, handed down a ruling in *Vanhorne's Lessee v. Dorrance*, which remains one of the most stirring defenses of property rights ever put on record:

> *It is evident; that the right of acquiring and possessing property, and having it protected, is one of the natural, inherent, and unalienable rights of man. Men have a sense of property: Property is necessary to their subsistence, and correspondent to their natural wants and desires; its security was one of the objects, that induced them to unite in society. No man would become a member of a*

community, in which he could not enjoy the fruits of his honest labour and industry. The preservation of property then is a primary object of the social compact.[71]

WAYNE HAGE, THE SAGEBRUSH REBEL

Wayne Hage was a man with such a sense of property. While the Wild West was the ultimate frontier to be conquered for history buffs, for Wayne Hage it became the backdrop for his own personal American revolution.[72]

A self-made man, Hage worked his way through undergraduate and graduate school before realizing his dream of having his own ranch. In 1978, Hage purchased Pine Creek Ranch in Nye County, Nevada, which adjoins the federally administered Toiyabe and Humbolt National Forests and Monitor Valley. A couple of months after Hage purchased the 752,000-acre ranch, which he and his wife Jean managed along with their five children, two government agents from the National Park Service appeared at his front door and informed Hage that they were going to buy his ranch. When they offered him about half of what he had just paid, Hage refused.

That's when the harassment, as Hage describes it, began. First, the U.S. Forest Service and Bureau of Land Management (BLM) filed a claim on the water rights to Hage's ranch—after Forest Service rangers fenced in a critical spring used to pipe water into the rangers' cabin. Since Pine Creek Ranch is comprised of mostly desert terrain, access to this water for cattle and wildlife was crucial.

Government interference in the daily operations of Hage's property was driving the ranch to the brink of collapse. Over a period of 105 days, Hage received forty certified letters and more than seventy personal visits, each citing him in violation of a creatively new bureaucratic regulation. In one instance, Hage sent a horse and rider to ride a 20-mile fence line to verify a violation, only to find that there was one staple missing in the entire fence line, dutifully earmarked with a bright blue flag. And there were forty-five counts of trespass, charging that Hage's cattle were grazing in the wrong locations. Yet on more than one occasion, eyewitnesses claimed to have seen the Forest Service move the cattle into a trespass area and then cite Hage for the violation.

Things became even more serious in 1991 when the Forest Service confiscated some of Hage's cattle. Hage had previously worked for the Forest Service and BLM and, therefore, knew that part of their unwritten procedure in dealing with people is to provoke confrontation. An aggravated confrontation becomes an easy, lawful way for a federal agency to pursue an individual if that citizen reacts and physically threatens the federal agents involved. This was the scenario with the infamous 1992 Ruby Ridge incident where federal agents shot and killed Randy Weaver's wife and son after Weaver engaged the agents. In the end, Weaver was found innocent of any charges after standing trial and was eventually awarded a $3.1 million settlement against the federal government.

In preparing to confiscate Hage's cattle, the Forest Service repeatedly sent out emails and made phone calls to various parties, portraying Hage as one "who can only be dealt with in very extreme measures." Hage amazingly kept his composure during the ordeal. When he drove to the site where his cattle had been confiscated, he found thirty Forest Service riders, armed with semi-automatic weapons and bulletproof vests. Some were stationed on high points, clearly expecting confrontation. But much to their dismay, Hage had done his homework, was aware of his rights, and knew to avoid the mistakes of others. Hage refused to be provoked to violence. Instead, he pulled out a 35-mm camera and said to the agents, "Smile pretty, boys." After confiscating more than one hundred head of Hage's cattle, the Forest Service handed him a bill for their costs in gathering the cattle. They then took the cattle to a sale yard, but it adamantly refused to auction off stolen cattle. The agents reportedly proceeded to hold their own sale and kept the profits.

Heavily armed agents came out to Hage's ranch on several occasions, but again Hage refused to let the confrontations turn violent. Instead, he took the federal government to court, filing a landmark case that put on trial the practices of federal land management and adjoining agencies set to drive landowners "off the range."[73] *Hage v. United States* stands for seeking justice and compensation against the Forest Service under the Fifth Amendment to the U.S. Constitution.[74] Hage cited the taking of private land and cattle, water rights, and irrigation ditch right-of-ways by the federal government. At trial, the court concluded that Hage indeed owned the water on his grazing allotment, ditch right-of-ways, and other property rights. The federal government, however, continued to argue that Hage's case was not really about personal property rights but responsible grazing. Government agents continued their attempts to enforce rules and regulations they claimed Hage broke.

The principles in Hage's case, however, go far beyond the issue of a man fighting to keep his ranch. "There are no such things as civil liberties if you do not have property rights," said Hage. "If a person's cattle, ditches and water, on his own ranch, aren't safe, any other property you have is not safe—they can take anything they want."[75]

One of the more alarming developments in recent years is the alignment of the federal government with overly aggressive environmental groups. Roy Elicker, an attorney for the National Wildlife Federation, revealed their strategy at a seminar designed to teach participants how to eliminate people such as Hage and his livestock from federal lands. It is to make "it so expensive in his operation and mak[e] so many changes for him to continue to run his cattle on the public lands that he goes broke." Elicker continued: "How to win is one at a time, one at a time, he goes out of business, he dies, you wait him out, and you win."[76]

Wayne Hage understood what he was up against. That is why he argued that property owners need to know their rights and stand up for them, especially concerning the attainment of property under the guise of environmentalism. "You either exercise your right to own property, or you yourself are the property of a coercive or tyrannic government."[77] Passionate about getting the government "back under control," Hage continued his fight over the years, despite pressure from the federal government to drop the case. To Hage, it was yet another set of circumstances determining the future of our freedoms in America. "The broad issue is whether me, my children, my friends, my fellow countrymen are going to be able to see a free society in the future."[78]

According to Hage, the Fifth Amendment, including its relevant clause stating "nor shall private property be taken for public use without just compensation," was placed in the Constitution because history taught those who founded the American system of government that the state, left unchecked, will always become a thief. "But all thieves lose their zeal for stealing when they are required to pay full value for what has been stolen."[79] No one else, he argued, is going to protect your rights if you are unwilling to defend them yourself.

In August 2004, in the midst of finalizing posttrial briefs of the thirteen-year-old lawsuit and in a move of apparent direct defiance of all court decisions, the Forest Service and BLM indicated that they were preparing to confiscate the remaining cattle on Hage's ranch. The federal government claimed that BLM could move forward with the confiscation unless they received a cease and desist order from a federal court. "The government refuses to recognize that I am not a trespasser on my own ranch," said Hage.

Until his death from cancer in June 2006, Hage remained committed to his belief that the cornerstone of a truly free society is the ownership of private property by the people. As he said, "A right undefended is a right waived."[80]

An editorial that appeared in the *Colorado Springs Gazette* after Hage's death captured it best: "We find something exhilarating and reassuring about the occasional flaring of sagebrush rebellions—in knowing that there are some Americans in the Wayne Hage mold, who aren't going to back down from what they see as Uncle Sam's bullying ways. Theirs is a spirit that's too stubborn to crush."[81]

KELO'S REVENGE

Susette Kelo is a sagebrush rebel in the Wayne Hage mold.

In July 1997, Kelo, a registered nurse, purchased her dream home in Fort Trumbull, Connecticut. From her dining room window on a clear day, she could see Montauk Point at the tip of Long Island. When she bought the small Victorian, it was so overgrown with weeds that she literally needed a hatchet to reach the front door. But soon thereafter, the house was lovingly converted into a little pink show home where Susette and her husband Tim lived in relative peace. That all changed the day before Thanksgiving 2000, when a notice was posted on their door by the New London Development

Corporation. It informed the Kelos that they would have to leave their home by March 2001—or the police would forcibly remove them and their belongings.

"There are no words to explain what it feels like to have someone try to take your home away from you," Susette said. "You have to worry all the time … worry about where you are going to live … worry about how you're going to continue to fight for what is yours." Moreover, "If the taking of our property were for a bridge, road, or firehouse, I would be prepared to sell without a fight. But the government should not be able to force me to sell my home for just any purpose."[82]

Susette decided to fight back. As she told the *Washington Post,* "I don't like being pushed around."[83] With eight of her neighbors, Kelo filed a lawsuit charging that New London's plan to redevelop the waterfront area where she lived was unconstitutional because the government wanted to take her property for private development, not as a "public use," as the Fifth Amendment requires.

In many areas of the United States, corporations are using their money and influence to persuade local governments to abuse their power of eminent domain (the power given to government in the Fifth Amendment to take private property for public use). Corporations make deals with local governments to build developments in their towns, promising to bring in more taxes and economic growth—that is, if the government will hand over the property of those who refuse to sell in the area where the corporation wants to develop.

There is little dispute over many kinds of public land use, such as schools, roads, and water treatment plants. In recent years, however, municipalities, often in conjunction with corporate interests, have expanded the interpretation of "public use." The reasons given include revitalizing dilapidated downtowns, removing urban blight, and boosting tourism and tax revenue. But when governmental abuse occurs, it often falls on the poor and lower middle classes because the poor are often ill equipped to fight back. This was the situation in which Susette Kelo and her fellow New Londoners found themselves.

New London, once a prominent whaling center and then a shipping and manufacturing hub, had slowly lost its industrial and commercial base. In 1997, Pfizer, the giant pharmaceutical firm that makes such drugs as Zoloft, Viagra, and Celebrex, began discussions with state and local officials about a $300 million research plant in New London that would bring in two thousand jobs. It was the first time a major manufacturer had expressed interest in moving to New London in more than one hundred years.

In a March 1999 letter, George M. Milne Jr., president of Pfizer's Central Research Division, wrote that the company's New London expansion "requires the world class redevelopment planned for the adjacent 90 acres," which included Kelo's neighborhood, encompassing about 115 properties. Milne said Pfizer needed a 200-room waterfront hotel, a conference center, a physical fitness area, extended-stay residential units, and eighty units of housing.

Kelo learned about the government's plan for her property when a real estate agent showed up on her doorstep in early 1998, telling her that her home was scheduled for demolition and that she had better sell quickly. Kelo had bought the two-bedroom, one-bath house for $53,000 in 1997. When the real estate agent offered her $68,000, Kelo told the agent to get off her property. Other area residents, unfortunately, were easier to persuade.

The issue of compensation was a major sticking point. When Kelo bought her house, the Fort Trumbull area was run down, wedged between a decommissioned military installation and a ramshackle marina and near a malodorous sewage treatment plant. But by the time demolition of the neighborhood began, the sewage smell had abated and there was a blue-chip corporate research center and an attractive waterfront park with bike trails and green lawns. When Pfizer decided to build a state-of-the-art day care center for the children of its employees, the corporation bought homes near its compound, paying prices considerably higher than the previous going rates. Although one house reportedly sold for $400,000, Kelo said the final government offer she received was $125,000.

Kelo decided to fight the condemnation and got support from area activists who also opposed the project. With the backing of the Institute for Justice, Kelo and the eight other property owners sued and won in the Connecticut Superior Court. New London, however, appealed to the state Supreme Court, which sided with the city. In June 2005, the U.S. Supreme Court, in a sharply divided and controversial 5–4 decision, ruled in favor of the city as well.

Justice John Paul Stevens recognized that "there is no allegation that any of these properties is blighted or otherwise in poor condition, rather, they were condemned only because they happen to be located in the development area."[84] Even after recognizing this, Stevens ruled on behalf of the city and against Kelo. In a stinging dissent, Justice Sandra Day O'Connor expressed her fear for what discriminatory effects and hardships the abuse of the government's eminent domain power would create. O'Connor stated that "the beneficiaries are likely to be those citizens with disproportionate influence and power in the political process, including large corporations and development firms. As for the victims, the government now has license to transfer property from those with fewer resources to those with more. The Founders cannot have intended this perverse result."[85]

In a rare opinion, Justice Clarence Thomas stated: "The losses will fall disproportionately on poor communities. Those communities are not only systematically less likely to put their lands to the highest and best social use, but are also the least politically powerful....The deferential standard this Court has adopted for the Public Use Clause is therefore deeply perverse. It encourages 'those citizens with disproportionate influence and power in the political process, including large corporations and development firms' to victimize the weak."[86]

Justice Thomas was right on target. *Kelo v. City of New London* should be viewed as a major threat to individual property rights, especially those of the poor and minority groups that do not have political power or influence. And the Court's decision, which kowtowed to big business and equated affluence with the "general good," should have come as no surprise because we live in a nation that increasingly resembles a corporate state. Corporations are capable of wielding undue influence over governments and legislatures. With the Court's decision in *Kelo* significantly weakening judicial limitations and oversight, there is little to prevent corporations from expanding even more.

In the Wake of Kelo

If one good thing came out of the New London debacle, it was its impact on the nation. The decision by Susette Kelo and her neighbors to stand and fight caused a firestorm of criticism. It was labeled "Kelo's revenge" because Americans were waking up and fighting back.

In eight states, from Arizona to South Carolina, voters made their voices heard on the issue of eminent domain. Many state governments have now limited the definition of "public use" so that property may not be taken solely for economic development. After the *Kelo* decision, almost every state legislature addressed the issue of eminent domain, and twenty-five states passed statutes providing increased protections against eminent domain abuse.[87]

While *Kelo* mobilized many state and local government leaders to protect their constituents' property rights, however, others were encouraged to exercise the power of eminent domain. The Institute for Justice reports that since *Kelo*, "Local governments have threatened or condemned more than 5,783 properties for private projects. That is more than half of the 10,282 properties threatened or taken by eminent domain for the benefit of private parties in the five years between 1998 and 2002."[88] Of the 5,783 properties, 354 were "filed/authorized condemnations," which are "eminent domain actions filed in court to take property, or votes by local government to specifically authorize filing eminent domain actions or giving private parties the power to file eminent domain actions."[89] The remaining 5,429 were "threatened condemnations," which are "government actions leading up to filing a condemnation action in court, or voting to authorize the filing of such action—including blight studies that are used to justify eminent domain, plans that call for replacing existing residents and businesses, statements that eminent domain may be used, and votes to make final offers to purchase property."[90]

Not all of these cases may involve abuse. But the drastic increase in the frequency and number of eminent domain cases indicates that governments feel more at liberty to use eminent domain after the *Kelo* decision and that developers are likely to capitalize on it.

The instances of eminent domain abuse are far-reaching. Since *Kelo*, at least sixteen places of worship (which pay no taxes) were taken for private uses (which will generate tax dollars).[91] Other attempted takings include the transfer of three family-owned seafood businesses to a larger private marina in Texas; the transfer of farmland to a shopping center anchored by a Lowe's in Illinois; developing 233 low-income and elderly families' properties in New Jersey into a senior community where townhouses cost more than $350,000; and developing middle-income, single-family homes on the waterfront into more expensive condominiums in New Jersey.[92]

There is, thankfully, some good news to report. Property owners in southwest Ohio won a major victory in July 2006 when the Ohio Supreme Court ruled that a portion of the state's eminent domain statute is unconstitutional. In a unanimous decision, the Ohio court ruled that the city of Norwood did not have the right to take two houses to make way for a high-end commercial and residential development. Justice Maureen O'Connor wrote that the court's decision balances "two competing interests of great import in American democracy: the individual's rights in the possession and security of property, and the sovereign's power to the private property for the benefit of the community."[93]

The court found that while economic factors may be considered when determining whether private property can be appropriated, those factors alone do not justify the taking of property. The court also ruled that use of the term "deteriorating area" as a standard for determining whether private property is subject to appropriation is unconstitutional because it inherently incorporates speculation as to the future condition of a property. "In addressing these important matters, we have benefited from the wisdom of other courts, which, by the masterly design of our government, are at the forefront of these critical constitutional questions," O'Connor wrote.[94] "Although the judiciary and legislature define the limits of state powers, such as eminent domain, the ultimate guardians of the people's rights, as evidenced by the appellants in these cases, are the people themselves."[95]

In August 2006, it was revealed that Susette Kelo's little pink cottage—the home that was the subject of a landmark U.S. Supreme Court case and a national symbol of the fight against eminent domain abuse—would be spared from the wrecking ball. After the U.S.

Supreme Court ruled that the City of New London, Connecticut, could take her home, Kelo was faced with an imminent eviction. Instead of resigning herself to losing her home, Kelo resubmitted a proposal that had been rejected by the city when it initially approached Kelo and the others about their property. The proposal was to preserve and move the home to a new location. This time, the city and the state of Connecticut agreed.[96]

RICH COLLINS: A FREE SPEECH SHOWDOWN IN A PRIVATE PARKING LOT

Rich Collins's story puts a somewhat different spin on the debate over property rights. Whereas Hage's and Kelo's experiences pitted their property interests against the government's eminent domain claims for the sake of the greater good, Collins found himself in a showdown between his free speech rights and private property interests. Collins, a seventy-year-old retired university professor, had decided to run for the Virginia State Legislature. But unlike his opponent, Collins lacked the funds to advertise in newspapers or on television, and so he took his campaign to the streets, handing out leaflets to people on a public sidewalk at a local shopping center.

It was there, on a summer day in 2005, while handing out his leaflets, that Collins learned a valuable lesson on the costs of practicing free speech principles. The manager of the shopping center approached Collins and asked him to stop handing out his leaflets. Standing on what he believed were his First Amendment rights, Collins refused. A disagreement ensued, the police were called, and the former professor was arrested, handcuffed, and charged with trespassing.

Collins eventually took the issue to court, arguing that his free speech rights had been violated. Some constitutional purists—especially those who find themselves strongly advocating for private property rights—were hard-pressed to side with Collins. Yet as his case worked its way through the courts, it became clear that the growing tension was not so much between the people and their government but between corporate entities and the people. Unfortunately for Collins, both the lower and appeals courts ruled that since the shopping center was not located on state property, the Constitution did not apply. However, this is contrary to other rulings in which the courts have indicated that First Amendment principles apply, even in private shopping centers.

In *New Jersey Coalition Against the War in the Middle East v. J.M.B. Realty Corp.*, the court held that privately owned regional and community shopping centers must permit leafleting on societal issues, subject to any reasonable conditions set by the shopping centers. The court relied on the basis of the free speech provisions of the New Jersey Constitution, declining to follow rulings of the U.S. Supreme Court that refuse to extend the First Amendment to expressive activity at privately owned shopping centers.[97]

The California Supreme Court also recognized a right of access to privately owned shopping centers for the purpose of engaging in political speech in *Robins v. Pruneyard Shopping Center*.[98] The state court based the right upon the state's constitution.[99] The Colorado Supreme Court has also interpreted its constitution as precluding the private owners of an enclosed shopping mall from excluding citizens engaged in nonviolent political speech in common areas of the mall where there was significant state involvement in the operation of the mall.[100] And in *Batchelder v. Allied Stores Int'l, Inc.*, the court held that the state constitution gave a candidate for office the right of access to a private shopping center to obtain signatures in support of his candidacy under a state constitutional provision regarding ballot access.[101]

It is evident that as the corporate world expands and takes up more and more space, places that traditionally were open to the public are suddenly being restricted. The old public squares where people used to meet and discuss issues have all but disappeared—even in smaller communities. This is the new reality in which we live.

Over the past 150 years, the corporation has risen from relative obscurity to become the world's dominant economic institution—even surpassing governments in power and influence. Corporations are consuming more and more property, which, with rising property values, forces many average Americans into the category of renters instead of owners. In effect, corporations govern our lives. They determine what we eat, watch, wear, do, where we can exercise our rights, and even what we think about the world and ourselves. We are inescapably surrounded by corporate ideology and culture, especially with the increasing control over the media by its corporate owners.

In his study of corporations, Joel Bakan, a law professor at the University of British Columbia, wrote: "They posture as infallible and omnipotent, glorifying themselves in imposing buildings and elaborate displays. Increasingly, corporations dictate the decisions of their supposed overseers in government and control domains of society once firmly embedded within the public sphere. The corporation's dramatic rise to dominance is one of the remarkable events of modern history, not least because of the institution's inauspicious beginnings."[102]

Although some corporations are beginning to appear concerned about people and the environment, Bakan claims that this is a mask, noting that "pious social responsibility themes now vie with sex for top billing in corporate advertising."[103] Bakan goes on to say that "good intentions, like good-looking girls, can sell goods."[104]

Two points must be made. First, those who founded this country and gave us the Constitution could not have foreseen the growth and influence of megacorporations. They certainly could not have contemplated that corporations, by way of a U.S. Supreme Court decision, would one day be treated as legal persons with rights and liabilities.[105] In the process, corporations, which are abstract entities, now have constitutional rights. But unlike real persons, a corporation does not have a conscience; neither does it operate from a moral base. The majority of corporations do not exist to help people but rather to make money, even at the expense of exploiting people.

As President Rutherford B. Hayes once observed, "Hundreds of laws of Congress and the state legislatures are in the interest of these men and against the interests of the workingmen. These need to be exposed and repealed. All laws on corporations, on taxation, on trusts, wills, descent, and the like, need examination and extensive change. This is a government of the people, by the people, and for the people no longer. It is a government of corporations, by corporations, and for corporations."[106]

MEGACORPORATIONS

Megacorporations increasingly operate unchecked and are often unaccountable to the people and to the government. The federal government's general response to corporate scandals has been sluggish and timid at best. As Professor Bakan recognizes, "Over the last three hundred years, corporations have amassed such great power as to weaken government's ability to control them."[107]

In 2000, the Institute for Policy Studies (IPS) issued a report stating that of the one hundred largest economies in the world in 1999, fifty-one were corporations and forty-nine were countries. The report also documented the rapid growth of corporations, stating that "between 1983 and 1999, the profits of the Top 200 firms grew 362.4 percent, while the number of people they employ grew by only 14.4 percent."[108] Wal-Mart is the prime example of rapid growth, which went from $4.7 billion in sales in 1983 (below the Top 200 threshold) to $166.8 billion in sales by 1999, making it the second largest firm in the world. Despite the exceptional emergence of Wal-Mart into the Top 200, over half of the corporations in the Top 200 list in 1983 remained in the list through 1999.

Of the Top 200 corporations in 1999, U.S. corporations comprised the highest percentage: 41 percent. One might think that the taxes on these corporations would benefit our social welfare, but this is not true. Over half of these U.S. corporations did not pay the full federal corporate tax rate between 1996 and 1998. And seven—Texaco, Chevron, PepsiCo, Enron, WorldCom, McKesson, and General Motors—paid less than zero in federal income taxes in 1998 because of rebates.

One prime area where corporations are spending these tax savings is political lobbying and campaigning. Ninety-four of the Top 200 firms have "government relations" offices located on or near Washington DC's K Street corridor. Eighty-two of the Top 200 U.S. companies contributed over $33 million through political action committees (not including soft money donations) for election campaigns in 2000, spending fifteen times more than labor unions. These expenditures most likely have a significant effect on political campaigns, as shown by the Center for Responsive Politics's report that 94 percent of those elected to the U.S. House of Representatives had outspent their opponents in campaigning. An IPS report concluded that "widespread trade and investment liberalization have contributed to a climate in which dominant corporations are enjoying increasing levels of economic and political clout that are out of balance with the tangible benefits they provide to society."[109]

Our political campaign laws and regulations are flawed. Candidates who have money to advertise themselves and their views in the most favorable light while attacking opponents' views have a clear advantage over those who do not possess similar funding. Since many voters are not well-informed and often fail to think critically, the most heavily advertised candidate often wins. And because corporations have a lot of money to support candidates, they can substantially influence political elections. Thus, those with the most money often control politics and the direction of the country.

As will be discussed in more detail in Chapter Eight, corporations also exert a powerful influence on people's views by way of the media. The media has become more a source of entertainment than education and is aimed at increasing profit. Many major media companies are owned by corporations and necessarily operate within the interests of the corporations. While corporations have a right to express their views and advocate their interests, they have an unfair advantage over smaller media companies and often threaten to expand and buy up these smaller companies. But even if the larger corporations do not acquire the smaller media companies, corporations have the money to purchase the most popular advertising time and exert their influence on multitudes of people. The average citizen, except in rare circumstances, has no access to the public through these media venues.

As private corporations combine with and become adjuncts of the government, they increasingly overshadow not only the livelihoods of private citizens but also our rights as individuals in a "free" society. This is occurring in several ways. As we saw with Rich Collins, corporations—having restructured society so as to make themselves the new social centers—have the power to suppress the right of free speech by private citizens. Corporations are also using their authority and influence to persuade the government to transfer individuals' private property rights to them, thus abusing the government's so-called power of eminent domain.

BUYING UP OUR LIBERTIES

In the end, it all comes down to property. The rising tensions over property rights go beyond mere disputes about material possessions; they reflect a lack of acknowledgment of a person's humanity. When the government forcibly takes one person's property and gives it to another, it devalues the worth of the original owner.

Will the battle for private property be relegated to a last stand for a final frontier? Or will it be the last straw that must fall before Americans wake up to the threats to their liberties and once again stand and fight for their freedoms? Our lives, liberties, and property are protected by the Constitution. Yet if we allow corporations to join powers with and use (or abuse) the government in order to take our property, then what will stop corporations from buying up our liberties, and then our lives?

Vox populi, vox Dei is the Latin phrase meaning, "The voice of the people is the voice of God." It is time for the voice of the people to be heard—loudly and clearly. So far, it has only been a faint moan.

CHAPTER EIGHT

Igniting the Spark for Justice and the Politics of Hope

i knew that i was dying.
something in me said, go ahead, die, sleep, become them,
accept.
then something else in me said, no, save the tiniest bit.
it needn't be much, just a spark.
a spark can set a whole forest on fire.
just a spark.
save it.

—Charles Bukowski

We have discussed at length the government's ongoing assaults on our freedoms. We have also studied the fusion of corporate America with government agencies and the subsequent effect on our rights. Now let us turn to the most important players in this unfolding drama—we the people. Where do we fit in? Do we have any say in what happens in our nation? Can we write our own ending? Or are we nothing more than actors in a play whose ending has already been determined?

I, for one, believe that as long as there is a spark of freedom left, there is hope. As the poet Charles Bukowski writes, "a spark can set a whole forest on fire." Our country may be in deep trouble, but there is still something that can be done to remedy the problems. It is understandable that many Americans feel overwhelmed, powerless, and discouraged in the face of the government's expansive powers, unlimited resources, and military might. Even so, that is no excuse for standing silently on the sidelines.

There is no better time to act than the present. Fear, apathy, and escapism will not carry the day. It is within our power to make a difference and seek corrective measures. Yet it is not merely that we should make a difference. Rather, we are compelled—required, if you will—to attempt in a nonviolent way to make a difference. We must be willing, if need be, to stand and fight.

The old African proverb "Even an ant can harm an elephant" speaks to the power of the people to stand against even the mightiest of opponents. The thick-skinned elephant is impervious to most insects and can trample countless ant colonies with its massive form. Yet a single ant will drive an elephant mad if it crawls into the elephant's trunk. If a tiny ant can create such chaos by targeting this vulnerability, imagine what an army of ants—or a nation of dissenters—could achieve.

This book can be a starting point, a handbook for enacting change, but the rest is up to you. I should warn you, however, that there is no ten-step plan to revolution, no top-ten list of issues that must be challenged, and no easy formula for success. As any activist can tell you, each situation is often completely without precedent. Nevertheless, the key to making a difference is in understanding that the first step begins with you. As Mahatma Gandhi said, "We need to be the change we wish to see in the world."[1]

WHAT CAN YOU DO?

While there is no how-to book for taking a stand against the loss of our freedoms and effectively resisting authoritarianism, there are certain things that are common to every successful struggle.

1. *Get educated.* Before you can stand and fight, you must understand what you're fighting for and what you will be going up against. Without knowledge, very little can be accomplished. Thus, you must know your rights. Take time to read the Constitution, something very few Americans have ever done. In particular, study *A Freedom Manifesto*, which follows this chapter. Study and understand history because the tales of those who seek power and those who resist it, as you will see, is an age-old one. The Declaration of Independence is a testament to this struggle and the revolutionary spirit that overcame tyranny. Understand the vital issues of the day so that you can

be cognizant of the threats to freedom. Stay informed about current events and legislation by way of television, the Internet, and a variety of newspapers. A good place to start is by availing yourself of books such as this one, as well as the books and articles cited in the endnotes to this book.

2. *Get involved.* One of the most important contributions an individual citizen can make is to become actively involved in local community affairs, politics, and legal battles. As the adage goes, "Think globally, act locally." America was meant to be primarily a system of local governments, which is a far cry from the colossal federal bureaucracy we have today. Yet if our freedoms are to be restored, understanding what is transpiring practically in your own backyard—in one's home, neighborhood, school district, town council—and taking action at that local level must be the starting point. Responding to unmet local needs and reacting to injustices is what grassroots activism is all about. Getting involved in local politics is one way to bring about change. This could mean running for office, attending and becoming actively involved in party conventions where grass-roots decisions are made, or serving on various commissions or political committees. I have seen instances where one person sitting on a local city council or zoning commission tipped the balance on crucial issues.

Short of running for office, personal contact with your local, state, and public officials is vital. Seek out opportunities to voice your concerns and call on your government representatives to account for their actions. Call, write letters, sign petitions, visit their offices—do whatever it takes to get their attention and remind them that they are your representatives and, thus, accountable to you. In all my years of working with various members of Congress, it has never ceased to amaze me how little input these men and women receive from the average citizen before casting their vote on legislation that will inevitably impact their constituents. One of the most powerful tools available to the individual, and individuals organized as a group, is the ballot box. If your representatives do not heed your advice on the central issues, then work to unseat them. This may involve running your own candidate. In this way, the ordinary citizen can affect the political process. Do not, however, make the mistake of thinking that politics is the only avenue for enacting change. Sometimes, you will need to take direct action rather than waiting on the bureaucrats to make a move. For example, establish a soup kitchen or shelter to help the poor. Start a recycling and street clean-up program to address problems with pollution and waste management.

3. *Get organized.* In going up against a more powerful adversary, it is critical that you understand your strengths and weaknesses and tap into your resources. Remember the analogy of the elephant and the ant: you can overcome the behemoth with enough cunning, skill, and organization. Play to your strengths and assets. Conduct strategy sessions to develop both the methods and ways to attack the elephant. Prioritize your issues and battles. Don't limit yourself to protests and paper petitions. Think outside the box. Time is short, and resources are limited, so use your resources in the way they count the most.

4. *Be creative.* Be bold and imaginative, for this is guerilla warfare—not to be fought with tanks and guns but through creative methods of dissent and resistance. Creatively responding to circumstances will often be one of your few resources if you are to be an effective agent of change. Every creative effort, no matter how small, is significant. As Jason Salzman points out in his book *Making the News*, "You need to nurture a war-room attitude, infused with creativity."[2] Salzman asks, "Would you dress in a pink ostrich costume and tell politicians to get their heads out of the sand? Or, if you were kicked out of a mall for breast-feeding, would you fight back and stage a 'breast-feed-in' with forty nursing moms—and the media—in tow?...If you opposed the Iraq war, would you find forty-nine other people, strip naked, and spell 'peace' with your bodies? Would you deliver manure to politicians and tell them they are full of !!**@??!!."[3]

You might be hesitant to do such things, but others, as you will see, were not. They succeeded in getting their point across when more traditional methods might have been less effective. This is what it means to think outside of the box. Even with limited resources, such creative acts will not only get people's attention, they will also attract the media's attention and help you get your message to a larger audience. "The most imaginative and theatrical people are going to win," remarked Colin Covert, a feature reporter at the *Star Tribune* in Minneapolis. "Don't expect good intentions to get you space. The fact that you're trying to fight cancer is great, but it's not news. If you do something interesting, we'll write about it."[4]

5. *Use the media.* Effective use of the media is essential. Attracting media coverage not only enhances and magnifies your efforts, it is also a valuable education tool. It publicizes your message to a much wider audience. It is through the media—television, newspapers, Internet sites, bloggers, and so on—that people find out about your growing resistance movement. Media coverage also alerts the people to many issues they may not otherwise know about. As Salzman notes, "Successful media campaigns are, above all else, entertaining. That doesn't necessarily mean amusing. In fact, some successful media campaigns are disgusting. But whether amusing or disgusting—they are engaging, and that is the key synonym for entertainment in the news business."[5]

Examples abound of individuals who use creative methods to raise awareness and get their message heard. For instance, it was New York's Working Families Party that dressed an activist as an ostrich to illustrate how various politicians have their "heads in the sand" over various issues such as the economy.[6] Hoping to raise awareness about the unfairness of their high utility bills, residents of a semirural area in Oregon attempted to pay their bills in pennies, chickens, and the shirts off their backs. A local TV station caught it on film.[7] The Coalition to Stop Gun Violence generated national coverage when it assembled 40,000 pairs of shoes of citizens killed by guns on the

National Mall in Washington DC. An ordinary rally might not have been half as effective.[8] In these ways, as Salzman rightly notes, activists move "social ills from behind locked doors into the public domain—into our communal backyard."[9]

6. *Start brushfires for freedom.* Take heart that you are not alone. You come from a long, historic line of individuals who have put their beliefs and lives on the line to keep freedom alive. What's more, recognize that you don't have to go it alone. Engage those around you in discussions about issues of importance. Challenge them to be part of a national dialogue. As I have often said, one person at a city-planning meeting with a protest sign is an irritant. Three individuals at the same meeting with the same sign are a movement. You will find that those in power fear and respect numbers. This is not to say that lone crusaders are not important. There are times when you will find yourself totally alone in the stand you take. However, an army of ants creates the impression that, not only are you not alone, but that something bigger is involved. There is power in numbers. Politicians understand this. So get out there and start drumming up support for your cause.

7. *Take action.* Be prepared to mobilize at a moment's notice. It doesn't matter who you are, where you're located, or what resources are at your disposal. What matters is that you recognize the problems and care enough to do something about them. Whether you're eight, twenty-eight, or eighty-eight years old, you have something unique to contribute. Radford Lyons certainly did his part to raise awareness about contaminated well water in Pike County, Kentucky. Appearing at a public hearing where a debate was underway over extending water lines out to homes in an area of contaminated wells, the eight-year-old pressed the point home when he offered hearing officials free lemonade made from the contaminated well water. By the end of the hearing, one official had promised to have the lines constructed.[10] As young Radford proved, you don't have to be a hero. You just have to show up and be ready to take action.

8. *Be forward-looking.* Beware of being so "in the moment" that you neglect to think of the bigger picture. Develop a vision for the future. Is what you're hoping to achieve enduring? Have you developed a plan to continue to educate others about the problems you're hoping to tackle and ensure that others will continue in your stead? Take the time to impart the value of freedom to younger generations, for they will be at the vanguard of these battles someday.

9. *Develop fortitude.* What is it that led to the successful protest movements of the past headed by people such as Martin Luther King Jr.? Resolve. King refused to be put off. When the time came, he was willing to take to the streets for what he believed and even go to jail if necessary. King risked having an arrest record by committing acts of nonviolent civil disobedience. That's how much he cared about his fellow human beings. He was willing to sacrifice himself. But first, he had to develop the intestinal fortitude to give him the strength to stand and fight. If you decide that you don't have the requisite fortitude, find someone who does and back them. A caveat is appropriate here. Before resorting to nonviolent civil disobedience, all reasonable alternatives should be exhausted. If there is an opportunity to alter the course of events through normal channels (for example, negotiation, legal action, or legislation), they should be attempted.

10. *Be selfless and sacrificial.* Freedom is not free—there is always a price to be paid and a sacrifice to be made. If any movement is to be truly successful, it must be manned by individuals who seek a greater good and do not waver from their purposes. It will take boldness, courage, and great sacrifice. Rarely will fame, power, and riches be found at the end of this particular road. Those who travel it inevitably find the way marked by hardship, persecution, and strife. Yet there is no easy way. As the abolitionist Frederick Douglass remarked in an 1857 speech:

The whole history of the progress of human liberty shows that all concessions yet made to her august claims have been born of earnest struggle. The conflict has been exciting, agitating, all-absorbing, and for the time being, putting all other tumults to silence. It must do this or it does nothing. If there is no struggle there is no progress. Those who profess to favor freedom and yet deprecate agitation are men who want crops without plowing up the ground; they want rain without thunder and lightning. They want the ocean without the awful roar of its many waters. This struggle may be a moral one, or it may be a physical one, and it may be both moral and physical, but it must be a struggle. Power concedes nothing without a demand. It never did and it never will.[11]

11. *Remain optimistic and keep hope alive.* Although our rights are increasingly coming under attack, we still have certain freedoms. We can still fight back. We have the right to dissent, to protest, and even to vigorously criticize or oppose the government and its laws. The Constitution guarantees us these rights. In a country such as the United States, a citizen armed with knowledge of the Bill of Rights and the fortitude to stand and fight can be that single ant that overcomes the elephant. But it will mean speaking out when others are silent. It won't be easy, but take heart. And don't give up. Practice persistence, along with perseverance, and the possibilities are endless. You can be the voice of reason. Use your voice to encourage others. Much can be accomplished by merely speaking out. Oftentimes, all it takes is one lone voice to get things started. So if you really care and you're serious and want to help change things for the better, dust off your First Amendment tools and take a stand—even if it means being ostracized by those who would otherwise support you.

SPIRIT OF RESISTANCE

Now that you have a better understanding of the key ingredients required in becoming an active citizen, it is time to take a closer look at some of the people and groups that have put these principles into action. Anthony Griffin is a good example.

Griffin, an African American attorney, challenged the prejudices of both African Americans and Caucasians when he defended the First Amendment rights of the Ku Klux Klan.[12] A small town in Texas, described by some as home to many fierce racists, was under a federal court order to integrate public housing.[13] African Americans who moved into the town, however, soon found themselves under such pressure and intimidation that they felt forced to leave. The Ku Klux Klan (KKK) quickly came under suspicion as the source of the threatening tactics. In order to confirm these suspicions, the Texas Commission on Human Rights decided to find out if any members of the Klan actually lived in this town. In 1993, the Commission went to court in an attempt to get the membership list of the Texas Knights of the KKK. The Klan immediately sought the help of the American Civil Liberties Union (ACLU) to protect the names of its members.

At that time, Griffin served as a volunteer lawyer for the Texas ACLU, as well as general counsel for the National Association for the Advancement of Colored People (NAACP) in Texas. When he agreed to take the ACLU case representing the KKK, Griffin lost his position with the Texas NAACP. In 1958, however, the NAACP had taken the state of Alabama all the way to the U.S. Supreme Court in order to protect the names of its members.[14] That case, *NAACP v. Alabama*, was successfully used in the 1970s in Texas—again by the NAACP—to prevent the state from obtaining its membership list. Thus, it seems inconsistent for the Texas NAACP to force Griffin out of its organization for representing the KKK's right to protect its membership list.

Griffin defended his decision to represent the KKK by explaining that the case was not about race; it was about the First Amendment rights of association and free speech. Griffin also pointed out that the First Amendment protects everyone, not just those found to be to our liking. And he said that a law silencing the KKK today would come around and silence the rest of us tomorrow. Griffin eventually won his case. The Texas Supreme Court ruled in favor of the KKK in 1994 by citing *NAACP v. Alabama.*

ORGANIZED RESISTANCE

The point is that one person can make a difference, and a group of highly organized individuals can magnify such an impact. This is why broad networks, coalitions, and movements are important.

Too often, we underestimate the potential strength of those who appear to be weak and powerless. But we would do well to remember that it was a seemingly weak and powerless group of patriots, fueled by immense courage, who established the basis of American freedom. Faced with overwhelming odds, a handful of ragtag rebels resisted the mighty British Empire and planted the seeds of democracy—all rooted in what they believed to be the right to resist illegitimate government actions.

That is what many consider the USA PATRIOT Act to be—an illegitimate government action. As author and journalist Nat Hentoff writes, the erosion of "the Bill of Rights began to be quickened when the president signed the USA Patriot Act."[15] Although the PATRIOT Act was hastily passed in October 2001 by an overwhelming majority in both houses of Congress (356–66 in the House, 98–1 in the Senate), many members, as we have seen, later confessed to barely reading it.

Under the PATRIOT Act as originally passed, many of the freedoms afforded in the Bill of Rights were greatly weakened. In the name of fighting terrorism, government officials were permitted, among other things, to: monitor religious and political institutions with no suspicion of criminal wrongdoing; prosecute librarians or keepers of any other records if they told anyone that the government subpoenaed information related to a terror investigation; monitor conversations between attorneys and clients; search and seize Americans' papers and effects without showing probable cause; and jail Americans indefinitely without a trial.

Pockets of resistance cropped up almost immediately as Americans across the country began to mobilize and fight back. Bill of Rights defense committees, small groups made up of concerned citizens, and community members determined to protect their towns from the government's overly broad reach, led the charge to oppose the PATRIOT Act. Their actions are reminiscent of the prerevolutionary Committees of Correspondence that were initiated by Samuel Adams and other Sons of Liberty in Boston in 1767.

Librarians began shredding their sign-in sheets of people using the computers in order to keep the data from falling into the hands of government agents. Others posted signs warning patrons that federal authorities might review their records. The Montana Library Association passed a resolution saying it considered parts of the PATRIOT Act "a present danger to the constitutional rights and privacy rights of library users."[16] Even young people got into the act. In Santa Cruz, California, some college students checked out any controversial books they could find, including *The Anarchist's Cookbook*, which contains instructions for making bombs. As one student said when interviewed by television analyst Jim Lehrer: "The group checkout was a protest against provisions of the Patriot Act that allow the FBI to more easily examine records in their hunt for foreign terrorists."[17]

The ants finally got the elephant's attention. In 2006, when Congress acted to reauthorize the PATRIOT Act, it included a safeguard that restricted some access by federal agents to library records.

More than four hundred communities and eight states covering 85 million people have passed resolutions affirming their commitment to civil liberties and condemning the PATRIOT Act as a threat to those rights. As of the fall of 2006, there were over 280 efforts under way in other communities to do the same. The town of Telluride, Colorado, placed the following on their welcome sign: "A civil liberties safe zone."

Among the first cities to adopt resolutions opposing the PATRIOT Act were Berkeley, Santa Cruz, and Sebastopol, California; Denver and Boulder, Colorado; Ann Arbor, Michigan; Santa Fe, New Mexico; Eugene, Oregon; Burlington, Vermont; and Madison,

Wisconsin. While the resolutions vary from city to city, they reflect communal criticism of the federal government's heightened powers under the PATRIOT Act. The resolution passed by the people of Madison, Wisconsin, states: "The City of Madison recognizes that such infringement of the constitutionally guaranteed rights of any person, under the color of law, is an abuse of power, a breach of the public trust, a misappropriation of public resources, a violation of civil rights, and is beyond the scope of governmental authority."

Many cities took their resistance beyond mere words. In Berkeley, California, public library director Jackie Griffin purged the records of all the returned books each day and erased the list of websites visited on the library's fifty Internet terminals. Officials in Portland, Oregon, declined to cooperate with federal agents who might have served warrants that would remain secret under the PATRIOT Act. And in Arcata, California, the City Council passed an ordinance barring city workers from enforcing the PATRIOT Act.[18]

"You're either part of the solution," wrote the 1960s African American activist Eldridge Cleaver, "or you're part of the problem."[19] As we see our freedoms increasingly under attack, we can take hope in the fact that communities across America are becoming part of the solution.

No Time for Weeping

Far from feeling powerless, these citizens, librarians, students, and others are doing something to resist the bureaucracy. American history shows that the most effective means of spurring social and political change is often to start protests, rallies, and petition drives that strive to further one's cause. Such public efforts are not only useful in their ability to gain support and band individuals together, they are also more likely to become the center of media attention and public debate.

An example is the American Freedom Campaign (AFC), an organization that strives to "restore our system of checks and balances" in cooperation with groups such as the Center for Constitutional Rights, Human Rights Watch, and others.[20] AFC has called for a new grassroots democracy movement in this time of constitutional crisis and advocates monthly national strikes known as Constitution Days, which began on November 6, 2007. AFC challenges people of all walks of life to participate in mass-action sit-ins in the most public spaces in their communities. They insist that if millions join the strikes, the nation's leaders will have no choice but to respond. While AFC recognizes that garnering support in the millions will not happen overnight, they believe the average American must begin somewhere, anywhere.[21]

Author and journalist Naomi Wolf, a founder of AFC, claims that all democratic movements began with a mere handful of citizens and steadily gained support and fervor. Such national sit-ins, she insists, will undeniably affect the American government—as it "only took three days of a widely observed National Moratorium to strike a real blow to the war in Vietnam."[22] Thus, the AFC and Wolf urge Americans to band together in any way possible: hold house parties, assemble with their neighbors, pass out users' guides to the Constitution, and take to the streets in masses to preserve the American sense of democracy and constitutionality. As Wolf states: "The time for weeping has to stop; the time for confronting must begin."[23]

LONE CRUSADERS

The Iraq war has produced widespread public discontent and led many individual citizens to take a stand against warfare and violence. Vicki Rottman is a sculptor from the state of Colorado. In 2003, Rottman decided to protest the war by standing silently in front of Denver's Wellington E. Webb Municipal Building on a weekly basis.[24] She got the idea from a similar movement that occurred in the late 1980s in the city of Jerusalem. A group of women, referring to themselves as "Women in Black," silently stood at busy city intersections in an attempt to force the public to acknowledge Israel's role in the region's violence and conflict.[25] Rottman claims that the formation of Women in Black opened her eyes to the staggering power of silence and its ability to often speak louder than words. Rottman continues to protest every Thursday in Denver, an action that has incited varying responses from the local population—from encouraging declarations from passing motorists to angry threats and accusations of treachery.

One might well ask what Rottman is accomplishing through her silent protestation. While she may not have made a tangible impact on the direction and strength of the war itself, many local citizens admit that Rottman's persistent efforts have not gone unnoticed. Since beginning her weekly protests, nearly thirty women have joined Rottman, standing silently alongside her every week in front of the city's municipal building. Women in other cities such as Boulder, Colorado, have formed similar groups that strive to voice their disapproval of the war against Iraq through silent assertion. Rottman believes that her efforts will inevitably compel at least a few of her fellow community members to think about the Iraq war in terms of its unnecessary violence and unjust cause. By holding weekly protests, Rottman—in the world of the elephant a very persistent ant—has encouraged others to do the same.

Whether such protests deal with matters regarding the Iraq war or our constitutional freedoms, it is often up to a lone crusader or protester to return such matters of importance to the public eye. On June 29, 2007, Reverend Billy (William Talen) was arrested and charged with two counts of second-degree harassment for reciting the forty-five words of the First Amendment during "Critical Mass." This protest, in New York City's Union Square Park, is a leaderless, unstructured, pro-environmental demonstration against the unfriendly way cities treat bicyclists. Police officers claimed that Talen's recitation was "obnoxious" and served no legitimate purpose.[26] His lawyers strongly disagreed, insisting that "there could hardly be a more legitimate place than a protest rally to recite the First Amendment, with its lines barring Congress from 'abridging the freedom of speech' and guaranteeing the rights 'of the people peaceably to assemble.'"[27] The charges against Talen appeared to be a clear and unjust infringement upon the constitutional rights granted to U.S. citizens by the First Amendment. Well-known for his various protests, Talen is also adept at using the media to magnify his message. Media coverage of the arrest not only raised awareness by informing the public of the injustices that still pervade today's society but also alerted the public to the responsibility and importance of fighting and taking a stand for one's unalienable rights and freedoms.

While Reverend Billy, an avid crusader against large businesses such as Starbucks and the leader of the "Church of Stop Shopping," is no stranger to the media and public spotlight, various small-town citizens have also made an effort to stand up for the rights they believe were intrinsically granted to them by the American Constitution.

In March 2007, Donald Bird, a seventy-two-year-old former Marine and resident of Rancho Tehama, California, was protesting outside his local television station headquarters. He was holding various signs that accused the television staff of being "cowards" for refusing to highlight his ongoing struggle to preserve the rights granted to him by the Constitution.[28] His anger and protests emerged from an incident that occurred two years prior when Bird was issued a speeding ticket and a fine of $192 for going 71 miles per hour in a 55 miles per hour zone. Rather than pay the ticket, Bird requested a trial by jury— a request that was ultimately denied. Bird, who has studied the Constitution at great length, became angry and concerned and cited the Seventh Amendment: "At suits of common law, where the value shall exceed twenty dollars, the right of a trial by jury shall be preserved."

The California legal system has refused to acknowledge Bird's concerns, claiming that California law restricts this constitutional right in cases of petty crimes and minor infractions. Bird has conducted his own singular protests in which he has accused California assemblymen and senators of failing to preserve the Constitution and defend the right of all Americans to be granted its freedoms. While many of Bird's fellow community and legislative members do not agree with his strict interpretation of the Constitution, others admire his willingness to take a stand for what he believes the Constitution embodies and bestows upon the American public. When asked what he hoped to accomplish through his many rallies and protests, Bird replied, "I am hopeful, even if I fail in my endeavor, it might plant the seed for other citizens to stand up for their rights."[29]

REVOLT OF THE GRANDMOTHERS

Grandmothers may seem to be an unlikely group to jumpstart a protest movement. But Grandmothers for Peace, founded in May 1982 by Barbara Wiedner, has become a global phenomenon.

Wiedner's awareness of the proximity of nuclear weapons to her home in Sacramento, California, during the height of the Cold War was the tipping point that spurred her to establish this nonprofit association.[30] She said: "It made me realize that if things did not change, my precious grandchildren could be part of the last generation on earth."[31] This reality check pushed Wiedner to stage weekly protests with others who felt the same way. As the media began to focus attention on her work, there was no turning back. The unique voice that emerged began to gain its own universal appeal.[32]

The organization is composed of two different kinds of members: the activists and the "stay at home" members. The activists are involved publicly with spreading the association's message—they participate in protests, marches, speeches, and the publication of newsletters to alert the public about what they stand for. The "stay at home" members keep in contact with elected officials, establish petitions, teach their loved ones the peaceful message, and fundraise.

As Grandmothers for Peace volunteers increased, it branched off into subgroups that protest for even more specific concerns. One subgroup that has gained a lot of attention is "Grandmothers Against the War," which was founded in November 2003 by Joan Wile. This group, which protests America's involvement in the Iraq war, took aim at President Bush, telling him he should stop "his illegal, immoral, indefensible, insane presence in Iraq."[33] They have branches throughout the country, but the city where they have made headlines is New York.

These women, who are totally dedicated to their campaign, hold demonstrative vigils every Wednesday in front of Rockefeller Center to show their antiwar sentiments.[34] As seventy-four-year-old Wile said, "I have totally, totally involved myself in this full-time for the past two and a half years."[35] And although not all the members have grandchildren, this has yet to slow down their enthusiasm for the cause at hand. They believe all grandchildren need this protection because "the world is a safer place 'in grandma's arms.'"[36]

These grannies stirred up things in New York City in October 2005 when they attempted to enlist in the United States military but were denied the opportunity. In protest, they sat down (some with more difficulty than others) in front of the entrance to the Times

Square military recruiting booth. They were soon charged with disorderly conduct and led away to jail.[37] Their incarceration, which lasted four to five hours, was of a different sort than most inmates. They were given somewhat special treatment, clearly because of their age and physical ability. All the grannies were placed in the women's section of the prison, and those who could not make it upstairs were kept on the ground floor. Throughout their entire stay, "morale was high with much laughter and chanting throughout the cell block."[38]

The New York Civil Liberties Union represented the arrested members in court. The judge set to rule on their case had found another similar group guilty for the same kind of action, and the grannies were ready to take whatever consequences were allotted to them.

After several days in the courtroom, including a chance for each charged member to have her say on the stand, Judge Neil E. Ross of the Manhattan Criminal Court found all eighteen grandmothers not guilty.[39] The judge said that "there was evidence to support the grannies' contention that they were not blocking the doorway to the recruitment center during their sit-in; anyone who so desired had free access."[40]

Although they won their case, the grannies still have a major war to fight. In addition to the Iraq war, Grandmothers Against the War has also taken on issues that are presently plaguing our nation, such as the dangers of nuclear power plants, radioactive waste, nuclear testing, the nuclearization and weaponization of space, and global militarism.[41]

These grannies vow to continue to fight for the issues that matter most, the concerns that most closely affect the family and the ones in which their grandchildren are not able to participate. These senior citizens agree on two points: it is their responsibility, rather than their grandchildren's, to make this message heard because "they're busy; we're retired."[42] They also concur that "they have reached a wonderful stage of life called: nothing left to lose."[43]

Political opposition has been a practice implemented throughout American history. Sometimes it is successful; at other times, it fails miserably. Different tactics have been used in order to spread messages that citizens feel are important. The Grandmothers Against the War have chosen to peaceably demonstrate and, if need be, practice civil disobedience. Whether they succeed in convincing one person or one million, the grannies continue undeterred in their mission. Such committed citizens put into practice principles that have roots as far back as the American Revolution.

A GOOD DOSE OF REALISM

As these vigilant citizens illustrate, it is important that individual Americans take a stand for their beliefs, causes, and freedoms. It is also imperative that the individual members of the American public fulfill their responsibilities as citizens—to preserve the rights granted to them and to influence and educate others in a way that may ultimately change the course of future policies and ideologies. At the same time, we must take care to remember that when we take a stand for what is right, we will not always "win" in the traditional sense. Winning is not why we stand and fight. We stand and fight for our convictions, for our rights, and for each other because, regardless of the anticipated impact and support of others, it is the right thing to do.

However, to be effective in standing and fighting the bureaucracy requires a good dose of realism. Although the opportunities for small victories are enormous, they often come with setbacks and great pain. This means that the question "What can I do?" must be realistically faced in terms of exactly where and who you are, what your capabilities might be, and what you want to accomplish. But it is essential to combine realistic expectations with high aspirations. To be an effective agent for change instead of merely a reactor, you must raise your aspirations far beyond the level of current expectations. In other words, aim high and let your reach exceed your grasp.

The shrewdest people in power—both government and corporate—understand this distinction. "That is why they level furious attacks against any high aspirations in general, and personal attacks against anyone who tries to articulate them specifically," notes Bertram Gross. "If articulated aspirations are broad enough to include the needs of the great majority of people, it may be more difficult to carry out the old divide-and-rule strategies. Instead of trying to get what they need and want, the reasoning goes, people should be brainwashed into wanting what they get. More apathy by the masses, they seem convinced, is the prerequisite for preserving democratic machinery."[44]

"TRUTH" IN MEDIA

The media certainly play a part in contributing to our apathy, "dumbing down" our populace and spoon-feeding us their particular take on current events. Anyone who relies exclusively on television news reporting for in-depth insight into what's happening in the world is making a serious mistake. Since Americans have, by and large, become nonreaders and primarily viewers of television, it has become an inescapable necessity for most that if they desire information on current events, they get it from watching TV news shows.

TV news networks, having fallen prey to the demands of a celebrity-obsessed and entertainment-driven culture, often provide viewers with what they want to see, rather than what is newsworthy. There tends to be little deviation among the networks. More time is often spent titillating and entertaining viewers with such "news" stories as Britney Spears's custody battle, Paris Hilton's recovery, and O. J. Simpson's latest skirmish with the law than educating them about pressing issues of concern

We have become accustomed to entertainment items presented as important breaking news. At the same time, critical news stories dealing with warfare, economics, and governance are often presented as entertainment items of a lesser sort. This is a reflection of the networks' misplaced priorities and sensibilities. While they cover the scandals involving celebrities for weeks, far less time is devoted to harder-hitting issues such as crime, welfare, homelessness, wars, and government corruption and accountability—and the countless other issues you should have been aware of without having to read about them in this book.

The lack of discernment on the part of television news watchers also plays a part. Surveys of viewing patterns indicate that, in an average household, the television set is in use over seven hours a day. Most people, believing themselves to be in control of the process, are scarcely bothered by this statistic. But it is a false sense of control. The fact is that television not only delivers programs to your home, it also delivers you to a sponsor. The fundamental point of television in America, including television news programs, is to get you to watch so that networks, performers, and others can increase their profits. That is why so-called news events are commingled with a bevy of vacuous entertainment items. It is to keep you glued to the set so that a product can be sold to you. Except for rare cases, television, it must be remembered, is not a public service. It is a business designed to make money.

This does not mean that television news is not important. There are things the public must know, whether they "like" it or not. This is a necessity in a democratic society. TV news should give people what they need, however, not necessarily what they want.

There are things that can be done to help you understand TV news. In their insightful book, *How to Watch TV News*, New York University professor Neil Postman and television journalist Steve Powers analyze some of them.[45]

First, it is important to recognize that TV news is not always a true reflection of the most critical things that happen in the world. Rather, it is what someone labeled a "journalist" or "correspondent" thinks is worth reporting.

Second, television personalities would prefer that you trust them, but it is in your best interests to judge and analyze what is reported. Although there are some very good TV journalists, the old art of investigative reporting has largely gone by the wayside. How often have you heard a reporter preface a "news" report with the statement, "This comes from official sources"? What this often means is that the government is speaking directly to you through a reporter. It cannot be trusted since the government has thousands of spin doctors whose job it is to present the government in the best possible light.

Third, as Postman and Powers argue, TV news is not communication but broadcast. It is, in other words, entertainment. Communication is between equals. And when you are being spoon-fed by advertisers, you are in no way equal. Although the news may have value, it is primarily a commodity to gather an audience, which will be sold to advertisers. That is why the program is called a news "show." It means that the so-called news is delivered as a form of entertainment. "In the case of most news shows," write Postman and Powers, "the package includes attractive anchors, an exciting musical theme, comic relief (usually from the weather people, especially men), stories placed to hold the audience, the creation of the illusion of intimacy, and so on. The point of this kind of show is that no one is expected to take the news too seriously. For one thing, tomorrow's news will have nothing to do with today's news."[46]

Fourth, never underestimate the power of commercials, especially to news audiences. People who watch the news tend to be more attentive, educated, and have more money to spend. They are a prime market for advertisers, and sponsors are willing to spend millions on well-produced commercials. Such commercials are often longer in length than most news stories and cost more to produce than the news stories themselves. And the content of many commercials, which often contradicts the messages of the news stories, cannot be ignored. Many commercials are aimed at prurient interests in advocating materialism, sex, overindulgence, pharmaceutical drugs, etc., which can have a demoralizing effect on viewers, especially children.

For various reasons, it is important to learn about the economic and political interests of those who own the "corporate" media. There are few truly independent news sources. In fact, corporate empires own the major news outlets. General Electric owns the entire stable of NBC shows, including MSNBC, which it co-owns with Microsoft (the "MS" in MSNBC stands for Microsoft).[47] Both GE and Microsoft have poured millions of dollars into political campaigns.[48] CBS is owned by Westinghouse, while Disney, which according to data compiled by the Federal Election Commission gave over $2.7 million to political campaigns during the 2000 and 2002 election cycles, owns ABC.[49] CNN is owned by the multinational corporation Time-Warner, while media mogul Rupert Murdoch owns Fox News Channel.[50]

The obvious question: How can a news network present objective news on a candidate that it financially supports? "One doesn't have to be a Marxist," note Postman and Powers, "to assume that people making a million dollars a year will see things differently from people struggling to make ends meet."[51] This is why it is so vitally important to get your news from more than one source. There are independent television news channels and shows that present a different view than what is seen on the corporate news networks. The Internet also provides a tremendous variety of news sources. There are some debate and interview shows on television and radio that provide alternative news. And there are local and national newspapers that provide a good source of information on current events.

Pay special attention to the language of newscasts. Because film footage and other visual imagery are so engaging on TV news shows, viewers are apt to allow language—what the reporter is saying about the images—to go unexamined. A TV newscaster's language frames the pictures, and, therefore, the meaning we derive from the picture is often determined by the reporter's commentary. TV by its very nature manipulates viewers. One must never forget that every television minute has been edited. The viewer does not see the actual event but the edited form of the event. Add to that the fact that the reporters editing the film have a subjective view—sometimes determined by their corporate bosses—that enters into the picture. When we see a political figure such as the president on TV, we are not seeing the person as he necessarily is. We are often seeing the image that his handlers have decided we should see. This generally goes for all politicians.

We would all do well to reduce by at least one-third the amount of TV news we watch. TV news generally consists of "bad" news—wars, torture, murders, scandals, and so forth. It cannot possibly do you any harm to excuse yourself each week from much of the mayhem projected at you on the news. Do not form your concept of reality based on television. TV news, it must be remembered, does not reflect normal everyday life. Studies indicate that a heavy viewing of TV news makes people think the world is much more dangerous than it actually is. One "study indicates that watching television, including news shows, makes people somewhat more depressed than they otherwise would be," say Postman and Powers.[52] This may lead to chronic depression and a constant state of alarm. There is, however, a bevy of commercials pitching drugs at you that allegedly relieve the anxiety and depression.

One of the reasons people are addicted to watching TV news is that they feel they must have an opinion on almost everything, which gives the illusion of participation in American life. But an opinion is all that we can gain from TV news because it only presents the most rudimentary and fragmented information on anything. On most issues, we don't actually know much about what is going on, which makes it all but impossible to form a true opinion. We should instead place greater emphasis on reading good books and newspapers and carefully analyzing issues in order to be better informed.

Finally, schools must begin teaching children how to watch TV news. Specific courses should be taught so that our future citizens can hopefully avoid the pitfalls that the television news monolith will continue to lay before coming generations. If not, they will have little clue about what is really happening, not only in their own town or country but in the world as well, and even less control over their futures.

If people strive for greater control over their lives, they will be less apt to be satisfied with so-called reforms that enhance the power of faceless government bureaucrats and corporate oligarchs. And they will be more willing to pitch in and help those already under the gun. The major media, however, will not tell you about most of the acts of dissent and resistance that take place every day in American society—the strikes, protests, and individual acts of courage in the face of authority, such as with many of the individuals already discussed.

There are more instances of citizen unrest and protest than we are led to believe. That is why it is important to read newspapers and magazines, search the Internet, and watch alternative and public access television news programs. For the few instances found, take comfort in the fact that there are likely hundreds more unreported acts of people standing for justice.

WHAT KIND OF REVOLUTIONARY WILL YOU BE?

The time to act is now. Martin Luther King Jr. eloquently addressed this need for urgency in the face of injustice and oppression in his "Letter from Birmingham City Jail." Dr. King wrote this stirring essay on April 16, 1963, while serving a sentence for participating in civil rights demonstrations in Birmingham, Alabama—one of the most racially segregated cities in the country at the time. Although King rarely bothered to defend himself against his opponents, he put pen to paper when eight prominent "liberal" Alabama clergypersons, all white, published an open letter castigating King for inciting civil disturbances through nonviolent resistance. The clergymen called on King to let the local and federal courts deal with the question of integration. King, however, understood that if justice and freedom were to prevail, African Americans could not afford to be long-suffering. Quoting U.S. Supreme Court Justice Thurgood Marshall, King wrote, "Justice too long delayed is justice denied."[53] Action was needed immediately. In his letter, King declared:

> We are caught in an inescapable network of mutuality, tied in a single garment of destiny. Whatever affects one directly affects all indirectly. Never again can we afford to live with the narrow, provincial "outside agitator" idea. Anyone who lives in the United States can never be considered an outsider anywhere in this country....Nonviolent direct action seeks to create such a crisis and establish such creative tension that a community that has constantly refused to negotiate is forced to confront the issue. It seeks so to dramatize the issue that it can no longer be ignored....We know through painful experience that freedom is never voluntarily given by the oppressor; it must be demanded by the oppressed....You express a great deal of anxiety over our willingness to break laws. This is certainly a legitimate concern....One may well ask, "How can you advocate breaking some laws and obeying others?" The answer is found in the fact that there are two types of laws: there are just and there are unjust laws. I would agree with Saint Augustine that "An unjust law is no law at all." ... Any law that uplifts human personality is just. Any law that degrades human personality is unjust....I submit that an individual who breaks a law that conscience tells him is unjust, and willingly accepts the penalty by staying in jail to arouse the conscience of the community over its injustice, is in reality expressing the

very highest respect for law....We can never forget that everything Hitler did in Germany was "legal" and everything the Hungarian freedom fighters did in Hungary was "illegal." It was "illegal" to aid and comfort a Jew in Hitler's Germany. But I am sure that if I had lived in Germany during that time I would have aided and comforted my Jewish brothers even though it was illegal....It is the strangely irrational notion that there is something in the very flow of time that will inevitably cure all ills. Actually time is neutral. It can be used either destructively or constructively. I am coming to feel that the people of ill will have used time much more effectively than the people of good will....But as I continued to think about the matter I gradually gained a bit of satisfaction from being considered an extremist. Was not Jesus an extremist in love—"Love your enemies, bless them that curse you, pray for them that despitefully use you." ... Was not Abraham Lincoln an extremist—"This nation cannot survive half slave and half free." Was not Thomas Jefferson an extremist— "We hold these truths to be self-evident, that all men are created equal." So the question is not whether we will be extremist but what kind of extremist will we be. Will we be extremists for hate or will we be extremists for love?[54]

The word "extremist" has taken on negative connotations over the years, but it is appropriate here. When talking about a revolution, there can be no room for timidity or lukewarm emotions. What we need is passion and dedication and courage. We need the sort of idealism that Martin Luther King Jr. embodied.

TEASPOON OF RESISTANCE

Idealism is a frame of mind. It is staring into the face of adversity and offering positives. In a world steeped in pessimism, where our minds are continually bombarded with superfluous, vacuous information and truth seems unwelcome, it is difficult to remain idealistic. But if you are to have any impact at all, you must maintain your idealism. Sometimes it will be all that is left to inspire hope and keep the flames of freedom burning.

Consider the renowned classic folksinger and writer Pete Seeger. Because of his activism, Seeger was targeted by the American government and was blacklisted during the McCarthy era of the 1950s. In 1955, the House Committee on Un-American Activities subpoenaed Seeger to appear before them. During the hearings, Seeger refused to disclose his political views and the names of his political associates. When asked by the committee to name for whom he had sung, Seeger replied, "I am saying voluntarily that I have sung for almost every religious group in the country, from Jewish and Catholic, and Presbyterian and Holy Rollers and Revival Churches, and I do this voluntarily. I have sung for many, many different groups—and it is hard for perhaps one person to believe, I was looking back over the twenty years or so that I have sung around these forty-eight states, that I have sung in so many different places."

Seeger was sentenced to one year in jail but, citing the First Amendment, successfully appealed the decision after spending four hours behind bars. He was also heavily involved in the African American civil rights movement and, through his songs, inspired a generation of activists. Despite his trials and tribulations over the years, Seeger maintained his idealism. In an interview I conducted with him when he was eighty-six years old, I asked him about his view of life and whether he was, at that age, still an optimist. He replied:

I think if we can learn within the next few decades to face the danger we all are in, I believe there will be tens of millions, maybe hundreds of millions, of human beings working wherever they are to do something good. I tell everybody a little parable about the "teaspoon brigades." Imagine a big seesaw. One end of the seesaw is on the ground because it has a big basket half full of rocks in it. The other end of the seesaw is up in the air because it's got a basket one quarter full of sand. Some of us have teaspoons and we are trying to fill it up. Most people are scoffing at us. They say, "People like you have been trying for thousands of years, but it is leaking out of that basket as fast as you are putting it in." Our answer is that we are getting more people with teaspoons every day. And we believe that one of these days or years—who knows—that basket of sand is going to be so full that you are going to see that whole seesaw going zoop! in the other direction. Then people are going to say, "How did it happen so suddenly?" And we answer, "Us and our little teaspoons over thousands of years." [55]

Pete Seeger's work is not done. There are countless others who have kept hope alive through their teaspoons of resistance. During the years when apartheid resister Nelson Mandela was in a South African prison with no hope of release, he and fellow prisoners devised small ways to defy the powers that be. "They smuggled messages and newspaper headlines cell-to-cell on scraps of toilet paper, sang or whistled freedom songs to raise their morale, and kept their dignity until even some of the guards began to show them respect." [56] They did this for twenty-seven years, "making a way out of no way," to borrow the phrase of sociologist Joseph Scott. [57]

As they resisted the Communists, the early human rights activists in Czechoslovakia faced ridicule and scorn, especially in their efforts to free political prisoners. Petitions they circulated demanding the release of dissidents had no success. But when the prisoners were finally released, they said the "mere fact that others had taken up their cause had sustained them during their incarceration." [58]

When Henry David Thoreau wrote, "Plant the seed of hope and caring and leave the garden to God," he was dismissed by many as eccentric. [59] Thoreau's essay "Civil Disobedience," however, was read by Leo Tolstoy. In turn, Mahatma Gandhi read Tolstoy. Martin Luther King Jr. read Gandhi, and millions were inspired to act during the civil rights movement by the words of King. [60]

In the 1840s, Wendell Phillips was a lone voice speaking out against slavery. Even though his cause seemed hopeless, he rode from home to home on horseback to urge Quakers to stop being slave owners because owning slaves was incompatible with Quaker principles. After hearing one of his passionate speeches condemning slavery as a "moral outrage," a friend asked, "Why are you so on fire?" To this, Phillips responded, "I am on fire because I have mountains of ice before me to melt."[61]

In the early 1960s, a small group of women and children held a demonstration in front of the White House to protest nuclear testing. Rain poured down, and no one seemed to notice them. Cold and frustrated, the protesters felt as though they were wasting their time. A few years later during a major march against nuclear testing, the keynote speaker told the crowd how he came to be involved in the issue. While driving through Washington DC one miserable rainy day, he noticed a group of women and children huddled in front of the White House protesting nuclear testing, and he was moved to take action.[62]

Every day, a solitary man stood with a protest sign at the entrance of a laboratory where work was being done on nuclear weapons. By silently standing at the entrance, all who passed were forced to consider the meaning of their life's work. A senior official said the presence of this lone protester played a significant role in his eventual decision to resign his job.[63]

The lesson is obvious: with the right attitude, anyone can make a difference. As Mahatma Gandhi once said, "What you do may seem terribly insignificant, but it is terribly important that you do it anyway."[64]

ONE PERSON COUNTS

Anyone, as history shows, can begin the process of change. We have seen this illustrated by the courageous people profiled throughout this book.

Rosa Parks is one person who made a difference in the civil rights movement. On December 1, 1955, this forty-three-year-old seamstress from Montgomery, Alabama, was returning home after a hard day's work. Riding in a crowded bus, she was sitting directly behind the white section, which was fully occupied. When more whites entered the bus, the driver ordered the African Americans to move further back to make room for the favored Caucasians. Although this was the established custom for African Americans, Parks decided that she would no longer be subservient to the powers that be and refused to move. The bus driver called the police, who arrested Parks. A few days later, the Montgomery Improvement Association, led by the Reverend Martin Luther King Jr., organized an African American boycott of all city buses. (The inspiration for this act of civil disobedience took place half a century earlier and half a world away. In 1893, Gandhi, sitting in a South African railroad car, was asked to move to make way for whites. Gandhi refused and was forcibly ejected. Gandhi's boycotts and nonviolent campaigns against the British domination of India greatly influenced Martin Luther King Jr.'s efforts at civil disobedience.)

Within a few years' time, civil rights boycotts and demonstrations—often involving whites as well—were being staged in hundreds of cities in the South and other parts of the country. The ants were organizing. However, while Rosa Parks has been credited with being the "Mother of the Modern-Day Civil Rights Movement," she wasn't solely responsible for putting the wheels of justice in motion. As former presidential advisor Bertram Gross explains, "Rosa Parks's refusal was a culmination of thousands of beginnings, some of which were recorded, most of which were forgotten, over many years; here was the unpredictable outcome of thousands of sparks that flickered briefly and at the time seemed to have no consequences."[65] Gross continues:

> *In the same city of Montgomery a few years earlier Vernon Jones, an African American preacher, had refused to vacate his seat under similar circumstances—and had gotten away with it. Also, the boycott led by Martin Luther King had had its origins in the responses of other lesser-known—and now unremembered—African Americans who felt that something must be done this time. In turn, King's vigorous leadership of the boycott*

*goes back to the wave of hope that swept over the South
after May 31, 1954, when the Supreme Court, responding to many years of pressure by the National Association for the Advancement of Colored People, ordered
school desegregation "with all deliberate speed."*[66]

As the 1960s dawned, it became clear that the courageous responses of thousands of African Americans to injustice were changing the course of history.

Defying the law—even committing civil disobedience—can alter
the law, as in the landmark case *Edwards v. South Carolina.*[67] On
March 2, 1961, nearly two hundred African Americans gathered at
Zion Baptist Church in Columbia, South Carolina. Carrying plac-
ards and picket signs, they marched without incident to the state capital grounds to express their grievances "to the citizens of South
Carolina, along with the Legislative Bodies of South Carolina."[68] The
objective of the demonstration was to protest the ill treatment of
African American citizens. U.S. Supreme Court Justice Potter Stewart described the situation:

*As they entered [the Capitol grounds] they were told
by the law enforcement officials that they had a right
as a citizen to go through the State House grounds,
as any other citizen has, as long as they were peaceful.
During the next half hour or 45 minutes, the[y] ...
walked in single file or two abreast in an orderly way
through the grounds.*[69]

The picketers peaceably assembled and expressed their grievances.
Not until they were told by the police to disband did they do more.
As Justice Stewart wrote: "Even then, they sang patriotic and religious songs after one of their leaders had delivered a religious
harangue. There was no violence or threat of violence on their part,
or on the part of ... the crowd."[70]

The protesters, because of their refusal to disband, were all
charged with a "breach of the peace." The mass arrest of 179 African

Americans was challenged in court, and the South Carolina Supreme Court ultimately upheld the arrests. On appeal, the U.S. Supreme Court overturned the validity of the arrests, stating that the "circumstances in this case reflect an exercise of these basic constitutional rights in their most pristine and classic form."[71]

As demonstrations spread, the governmental bureaucracy was forced to make a fundamental change in the law and alter the social and cultural landscape of America. This resulted in the Civil Rights Act of 1964, which was signed into law on July 2 by President Lyndon Johnson, with Martin Luther King Jr. standing by his side.

FASCISM?

Martin Luther King Jr. was one of the first to recognize that as a nation we seem to have significantly passed from a nation of laws to a nation of men. Whereas the United States Constitution was once the rule of law, guarding our freedoms and shielding us from government abuses, many have now largely abdicated their duties as citizens, leaving bureaucrats and corporate entities to steer our ship of state. "This is the first time in our history," writes Catholic University professor Morris Berman, "that we rewrote the law to make torture legal, or seriously contemplated canceling a presidential election. Nor has there been any widespread objection on the part of the American people to these developments. Indeed, the dust settled on them fairly quickly; they too just became part of the 'natural' political landscape."[72]

In an address to the nation shortly after 9/11, George W. Bush remarked: "That spirit of optimism and courage still beckons people across the world who want to come here. And that spirit of optimism and courage must guide those fortunate enough to live here."[73] Sounding like such predecessors as John F. Kennedy, President Bush's point was that we are living in an age of optimism, much like some of those bygone eras of the past. Yet this is a far cry from the reality of the world in which we live, where self-interest, privatization, and corporatization continue to triumph over the rule of law.

If we really want to combat terrorism while maintaining the freedoms given to us by the founders in the Constitution and Bill of

Rights, we must reject our cynicism and apathy and resurrect the "spirit of optimism, idealism, and courage" that motivated earlier generations to stand and fight. We can only do that by shifting domestic values from any self-centered concerns to a willingness to sacrifice in order to salvage our freedoms and values.

Were he alive today, King no doubt would be speaking out against the loss of our freedoms and standing against the growth of governmental power. He would be taking the American people to task for their disinterest and apathy, which have empowered government leaders to play fast and loose with the Constitution and the rule of law.

Some view the entrenched uncertainty and apathy exhibited by the majority of Americans as a sign that America is ripe for some sort of fascist government. Such a postulated scenario should not be dismissed lightly.

Chris Hedges, the Pulitzer Prize-winning journalist and former *New York Times* war correspondent, states in *American Fascists*, his book on the emergence of the Christian Right, that fascism has already gained a foothold in American society. By fascism, he means a centralized government that closely aligns with corporate powers to control all aspects of a country's social, economic, military, and governmental structures. Hedges prefaces his book with Umberto Eco's essay, "Eternal Fascism: Fourteen Ways of Looking at a Blackshirt."[74]

Laurence W. Britt, a former corporate executive, compiled a list of fourteen characteristics that have existed in the seven most prominent fascist and proto-fascist states of the twentieth century.[75] Although Britt never claims that the United States is a fascist state, he implies that the nation is more than likely headed in that direction: "Fascism's principles are wafting in the air today, surreptitiously masquerading as something else, challenging everything we stand for. The cliché that people and nations learn from history is not only overused, but also overestimated; often we fail to learn from history, or draw the wrong conclusions. Sadly, historical amnesia is the norm."[76]

What are some of the principles of fascism that we should consider relevant to us today? Britt's list follows:

+ Powerful and continuing expressions of nationalism
+ Disdain for the importance of human rights
+ Identification of enemies/scapegoats as a unifying cause
+ The supremacy of the military/avid militarism
+ Rampant sexism
+ A controlled mass media
+ Obsession with national security
+ Religion and ruling elite tied together
+ Power of corporations protected
+ Power of labor suppressed or eliminated
+ Disdain and suppression of intellectuals and the arts
+ Obsession with crime and punishment
+ Rampant cronyism and corruption
+ Fraudulent elections[77]

In *The End of America: A Letter of Warning to a Young Patriot*, author and political activist Naomi Wolf goes one step further by drawing some ominous parallels with former fascist regimes and our present situation. Wolf's ten steps to creating a dictatorship should elicit a shiver of recognition in all who have been paying close attention, especially over the past few years:

+ Invoke a terrifying internal and external enemy
+ Create secret prisons where torture takes place
+ Develop a thug caste or paramilitary force that is not answerable to the citizens
+ Set up an internal surveillance system
+ Infiltrate citizens' groups
+ Engage in arbitrary detention and release
+ Target key individuals
+ Control the press
+ Declare all dissent to be treason
+ Suspend the rule of the law[78]

It doesn't take a political scientist to recognize that there are ominous parallels to past dictatorial or fascist regimes in America today.

All the social analyses of the "it can never happen here" variety are, as Professor Morris Berman writes, "tied to a critique of popular culture that points to the existence of a large mass of people who are unable to think for themselves, operate out of an emotive basis, confuse entertainment with education, and desperately want to be 'filled' from the outside."[79]

How can we keep any sense of optimism when the government may be headed toward a proto-fascist structure? Simply put, the government must be held to its end of the bargain and forced to practice what it preaches. At the same time, we must be realistic, knowing that confronting the government in an era where governmental power is so expansive will be difficult. This is why it is so important to maintain our idealism. We must remember that despite the awesome powers the president has claimed, the Supreme Court can overrule the chief executive. And Congress, if it exercises constitutional oversight, can limit both presidential actions and Supreme Court decisions. In the end, it is still the people who hold the ultimate power.

Co-Belligerents for Freedom

Although we may not realize it, our strength in taking back the twenty-first century may very well be in bipartisanship. "If progress is to be made on the important issues facing America," write authors Cal Thomas and Bob Beckel, "then common ground is necessary in a system of government dominated by two major parties that have conflicting ideas on most issues."[80] The countermovement of the 1960s, for example, did not take off on the wings of one party, and the same is true now.

From zero tolerance in schools to free speech infringements, federal surveillance and immigration, conservatives and liberals are increasingly finding themselves on the same side. Many partner in opposing zero tolerance and other school-related measures, deferring to the health and well-being of their children. They are jointly fighting to limit the overarching power of law enforcement and remove barriers to free speech, whether it be expanding political speech zones or in regard to other political protests. Many on both sides have increasingly opposed such federal legislation as the USA PATRIOT Act.

One thing is definitely clear: in a day and age when the government often poses dire threats to our freedoms, Americans need to stop rallying around political parties and start rallying around the Constitution. Liberty is a fragile commodity. People must be informed about their rights, realizing that democracy is not self-executing. We have to do it together.

We need a new national mood. We need to join together, no matter our beliefs or ideologies, and devote ourselves to ensuring that the liberties guaranteed to us in the Bill of Rights are secured for future generations. Either we believe in an open and free society, or we do not. If not, then the alternative is a controlled, authoritarian society.

There are hopeful signs—some of which are illustrated by the courageous citizens profiled in this book, among others. People are making a difference in their communities. Simply picking up a copy of the *Washington Post* on an ordinary Saturday in July can demonstrate that the tide may be turning. In Dumfries, Virginia, a small town about thirty miles from Washington DC, police chief Calvin Johnson wrote an apology to a few homeless men for throwing out their belongings during a raid of an illegal homeless camp in the woods.[81] Although the officers were just doing their job, the police department made efforts to replace the belongings that were discarded. The department stressed that "this was not the way the town wanted to be known, not the way it wanted to act."[82] Upon hearing of the raid, fifteen community members phoned the department and offered to donate clothes and shaving kits. One of these bags met a raid victim with a note reading, "From a neighbor. Good Luck." This story portrays how a community's acts of compassion go a long way.

Countless community efforts are making a difference. In Manassas, Virginia, a zoning ordinance that targeted immigrants like the Chavez family was repealed within one month of its creation. This ordinance, which was designed to combat overcrowding, restricted households to immediate relatives plus one unrelated person. The definition of "family" excluded aunts, uncles, nieces, nephews, cousins, and other members of the extended family. This naturally restricts Latinos, who tend to have larger extended families. Ricardo Juarez, a Manassas neighbor, boasted, "This shows us that the abuse of power can be defeated by the community."[83] Consequently, Latino families will now sleep easier. However, there are always victims. After being given thirty days to comply before the ordinance was challenged, the Chavez family decided to move to North Carolina where the living was cheaper and they wouldn't have to rent out rooms. The Chavez family is not alone. Many Americans whose civil liberties are infringed daily feel merciless at the hands of the government and its overreaching powers.

The most effective solution in countering the growth of governmental bureaucracy is for fellow conservative and liberal citizens to join together to stop the erosion of rights and bring the government, at all levels, under control. In other words, we must become cobelligerents for freedom. If we continue to fight among ourselves, however, we will remain victims to those who wield the power.

Although the two great political ideologies existed when America was born, they agreed on at least one thing: freedom. As historian Arthur Schlesinger has recognized: "The two jostling strains in American thought agree more than they disagree. Both are committed to individual liberty, the constitutional state, and the rule of law. Both have their reciprocal functions in preserving the body of the politic. Both have their indispensable roles in the dialectic of public policy. They are dissolute partners in the great adventure of democracy."[84]

Much like the Cold War that raged in varying degrees up until the 1980s, America is confronted with a "war on terror" that seems as if it will last indefinitely. But that doesn't mean we should hand over our basic liberties in the meantime. We should be cautious. We should be vigilant of the terrorists who may be lurking among us, but we should not let our fears get the best of us. As the Constitution's Preamble proclaims, it is up to "we the people" to maintain our freedoms. We have no one to bail us out, but we do have each other.

In talking about America's two great political ideologies, Ralph Waldo Emerson remarked, "Each exposes the abuses of the other; but in a true society, in a true man, both must combine."[85] Although we may disagree about many things, as a people we must come together in the fight for our freedoms. As Thomas Paine, in attempting to arouse a nation to resist tyranny, wrote in December 1776, "I call not upon a few, but upon all: not on this state or that state, but on every state; up and help us; lay your shoulders to the wheel; better to have too much force than too little, when so great an object is at stake."[86]

THE CHANGE
MANIFESTO

*The only thing necessary for the triumph of evil, is for
good men to do nothing.*

—Edmund Burke, eighteenth-century British statesman and
author who supported the American colonists

Now that you know what's wrong and that you can make a difference, all you need are the tools. Hence, *The Change Manifesto*.

We are not helpless. We have a rich history. We often forget, as we
have become complacent and apathetic, that America began with a
revolution. Fueled by a group of rebels, America was born.

The colonists stood their ground. They knew they had rights.
When those rights had been systematically violated, the colonists decided to resist. And, as we shall see, this resistance cost them dearly.
But early Americans knew, as did others such as Edmund Burke, that
if they didn't stand against evil, evil would triumph.

How to stop evil from triumphing? That was the central purpose behind the Constitution and the Bill of Rights. The colonists knew that winning the War of Independence was only the first step in fighting evil. They
needed a constitution and a clear statement of rights to protect them—
as well as future generations of Americans—from the government. Thus,
the Constitution and the Bill of Rights, along with the fortitude to stand
up for what you believe, are the necessary tools by which we can maintain our freedoms against the present governmental onslaught.

The Change Manifesto (Chapters Nine and Ten) is a recounting of
the history of resistance and a primer on the Bill of Rights. Study the
Manifesto. And, above all else, use it to speak truth to power.

CHAPTER NINE

No Time for Sunshine Patriots

These are the times that try men's souls. The summer soldier and the sunshine patriot will, in this crisis, shrink from the service of their country; but he that stands it now deserves the love and thanks of man and woman. Tyranny, like hell, is not easily conquered; yet we have this consolation with us, that the harder the conflict, the more glorious the triumph.

—Thomas Paine, December 1776

The freedoms that we often take for granted did not come about through happenstance. They were hard won through the sheer determination, suffering, and sacrifice of thousands of patriotic Americans who not only believed in the cause of liberty but also acted on that belief. The success of the American Revolution owes much to these men and women. In standing up to the British Empire and speaking out against an oppressive regime, they exemplified courage in the face of what must have seemed like an overwhelming foe.

We elevate the events of the Revolution to near-mythical status all too often and forget that the real revolutionaries were people just like you and me. Caught up in the drama of Redcoats marching, muskets exploding, and flags waving in the night, we lose sight of the enduring significance of the Revolution and what makes it relevant to our world today. Those revolutionaries, by and large, were neither agitators nor hotheads. They were not looking for trouble or trying to start a fight. Like many today, they were simply trying to make it from one day to another, a task that was increasingly difficult as Britain's rule became more and more oppressive.

The American Revolution did not so much start with a bang as with a whimper—a literal cry for relief from people groaning under the weight of Britain's demands. The seeds of discontent had been sown early on. By the time the Stamp Act went into effect on November 1, 1765, the rumbling had become a roar.

The Stamp Act, passed by the British Parliament with no representation from the colonies (thus raising the battle cry of "no taxation without representation"), required that revenue stamps be affixed to all printed materials. It was an onerous tax that affected every colonist who engaged in any type of business. Outraged at the imposition, the colonists responded with a flood of pamphlets, speeches, and resolutions. They staged a boycott of British goods and organized public protests, mass meetings, parades, bonfires, and other demonstrations.

Mercy Otis Warren was an active propagandist against the British and a prime example of the critical, and often overlooked, role that women played in the Revolution. Historian Nina Baym writes, "With the exception of Abigail Adams, no woman in New England was more embroiled in revolutionary political talk than Mercy Otis Warren."[1] Warren penned several plays as a form of protest, including *The Group* in 1775. As Baym writes: "*The Group* is a brilliant defense of the revolutionary cause, a political play without a patriot in it. In letting the opposition drop their masks of decency, Warren exposes them as creatures of expediency and selfishness, men who are domestic as well as political tyrants."[2]

Although Parliament repealed the Stamp Tax in 1766, it boldly moved to pass the Townshend Acts a year later. The Townshend Acts addressed several issues. First, any laws passed by the New York legislature were suspended until the colony complied with the Quartering Act, which required that beds and supplies be provided for the king's soldiers. Duties (or taxes) were imposed on American imports of glass, lead, paint, paper, and tea.

Americans responded in outrage through printed materials and boycotts. In *Letters of a Pennsylvania Farmer*, which appeared in newspapers and pamphlets, attorney John Dickinson argued that Parliament had no right to levy taxes for revenue. He also cautioned that the cause of liberty be advanced with moderation. But as historians George Brown Tindall and David Emory Shi write, "Such conciliatory language led John Adams to dismiss Dickinson as a 'piddling genius.'"[3] Samuel Adams responded by organizing protests in Boston and, with James Otis, in 1768 circulated a letter throughout the colonies that reiterated their concerns about the illegality of British taxation and asked for support from the other colonists. When an official in London ordered that the letter be withdrawn, they refused. By 1773, Samuel Adams had convinced the Boston town meeting to form a "Committee of Correspondence," a group of protesting American colonists. The committee issued a statement of rights and grievances and invited other towns to do the same.

Thereafter, Committees of Correspondence sprang up across Massachusetts. And in 1773, the Virginia Assembly proposed the formation of Committees of Correspondence on an inter-colonial basis. A network of committees spread across the colonies, mobilizing public opinion and preventing colonial resentments from boiling over. As a result, the Committees of Correspondence played a critical role in the unification of the colonies. Author Nat Hentoff writes:

> In 1805, Mercy Otis Warren—in her History of the Rise and Progress and Termination of the American Revolutions, emphasized: "Perhaps no single step contributed so much to cement the union of the colonies, and the final acquisition of independence, as the establishment of the Committees of Correspondence ... that produced unanimity and energy throughout the continent." These patriots spread the news throughout the colonies about such British subversions of fundamental liberties as the general search warrant that gave British customs officers free reign to invade homes and offices in pursuit of contraband.[4]

Slowly, but surely, the colonists were uniting and the British were losing ground. Probably the most famous example can be found in the acts of protest that came to be known as the Boston Tea Party. On the night of December 16, 1773, a group of men dressed as Indians boarded three ships that were carrying tea. Cheered on by a crowd along the shore, they threw 342 chests of tea overboard in protest of a tax on the tea. Many American merchants were aghast at the wanton destruction of property. A town meeting in Bristol, Massachusetts, condemned the action. Ben Franklin even called on his native city to pay for the tea and apologize. But as historian Pauline Maier notes, the Boston Tea Party was a last resort for a group of people who had stated their peaceful demands but were rebuffed by the British: "The tea resistance constituted a model of justified forceful resistance upon traditional criteria. As with the Stamp Act, resistance was necessary because, as John Adams wrote, the tea duty represented 'an attack upon a fundamental principle of the constitution,' against which all efforts short of force had failed. Payment of the duty had to be prevented, yet volatile confrontations and the destruction of private property were to be avoided where possible."[5]

In an attempt to bring the colonies back under their control, the English Parliament passed the Coercive Acts in 1774. Like the Townshend Acts, they had several effects, such as closing the Boston Port until the city paid for the tea that was destroyed during the Boston Tea Party. Under the law, soldiers could be lodged in private homes and the governor of Massachusetts was authorized to transfer the trials of British officials accused of wrongdoing to England, thus ensuring leniency for them. The Massachusetts council and law enforcement officers would be appointed by the British authorities, rather than being elected; sheriffs were to select jurors; and town meetings were not to be held without the governor's consent, except for the annual election of town officers.

Instead of tamping down on the brewing rebellion, the Coercive Acts further galvanized the colonies, emboldened resistance, and created a greater sense of solidarity among the colonists, who took up collections and sent provisions to Boston to help with the resistance.

In Virginia, Thomas Jefferson proposed to set aside a day of fasting and prayer for the date that the Boston Port was to be shut down. As similar ideas were springing up in other colonies, George Washington wrote that "the crisis is arrived when we must assert our rights, or submit to every imposition, that can be heaped upon us, till custom and use shall make us as tame and abject slaves, as the blacks we rule over with such arbitrary sway."[6]

The real revolution clearly began long before the first shots were fired at Lexington and Concord. Late in the summer of 1774, more than half a year before the "shot heard round the world," tens of thousands of farmers seized political authority from British-appointed officials in Massachusetts. Hats in hand, judges and members of the governor's council resigned their posts. Muskets in tow, the farmers took over. "This was the true beginning of the American Revolution; the later battles at Lexington and Concord constituted a counterrevolution as the British tried to regain control of a countryside they had previously lost," writes historian Ray Raphael.[7]

The rebellion was in full swing. Colonists formed the Continental Congress and in early 1775 urged the colonies to mobilize their militias. America was primed for bloodshed. The British remained encamped in Boston while American militia units openly trained in surrounding towns. The Continental Congress's call for an end to importing goods from Great Britain had a dramatic impact, cutting trade with British merchants by as much as 88 percent. Both sides became increasingly recalcitrant. Neither wanted to compromise in any way.

Virginia colonists strengthened their militia and debated how to respond to British actions in Boston. In March 1775, Virginia delegates met in Richmond to consider the resolutions of the Continental Congress. It was there that Patrick Henry gave his rousing speech to enflame the delegation and shore up support for the declarations:

> *There is no retreat but in submission and slavery. Our chains are forged. Their clanking may be heard on the plains of Boston. The war is inevitable—and let it come. I repeat it, sir, let it come.*

It is in vain, sir, to extenuate the matter. Gentlemen may cry peace, peace!—but there is no peace. The war is actually begun. The next gale that sweeps from the north will bring to our ears the clash of resounding arms. Our brethren are already in the field. Why stay we here idle? What is it that gentlemen wish? What would they have? Is life so dear, or peace so sweet, as to be purchased at the price of chains and slavery? Forbid it, Almighty God. I know not what course others may take, but as for me: give me liberty, or give me death![8]

The colonial militias were soon raiding military stores and gathering arms and gunpowder. General Thomas Gage, the military governor of Massachusetts, issued orders to seize the militia's supply depot at Concord and arrest leaders of the Provincial Congress. As British forces gathered in Boston, Paul Revere and William Dawes set out on their famous rides to warn the people.

Early in the morning of April 19, 1775, approximately seventy-seven minutemen (so called because they needed to be prepared to fight at a minute's notice) lined up in Lexington, along the route the British were traveling to Concord. As the Americans faced off against a sea of British soldiers numbering in the hundreds, a shot was fired from an unknown source. The British soldiers then fired a volley and charged the minutemen with bayonets, killing eight and wounding ten, but courage was running high. As historians George Brown Tindall and David Emory Shi write, "One wounded American patriot, whose wife and son were watching the spectacle, crawled 100 yards to die on his front doorstep."[9]

The British made it to Concord. But at North Bridge, the Americans were ready and killed fourteen British soldiers. As the British tried to march back to Boston, their casualties increased to 250, as "the embattled farmers from 'every Middlesex village and farm' sniped from behind stone walls, trees, barns, houses, all the way back to Charlestown peninsula."[10]

We would do well to remember that, in the end, it was the courage and resolve of common, everyday people that carried the day.

Courage was a key ingredient in the makeup of the revolutionaries. The following vignette offers a glimpse of one man's strong stand in the face of the British army:

> *Two months before the battles of Lexington and Concord, the British sent Colonel Leslie with 240 men to seize arms and ammunition which the rebels had stored in Salem. As the troops approached town, residents halted their progress by lifting the Northfield drawbridge. Several inhabitants climbed onto the raised leaf of the bridge and engaged in a shouting match with Colonel Leslie on the other side. William Gavett, an eyewitness, reported the incident: "In the course of the debate between Colonel Leslie and the inhabitants, the colonel remarked that he was upon the King's Highway and would not be prevented passing over the bridge. Old Mr. James Barr, an Englishman and a man of much nerve, then replied to him: 'It is not the King's Highway; it is a road built by the owners of the lots on the other side, and no king, country or town has anything to do with it.'" Colonel Leslie was taken aback, but he pressed the issue; James Barr held firm, knowing he was in the right. In the end, Leslie promised to march only fifty rods "without troubling or disturbing anything" if the residents of Salem would lower the bridge. The bridge came down, Leslie kept his word, and the opening battle of the American Revolution was postponed. Old James Barr had taken on the British empire with a few simple words.*[11]

COURAGE AND COMMON SENSE

While courage was vital to the revolutionary cause, it alone was not enough. Thomas Paine understood this. A man of humble origins, Paine gave voice to the American people through his writings. *Common Sense*, published on January 9, 1776, when Paine was thirty-seven years old, stirred the nation to revolution. The pamphlet helped to inspire widespread calls for independence that would culminate in the Declaration of Independence. Within three months of its publication, more than 100,000 copies were in circulation—an unbelievable number considering that there were only three million people in all thirteen British colonies. Written in plain language, Paine tore down the notion of monarchical rule, American dependence on Britain for economic prosperity, and British benevolence: "O ye that love mankind! Ye that dare oppose not only the tyranny but the tyrant, stand forth! Every spot of the old world is overrun with oppression. Freedom hath been hunted round the globe. Asia and Africa have long expelled her. Europe regards her like a stranger, and England hath given her warning to depart. O receive the fugitive, and prepare in time an asylum for mankind!"[12]

Paine's writings also inspired the American colonial army. In *The American Crisis*, Paine wrote: "These are the times that try men's souls: The summer soldier and the sunshine patriot will, in this crisis, shrink from the service of his country; but he that stands it NOW deserves the love and thanks of man and woman. Tyranny, like Hell, is not easily conquered. Yet we have this consolation with us, that the harder the conflict, the more glorious the triumph."[13] This pamphlet, which was read in the American army camps, bolstered the often-shaky morale of the patriots.

There was much to be anxious about. The colonists were inexperienced in the ways of war. They had no army. As General Nathanael Greene, George Washington's ablest commander, noted, few in the Continental Army had engaged in combat, and they were hard-pressed to "stand the shocking scenes of war, to march over dead men, to hear without concern the groans of the wounded."[14] The realities of war and military life consisted not only of combat but also death by accidental gunshot and poor sanitary conditions. If the British captured the colonists, there were floggings, torture, and even executions.

In spite of all this, the ragtag band of inexperienced recruits believed they could prevail because they were fighting for the future of freedom and their homeland—things they believed were worth dying for. These beliefs bolstered their courage, fueled the resistance, and gave them the moral resolve to persevere against the larger, better trained, better equipped, and more experienced British army.

Captain Nathan Hale epitomized the courageous colonial spirit. After volunteering to go behind enemy lines to scout out their troop movements, he was captured by British troops on Long Island in September 1776. An American officer with the British, possibly Hale's own cousin, had recognized and betrayed him. Hale was taken to Manhattan and summarily hanged as a spy. His famous last words and the bearing in which Hale spoke them made him a legend. Even the British officers who witnessed the execution admired his courage. William Hull, an officer in the American army, gave this account:

> *"On the morning of his execution,"* continued the officer, *"my station was near the fatal spot, and I requested the Provost Marshal to permit the prisoner sit in my marquee, while he was making the necessary preparations. Captain Hale entered: he was calm, and bore himself with gentle dignity, in the consciousness and rectitude and high intentions. He asked for writing materials, which I furnished him: he wrote two letters, one to his mother and one to a brother officer."* He was shortly after summoned to the gallows. But a few persons were around him, yet his characteristic dying words were remembered. He said, "I only regret that I have but one life to lose for my country."[15]

While few could hope to face death as stoically as Hale, there were many, far less famous and now long forgotten, who shared his bravery. "Weakness," writes historian Charles Royster, "was unpatriotic."[16] And retreat was not an option. As the Reverend Robert Cooper sermonized in *Courage in a Good Cause*: "To draw back, if you were even before the cannon's mouth, would fix both awful guilt and indelible disgrace upon you....If then you would escape deep guilt before God, and lasting contempt among men, forward you must go, wheresoever the drum shall beat, and the trumpet sound for battle. You have, in a word, no alternative, but either to venture your lives bravely, or attempt to save them ignominiously; to run the hazard of dying like heroes, or be certain of living like cowards."[17]

Colonial men were not the only heroes of their day. The American soldiers' fortitude was often strengthened and made possible by the courage of their female counterparts. As we have seen with Mercy Otis Warren, women directly contributed to the war effort and inspired men to live up to their ideals. "Not only would women's inspiration encourage men's valor," Royster recognizes, "but women's valor would threaten the weak man with an ignominious contrast."[18]

Women inspired the men by attending drills and parades and making their support known. They also made musket balls from pots and pans, served as couriers for the army, and raised money for the soldiers. Wives often followed their husbands to camp and, as a result, suffered the same effects of hunger, cold, and sickness that the men faced. Some women even stood in line as soldiers. At Fort Washington, Margaret Corbin took her husband's place in line when he fell at his artillery post. Mary Ludwig Hays, also known as Molly Pitcher, did the same after her husband dropped from heat exhaustion. Deborah Sampson "joined a Massachusetts regiment as 'Robert Shurtleff' and served from 1781 to 1783 by the 'artful concealment' of her sex."[19] In such ways, women's sacrifices and courage during the war served the cause directly and were a testament to the fact that the revolution was not a rebellion dreamed up by intellectual elites but rather a concerted stand by the people—young, old, male, female, rich, and poor alike.

TYRANNY OF THE MAJORITY

As is often the case during war, while there were numerous instances in which the colonists showed uncommon valor, people's passions also got the best of them at various times, resulting in a mob mentality. Before the Stamp Act was to take effect, for instance, a mob carried an effigy of Boston's stamp agent through the streets, destroyed the stamp office, and burned the effigy. "Somewhat later another mob sacked the homes of Lieutenant-Governor Thomas Hutchinson and the local customs officer," note Tindall and Shi.

"Loyalists deplored such riotous violence, arguing that the American rebels were behaving more tyrannically than the British."[20]

Although this may have been an overstatement, the loyalists (Americans who supported the British) had a point. Americans themselves generally seemed to concede this fact and shifted from violence to more peaceful means of protest. Such violent actions became politically counterproductive. Rather than resort to violence, Americans decided to boycott English goods and thereby put pressure on British merchants. As Pauline Maier notes, "This retreat from violence to ostracism signaled a new awareness that the 'enemies of liberty' themselves had rights."[21] One writer from that time period is quoted as saying: "Let us not ... while we are opposing an act, which we think ... destructive of our rights, liberties, and estates, be guilty of so glaring an inconsistency, as to injure the rights and property of a fellow subject."[22]

While the boycotts were effective in forcing the British to modify the Townshend Acts, they did not put an end to rash acts of violence. Fueled by rising tensions over their presence in Boston, crowds heckled and ridiculed the British soldiers, whom they referred to as "lobster backs" because of their red coats. On March 5, 1770, a group of colonists began taunting and snowballing a British soldier. As tensions escalated, "a soldier was knocked down, rose to his feet, and fired into the crowd. When the smoke cleared, five people lay on the ground dead or dying, and eight more were wounded."[23] This tragic incident would become known as the Boston Massacre.

Unlawful violence by American colonists began to escalate against those who supported the British. This led to deplorable actions, such as tarrings and featherings. A Connecticut resident who spoke in favor of the king "was assaulted by a Mob, stripped naked, & hot Pitch was poured upon him, which blistered his Skin. He was then carried to a Hog Sty & rubbed over with Hog's Dung. They threw the Hog's Dung in his Face, & rammed some of it down his Throat; & in that condition exposed to a Company of Women. His House was attacked, his Windows broke, when one of his Children was sick, & a Child of his went in Distraction upon this Treatment. His Gristmill was broke, & Persons prevented from grinding at it, & from having any Connections with him."[24]

The potential for widespread, undisciplined mob violence resulted in new calls for restraint. In 1774, John Adams complained, "These tarrings and featherings, this breaking open Houses by rude and insolent Rabbles, in Resentment for private Wrongs or in pursuance of private Prejudices and Passions, must be discountenanced."[25]

These events would serve to instruct future lawmakers that not only the government, but the people as well, at times needed to avoid violence in order for freedom to flourish. Part of the motivation behind the Bill of Rights may have been the colonials' harsh treatment of loyalists during the Revolution. "American schoolchildren have always been taught that the Bill of Rights was meant to insure against the tyrannical abuses of Old World governments, but the new American states had also been abusive to basic civil liberties," writes historian Ray Raphael. "Many of the Revolutionaries, once the war had ended, recoiled at the consequences of popular fury, the 'tyranny of the majority' they had witnessed firsthand. The War for Independence had proven that Americans needed protection—not just from kings, but from themselves."[26] Thus, the Bill of Rights was created, in part, to protect the minority on those occasions when the majority got out of control.

SECURING RIGHTS: THE CONSTITUTION

For most Americans, the account of how America won its independence from Britain usually ends with the signing of the Declaration of Independence and America's subsequent success in winning the war. Yet as the Philadelphia physician Benjamin Rush observed in 1786: "There's nothing more common than to confound the terms of the American revolution with those of the late American war. The American war is over: but this is far from being the case with the American revolution. On the contrary, nothing but the first act of the great drama is closed."[27]

Rush recognized that winning independence was only the first part of a greater story. In his mind, the Revolution was more than a struggle for independence and home rule. It had also become a movement to establish new forms of government, molded on such principles that made the people the only proper source of political authority. It was time to ponder a government that could, as the Declaration of Independence declares, hold the colonies together as "the United States of America."

A Second Continental Congress was formed, and an attempt was made to draft a constitution. The newly created states eventually ratified this constitution as the Articles of Confederation in 1781. Although the Articles were a remarkable achievement, they did not create a union or a more centralized government. As the years passed, the weaknesses of a loose confederation became increasingly apparent. The Articles of Confederation had proven ineffective to many. "Self-interest led bankers, merchants, and mechanics to promote a stronger central government," write historians Tindall and Shi. "Many public-spirited men saw it as the only alternative to anarchy. Gradually people were losing the fear of a tyrannical central authority as they saw evidence that tyranny might come from other quarters, including the common people themselves."[28]

It became clear to many of the national leaders that constitutional reform was needed, and it began in Virginia. In January 1786, the Virginia legislature adopted a resolution inviting the other states to send delegates to a convention where they could discuss necessary changes in the Articles. The Virginia delegation to this meeting included James Madison, who was later called the "Father of the Constitution."

In the intervening months, the movement for general constitutional reform gathered strength. In February 1787, the Continental Congress added its own endorsement of the convention. Twelve of the thirteen state legislatures eventually appointed delegates. The lone holdout was Rhode Island, a determinedly anti-federal state.

Although the purpose of the convention was to revise the Articles, the final product was a proposal for a new Constitution. When drafts of the new Constitution were circulated, many were surprised that a completely new form of government was in the works. Initial reactions were mixed. Thomas Jefferson, who was in Paris at the time of the convention, had decidedly contrary views of the Constitution.

In a November 13, 1787, letter to William Stephens Smith, he voiced his concerns and even questioned the need for a new Constitution:

> *God forbid we should ever be 20 years without such a rebellion. The people can not be all, and always, well informed. The part which is wrong will be discontented in proportion to the importance of the facts they misconceive. If they remain quiet under such misconceptions it is a lethargy, the forerunner of death to the public liberty.*

> *And what country can preserve its liberties if the rulers are not warned from time to time that their people preserve the spirit of resistance? Let them take arms. The remedy is to set them right as to facts, pardon and pacify them. What signify a few lives lost in a century or two? The tree of liberty must be refreshed from time to time with the blood of patriots and tyrants. It is its natural manure.*[29]

The Fathers of the Constitution—the fifty-five delegates who met in Philadelphia during the sweltering days of 1787—were not inclined to rebellion. They created a conservative document that called for a federal plan of government, a system of separation of powers with checks and balances, and a procedure for orderly change to meet exigencies of the future. By checking both the power of the government and the power of the people, the Constitution attempted to achieve a balance among powers.

For the most part, the delegates' differences on political philosophy fell within a narrow range. On certain fundamental issues, they generally agreed that government derived its just powers from the consent of the people, but society must be protected from the tyranny of the majority; that the people at large must have a voice in their government, but checks and balances must be provided to keep any one group from arrogating power; that a stronger central authority was essential, but all power was subject to abuse.

They assumed, as James Madison did, that if people were "angels, no government would be necessary."[30] Even the best people were naturally selfish, and government, therefore, could not be founded altogether upon a trust in goodwill and virtue. Yet by a careful arrangement of checks and balances, by checking power with countervailing power, the framers hoped to devise institutions that could constrain individual selfishness and channel self-interests to benefit the public good.

THE BILL OF RIGHTS

The proposed Constitution would not become effective unless nine states ratified it. The most important reason some states initially opposed ratification of the Constitution was because it did not include a bill of rights. The Constitutional Convention had considered including a bill of rights, but the motion to have a committee prepare such a document was quickly and easily defeated. Roger Sherman of Connecticut suggested that because the Constitution did not give the federal government the power to infringe upon fundamental rights, a bill of rights was unnecessary. The majority of the delegates shared this view.

Supporters of the Constitution became known as Federalists, and opponents of the Constitution were labeled Anti-Federalists. Anti-Federalists criticized the Constitution for several reasons, one being its failure to include a bill of rights. Richard Henry Lee despaired at the absence of protection of "those essential rights of mankind without which liberty cannot exist."[31] Although the Anti-Federalists disliked the Constitution for a number of reasons, they focused on its omission of a bill of rights because that was their best argument for enlisting public support to defeat it: "From the start of the ratification controversy, the omission of a bill of rights became an Anti-Federalist mace with which to smash the Constitution," writes historian Leonard W. Levy. "Its opponents sought to prevent ratification and exaggerated the bill of rights issue because it was one with which they could enlist public support. Their prime loyalty belonged to states' rights, not civil rights."[32]

Samuel Adams at first opposed the ratification of the Constitution but later changed his mind when it was agreed that a series of amendments would be introduced to protect fundamental rights. These rights included, among others, the freedom of the press, the right to bear arms, the right to petition government for a redress of grievances, and the right to be secure against unreasonable searches and seizures. Adams had feared that without a bill of rights, the federal government would take over the powers of the state governments "and sink both in despotism."[33] As Adams proclaimed: "I mean, my friend, to let you know how deeply I am impressed with the sense of the importance of amendments; that the good people may clearly see the distinction—for there is a distinction—between the federal powers vested in Congress and the sovereign authority belonging to the several states, which is the palladium of the private and personal rights of the citizens."[34]

Several of the states agreed to ratify the Constitution on the condition that amendments would be proposed to ensure fundamental rights. But the existence of the Bill of Rights is due in great part to the extraordinary efforts and courage of James Madison, who actually drafted the amendments and pushed them through Congress.

Madison initially thought that a bill of rights would be "unnecessary and dangerous."[35] Neither the Federalists nor the Anti-Federalists opposed a bill of rights in principle. But, as Levy recognizes, "many Framers argued, as did Alexander Hamilton in *The Federalist*, No. 84, 'that the Constitution is itself, in every rational sense, and to every useful purpose, a Bill of Rights.'"[36] The danger of a bill of rights, Madison and other Federalists believed, was that by listing rights, the drafters might accidentally omit some from the list and thus fail to protect those rights omitted. As experience had shown them, state bills of rights had overlooked a number of rights that went unprotected. Federalists concluded that the problem could be avoided by forming a government of limited powers and avoiding an express list of rights.

In this way, a bill of rights was unnecessary, Federalists argued, because the Constitution did not grant the federal government the power to deprive the people of their fundamental rights. A bill of rights, then, would lead people to believe that the Constitution empowered the federal government to deprive the people of those rights in the first place. "As Alexander Hamilton phrased it in the eighty-fourth paper of *The Federalist*, 'Why declare things should not be done which there is no power to do?'"[37]

Experience had shown Madison and others that state bills of rights had failed to protect the people during crises. The framers of the Constitution tended to be skeptical about the value of so-called barriers against "overbearing majorities," as Madison said.[38] He had seen repeated violations of bills of rights in every state. As realists, the framers believed that constitutional protections of rights meant little during times of popular hysteria. And any member of the Constitutional Convention could have cited examples of gross abridgments of civil liberties in states that had bills of rights—not to mention the excesses observed during the Revolution.

In the end, Madison recognized the political necessity of allaying the fears of Anti-Federalists. Madison believed there was a moral obligation imposed by those ratifying conventions that had approved the Constitution with the understanding that a bill of rights would be offered to the states.

While several of the arguments that Madison would later use to support his change of position on a bill of rights were strong, they can be traced directly to arguments made earlier by Thomas Jefferson. In his first letter to Madison on the subject of the Constitution, Jefferson began with praise but ended with what he did not like: "First the omission of a bill of rights."[39] After listing rights he thought deserved special protection, starting with the freedoms of religion and the press, Jefferson dismissed as campaign rhetoric justifications for the omission of a bill of rights and concluded: "Let me add that a bill of rights is what the people are entitled to against every government on earth, general or particular, and what no just government should refuse, or rest on inference."[40]

Jefferson's personal opinion refuted Federalist concerns about the Bill of Rights with clear logic. Concerning the Federalist argument that a bill of rights was unnecessary because the Constitution did not grant the federal government the power to deprive the people of fundamental rights, Jefferson responded that "because the Constitution protected some rights but ignored others, it raised implications against them, making a bill of rights 'necessary by way of supplement.'"[41]

Many of the Founding Fathers, as we have seen, were concerned that majorities could become oppressive and override the decisions of so-called well-reasoning men. As John Winthrop of Massachusetts wrote, a bill of rights "serves to secure the minority against the usurpations and tyranny of the majority."[42] With regard to such concerns about overbearing majorities, Jefferson believed that an independent court could withstand oppressive majority impulses by holding unconstitutional any acts violating a bill of rights. Jefferson was anticipating the role of the courts in curbing the power of the government, even if it feigned to speak for the people. Jefferson added "that a bill of rights 'will be the text whereby to try all the acts of the federal government.'"[43]

With regard to the position that compiling a list of rights runs the danger of omitting some rights, Jefferson replied with the adage that half a loaf is better than none. Even if all rights could not be secured, "Let us secure what we can."[44] Others believed that a bill of rights was a good education tool in that it taught "truths" upon which freedom depends.

Incredibly, when Madison introduced his proposals for the Bill of Rights in the First Congress, the Federalists thought the House had more important matters with which to deal. And the Anti-Federalists feared that the adoption of such amendments would effectively ruin their quest to oppose the Constitution. But Madison persevered and, on June 8, 1789, made a long, memorable speech before an apathetic House of Representatives, introducing amendments culled mainly from state constitutions and state ratifying convention proposals, especially Virginia's. All power, he argued, was subject to abuse and should be guarded against by constitutionally securing "the great rights of mankind."[45]

Madison argued that the government had only limited powers but that it might, unless prohibited, abuse its discretion. The great objective he had in mind, Madison declared, was to limit the powers of government, thus preventing legislative as well as executive abuse and, above all, preventing abuses of power by "the body of the people, operating by the majority against the minority."[46] Madison also used Jefferson's argument that the Bill of Rights would encourage courts to "check" the other branches of the federal government.

Madison's political courage and determination cannot be overstated. He was insistent, compelling, unyielding, and ultimately triumphant. By the end of the summer, Congress proposed to the states the amendments that eventually became the Bill of Rights. Madison's accomplishment in the face of congressional opposition and apathy entitles him to be remembered as the "father of the Bill of Rights," even more than the "father of the Constitution."

LESSONS LEARNED FROM TYRANNY

The Bill of Rights, consisting of the first ten amendments to the U.S. Constitution, ensures that the government cannot take away basic, fundamental liberties. Historian Leonard W. Levy writes, "The triumph of individual liberty against government power is one of history's noblest themes, epitomized by the Bill of Rights."[47]

The Bill of Rights was ratified and became part of the U.S. Constitution on December 15, 1791. Its function is succinctly stated by Levy:

The purpose of a bill of rights is to remove certain rights from political controversy, and place them as fundamental legal principles.

One's rights to life, liberty, or property, to freedom of speech and press, to freedom of worship and assembly, to the equal protection of the laws, do not or should not depend upon the outcome of any elections. By giving them and other rights—the great ideals of liberty, equality and fairness—constitutional status, we declare them to be rights that government cannot impair or deny, and we entrust a special body of defenders, the courts, to protect them.[48]

The Bill of Rights was created primarily to reinforce fundamental freedoms that had been threatened during revolutionary times—both by government and overreactions by some of the people.

In the years leading up to the American Revolution, there was a general concern among Americans that the British were gradually gaining more and more power over the colonies or, in the words of historian Bernard Bailyn, of "enslaving the colonies" and "bringing them under arbitrary government."[49] With increasing clarity, the Americans saw British officials as conspirators in a plan to dominate the colonies and take away long-enjoyed freedoms.

As time went on, various colonies experimented with constitutions in reaction to these concerns. Some states included bills of rights to ensure that people's basic freedoms would neither be infringed upon nor eradicated by the government. The Bill of Rights, as we know it today, thus originated from the revolutionary generation's experience with a tyrannical regime.

Several of the freedoms listed in the Bill of Rights can be traced to the harsh experiences of the colonists. The First Amendment, for example, includes the people's right to assemble. Before the Revolutionary War began, the British Parliament enacted the Massachusetts Government Act. This was one of several measures—collectively known as the Coercive Acts—enacted by Parliament following the infamous Boston Tea Party. Under the Coercive Acts, "no town meeting could be held without the governor's consent, except for the annual election of town officers."[50] This measure essentially gave the British-controlled governor veto power over the people's ability to organize themselves and discuss political matters.

The Third Amendment, which states that soldiers shall not be quartered in a person's house during times of peace without the homeowner's consent, can also be traced to colonial experiences. In 1765, the Quartering Act required the colonies to supply British troops with food, lodging, and other provisions. It also demanded that the colonists provide British troops with barracks or let them use inns and vacant buildings. In 1774, the Coercive Acts even required the American colonists to provide lodging for soldiers in their private homes.

The Third Amendment also states that soldiers shall not be quartered in a person's house during times of war, except in accordance with the law. Some Americans had first-hand experiences with troops being quartered in their homes. During the Revolution, a housewife on Long Island named Lydia Mintern Post was forced to provide housing for some Hessian troops during the British occupation. Historian Ray Raphael writes:

> *When the Hessians received their monthly ration of rum, the hostess wrote, "we have trying and grievous scenes to go through; fighting, brawls, drumming and fifing, and dancing the night long; card and dice playing, and every abomination going on under our very roofs." Whether drunk or not, the soldiers would "take the fence rails to burn, so that the fields are left open, and the cattle stray away and are often lost; burn fires all night on the ground, and to replenish them, go into the woods and cut down all the young saplings, thereby destroying the growth of ages." What bothered Lydia the most, however, was that the Hessians made baskets for her daughters and taught German to her son. "The children are fond of them," she conceded. "I fear lest they should contract evil."*[51]

The Fourth Amendment, which provides that the people have a right to be secure in their persons and property against unreasonable searches and seizures, arose out of colonial experiences as well. It also states that valid warrants require "probable cause" and a particular description of the place to be searched and the persons or objects to be seized.

Before the American Revolution, there was virtually no right to be secure against unreasonable searches and seizures. During colonial times, British judges issued "writs of assistance," or general search warrants, which allowed officers to enter any place during the day. All that was needed for a judge to issue the warrant was an officer's assertion of a mere suspicion of illegal activity. As a consequence, British soldiers entered homes and places of business, virtually at will. As time went by, these general warrants were used with increasing frequency. The effects on the American people were devastating and long lasting. As one colonist wrote, "our houses, and even our bedchambers, are exposed to be ransacked, our boxes, trunks, and chests broke open, ravaged, and plundered by wretches whom no prudent man would venture to employ even as menial servants."[52]

In 1760, James Otis, a renowned colonial attorney, was hired to fight against the legality of these general warrants in court. Otis "condemned writs of assistance because they were perpetual, universal (addressed to every officer and subject in the realm), and allowed anyone to conduct a search in violation of the essential principle of English liberty that a peaceable man's house is his castle."[53] Otis's argument was particularly daring because it was radical at that time to challenge an act of Parliament as unconstitutional. Although Otis did not win the case, it was highly publicized throughout the colonies. Because of Otis's stand for freedom, Americans found a cause and a constitutional argument. As a result, inspired crowds frequently prevented enforcement of the writs by British soldiers. Years after James Otis's courtroom speech, John Adams considered Otis's stand to be the beginning of the American movement toward independence: "Otis was a flame of Fire! ... Then and there was the first scene of the first Act of Opposition to the arbitrary Claims of Great Britain. Then and there the child Independence was born."[54]

Among other rights, the Sixth Amendment guarantees criminal defendants the right to an impartial jury of their peers. During colonial times, Americans were repeatedly threatened and subjected to unfair trial procedures. In the late 1760s, the British Parliament aggressively moved to collect information on American troublemakers and return the accused to England for trial. This was in response to a declaration from a convention of Massachusetts delegates who stated their aversion to having British soldiers on American soil, which they saw as endangering their freedoms.

Americans were understandably concerned with being arrested and transported to England for trial. New Yorkers were alarmed by what appeared to be attempts to undermine the jury system. Bernard Bailyn writes, "In New York the same executive who had fought the permanent tenure of judges insisted on the legality of allowing jury decisions, on matters of fact as well as of law, to be appealed to the governor and Council."[55] Although this effort to undermine jury verdicts was ultimately defeated, it nevertheless reinforced the need by Americans to resist such British encroachments.

Americans were even more outraged over the formation of four new British vice-admiralty courts, which were set up to administer law "maritime and civil" and handle trade, navigation, and marine matters. Comprised of politically appointed judges, these courts played a dual role in port towns and were the arbitrator of all conflicts that concerned the ocean commerce of the province, as well as the agency that heard and determined cases involving infringements of the British Navigation Acts. When Great Britain decided to step up enforcement of the Trade and Navigation Acts, the authority of the courts was further expanded to include enforcement of customs and criminal charges for smuggling, and so on. Because no jurymen were called to judge their peers, the vice-admiralty courts have been viewed as the ugly duckling of the provincial legal structure. And the absence of juries offended Americans and instilled even more fear about what was being planned for them.

THE NEED FOR A BILL OF RIGHTS

The creation of the Bill of Rights was heavily influenced by what Americans considered to be the need to preserve long-held historical rights. These included the Second Amendment right to bear arms, the Fifth Amendment right against double jeopardy, and the Eighth Amendment safeguards against excessive bail, excessive fines, and cruel and unusual punishment.

The need for a bill of rights was also based in part on the notion that human beings are born with natural rights and that these rights are established in an agreement between the people and the government. As Leonard Levy writes, "Over a period of a century and a half, America became accustomed to the idea that government existed by consent of the governed, that the people created the government, that they did so by a written compact, that the compact reserved their natural rights, and that it constituted a fundamental law to which the government was subordinate."[56]

By the time of the American Revolution in 1776, the belief had existed for centuries that the people possessed certain inherent and inalienable rights apart from what the government allowed. Throughout the Revolution, the colonists sought to preserve what they thought were rights rooted in history. Although they succeeded in creating many new rights, the revolutionaries convinced themselves that they were in actuality defending essential rights found in such ancient British documents as the Magna Carta.

Known as the "Great Charter" of English liberties, the Magna Carta was forced on King John by English barons in 1215. In sixty-three paragraphs, these English barons set forth various grievances against the king, while asserting their liberties. The final paragraph declares with clarity their intentions: "The men in our kingdom have and hold all the aforesaid liberties, rights, and concessions, well and peaceably, freely and quietly, fully and wholly, for themselves and their heirs, of us and our heirs, in all respects and in all places forever, as is aforesaid."

Americans believed that such documents as the Magna Carta already limited the British government. By 1776, however, Americans had progressed far beyond the English in securing their rights. The English constitutional documents limited only the king and protected few rights. Americans had developed a more expansive view of freedom and, thus, wanted more in terms of their rights.

Yet one thing was clear: the rights already established under British law would be the starting point for Americans. When the Bill of Rights was drafted, the amendments were based on lessons learned from the Magna Carta of 1215. As Levy notes, the "Fourth Amendment emerged not only from the American Revolution; it was a constitutional embodiment of the extraordinary coupling of Magna Carta to the appealing fiction that 'a man's house is his castle.'"[57] By the time of the Bill of Rights, therefore, the argument that one has a right to privacy in one's home was over five hundred years old.

In addition to the Magna Carta, the English Declaration of Rights of 1689 was highly influential. The Bill of Rights contains several clauses and phrases—particularly in the Third and Eighth Amendments—that are similar to those found in the English Declaration of Rights. The English Declaration of Rights, for example, accused James II of, among other things, "'quartering of Souldiers contrary to Law,' requiring excessive bail of accused criminals, and inflicting 'illegall and cruell punishments.'"[58]

Even before the Revolution, the American colonists were well on their way to formulating a declaration of rights. In 1774, the First Continental Congress adopted a Declaration of American Rights. During the Revolution, various colonies created bills of rights to secure "time-honored" individual rights. The states' experiences with these bills of rights provided an important foundation for the later creation of the federal Bill of Rights. The first eight amendments of the Bill of Rights are based heavily upon the Virginia Declaration of Rights of 1776. Drafted by George Mason, the Virginia Declaration of Rights may be considered "the first modern bill of rights" since it was the first such charter to secure individual rights over time against the will of the majority in legislatures.[59]

The bills of rights from one time period to another were not always carbon copies. For the most part, our present Bill of Rights was based on a continuation of what the revolutionary generation thought to be a long history of rights dating back through colonial times to older English law. And the unique American experience that led up to the War of Independence both colored and shaped the broad range of freedoms we enjoy today.

The Bill of Rights was introduced in part for political reasons, as Federalists sought to gain Anti-Federalist support for the Constitution. The Bill of Rights was also composed because the people of the states demanded it before ratifying the Constitution.

The ultimate reason the Bill of Rights was created was because it made sense—it served as a check on government power over time. As U.S. Supreme Court Justice Antonin Scalia writes, the "Founders were right when they feared that some (in their view misguided) future generation might wish to abandon liberties that they considered essential, and so sought to protect those liberties in a Bill of Rights."[60] In this sense, the Bill of Rights is valuable because it endures over time. It provides people today with the opportunities for the free and peaceful political activity that the revolutionary generation had hoped for.

A RISING SUN

During the Revolution, Americans resisted what they perceived was tyranny. Their courage was displayed in protests, combat, and politics, and many died in the name of freedom and rights. Fear of government and distrust of power led the people to form a new government—one that they hoped would limit the tyranny of government. Most importantly, the people got involved.

The American Revolution required common, ordinary people to think about the far-reaching consequences of their everyday decisions and choose a side in the conflict. In this sense, the people of the revolutionary age became important players in history. This is something the current generation can do as well. As John F. Kennedy explained, "In a democracy, every citizen, regardless of his interest in politics, 'holds office'; every one of us is in a position of responsibility; and, in the final analysis, the kind of government we get depends upon how we fulfill those responsibilities. We, the people, are the boss, and we will get the kind of political leadership, be it good or bad, that we demand and deserve."[61]

Although there is no single reason as to why the Bill of Rights was created, the responsibility of future generations was—and is—clear. In his final address to the Constitutional Convention, Benjamin Franklin reminded his colleagues once more that the strength of any government rested on the virtue of the people. "This [government] is likely to be well administered for a course of years, and can only end in despotism, as other forms have done before it, when the people shall become so corrupted as to need despotic government, being incapable of any other."[62] Franklin challenges us, "we the people," to reaffirm the Bill of Rights and take advantage of our freedoms in order for them to survive.

No matter how dire the situation may be, there is hope for the future—a hope that resided with those who gave us the Bill of Rights. Franklin seemed optimistic about the future of the nation at that time. James Madison described the Constitutional Convention as it came to a close:

> *Whilst the last members were signing it, Doctor Franklin, looking towards the president's chair, at the*

back of which a rising sun happened to be painted, observed to a few members near him, that painters had often found it difficult to distinguish in their art a rising from a setting sun. I have, said he, often and often in the course of the session, and the vicissitudes of my hopes and fears as to its issue, looked at that behind the president, without being able to tell whether it was rising or setting. But now at length I have the happiness to know that it is a rising and not a setting sun.[63]

The American people should be inspired by their history. But, ultimately, that is not enough. Courage does not come from merely reading stories. It comes from within. Only when that inner courage is found can one serve the purpose of the Bill of Rights and engage in the free and lawful advocacy that the revolutionaries intended. As John F. Kennedy put it:

To be courageous ... requires no exceptional qualifications, no magic formula, no special combination of time, place and circumstance. It is an opportunity that sooner or later is presented to us all. Politics merely furnishes one arena which imposes special tests of courage. In whatever arena of life one may meet the challenge of courage, whatever may be the sacrifices he faces if he follows his conscience—the loss of his friends, his fortune, his contentment, even the esteem of his fellow men—each man must decide for himself the course he will follow. The stories of past courage can define that ingredient—they can teach, they can offer hope, they can provide inspiration. But they cannot supply courage itself. For this each man must look into his own soul.[64]

CHAPTER TEN

The Great Rights of Mankind

At the time of their adoption, the Bill of Rights represented the high point of a courageous struggle to pass on the relatively new idea that rule of law must forever stand as a check upon governmental power.

—New York University law professor Bernard Swartz

Much has transpired since the United States Constitution was ratified and the 462 words that make up the Bill of Rights—the first ten amendments to the Constitution—became an integral part of America's legal and political fabric. Our nation has made great strides in protecting the rights of minorities, as well as advancing the cause of freedom worldwide. Unfortunately, it has also perpetrated vast injustices and facilitated countless violations of human rights. The U.S. Supreme Court has played a pivotal role in shaping these rights, sometimes affirming and at other times limiting the freedoms set out in the Bill of Rights. Yet the Court does not bear sole responsibility for the current state of our freedoms. Although our civil liberties are in a state of disrepair, due in large part to a government that increasingly justifies encroachments on our rights as necessary in its so-called "war on terror," the blame cannot entirely be placed at the feet of government leaders.

"We the people" are the first and best guardians of our rights. We are the Constitution's first line of defense. The credit, as well as the blame, rests with us. As a sign in President Harry S Truman's office proclaimed, "The buck stops here."

While the war for independence ended more than two hundred years ago, the struggle to safeguard our freedoms will never be over.

When we lose sight of that truth, when we become too comfortable and complacent with the status quo, is when we are most vulnerable to attack. And because of our apathy and ignorance of the government's explosive growth and expansive powers, we have no one to blame but ourselves.

Surveys reveal that Americans are inexcusably illiterate about the Bill of Rights. Most Americans cannot name the five freedoms guaranteed in the First Amendment.[1] And about half of those surveyed believe the First Amendment goes too far in the rights it guarantees.[2] Fault for this lack of constitutional savvy lies in part with our educational system. When high school seniors were tested several years ago, just one in four could name two ways the American political system prevents the exercise of "absolute arbitrary power" on the part of the government. Among the possible answers on a multiple choice test were such basics as the Bill of Rights, an independent judiciary, civilian control of the military, and the right to vote. Not one in ten seniors could identify two ways that democracy benefits from the active participation of its citizens.[3] And in a 1998 poll conducted by the National Constitution Center, not one in fifty American teenagers could identify James Madison as the father of the U.S. Constitution. Less than half could name the three branches of the federal government.[4]

Educators do not fare much better in understanding and implementing the Constitution in the classroom. A study conducted by the Center for Survey Research and Analysis at the University of Connecticut found that while educators seem to support First Amendment rights in principle, they are reluctant to apply such rights in the schools. They support severe restrictions on freedom by forbidding student distribution of political and religious materials, thus endorsing a hypocritical double standard where belief and action collide. This is nowhere better illustrated than in the zero-tolerance policies that expel children from school for innocent acts and speech without a hearing and regardless of circumstances. This obviously creates confusion for students when it comes time to learn about the Bill of Rights.[5]

Government leaders and politicians are also ill-informed. Although they take an oath to uphold, support, and defend the Constitution against enemies foreign and domestic, their lack of education about our fundamental rights often causes them to be enemies of the Bill of Rights. Anyone taking public office should have a working knowledge of the Constitution and the Bill of Rights and should be held accountable for upholding their precepts. One way to ensure this would be to require government leaders to take a course on the Constitution and pass a thorough examination before being allowed to take office.

Sadly, those precious 462 words of freedom that make up the Bill of Rights are in danger of being swallowed up in the mire of ignorance, misunderstanding, and apathy that seems to hold our nation captive. As the many great freedom fighters discussed in the previous pages demonstrate, only active involvement from an informed citizenry can maintain our democratic form of government. But before we can take action, we must be educated on our basic freedoms.

The following is a primer on the Bill of Rights, as well as the all-important Writ of Habeas Corpus. Study it. Use it. And above all, cherish it.

AMENDMENT I: FREEDOM OF RELIGION, SPEECH, PRESS, AND ASSEMBLY

Congress shall make no law respecting an establishment of religion, or prohibiting the free exercise thereof; or abridging the freedom of speech, or of the press; or the right of the people peaceably to assemble, and to petition the Government for a redress of grievances.

At the time of our nation's inception, the founders believed that the open, free exchange of ideas was necessary for the survival of a representative democracy. As Benjamin Franklin proclaimed, "Whoever would overthrow the liberty of a nation must begin by subduing the freeness of speech."[6] To protect this principle, the founders established the freedoms of speech and the press in the First Amendment. In recalling their wisdom, U.S. Supreme Court Justice Hugo Black wrote, "The Framers knew that free speech is the friend of change and revolution. But they also knew that it is always the deadliest enemy of tyranny."[7]

The First Amendment has come to symbolize the right of "a single minority of one" to express views that differ from those of the popular majority in the areas of speech, religion, and expression. As a federal judge recognized, history has shown us that "pleasing speech is not the kind that needs protection."[8] According to the U.S. Supreme Court, the First Amendment has become the fortress for protecting the "uninhibited, robust, and wide-open" discussion of controversial and often unpopular issues in public places.[9]

The First Amendment also includes the right to freely express one's religion. It does so by guaranteeing every person the right to express any religious belief, or none at all, while at the same time prohibiting the government from favoring any particular religion over another. The government cannot dictate how we should act or what we should believe, especially when it comes to religion.

The First Amendment Today

The freedom to speak your mind. To worship. To pray without interference. To protest in peace. These rights are still protected by the First Amendment. The freedom to speak one's mind on issues of the day, exercise religious beliefs, remain educated through a free press, associate with others, and petition the government when you have been wronged is just as important today as it was in 1791. If our First Amendment protections are to remain intact, however, it will require courageous individuals who are willing to take a stand in defense of them.

There is much to defend today. Despite the clear protections found in the First Amendment, the freedoms described therein are under constant assault, from school officials stripping students of their right to express their faith, to local governments and police forbidding citizens from expressing unpopular views in public to members of the press being threatened with jail time for reporting on important government programs.

For instance, in September 2007, University of Florida student Andrew Meyer was brutally dealt with by police for exercising his First Amendment rights at a forum featuring Senator John Kerry.

Meyer was tasered and then arrested by police when he refused to leave the microphone after his allotted time to ask his question—a question that Senator Kerry stated he was prepared to answer.[10]

On July 4, 2004, Nicole and Jeffery Rank of Corpus Christi, Texas, were handcuffed and removed from a rally at the West Virginia state capitol, where President Bush was giving a speech, for refusing to cover their T-shirts, which bore anti-Bush slogans. They were later released without charge—unsurprising given that their only "crime" had been to express themselves—and the federal government later settled a lawsuit the Ranks initiated for $80,000.[11] What the case revealed is that the U.S. Secret Service has a manual for dealing with such dissenters, including removing those who want to act on their free speech rights from such events.[12]

In Washington DC, a woman who opposed China's practice of religious oppression was arrested for publicly protesting during an official government ceremony for Chinese President Hu Jintao.[13] Also in our nation's capital, police removed a congressman's wife from President Bush's 2006 State of the Union Address because her shirt proclaimed the message, "Support the Troops—Defending Our Freedom."[14]

Infringements on First Amendment rights have reached such extremes that government officials are even attempting to dictate what we can and cannot wear. Various cities, for example, have begun cracking down on the so-called "baggy pants" trousers worn below the underwear. The style, which developed in prisons because inmates were not provided with belts, has become fashionable in certain communities. Some local officials have adopted a harsh stance on this form of expression. In Delcambre, Louisiana, "offenders" face a $500 fine or six-month jail sentence for wearing their pants in this style.[15] An ordinance in Mansfield, a town of 5,496 near Shreveport, subjects offenders to a fine (as much as $150 plus court costs) or jail time (up to fifteen days).[16] Larger cities such as Atlanta, Georgia, have considered introducing a similar ordinance.

The press, which is essential to the preservation of liberty, has also come under attack from the government. One of the principles that ensures a free press is that journalists are not required to reveal their sources. This is one way that government whistleblowers can feel free to come forward and reveal information that is of public importance, such as governmental corruption and abuse, without fearing exposure. If journalists were required to reveal their sources, scandals involving government corruption and wrongdoing such as Watergate might never be brought to the attention of the media and, thus, the American people.

Despite the importance of this journalistic safeguard, the freedom of the press has come under attack in recent years. During the federal government's investigations into steroid abuse and the Bay Area Laboratory Co-Operative (BALCO), a service business for blood and urine analysis and food supplements, two journalists from the *San Francisco Chronicle* were threatened with prison time—up to eighteen months, the length of the grand jury investigation—for refusing to reveal their sources. The sentence would have been longer than the combined sentences for all those convicted in the BALCO case.[17] Although the issue was eventually settled when the whistleblower came forward, the fact that the U.S. Department of Justice was so eager to attack the fundamental right of the press—the prohibition on journalists being forced to name sources—shows how the most basic rights enshrined in the Bill of Rights are being undermined.

Former U.S. Attorney General Alberto Gonzales threatened the press for reporting information about the "war on terror" that the government deemed "classified." Gonzales insisted that the government had the authority to prosecute and, thus, intimidate journalists who published alleged classified information, implying that the freedom of the press was not quite as free as Americans previously may have thought. When asked whether he was open to the possibility that the *New York Times* should be prosecuted for its disclosures in December 2005 concerning a National Security Agency surveillance program, Gonzales said his department was trying to determine "the appropriate course of action in that particular case."[18]

As this book shows, battles are continually being fought across America to protect our First Amendment rights. However, Americans should not be silenced by the government for lawfully exercising their First Amendment freedoms.

Amendment II: To Keep and Bear Arms

A well regulated Militia, being necessary to the security of a free State, the right of the people to keep and bear Arms, shall not be infringed.

At the time of our nation's founding, Americans relied on firearms to procure food and protect themselves from those who would harm them. With the Revolutionary War only a few years behind them, the founders understood that the people of this country had to be able to defend themselves if they were to preserve their newly acquired freedoms.

The Second Amendment, as one federal appeals court has held, "protects the right of individuals to privately keep and bear their own firearms that are suitable as individual, personal weapons ... regardless of whether the particular individual is then actually a member of the militia."[19] Patrick Henry, the fiery patriot of the American Revolution, said, "The great object is that every man be armed....Everyone who is able may have a gun."[20] Richard Henry Lee, a fellow Virginian and member of the first Senate, wrote: "To preserve liberty, it is essential that the whole body of the people always possess arms, and be taught alike, especially when young, how to use them."[21] George Mason, also a Virginian, declared: "To disarm the people [is] the best and most effective way to enslave them."[22]

Some have argued in recent years that the Second Amendment only applies to the militia—not to the right of individuals—to possess guns. George Mason refuted this argument long ago at the time of the Second Amendment's passage when he proclaimed: "What is the militia? It is the whole people, except for a few public officials."[23] American statesman Samuel Adams proclaimed that the "Constitution shall never be construed to authorize Congress to infringe the just liberty of the press or the rights of conscience; or to prevent the people of the United States who are peaceable citizens from keeping their own arms."[24]

The Second Amendment Today

The case is often made that gun ownership in America should be restricted to law enforcement and government officials. Renowned Harvard law professor Laurence Tribe, however, has recognized that individual Americans have the right to "possess and use firearms in defense of themselves and their homes" and that the "government may not disarm individual citizens without some unusually strong justification."[25]

While individuals still possess the right to "keep and bear arms," Congress and state legislatures have regulated the ownership and use of firearms through modern gun control laws. Federal law regulates the types of firearms citizens may own, outlines various criteria for gun ownership such as age, training, and criminal history, mandates how firearms must be registered, and regulates how firearms must be displayed. Two of the most notable gun control measures passed by Congress are the Gun Control Act of 1968, which established a tracking system that permits the federal government to track the owners of each gun and prohibits convicted felons from owning a gun, and the 1986 Firearm Owners Protection Act, which restricts the availability and ownership of certain automatic weapons. In January 2008, President Bush signed the first new gun-control legislation in fourteen years. The NICS (National Instant Check System) Improvement Amendments Act of 2007 provides up to $250 million a year to states and state courts to automate records on mentally ill people and forward the information to the FBI. That information is included in the National Instant Criminal Background Check System, which prevents anyone from buying a gun who is seriously mentally ill, a criminal, or somebody who has a restraining order against them for domestic violence. Most of these laws are in response to tragic deaths that result from the misuse of firearms, as well as the need to control the criminal use of guns.

Those who founded this country, however, had no intention of decrying the ownership of weapons such as hunting rifles and handguns for use by ordinary Americans. As James Madison, the father of the Constitution, wrote, "The advantage that Americans have over every other nation is that they are armed." When Patrick Henry proclaimed, "The great objective is that every man be armed; everyone who is able may have a gun," he clearly saw the Second Amendment as giving individuals the right to bear arms.[26]

Despite these sentiments, gun control bans have become increasingly popular in cities across the nation. In the District of Columbia, an absolute ban on handguns has been in place for the past thirty years. Like most gun-control bans, it was justified as constitutional by proponents on the basis that the Second Amendment applies to militias, not to individuals. The word "people" in the Second Amendment, however, is the same word used in the First Amendment (guaranteeing "the right of the people peaceably to assemble") and in the Fourth Amendment (guaranteeing "the right of the people to be secure ... against unreasonable searches and seizures"). Those rights clearly belong to individuals, not to states. In a Fourth Amendment case from 1990, the U.S. Supreme Court held that when the phrase "the people" is used in the context of the Second Amendment, it means "a class of persons who are part of a national community."[27] The U.S. Supreme Court agreed in late 2007 to make a ruling on the issues in the District of Columbia case.

The Second Amendment is still seen as allowing the possession of other guns, such as rifles and shotguns, for recreational purposes. Some notable Second Amendment advocates stress that as local police departments become more and more like paramilitary units, dressed in black riot gear and armed with assault weapons, the ability of the citizenry to protect itself from the government will become much more difficult. They point to instances such as New Orleans after Hurricane Katrina, where one of the government agents' first orders in restoring order was that no individuals have a gun, while they themselves brandished automatic assault rifles.[28]

AMENDMENT III: THE QUARTERING AMENDMENT

No Soldier shall, in time of peace be quartered in any house, without the consent of the Owner, nor in time of war, but in a manner to be prescribed by law.

Since the time of our nation's founding, Americans' homes have been their most important physical possession. The colonists took to heart eighteenth-century British Prime Minister William Pitt's sentiment: "Every man's home is his castle."[29] The Third Amendment addressed the framers' particular grievance with the Quartering Act of 1774, a policy that forced the colonists to provide accommodations for British troops in their homes at night, while these same soldiers terrorized their towns by day.[30] This constant invasion of the colonists' privacy by the British soldiers was condemned in the Declaration of Independence and was ultimately outlawed by the Third Amendment.

The Third Amendment Today

America was born during a time of martial law. Government troops stationed themselves in homes and trespassed on property without regard for the rights of owners.

People often question whether the Third Amendment is germain to our lives today. Although it is generally true that Americans' homes have been safe from soldiers since the Revolutionary War and the military may not threaten private property per se, the Third Amendment is still critically relevant. The right to keep the government out of our homes is an important safeguard against government abuse, and it also reinforces the principle that civilian authority is superior to the military. History clearly shows that citizens of martial states and of military dictatorships are rarely free. Subordinating the military to elected leaders is vital to a democracy.

We must remember that governments have a tendency to seek more and more control, especially in the wake of catastrophes and natural disasters. Many see the federal government's response to tragic events such as 9/11 and Hurricane Katrina as evidence that the United States is approaching a police state that wouldn't hesitate to declare martial law. With the increased military presence, we must be particularly vigilant about protecting the rights afforded by the Third Amendment, as well as the rest of the Bill of Rights.

AMENDMENT IV: SEARCHES, SEIZURES AND WARRANTS

The right of the people to be secure in their persons, houses, papers, and effects, against unreasonable searches and seizures, shall not be violated, and no Warrants shall issue, but upon probable cause, supported by Oath or affirmation, and particularly describing the place to be searched, and the persons or things to be seized.

Like the Third Amendment, the first half of the Fourth Amendment was included in the Bill of Rights in response to the oppressive way British soldiers treated American colonists through their use of "Writs of Assistance." These were court orders that authorized customs officers to conduct general searches of premises for contraband. The exact nature of the materials being sought did not have to be detailed, nor did their locations. The powerful new court orders enabled officials to inspect not only shops and warehouses, but also private homes. It quickly became apparent to many colonists that their homes were no longer their castles.[31] These searches resulted in the violation of many of the colonists' rights and the destruction of much of the colonists' personal property.

Revolutionary patriot James Otis was advocate general when the legality of these warrants came under question by the colonists. Called upon to defend that legality, he promptly resigned his office. Otis stated:

Now, one of the most essential branches of English liberty is the freedom of one's house. A man's house is his castle; and whilst he is quiet, he is as well guarded as a prince in his castle. This writ, if it should be declared legal, would totally annihilate this privilege. Custom-house officers may enter our houses when they please; we are commanded to permit their entry. Their menial servants may enter, may break locks, bars, and everything in their way; and whether they break through malice or revenge, no man, no court can inquire. Bare suspicion without oath is sufficient.[32]

After living through oppressive policies such as this, the founders wanted to ensure that Americans would never have to face intrusive government measures again. Thomas Jefferson wrote, "This I hope will be the age of experiments in government and that their basis will be founded in principles of honesty, not of mere force."[33]

The Fourth Amendment requires that a warrant signed by a judge be issued in order for authorities to arrest an individual. For a valid warrant to be issued, the circumstances must pass the legal test for probable cause—that "more likely than not," criminal activity is afoot. At the time of the founding, even after a warrant had been issued, law enforcement authorities were still required to follow a certain procedure prior to a search. This included knocking on the door and announcing their presence before entering a dwelling.[34]

The Fourth Amendment Today

The Fourth Amendment prohibits the government from searching your home without a warrant, which must include specific information such as the person's name and address to be searched. But what about other kinds of invasions? Your phone, mail, computer, medical records—they're all personal and private but also at risk for unwarranted electronic intrusions. The Fourth Amendment's protections against unreasonable searches and seizures go far beyond an actual police search of your home. The U.S. Supreme Court has defined the Fourth Amendment to mean that you have a reasonable expectation of privacy for your personal information as well.

By creating numerous exceptions, however, the Supreme Court has effectively diminished many of the Fourth Amendment's protections. In *United States v. Leon*, the Supreme Court held that evidence seized by officers objectively and in good faith was admissible, despite the fact that the warrant used to gather the evidence was later found to be defective.[35] The Supreme Court has ruled that grand juries may use evidence that is allegedly obtained illegally in questioning witnesses because to hold otherwise would interfere with grand jury independence and the time to contest the illegal search is after the accused is charged.[36] The Supreme Court has also held that the Fourth Amendment does not apply in certain situations: (1) probation or parole revocation hearings; (2) tax hearings; (3) deportation hearings; (4) when government officials illegally seize evidence outside the United States; (5) when a "private actor" (i.e., not a government employee) illegally seized the evidence; or (6) when the illegally seized evidence is used to impeach the defendant's testimony.

Since 9/11, the federal government has sought and acquired more power than at any other period in our nation's history, much of which undermines the rights afforded by the Fourth Amendment. Laws granting unprecedented police powers such as the USA PATRIOT Act, along with secret surveillance programs, have caused concern among many about the fundamental rights secured by this Amendment. As discussed earlier, the PATRIOT Act includes provisions such as the "Sneak and Peak" clause that permits police to enter and search a person's home with a secret search warrant and without informing the person for months afterwards. Then-U.S. Attorney General John Ashcroft gave legitimacy to these "black bag jobs," which were a throwback to former FBI director J. Edgar Hoover. Under the "Sneak and Peak" provision, the FBI, with a warrant, can also secretly enter a person's home and plant a "Magic Lantern" on the computer. These devices (also known as the keystone logger) are almost impossible to detect and, once installed, create a record of every time a key is pressed on the computer. The FBI can then recover this record during their next break-in. These "legal" break-ins and uses of "Magic Lanterns" are not limited to terrorists but are used in regular criminal investigations of American citizens as well.[37]

Police raids of American homes have greatly increased in recent years. Often the police even fail to knock and announce their presence before breaking down doors. In 2006, the U.S. Supreme Court ruled that evidence found by police officers who enter a home to execute a search warrant without first following the requirement to "knock and announce" can be used at trial, despite that constitutional violation.[38] And cities and towns across America are installing twenty-four-hour surveillance cameras that watch your every move, making it possible for the government to "search" you anytime you're in public. There are obvious parallels between these developments and the general search warrant exercised by the British during the colonial period, which was so despised by Americans.

Under the USA PATRIOT Act, the FBI initially could obtain a warrant from the secret Foreign Intelligence Surveillance Court, which allowed the FBI to secure lists of books borrowed and bought by patrons from libraries and bookstores.[39] The librarian or bookstore owner was prohibited from informing anyone, including the person whose privacy had been breached, that such a search had occurred. A much lower standard of proof than the normal "probable cause" was initially required for such searches. It has now been further reduced to having to be "relevant to an ongoing criminal investigation."[40]

The Protect America Act of 2007 allows for the massive, untargeted collection of international communications without a court order or meaningful oversight by either Congress or the courts. The Act grants the U.S. Attorney General—not a court or independent body—the authority to issue year-long program warrants for surveillance of people reasonably believed to be outside the United States. But it permits the government, with few limitations, to listen to all international communications where one party is in the United States. The act contains no protections for the domestic end of the phone call or email, leaving decisions about the collection, mining, and use of American citizens' private communications up to government agents.[41]

As these threats surrounding the continuing war on terrorism increase, Americans' rights under the Fourth Amendment will become even more relevant. While some might see the temporary necessity in such laws during a national security emergency, it must be pointed out that the "war on terror" has no finite duration. There will always be some form of terrorist threat to the United States. Although some provisions under the PATRIOT Act have been questioned by the courts, it is worrisome that the other provisions under the act are not subject to "sunset" clauses (which automatically set a date when legislative provisions terminate) but can remain in effect permanently, thereby effectively condemning portions of the Bill of Rights to history.[42]

Amendment V: A Bundle of Rights

> *No person shall be held to answer for a capital, or oth-erwise infamous crime, unless on a presentment or in-dictment of a Grand Jury, except in cases arising in the land or naval forces, or in the Militia, when in actual service in time of War or public danger; nor shall any per-son be subject for the same offence to be twice put in jeopardy of life or limb; nor shall be compelled in any criminal case to be a witness against himself, nor be de-prived of life, liberty, or property, without due process of law; nor shall private property be taken for public use, without just compensation.*

The Fifth Amendment consists of rights that are meant to protect citizens in the event that the government attempts to overreach its authority. John Jay, colonial statesman and the first chief justice of the U.S. Supreme Court, wrote, "It is the undoubted Right and unalien-able Privilege of a Freeman not to be divested or interrupted in the in-nocent use of Life, Liberty, or Property but by Laws to which he has assented, either personally or by his representatives."[43]

The initial act of protection found in the Fifth Amendment pro-vides a citizen accused of a crime the right to a grand jury. The grand jury, which is a group of people from the community, must determine whether the prosecutor has enough evidence to bring the accused to trial. It is likely that the founders included this particular protection against overzealous prosecutors because of an event that occurred in New York during the 1730s. There British authorities failed three times to convince a grand jury to bring a fellow American colonist to trial for publishing material critical of a political official.[44]

The Fifth Amendment also protects a criminal defendant from being tried twice for the same offense. Many of the founders had stud-ied the work of William Blackstone, the renowned scholar of English common law, who proclaimed that it was a "universal maxim of the common law of England, that no man is to be brought into jeopardy more than once of the same offence."[45] While there are a handful of exceptions, a criminal defendant who is tried and found not guilty by a judge or jury may not be tried again for the same crime. This is true even if more incriminating evidence is later discovered.

Because many early Americans accused of a crime chose to represent themselves at trial, the framers decided to provide criminal defendants with the right to not testify against themselves. Often referred to as "pleading the Fifth," this right guarantees that no person will have to say anything that would criminalize oneself.

The Fifth Amendment also assures every American the right to "due process." This means that the government may not deprive anyone of "Life, Liberty, and Property" without first providing that person with a fair hearing before an impartial judge.[46] As U.S. Supreme Court Justice Felix Frankfurter once explained, "The history of liberty has largely been the history of the observance of procedural safeguards."[47]

The final protection afforded to an individual by the Fifth Amendment is that the government, under its eminent domain authority, cannot take a citizen's private property unless it is for a valid public use. Even then, according to the Fifth Amendment, the government must pay the property owner "just compensation."

The Fifth Amendment Today

As it was in 1791, the Fifth Amendment continues to be very important today. Americans are protected against being tried repeatedly for the same crime. The government cannot bring you to trial again and again for the same offense, hoping to get the result they want. This means that if you are suspected of committing a crime, it's up to the state to prove its case against you. You are innocent until proven guilty, and governmental authorities cannot deprive you of your life, your liberty, or your property without following strict legal codes of conduct or "due process."

The Fifth Amendment also protects private property against a government taking. As discussed in Chapter Seven, in 2005 the U.S. Supreme Court ruled in *Kelo v. City of New London* that local governments could take private property from one person and transfer that property to a corporate entity with the expectation that the property would become more useful to the public. The ruling drew a sharp dissent from Justice Sandra Day O'Connor, who warned that it will allow governments to seize any property simply to allow developers to upgrade it. O'Connor wrote, "Nothing is to prevent the state from replacing any Motel 6 with a Ritz-Carlton, any home with a shopping mall."[48]

Since that decision, several local governments have declared their intent to take people's homes in order to convert them into office complexes, shopping centers, and megastores. As local governments continue to search for ways to increase tax revenue, hardworking homeowners must be wary about their homes being taken away. Designating such possessions as necessary for the "public use" is often a sham, with the desire to increase tax revenues being the real motivation of local governments. Since the *Kelo* decision, some state legislatures have passed laws that ensure that such possession takings cannot occur. But unless the American public remains educated and focused on preserving this important constitutional right, the government could take it, along with their homes.

Aside from the Takings Clause, the other rights guaranteed under the Fifth Amendment also remain relevant. Those facing a criminal charge by the federal government are entitled to avail themselves of the grand jury process, to represent themselves in a criminal trial, and not be tried for the same offense twice. Similarly, Americans are assured of fair and equal treatment by the government under the Fifth Amendment's Due Process Clause.

While this maxim is generally held to be true, in the post-9/11 years, the president and Congress have attempted to deny due process to those it believes have some connection to the "war on terror." The Presidential Military Order of November 13, 2001, gave the president the power to detain noncitizens suspected of connections to terrorists or terrorism as "enemy combatants." They could be held indefinitely without charge, without a court hearing, and without access to a lawyer. Not only have noncitizens been held in such a manner but so, too, were American citizens who were captured on American soil, rather than on a foreign battlefield. Such acts were in flagrant violation of the Due Process Clause, which allows for charges to be challenged in court, thus preventing someone being held in prison indefinitely. Despite successful legal challenges to these laws in the U.S. Supreme Court, Congress passed the Military Commissions Act in 2006, which eliminated habeas corpus (or the right to be heard in a court of law) in a way that allows noncitizen enemy combatants to be held indefinitely in a military prison, often without access to a civilian defense attorney. The legislation's denial of habeas corpus rights to noncitizens detained at Guantanamo Bay has been challenged before the U.S. Supreme Court.[49]

AMENDMENT VI: RIGHT TO SPEEDY PUBLIC TRIAL BY JURY

In all criminal prosecutions, the accused shall enjoy the right to a speedy and public trial, by an impartial jury of the State and district wherein the crime shall have been committed, which district shall have been previously ascertained by law, and to be informed of the nature and cause of the accusation; to be confronted with the witnesses against him; to have compulsory process for obtaining witnesses in his favor, and to have the Assistance of Counsel for his defense.

The Sixth Amendment spells out the right to a "speedy and public trial." An accused person is entitled to confront the witnesses against him and demand to know the nature of the charges. In addition, the government cannot keep someone in jail for unspecified offenses. We also have the right to be tried by a jury of our peers and be represented by an attorney. This means that our guilt or innocence in criminal proceedings is decided by our fellow citizens, not simply by panels of judges or unaccountable politicians.

At the height of its political power in the mid-1500s, the British legal system included an underground court known as the Star Chamber. These panels consisted of three judges and were held in secret with no indictments, no right of appeal, no juries, and no witnesses.

To ensure that this conduct would not continue, the founders enacted the Sixth Amendment, which guarantees a criminal defendant the right to a speedy trial open to all members of the public. Thomas Jefferson declared, "I consider [trial by jury] as the only anchor ever yet imagined by man by which a government can be held to the principles of its constitution."[50] Because the text of the Constitution permits all criminally accused defendants "to have the assistance of counsel for … defense," the U.S. Supreme Court has determined that a criminally charged defendant who is unable to afford an attorney shall have one appointed free of charge if he or she desires.[51]

The reasons behind these rights are twofold: first and foremost, a defendant benefits from a speedy and public trial by jury because an open trial suggests a fair hearing of his or her grievances. Second, democratic society benefits from the ability to witness local courts of law in action.

The Sixth Amendment Today

Americans still possess the right to a speedy and public trial by jury. In recent years, however, the government has demonstrated its willingness to ignore important constitutional safeguards found in the Sixth Amendment. Consider what happened at Guantanamo Bay: detainees were kept without charge, not informed of the evidence against them, and denied access to a lawyer. Even American citizens such as Jose Padilla were treated in like fashion until the U.S. Supreme Court intervened. Now, under the Military Commissions Act, such treatment is reserved for noncitizens.

Despite the Sixth Amendment's guarantee of public trials, nearly all records are being kept secret for more than 5,000 defendants who completed their journey through the federal courts over the last three years. As Lucy Dalglish, executive director of the Reporters Committee for Freedom of the Press, observed about these "secret dockets": "In this country, we don't prosecute and lock up convicts and have no public track record of how we got there. That violates the defendants' rights not to mention the public's right to know what its court system is doing."[52] At least one government official, former Attorney General John Ashcroft, has suggested that the government could ignore the

Sixth Amendment altogether and lock American citizens up indefinitely, simply by labeling them so-called "enemy combatants."[53]

Reports of contracts for new internment camps being awarded to private contractors have also raised considerable alarm among those who fear that the camps may be intended for American citizens. In 2006, the Department of Homeland Security awarded a $385 million contract to a former subsidiary of the Halliburton Corporation to build detention camps in the United States, reportedly for use in rounding up illegal immigrants. But Daniel Ellsberg sees more nefarious motives at work. "Almost certainly this is preparation for a roundup after the next 9/11 for Mid-Easterners, Muslims and possibly dissenters," says Ellsberg, a former military analyst who in 1971 released the Pentagon Papers, the U.S. military's account of its activities in Vietnam. "They've already done this on a smaller scale, with the 'special registration' detentions of immigrant men from Muslim countries, and with Guantanamo."[54]

Such a scenario would not necessarily represent a new course with respect to Americans. Recall, for example, the large-scale detainment of Japanese and Japanese Americans who had committed no crimes in internment camps during World War II. Remember, too, that thousands of protesters were arrested and taken to Pier 57, a condemned bus depot in New York, during the Republican National Convention in 2004.[55] Ellsberg may not be too far off the mark in wondering whether Arab Americans and Muslims might be next.

AMENDMENT VII: RIGHT TO A JURY TRIAL IN CIVIL DISPUTES

In suits at common law, where the value in controversy shall exceed twenty dollars, the right of trial by jury shall be preserved, and no fact tried by a jury, shall be otherwise re-examined in any Court of the United States, than according to the rules of the common law.

American law is based on centuries-old English common law, the accumulated body of laws that are based on common sense rulings and which preserve the rights of the people. Property ownership is a fundamental right of free people, and common law establishes the rules we abide by. In a legal dispute over property, citizens have a right to a jury trial.

The text of the Declaration of Independence explicitly criticizes King George III for "depriving us in many cases, of the benefits of trial by jury." Similar to the Sixth Amendment's guarantee of a jury trial for those accused of a crime, the Seventh Amendment guarantees a jury trial for civil disputes. The founders believed that the flames of freedom burn brightest when citizens from all walks of life are able to apply the law to the facts of a case. As Alexander Hamilton proclaimed: "I cannot readily discern the inseparable connection between the existence of liberty, and the trial by jury in civil cases."[56]

A jury's role is to examine the facts, while a judge determines and explains the law. These two roles are a fundamental part of our legal system. Judges are not allowed to overstep their bounds and become a jury of one.

The Seventh Amendment Today

The Seventh Amendment right to a civil trial remains relatively healthy. America's courts are full of private lawsuits where people are attempting to convince a jury that someone wrongfully injured them, violated their civil rights, or terminated their employment. But even the Seventh Amendment isn't safe from today's assault on liberty.

Many modern courts use a legal theory known as the "complexity exception," whereby a judge may take a civil lawsuit out of the hands of a jury because the issues are supposedly too complicated for the jurors to understand. This is most common in patent disputes, which often involve complex scientific principles. But this is in direct contravention of the Seventh Amendment. What gives the government the authority to determine that something is too complicated for a jury to understand?

Many corporations such as credit card companies and others that deal with consumer agreements are also attempting to surreptitiously undermine Americans' Seventh Amendment rights by nullifying the customer's right to sue. Hidden within the fine print of the often lengthy consumer contracts is the provision that customers can no longer take the corporation to court but, rather, must appear before an arbitration panel—a body that often limits the evidence that can be presented, prevents cross-examination, and does not allow an appeal of their decision.

AMENDMENT VIII: CRUEL AND UNUSUAL PUNISHMENT

Excessive bail shall not be required, nor excessive fines imposed, nor cruel and unusual punishments inflicted.

In a speech before the Virginia House of Burgesses, Patrick Henry stated: "I have but one lamp by which my feet are guided; and that is the lamp of experience. I know of no way of judging the future but by the past."[57] The past, as the founders knew it, was one shadowed by the threat of torture for any who disagreed with government policies. Torture in the form of "pillorying, disemboweling, decapitation, and drawing and quartering" was commonplace throughout medieval Europe.[58] Believing that inhumane punishments had no place in a nation founded upon the principle of liberty, the founders enacted the Eighth Amendment, which prohibits cruel and unusual punishment. The colonists were also wary of authority figures and were particularly concerned about guarding against an abuse of power by such individuals. The Eighth Amendment spoke to this concern by prohibiting judges from imposing arbitrary punishments upon individuals who came before the court.[59]

In some countries, "disloyal or troublesome" citizens are jailed indefinitely on trumped-up charges. If they cannot pay their bail, they don't get out. The U.S. Constitution, however, recognizes that those accused of crimes have rights. The Bill of Rights guarantees the basic human right of people to be treated with respect, even if they are convicted criminals. In this way, the Eighth Amendment is similar to the Sixth: it protects the rights of the accused, the people most susceptible to abuse because they have the least resources. And it prohibits the use of cruel or unusual punishment.

The Eighth Amendment Today

What exactly constitutes "cruel and unusual" punishment? The U.S. Supreme Court has struggled to establish a conclusive answer to this question. A few Supreme Court justices subscribe to the idea that what was considered "cruel and unusual" at the time of our nation's founding more than two hundred years ago should still shape our idea of what is considered "cruel and unusual" today. A majority of the Court, however, has determined that what constitutes "cruel and unusual" should be dependent on the "evolving standards of decency that mark the progress of a maturing society."[60]

Given such a benchmark as "evolving standards of decency," one might think that Americans are safe from being subjected to punishment that the average person would consider cruel and unusual. Yet that is not so. It should be noted that while the Supreme Court has determined that executing mentally retarded people is "cruel and unusual," it has left it up to the states to determine whether a particular inmate qualifies as "mentally retarded." Consequently, mentally retarded inmates are still being executed for lack of uniform guidelines and standards.

Lethal injection is one form of execution that has come under great scrutiny, especially in recent years, and is often painted as a civilized and benign way to die. Lethal injection was supposed to end the debate about how states execute prisoners. As U.S. Supreme Court Justice Antonin Scalia stated in the 1994 case *Callins v. Collins*, "How enviable a quiet death by lethal injection."[61] Over the past few years, however, growing concerns have been raised that lethal injection may actually inflict greater pain on the condemned, which raises the specter of constitutional violations.

Despite reports indicating that death by lethal injection causes extreme pain when not properly performed, thirty-seven states still use this method.[62] In December 2006, Governor Jeb Bush halted executions in Florida after the botched execution by lethal injection of Angel Diaz. Diaz took thirty-four minutes to die—twice the usual time—after the needles carrying the drugs were inserted into the flesh of his arms, rather than his veins. Coroners found chemical burns on his arms, suggesting that Diaz suffered considerable pain during the execution.[63]

Concerns about the reliability of the lethal injection protocol were raised with the Supreme Court. Central to these concerns is the possibility that an inmate about to be executed who is not properly sedated by the first drug and then paralyzed by the second drug is able to feel the effects of the painful third killing drug but unable to express that pain due to his paralytic state. The Court was asked to determine whether this scenario is likely and, if so, whether it constitutes cruel and unusual punishment. And in April 2008, the Supreme Court upheld the constitutionality of lethal injections. [64]

The Supreme Court's decision to review the case followed in the wake of lower court rulings throughout the country that have found the scenario described above to be at risk of, or actually, occurring. In California, the state with the largest death row population,[65] Judge Jeremy Fogel of the U.S. District Court for the Northern Circuit of California delivered a damning judgment in December 2006, wherein he stated that California's lethal injection procedure represents "an undue and unnecessary risk" of a violation of the constitutional prohibition against cruel and unusual punishment. "This is intolerable under the Constitution," Judge Fogel declared. "The state's implementation of California's lethal injection protocol lacks both reliability and transparency."[66]

In addition to the debate raging over what constitutes cruel and unusual punishment, there is an equally contentious dispute about whether criminal penalties, including the death penalty, are handed out based on factors unrelated to the crime, such as a defendant's race, socioeconomic class, and quality of legal representation. According to the U.S. General Accounting Office, in "82 percent of the studies reviewed, race of the victim was found to influence the likelihood of being charged with capital murder or receiving the death penalty, that is, those who murdered whites were found more likely to be sentenced to death than those who murdered blacks."[67] These, and other concerns, have contributed to a growing national movement calling for a moratorium on the death penalty.

Amendment IX: Rights Retained by the People

The enumeration in the Constitution, of certain rights, shall not be construed to deny or disparage others retained by the people.

The framers of our Constitution were so concerned about civil liberties that they wished to do everything conceivable to protect our future freedoms and guard against government encroachment. But some framers, as we have seen, opposed a declaration of rights because it might appear that these were the only rights the people possessed. The Ninth Amendment remedied this by providing that rights not listed were nonetheless maintained by the people.

The Ninth Amendment represents two of the most significant themes of our Constitution. The first is popular sovereignty, which holds that a government exists only to serve the interests of its people because the people themselves are the source of the government's power. Popular sovereignty—the belief that the power to govern flows upward from the people, rather than downward from the rulers—is a hallmark of America's freedom. This means that our rights are inherently ours, and we the people created our government to protect them. The government did not, nor did it ever, have the power to grant us our rights. This amendment assures that the national government never forgets this important principle. As James Madison noted, "The ultimate authority resides in the people alone."[68] And as the Declaration of Independence affirms, "Governments ... deriv[e] their just Powers from the Consent of the Governed."

The second theme is the "presumption of liberty." No one should ever be forced to bear the burden of proving why he or she should be able to exercise a particular right. Because the people are the source of the government's power, the government should always bear the burden of showing why a right should be restricted whenever it attempts to restrict one. After all, the Declaration of Independence states that we are "endowed ... with certain unalienable Rights ... among these are Life, Liberty, and the Pursuit of Happiness...."

In sum, the Ninth Amendment serves as a meaningful check on federal power and a significant guarantee of individual liberty. It is also an important reminder that the rights guaranteed in the Bill of Rights, along with the limitations placed on the government, were never intended to be an exhaustive list; rather, the Bill of Rights is merely a starting point. The founders understood that the balance of power should always fall in favor of the people, not the government. Indeed, the real power and authority under our Constitution, as clearly demonstrated in the Ninth Amendment, rests in those three revolutionary words: "we the people."

The Ninth Amendment Today

The government continues to pass more and more laws that restrict our freedoms, and government officials claim they have an "important government interest" in doing so. All the while, courts have all but ignored the Ninth Amendment, usually claiming that it is impossible to interpret its limits. As our homes are taken by the government, police intrusively break into our residences without even knocking or announcing their presence, and government agents listen in on our phone conversations and read our emails, the freedoms enshrined in the Bill of Rights are in jeopardy, including those not specifically named but protected nonetheless by the Ninth Amendment. When the government can violate the non-enumerated rights granted in the Ninth Amendment, it is only a matter of time before it will trample the enumerated rights of the people explicitly spelled out in the rest of the Bill of Rights.

Yet it is up to the American people to reclaim the rights that are being taken away from them by the government. Unless more people take a stand for their liberties, it won't just be the Ninth Amendment that is ignored.

AMENDMENT X: RESERVED POWERS OF THE STATES

The powers not delegated to the United States by the Constitution, nor prohibited by it to the States, are reserved to the States respectively, or to the people.

Ours is a federal system of government, with power divided among local, state, and national entities. This doctrine, known as "federalism," describes the unique relationship that each state has with the national or federal government. As a function of this system, independent state and local governments retain significant decision-making power for the people of their states. As James Madison asserted: "The powers reserved to the several states will extend to all objects, which, in the ordinary course of affairs, concern the lives, liberties and prosperities of the people, and the internal order, improvement, and prosperity of the state."[69] The Tenth Amendment reminds the national government that the people and the states retain every authority that is not otherwise mentioned in the Constitution.

These state governments are also subject to federal interests composed of values and goals that citizens of every state within the United States share. Federal and state flags illustrate an example of federalism in practice. While each state government building flies a red, white, and blue flag to symbolize its affiliation with the federal government, each state also has its own unique flag to symbolize the characteristics unique to that state which make it different from the forty-nine other states in the Union.

Because the Tenth Amendment only applies to the federal government, it serves as a reminder that federal power is limited and that laws unique to a particular state, as unusual as they might be, may only be struck down in favor of a prevailing federal interest and under extreme circumstances. An example of a prevailing federal interest is found in the 1954 case *Brown v. Board of Education of Topeka*. Although Kansas had a state law that permitted segregated schools, the federal interest in desegregation was so strong that the U.S. Supreme Court found this state law to be unconstitutional.[70]

The Tenth Amendment Today

With few exceptions, the old-fashioned town hall meeting has become a thing of the past. And to a certain extent, so is the power given to the states and the people in the Tenth Amendment. Like several other amendments in the Bill of Rights, the Tenth Amendment has practically been rendered moot by the national government and the courts.

Indeed, the federal government has grown so large that it has made local and state legislatures relatively irrelevant. Through its many agencies, the federal government has stripped states of the right to regulate countless issues that would be better governed at the local level.

Issues such as defining marriage and criminalizing flag burning are recent examples of the federal government's attempts through legislation to regulate issues that are almost purely local in nature. The so-called "hate crime" legislation that the federal government has been proposing over the past few years is yet another example of the federal government's increased role in the day-to-day lives of Americans. Hate crime legislation defines a hate crime as an act of violence committed against an individual because of the victim's race, religion, national origin, gender, sexual orientation, gender identity, or disability and represents a violation of the Tenth Amendment's limitations on federal power. Under the U.S. Constitution, there are only three federal crimes: piracy, treason, and counterfeiting. All other criminal matters are left to the individual states. Any federal legislation dealing with criminal matters not related to these three issues usurps state authority over criminal law and takes a step toward turning the states into mere administrative units of the federal government.

There has been no evidence that local governments are failing to prosecute the crimes covered under hate crime legislation; thus, the federal government has no justification for claiming a necessity to intervene. Instead of increasing the effectiveness of law enforcement, hate crime laws undermine equal justice under the law by requiring that law enforcement and judicial system officers give priority to investigating and prosecuting hate crimes.

As discussed in Chapter Four, eventually each state's driver's license will have to conform to federal standards in order for its citizens to conduct business or do routine things such as board an airplane. This Real ID program is yet another move toward the centralization of power, impacting the rights of states to regulate themselves.

We must remember that Congress and the president periodically assume more power than the Constitution grants them. It is up to the people and the states to make sure they obey the law of the land.

Habeas Corpus

The privilege of the writ of habeas corpus shall not be suspended, unless when in cases of rebellion or invasion the public safety may require it.

—Article I, Section 9, U.S. Constitution

Habeas corpus, a fundamental tenet of English common law, does not appear anywhere in the Bill of Rights. Its importance was such that it was enshrined in the Constitution itself. And it is of such magnitude that all other rights, including those in the Bill of Rights, are dependent upon it. Without habeas corpus, the significance of all other rights crumbles.

The right of habeas corpus was important to the framers of the Constitution because they knew from personal experience what it was like to be labeled enemy combatants, imprisoned indefinitely, and not given the opportunity to appear before a neutral judge. Believing that such arbitrary imprisonment is "in all ages, the favorite and most formidable instrument of tyranny,"[71] the founders were all the more determined to protect Americans from such government abuses.

The History of Habeas Corpus

Translated as "you should have the body," habeas corpus is a legal action, or writ, by which those imprisoned unlawfully can seek relief from their imprisonment. Derived from English common law, habeas corpus first appeared in the Magna Carta of 1215 and is the oldest human right in the history of English-speaking civilization. The doctrine of habeas corpus stems from the requirement that a government must either charge a person or let him go free.

While serving as president, Thomas Jefferson addressed the essential necessity of habeas corpus. In his first inaugural address on March 4, 1801, Jefferson said, "I know, indeed, that some honest men fear that a republican government cannot be strong; that this government is not strong enough." But, said Jefferson, our nation was "the world's best hope" and, because of our strong commitment to democracy, "the strongest government on earth." Jefferson said that the sum of this basic belief was found in the "freedom of person under the protection of the habeas corpus; and trial by juries impartially selected. These principles form the bright constellation which has gone before us, and guided our steps through an age of revolution and reformation."[72]

In the two centuries since the Constitution was ratified, habeas corpus has only been suspended twice. It was first suspended on April 27, 1861, in Maryland and parts of Midwestern states by President Abraham Lincoln in response to riots and local militia action, as well as the threat that Maryland would secede from the Union. The second suspension of habeas corpus occurred during Reconstruction, in the early 1870s, when President Ulysses S. Grant responded to civil rights violations by the Ku Klux Klan. It was then limited to nine counties in South Carolina.

Throughout the twentieth century, the U.S. Supreme Court has repeatedly confirmed the importance of the right of habeas corpus. And one federal appeals court observed that the Supreme Court has "recognized the fact that 'the writ of habeas corpus is the fundamental instrument for safeguarding individual freedom against arbitrary and lawless state action.'"[73]

Habeas Corpus Today

In 1996, following the Oklahoma City bombing, Congress passed the Antiterrorism and Effective Death Penalty Act (AEDPA), which limited the use of the federal writ of habeas corpus in two ways. First, it imposed a one-year statute of limitations on bringing the writ, which meant that those imprisoned were unable to apply for release after being imprisoned for over a year. Second, it dramatically increased the federal judiciary's deference to decisions previously made in state court proceedings either on appeal or in a state court habeas corpus action. This means that federal judges were prohibited from examining a case purely on its merits and were instead forced to follow previous decisions.

AEDPA also required that if any constitutional right was to be invoked in order to vacate a conviction rooted in a mistake of law by the state court, it must have "resulted in a decision that was contrary to, or involved an unreasonable application of, clearly established Federal law, as determined by the Supreme Court of the United States."[74] In other words, actual innocence—surely the whole point of habeas corpus—has been removed as a ground for challenging one's incarceration.

Following 9/11, President Bush made several attempts with varying degrees of success to revoke the right of habeas corpus. As well as the obvious example of denying habeas corpus proceedings to those detained at Guantanamo Bay, the president attempted, more surreptitiously, to grant himself the power to be able to revoke this basic right for every American citizen.

As discussed in Chapter One, prior to the midterm elections of 2006, which transformed the makeup of Congress, the Bush administration advocated the inclusion of two stealth provisions into a mammoth defense budget bill. The additions made it easier for the government to declare martial law and establish a dictatorship. The inclusion of a seemingly insignificant rider into the huge defense bill (the martial law section of the 591-page Defense Appropriations Act takes up just a few paragraphs) allows any president to use the military as a domestic police force in response to a natural disaster, disease outbreak, terrorist attack, or any "other condition." According to this law, a president will not have to notify Congress of his intent to use military force against the American people—he or she simply has to notify them after having done so. The defense budget provision's vague language left the doors wide open for rampant abuse, such as suspending the writ of habeas corpus.

Habeas corpus concerns are also apparent in this law, which facilitates militarized police roundups and the detainment of protesters in detention camps. The stated purpose of these camps is to provide "temporary detention and processing capabilities."[75] The plan calls for preparing for "an emergency influx of immigrants, or to support the rapid development of new programs" in the event of other emergencies, such as "a natural disaster."[76] However, Americans are incredibly naïve if they believe these camps will be used only to house illegal aliens. We would do well to remember that

American citizens who protested at the 2004 Republican National Convention were detained.[77]

Also discussed in Chapter One, President Bush went further when, on May 9, 2007, he issued a "presidential directive" that allows him to assume control of the federal government following a "catastrophic emergency."[78] Although the directive doesn't specifically identify the types of emergencies that would qualify as "catastrophic," the language is so broad that it could include almost anything that might have a major impact on the country. This directive would in effect make any president the final authority in such an emergency, as it states clearly that there will be a cooperative effort among the three branches of government that will be coordinated by the president. Each branch of government—the executive, legislative, and judicial—is supposed to be equal in power. Yet if the president is coordinating these efforts, it essentially puts him in charge of every branch of the government.

For suspected terrorists, it is important to note that those detained have not been held in a manner similar to how civilians would be detained by the police—that is, based upon probable cause. Many have been handed over by bounty hunters and arrested upon information obtained through vigorous interrogation. The evidence against many of the detainees, as well as its reliability, is extremely weak, if not downright nonexistent. This is why some speculate that the reason the president and Congress have attempted to prevent these detainees from having habeas corpus rights is that the evidence against them is not strong enough to stand up to the scrutiny of civilian courts.

The first effort by President Bush to avoid habeas corpus proceedings for suspects was the Presidential Military Order of November 13, 2001. This gave the president the power to detain as "enemy combatants" noncitizens suspected of having a connection to terrorists or terrorism. These individuals could then be held without charge indefinitely, without a court hearing and without access to a lawyer.

Not only have noncitizens been held in such a manner, but so too were American citizens, including those such as Jose Padilla who were captured on American soil, rather than on a foreign battlefield. Many legal and constitutional scholars have contended that these provisions are in direct opposition to the Constitution and the Bill of

Rights, particularly with regard to American citizens. The U.S. Supreme Court agreed, declaring that American citizens have a right to habeas corpus even when declared to be enemy combatants. It also affirmed the basic principle that a citizen's right to habeas corpus could not be revoked.[79] And the Court in *Rasul v. Bush* stated that the policy of preventing the detainees access to the protections of habeas corpus was unconstitutional.[80]

President Bush and Congress, however, were not deterred by the Supreme Court's rulings that habeas corpus rights—at least for noncitizens—could not be violated and passed legislation designed to prevent prisoners at Guantanamo Bay from having habeas corpus hearings. The 2006 Department of Defense Appropriations Act states in Section 1005(e) that "no court, justice, or judge shall have jurisdiction to hear or consider an application for a writ of habeas corpus filed by or on behalf of an alien detained by the Department of Defense at Guantanamo Bay, Cuba."

This ruling was challenged in *Hamdan v. Rumsfeld*. Salim Ahmed Hamdan petitioned for a writ of habeas corpus, challenging that the military commissions set up by the Bush administration to try detainees at Guantanamo Bay "violate both the UCMJ [Uniform Code of Military Justice] and the four Geneva Conventions." The U.S. Supreme Court, in a 5–3 ruling, rejected Congress's attempts to strip the court of jurisdiction over habeas corpus appeals by detainees at Guantanamo Bay.[81]

Following this legal setback for the Bush administration, Congress launched yet another attack on habeas corpus by passing the Military Commissions Act in 2006. The act eliminated habeas corpus by allowing noncitizen enemy combatants to be held indefinitely in a military prison without access to a lawyer. The legislation's denial of habeas corpus rights to noncitizens detained at Guantanamo Bay has since been challenged and considered by the U.S. Supreme Court.[82]

WHO DOES THE CONSTITUTION PROTECT?

The Bill of Rights and habeas corpus are fundamental to preserving our rights. Yet because the Constitution is a uniquely American document, the question has arisen: to whom do its protections and rights apply? Is it universal in its application, or are only citizens of the United States beneficiaries of it?

When addressing whom the Constitution protects, there is a necessary distinction to make, aside from whether the subject is a citizen, and that is whether the citizen or person is physically in the United States. Many U.S. statutes apply to conduct that occurs abroad, and the Bill of Rights, as well as the rest of the Constitution, protects citizens wherever they go in the world.

A different principle applies to territories ruled by the United States that are constitutionally distinct from the United States itself. In 1990, the U.S. Supreme Court in *U.S. v. Verdugo-Urquidez* ruled that the Fourth Amendment did not apply to a search by U.S. government agents of a noncitizen's property in Mexico. The Court held that "the people" intended to be protected by the Fourth Amendment were the people of the United States and that the defendant in this case lacked a sufficient relationship with the United States to call upon the U.S. Constitution for protection. Therefore, according to this logic, noncitizens abroad lack any constitutional rights, even when they confront the U.S. government there.[83]

Fourth Amendment protections do extend to all persons who come within the territorial jurisdiction of the United States, however, as the person enjoys constitutional rights while within U.S. borders, even when here illegally.[84] In 1975, Texas passed a law authorizing school districts to stop accepting children who were not legally admitted into the United States. In 1982, the U.S. Supreme Court ruled that the law violated the Fourteenth Amendment. The Court held that the Equal Protection Clause of the Fourteenth Amendment requires the state to provide free public schooling to children of undocumented workers on an equal basis with other children in the state.[85]

The Fifth Amendment rights of noncitizens were discussed in *Matthews v. Diaz*.[86] The U.S. Supreme Court recognized that the Fifth Amendment protects aliens whose presence in the United States is unlawful from invidious discrimination from the federal government.

Similarly, the Fourteenth Amendment's Equal Protection Clause requires states to provide equal protection under the law to all persons, regardless of citizenship, within their jurisdictions.

FIGHT TO KEEP THEM

Since the ratification of the Constitution with its provision for habeas corpus and the original ten amendments—those 462 words that make up the Bill of Rights—appended to it, there have been seventeen other amendments, bringing the grand total to twenty-seven. Not all the subsequent amendments deal with essential rights, the grand exceptions being the Thirteenth and Fourteenth Amendments, which guarantee equality, forbid slavery, and assure the right to vote. One disastrous amendment, the Eighteenth, which dealt with Prohibition, was repealed by the Twenty-First Amendment. Nevertheless, the original Bill of Rights and the Writ of Habeas Corpus, for all intents and purposes, remain standing. However, we must keep in mind always that the freedoms guaranteed in the Great Writ and those 462 words will only survive as long as we fight to keep them. The time to stand and fight to keep them is now.

Endnotes

Author to Reader: We Are Not What We Set Out to Be

1 *Inaugural Addresses of the Presidents of the United States* (Washington, DC: U.S. G.P.O., 1989) http://www.bartleby.com/124/.

2 Nancy Gibbs, "Apocalypse Now," *Time*, June 23, 2002, http://www.time.com/time/covers/1101020701/story.html. *See also* Carol Memmott, "'Left Behind' series: Like manna from heaven," *USA Today*, February 2, 2005, http://www.usatoday.com/life/books/news/2005-02-28-left-behind_x.htm and the website for the *Left Behind* series at http://www.leftbehind.com/channel-books.asp?channel ID=95.

3 As quoted in Morris Berman, *Dark Ages America: The Final Phase of Empire* (New York: W.W. Norton and Co., 2006), p. 282.

4 "Education Notebook: The Facts on Federal Education Spending," The Heritage Foundation, November 9, 2006, http://www.heritage.org/Research/Education/EdNotes49.cfm.

5 "The Illiteracy Time Bomb," *Business Week* (February 14, 2002), http://www.businessweek.com/smallbiz/content/feb2002/sb2002 0214_7072.htm.

6 "Poll: 1 in 4 adults did not read a single book last year," *Associated Press* (August 22, 2007).

7 Berman, *op. cit.*, p. 6.

8 "Still Misinformed," *Kansas City Star* (October 6, 2004), p. A2, reporting on a *USA Today*/Gallup Poll (on Saddam Hussein and 9/11).

[9] Thomas de Zengotita, "The Numbing of the American Mind: Culture as Anesthetic," *Harper's* (April 2002), p. 3, http://www.harpers.org/archive/2002/04/0079134., http://www.findarticles.com/cf_O/m1111/1823_304/84184700/print.ihtml.

[10] Alex Marshall, *How Cities Work* (Austin: University of Texas Press, 2000), pp. 189–90.

[11] Robert Putnam, *Bowling Alone: The Collapse and Revival of American Community* (New York: Simon & Schuster, 2000).

[12] Berman, *op. cit.*, p. 45.

[13] *Ibid.*

[14] "Video shows shoppers stepping over dying woman," *Associated Press*, (July 5, 2007), http://www.msnbc.msn.com/id/19586738.

[15] Darren W. Davis, *Negative Liberty: Public Opinion and the Terrorist Attacks on America* (New York: Russell Sage Foundation, 2007), p. 114.

[16] Joseph Wershba, "Edward R. Murrow and the Time of His Time," *Eve's Magazine*, http://www.evesmag.com/murrow.htm.

[17] Edward R. Murrow, "A Report on Senator Joseph R. McCarthy," *See It Now*, broadcast March 9, 1954 by CBS-TV.

[18] Davis, *op. cit.*

[19] *Ibid.*

[20] Lisa Anderson, "Changed Lives," *Chicago Tribune*, (March 10, 2002), p. 1.

[21] David Brooks, "The Happiness Gap," *New York Times* (October 30, 2007), http://www.nytimes.com/2007/10/30/opinion/30brooks.html.

[22] *Ibid.*

[23] Anne-Marie Slaughter, *The Idea That Is America: Keeping Faith with Our Values in a Dangerous World* (New York: Basic Books, 2007), p. ix.

[24] As quoted *ibid.*, pp. xvii–xviii.

[25] *Ibid.*, p. xviii.

Chapter One: A Government of Wolves

[1] "ACLU Written Statement of Nadine Strossen, President, and Timothy Edgar, Legislative Counsel, before the United States Commission on Civil Rights at a Hearing on 'Security and Liberty,'"

March 19, 2004, http://www.aclu.org/safefree/general/17493leg20040319.html.

[2] Bruce Fein, "Are Civil Liberties at Risk in the War on Terror?" *Cato Policy Report* (September/October 2007), http://www.cato.org/pubs/policy_report/v29n5/cpr29n5-4.html

[3] Chalmers Johnson, *Nemesis: The Last Days of the American Republic* (New York: Metropolitan Books, 2006), pp. 13–14.

[4] David A. Fahrenthold, "Federal Grants Bring Surveillance Cameras to Small Towns" *Washington Post*, January 19, 2006,, http://www.washingtonpost.com/wp-dyn/content/article/2006/01/18/AR2006011802324_pf.html.

[5] "College's librarians barred from wearing American pride stickers," *Associated Press*, September 19, 2001, http://www.freedomforum.org/templates/document.asp? documentID=14927.

[6] "Big Brother Is Watching, Listening" *CBS News*, broadcast May 15, 2002, by CBS-TV, http://www.cbsnews.com/stories/2002/05/15/eveningnews/main509140.shtml.

[7] "Things Getting Sticky for Owner of Sticker," *Salt Lake Tribune*, September 1, 2004.

[8] Richard Willing, "With only a letter, FBI can gather private data," *USA Today*, July 6, 2006, http://www.usatoday.com/news/washington/2006-07-05-fbi-letters_x.htm.

[9] John Solomon, "FBI Finds It Frequently Overstepped in Collecting Data," *Washington Post*, June 14, 2007, http:/www.washingtonpost.com/wp-dyn/content/article/2007/06/13/AR2007061302453_pdf.

[10] "Kindergartner's suspension appealed to Supreme Court," *Associated Press*, September 20, 2003, http://www.firstamendmentcenter.org/news.aspx?id=11952.

[11] Shaila K. Dewan, "City to Pay $1.6 Million in Fatal, Mistaken Raid," *New York Times*, October 29, 2003.

[12] *Kelo v. City of New London*, 545 U.S. 469 (2005), http://www.supremecourtus.gov/opinions/04pdf/04-108.pdf.

[13] "Many Defendants' Cases Kept Secret," *Associated Press*, March 4, 2006, http://www.cbsnews.com/stories/2006/03/04/ap/national/mainD8G4SFRG1.shtml.

14 "Profile: Jose Padilla," *BBC News*, November 22, 2005, http://news.bbc.co.uk/1/hi/world/americas/2037444.stm.

15 Jonathan Turley, "Camps for Citizens: Ashcroft's Hellish Vision," *Los Angeles Times*, August 14, 2002, http://www.truthout.org/docs_02/08.15B.ashcr.camps.htm.

16 Nat Parry, "Bush's Mysterious 'New Programs,'" *Consortium News*, February 21, 2006, http://www.consortiumnews.com/2006/022106a.html.

17 Scott Shane, "Locked Up in Land of the Free," *Baltimore Sun*, June 1, 2003, http://www.commondreams.org/headlines03/0601-01.htm.

18 Peter Slevin, "U.S. Prison Study Faults System and the Public," *Washington Post*, June 8, 2006, http://www.washingtonpost.com/wp-dyn/content/article/2006/06/07/AR2006060702050.html.

19 Shane, *op. cit.*

20 Michael Lind, "The Weird Men Behind George W. Bush's War," *New Statesman*, April 7, 2003, http://www.newstatesman.com/200304070003.

21 Arthur S. Miller, *The Modern State: Private Governments and the American Constitution* (Westport, CT: Greenwood Press, 1976), as quoted in Bertram Gross, *Friendly Fascism: The New Face of Power in America* (Cambridge, MA: South End Press, 1980), p. 189.

22 Gross, *op. cit.*, p. 190.

23 Russell Mokhiber and Robert Weissman, "Corporate Focus: Bush Rolls Out the Red Carpet for Big Business," *AlterNet*, January 16, 2001, http://www.alternet.org/module/printversion/10351.

24 Jane Mayer, "Contract Sport: What did the Vice-President do for Halliburton?" *The New Yorker*, February 16, 2004, http://www.newyorker.com/archive/2004/02/16/040216fa_fact?printable=true.

25 Morris Berman, *Dark Ages America: The Final Phase of Empire* (New York: W.W. Norton and Co., 2006), p. 219.

26 Graham Paterson, "Alan Greenspan claims Iraq war was really for oil," *Times Online*, September 16, 2007, http://www.timesonline.co.uk/tol/news/world/article2461214.ece?print=yes&randnum=11.

[27] Thomas Jefferson to M. de Meunier, January 24, 1786.

[28] Thomas Jefferson to Horatio G. Spafford, March 17, 1814.

[29] Gross, *op. cit.*, p. 190.

[30] James Madison, *Memorial and Remonstrance* (1785), http://www.infidels.org/library/historical/james_madison/memorial.html.

[31] White House Transcript, "President Bush Attends Veterans of Foreign Wars Convention, Discusses War on Terror," August 22, 2007, http://www.whitehouse.gov/news/releases/2007/08/20070822-3.html.

[32] Executive Order, "Blocking Property of Certain Persons Who Threaten Stabilization Efforts In Iraq" (July 17, 2007), http://www.whitehouse.gov/news/releases/2007/07/20070717-3.html.

[33] Walter Pincus, "Destabilizing Iraq, Broadly Defined," *Washington Post*, July 23, 2007, http://www.washingtonpost.com/wp-dyn/content/article/2007/07/22/AR2007072201141.html.

[34] Rebecca Carr and Ken Herman, "Government secrecy up despite exposure of issue," August 31, 2007, http://seattlepi.nwsource.com/national/329978_secrecy02.html.

[35] Statement of Michelle Boardman, Deputy Assistant Attorney General, Office of Legal Counsel, United States Department of Justice, Testimony Before the Committee on the Judiciary, United States Senate. *Presidential Signing Statements*, 109th Cong., 2nd sess., June 27, 2006, http://www.fas.org/irp/congress/2006_hr/062706boardman.html.

[36] "Making Martial Law Easier," *New York Times*, February 19, 2007, http://www.nytimes.com/2007/02/19/opinion/19mon3.html?ei=5088&en=b6389062c9533ffe&ex=1329541200.

[37] Jane Smiley, "What Would You Do If Bush Declared Martial Law?" *Huffington Post*, February 20, 2007, http://www.huffingtonpost.com/jane-smiley/what-would-you-do-if-bush_b_41674.html.

[38] John Warner, National Defense Authorization Act for Fiscal Year 2007, Public Law 109-364, Section 1076, http://frwebgate.access.gpo.gov/cgi-bin/getdoc.cgi?dbname=109_cong_public_laws&docid=f:publ364.109.pdf.

[39] Jonathan Alter, "I Know What You Did Last Summer," *Newsweek*, August 20, 2007, http://www.msnbc.msn.com/id/20226453/site/newsweek/.

[40] Aziz Huq, "Data-Mining Our Liberties," *Nation*, August 7, 2007, http://www.thenation.com/doc/20070813/huq2.

[41] William Fisher, "Bush Administration Ramps Up Secrecy," *Truth/Report*, September 10, 2007, http://www.truthout.org/docs_2006/printer_091007A.shtml.

[42] *Ibid.*

[43] Edward Alden, "Dismay at Attempt to Find Legal Justification for Torture," *Financial Times*, June 10, 2004, http://www.truthout.org/cgi-bin/artman/exec/view.cgi/4/4841.

[44] W. Taylor Reveley III, *War Powers of the President and Congress* (Charlottesville: University of Virginia Press, 1981), p. 29.

[45] Wikipedia, "Alien and Sedition Acts," http://en.wikipedia.org/wiki/Alien_and_Sedition_Acts.

[46] Church Committee, *Dr. Martin Luther King, Jr., Case Study*, Book III, Church Committee, United States Senate, April 23, 1976, http://www.icdc.com/~paulwolf/cointelpro/churchfinalreportI-IIb.htm. *See also* Allan Jalon, "A Break-In to End All Break-Ins: In 1971, stolen FBI files exposed the government's domestic spying program," *Los Angeles Times*, March 8, 2006, http://www.commondreams.org/views06/0308-27.htm.

[47] Transcript, "Address to a Joint Session of Congress and the American People," September 20, 2001, http://www.whitehouse.gov/news/releases/2001/09/20010920-8.html.

[48] *Ibid.*

[49] "Tommy Franks: Martial Law Will Replace Constitution After Next Terror Attack," *Newsmax*, November 21, 2003, http://www.propagandamatrix.com/211103martiallaw.html.

[50] Kevin Baker, "We're in the Army Now," *Harper's Magazine*, October 2003, p. 46.

[51] *Skinner v. Railway Labor Executives Association*, 489 U.S. 602, 635 (1989) (Marshall, J., dissenting).

[52] Berman, *op. cit.*, p. 13.

[53] Thomas Jefferson to Henry Lee, May 8, 1825.

54 Thomas Jefferson to Robert C. Weightman, June 24, 1826.

55 Thomas G. West and Douglas A. Jeffrey, *The Rise and Fall of Constitutional Government in America: A Guide to Understanding the Principles of the American Founding* (Claremont, CA: The Claremont Institute, 2006), p. 8.

56 *Ibid.*, p. 10.

57 Earl Warren, *A Republic, If You Can Keep It* (Quadrangle Books, 1972), p. 104.

58 Henry Grunwald, "The Morning After the Fourth: Have We Kept Our Promise?" *Time*, July 14, 1975, p. 19.

59 Bill Moyers, "Prudence Reigns," *Newsweek*, July 28, 1975, p. 72.

60 Thomas Jefferson to William C. Jarvis, September 28, 1820. *The Writings of Thomas Jefferson*, edited by H. A. Washington, U.S. Congress, 1853–54, 7:179.

61 Thomas Jefferson, James Madison, et al., *Report to the Commissioners Appointed to fix the Site of the University of Virginia*, August 4, 1818, http://press-pubs.uchicago.edu/founders/documents/v1ch18s33.html.

62 *Ibid.*

63 Thomas Jefferson to James Madison, 1787, *The Writings of Thomas Jefferson*, edited by H.A. Washington, U.S. Congress, 1853–54, 2:332.

64 "Homer Simpson, Yes; First Amendment? 'Doh!'" *Associated Press*, March 1, 2006, http://www.editorandpublisher.com/eandp/news/article_display.jsp?vnu_content_id=1002113807.

65 "Americans' Awareness of First Amendment Freedoms," McCormick Tribune Freedom Museum, March 1, 2006, http://www.freedommuseum.us/assets/pdf/e4/pressrelease/survey_results_report_final.pdf.

66 "New National Poll Finds: More Americans Know Snow White's Dwarfs than Supreme Court Judges, Homer Simpson than Homer's Odyssey, and Harry Potter than Tony Blair," August 14, 2006, home.businesswire.com.

67 Jennifer Harper, "Superman Tops Supremes," *Washington Times*, August 15, 2006, http://www.washingtontimes.com.

68 "New National Poll," *op. cit.*

[69] David Yalof and Ken Dautrich, "Future of the First Amendment," January 31, 2005, http://firstamendment.jideas.org/downloads/future_ch1.pdf.

[70] West and Jeffrey, *op. cit.*, p. 14.

[71] Street Law and The Supreme Court Historical Society. "Nixon's Views on Presidential Power: Excerpts from an interview with David Frost" (May 19, 1971), http://www.landmarkcases.org/nixon/nixonview.html.

[72] West and Jeffrey, *op. cit.*, p. 19.

[73] Alexis de Tocqueville, *Democracy in America* (New York: Harper Perennial, 1988), p. 63.

[74] As quoted in Simon Blackburn, *Being Good* (USA: Oxford University Press, 2001), p. 2.

[75] Crane Brinston, John B. Christopher, and Robert Lee Wolff, *A History of Civilization,* 2nd ed. (Englewood Cliffs, NJ: Prentice-Hall, 1963), 2:484.

[76] Kenneth Dolbeare, "Alternatives to the New Fascism" (paper delivered at the American Political Science Association, September 1976), as quoted in Gross, *op. cit.*, p. 2.

[77] As quoted in Cal Thomas and Bob Beckel, *Common Ground: How to Stop the Partisan War That Is Destroying America* (New York: William Morrow, 2007), p. 174.

[78] Edwin R. Bayley, *Joe McCarthy and the Press* (Madison: University of Wisconsin Press, 1981), p. 193.

[79] Warren, *op. cit.*, p. 1.

[80] *United States v. Schwimmer*, 279 U.S. 644, 654-55 (1929) (Holmes, J., dissenting).

[81] Warren, *op. cit.*, pp. 6–7.

[82] John W. Whitehead, "We the People," introductory essay to *Pocket Constitution* (Charlottesville, VA: The Rutherford Institute, 2007), p. 6.

Chapter Two: Police Overkill

[1] Ron Paul, "It Can't Happen Here," *LewRockwell.com*, December 21, 2004, http://www.lewrockwell.com/paul/paul225.html.

[2] U.S. Department of Justice, "Federal Law Enforcement Statistics," Bureau of Justice Statistics, http://www.ojp.usdoj.gov/bjs/fedle.htm.

[3] Virginia Department of Game and Inland Fisheries, "'Game Warden' Name Changing to 'Conservation Police Officer,'" April 25, 2007, http://huntfishva.com/news/release.asp?id=125.

[4] Joseph Farah, "The federalization of cops," *World Net Daily*, June 7, 2000, http://www.wnd.com/news/article.asp?ARTICLE_ID=14985.

[5] Speech delivered by James Madison at the Constitutional Convention, June 29, 1787, *The Papers of James Madison, Vol. II* (J. & H.G. Langley, 1841), p. 992.

[6] Nicolaus Mills, *The Triumph of Meanness: America's War Against Its Better Self* (Boston: Houghton Mifflin, 1997), p. 6.

[7] *Ibid.*

[8] *Ibid.*, p. 7.

[9] Arash Ghadishah, *ABC News*, "Fla. Police Tape Is No Laughing Matter to Protester," August 10, 2006, http://abcnews.go.com/US/LegalCenter/story?id=2296783.

[10] *Ibid.*

[11] Amnesty International, "USA: Excessive and Lethal Force: Deaths and Ill-Treatment Involving Police Use of Tasers," AMR 51/139/2004, November 30, 2004, http://web.amnesty.org/library/index/engamr511392004.

[12] *Ibid.*, 46n, which cites a series of articles by Nick Budnick, *Williamette Week*, originally published February 4, 2004, February 11, 2004, and February 18, 2004.

[13] "Meet the new shock jocks," *Guardian Unlimited*, August 21, 2005, http://www.guardian.co.uk/theguardian/2005/aug/19/guardianweekly.guardianweekly12.

[14] Alex Berenson, "As Police Use of Tasers Rises, Questions Over Safety Increase," *New York Times*, June 18, 2004, http://www.nytimes.com/2004/07/18/national/18TASER.html?ei=5090&en=2c9c37c0dfaef9a6&ex=1247803200&partner=rssuserland&pagewanted=print&position=.

[15] Phuong Cat Le and Hector Castro, "Police are too quick to grab for Taser's power, say critics," *Seattle Post-Intelligencer*,

November 30, 2004, http://seattlepi.nwsource.com/local/201700_taser30.html.

[16] Hector Castro, "Pregnant woman 'Tasered' by police is convicted," *Seattle Post-Intelligencer*, May 10, 2005, http://seattlepi.nwsource.com/local/223578_taser10.html.

[17] Matt Garfield, "Police Taser 75-year-old at nursing home," *The Herald*, October 20, 2004, http://www.infowars.com/print/ps/taser_oldwoman.htm.

[18] "Excessive and Lethal Force: Deaths and Ill-Treatment Involving Police Use of Tasers," *op. cit.*

[19] "Student Arrested, Tasered at Kerry Event," *Associated Press*, September 18, 2007, http://www.abcnews.go.com/print?id=3616977.

[20] UN General Assembly, Thirty-Fourth Session, Article 3, *Code of Conduct for Law Enforcement Officials*, UN General Assembly Resolution A/RES/34/169, 1979. http://www.unhchr.ch/html/menu3/b/h_comp42.htm.

[21] Radley Balko, *Overkill: The Rise of Paramilitary Police Raids in America* (Washington DC: Cato Institute, 2006), p. 5, http://www.cato.org/pubs/wtpapers/balko_whitepaper_2006.pdf.

[22] As quoted in *ibid.*, p. 15.

[23] *Ibid.*, p. 3.

[24] *Ibid.*, p. 18.

[25] *Ibid.*, p. 4.

[26] *Ibid.*

[27] *Ibid.*, p. 44.

[28] *Ibid.*, p. 5.

[29] Eugene V. Walker, *Terror and Resistance* (Oxford University Press, 1969), as quoted in Bertram Gross, *Friendly Fascism: The New Face of Power in America* (Cambridge, MA: South End Press, 1980), p. 305.

[30] Balko, *op. cit.*, p. 8

[31] *Ibid.*

[32] Kelly Hearn, "Rumsfeld's Ray Gun," *AlterNet*, August 19, 2005, http://www.alternet.org/story/24044/?comments=view&cID=43722&pID=25941.

[33] Greg Gordon, "Invisible beam tops list of nonlethal weapons," sacbee.com (*Sacramento Bee* online content), June 1, 2004, http://dwb.sacbee.com/content/news/story/9499345p-10423294c.html.

[34] "Weapons Freeze, Microwave Enemies," *Associated Press*, August 2, 2004, http://www.wired.com/science/discoveries/news/2004/08/64437?currentPage=2.

[35] Hearn, *op. cit.*

[36] *Ibid.*

[37] Balko, *op. cit.*, p. 9.

[38] *Ibid.*, p. 12.

[39] *Ibid.*, pp. 12–13.

[40] As quoted in *ibid.*, p. 14.

[41] *Ibid.*, p. 17.

[42] *Ibid.*, p. 14.

[43] *Ibid.*, pp. 43–44.

[44] *Private Warriors,* Frontline Frequently Asked Questions, http://www.pbs.org/wgbh/pages/frontline/shows/warriors/faqs/.

[45] "High pay—and high risks—for contractors in Iraq," *CNN.com*, April 2, 2004, http://www.cnn.com/2004/WORLD/meast/04/01/iraq.contractor/.

[46] *Ibid.*

[47] Ranae Merle, "Storm-Wracked Parish Considers Hired Guns: Contractors in Louisiana Would Make Arrests, Carry Weapons," *Washington Post*, March 14, 2006.

[48] Bill Sizemore, "Blackwater Employees Create a Stir in New Orleans," *Virginian-Pilot*, September 15, 2005.

[49] *Ibid.*

[50] *Ibid.*

[51] Jeremy Scahill and Daniela Crespo, "Overkill: Feared Blackwater Mercenaries Deployed in New Orleans," *Truthout*, September 10, 2005, http://www.truthout.org/docs_2005/091005A.shtml.

[52] *Ibid.*

[53] *Ibid.*

[54] *Ibid.*

[55] Jeremy Scahill, "Blackwater Down," *Nation*, October 10, 2005, http://www.thenation.com/doc/20051010/scahill.

[56] *Ibid.*

[57] Sabrina Tavernise, "U.S. Contractor Banned by Iraq Over Shootings," *New York Times*, September 18, 2007, http://www.nytimes.com/2007/09/18/world/middleeast/18iraq.html?ref=world&pagewante.

[58] Joel Brinkley and James Glanz, "Contractors in Sensitive Roles, Unchecked," *New York Times*, May 7, 2004, http://query.nytimes.com/gst/fullpage.html?res=9F06E5D7163CF934A35756C0A9629C8B63.

[59] James Dao, "Private Guards Take Big Risks, For Right Price," *New York Times*, April 2, 2004.

[60] *Education on Lockdown: The Schoolhouse to Jailhouse Track*, (Washington, DC: Advancement Project, March 2005), p. 11.

[61] Stephen King, *Danse Macabre* (New York: Everest House, 1981), p. 13.

[62] Gross, *op. cit.*, p. 310.

Chapter Three: No Place to Hide

[1] "Surveillance Society: The Experts Speak," *BusinessWeek*, August 8, 2005, http://www.businessweek.com/magazine/content/05_32/b3946008_mz001.htm.

[2] Rick Weiss, "Dragonfly or Insect Spy? Scientists at Work on Robobugs," *Washington Post*, October 9, 2007, http://www.washingtonpost.com/wp-dyn/content/article/2007/10/08/AR2007100801434.html.

[3] *Ibid.*

[4] "CIA exhibits spy gadgets with Bond edge," *CNN.com*, October 28, 2003, http://www.cnn.com/2003/TECH/10/28/tech.cia.reut/.

[5] Weiss, *op. cit.*

[6] *Ibid.*

[7] "CIA exhibits spy gadgets with Bond edge," *op. cit.*

[8] *Ibid.*

[9] Humphrey Hawksley, "Big Brother is watching us all," *BBC News*, September 15, 2007, http://news.bbc.co.uk/2/hi/programmes/from_our_own_correspondent/6995061.stm.

[10] *Ibid.*

[11] *Ibid.*

[12] *Ibid.*

[13] John W. Whitehead and Steven H. Aden, "Forfeiting 'Enduring Freedom' for 'Homeland Security,': A Constitutional Analysis of the USA Patriot Act and the Justice Department's Anti-Terrorism Initiatives," *AU Law Review* 51, no. 6 (August 2002), http://www.wcl.american.edu/journal/lawrev/51/51-6.cfm.

[14] "Post-ABC Poll: Terrorist Attacks," *Washington Post*, September 11, 2001, http://www.washingtonpost.com/wp-srv/politics/polls/vault/stories/data091201.htm.

[15] John W. Whitehead, "Expansive Police Powers Threaten Our Constitutional Rights," *The Rutherford Institute*, November 5, 2001, http://www.rutherford.org/articles_db/commentary.asp?record_id=137.

[16] Robert O'Harrow, Jr., *No Place to Hide* (New York: Free Press, 2005), p. 4.

[17] David Murakami Wood and Kirstie Ball, eds. "A Report on the Surveillance Society," *Data Protection Commissioner*, September 2006, http://www.dataprotection.ie/viewdoc.asp?Userlang=&DocID=386&StartDate=01+January+2007.

[18] Cara Buckley, "New York Plans Surveillance Veil for Downtown," *New York Times*, July 9, 2007, http://www.nytimes.com/2007/07/09/nyregion/09.ring.html.

[19] John McElhenny, "Smile, you're on security camera," *Boston Globe*, March 28, 2004, http://www.boston.com/news/local/massachusetts/articles/2004/03/28/smile_youre_on_security_camera/.

[20] Ron Paul, speaking before the U.S. House of Representatives, "Is America a Police State?" June 27, 2002, http://www.house.gov/paul/congrec/congrec2002/cr062702.htm.

[21] Christine Wallgren, "Smile, kids, you're on school bus camera," *Boston Globe*, October 7, 2007.

[22] Annie Cutler, "'Big Brother' in Utah's schools: students under video surveillance," *ABC 4 News*, broadcast October 9, 2007 by ABC-TV.

[23] Pamela Smith, "LR School District Introduces High-Tech Surveillance Method," *KATV7*, broadcast October 17, 2007, by ABC-TV.

[24] "Civil Liberties & Facial Recognition Software," *About.com*, http://web.archive.org/web/20060301220151/terrorism.about.com/od/civillibertiesissues/i/facialrecsoft_2.htm, accessed on February 25, 2008.

[25] Robert Block, "US to Expand Domestic Use of Spy Satellites," *Wall Street Journal*, August 15, 2007, http://online.wsj.com/public/article/SB118714764716998275.html.

[26] Joby Warrick, "Domestic Use of Spy Satellites to Widen Law Enforcement Getting New Access to Secret Imagery," *Washington Post*, August 16, 2007.

[27] "US agencies boost satellite use," *BBC News*, September 16, 2007, http://news.bbc.co.uk/2/hi/americas/6949358.stm.

[28] Warrick, *op. cit.*

[29] Block, *op. cit.*

[30] John Solomon, "FBI Finds It Frequently Overstepped in Collecting Data," *Washington Post*, June 14, 2007, http://www.washingtonpost.com/wp-dyn/content/article/2007/06/13/AR2007061302453.html.

[31] Margot Roosevelt, "Psst, Your Car is Watching You," *Time*, August 7, 2006, http://www.time.com/time/magazine/article/0,9171,1223380,00.html.

[32] *Ibid.*

[33] *Ibid.*

[34] David Spark, "LAPD Systems Keep An Eye Out for Crime: Video surveillance, criminal recognition projects put to the test on city streets," *eWeek*, January 2, 2006, http://www.mywire.com/pubs/eWeek/2006/01/02/1121422?extID=10051.

[35] Gregg Easterbrook, "Lights, Camera, Action," *New Republic*, February 28, 2005, http://www.tnr.com/doc.mhtml?i=w050228&s=easterbrook022805.

36 Spark, *op. cit.*

37 Julie Wakefield, "A Face in the Crowd," *Mother Jones*, November/December 2001, http://www.motherjones.com/news/outfront/2001/11/surveillance.html.

38 Thomas Frank, "Airport security arsenal adds behavior detection," *USA Today*, September 25, 2007, http://www.usatoday.com/travel/flights/2007-09-25-behavior-detection_N.htm.

39 Eric Lipton, "Faces, Too, Are Searched at U.S. Airports," *New York Times*, August 17, 2006, http://www.nytimes.com/2006/08/17/washington/17screeners.html?_r=1&pagewanted=print&oref=slogin.

40 Ellen Nakashima, "FBI Prepares Vast Database of Biometrics," *Washington Post*, December 22, 2007, http://www.washingtonpost.com/wp-dyn/content/article/2007/12/21/AR2007122102544_.

41 *Ibid.*

42 *Ibid.*

43 *Ibid.*

44 *Ibid.*

45 George Orwell, *1984* (New York: Harcourt, Brace and World, 1949), pp. 8–9.

46 Wade Roush, "Googling Your TV," *Technology Review*, August 24, 2006, http://www.technologyreview.com/Infotech/17354/?a=f.

47 *Ibid.*

48 "Google Censors Itself for China," *BBC News*, January 25, 2006, http://news.bbc.co.uk/1/hi/technology/4645596.stm.

49 *Ibid.*

50 "Search Engines Records and How They Can Be Used," *All Things Considered*, National Public Radio, January 20, 2006, http://www.npr.org/templates/story/story.php?storyId=5165533.

51 "Google developing eavesdropping software," *Register*, September 3, 2006, http://www.theregister.co.uk/2006/09/03/google_eavesdropping_software/.

52 Jacques Ellul, *The Technological Society* (New York: Vintage, 1964), p. 274.

53 *Ibid.*, p. 275.

54 David Cole and John W. Whitehead, "I Think We're Being Watched," *Legal Times*, August 27, 2007, www.legaltimes.com.

55 Sheldon Alberts, "Surveillance society keeps an eye out," *Ottawa Citizen*, September 3, 2006, http://www.canada.com/ottawaciti-zen/news/story.html?id=8a36b5db-9dc7-4e1c-b796-d6ef0834170a&k=47526.

56 O'Harrow, *op. cit.*, p. 125.

57 *Ibid.*, p. 126.

58 Neil Postman, *Technopoly: The Surrender of Culture to Technology* (New York: Alfred A. Knopf, 1992), p. 67.

59 "NSA: Spying at Home," *Washington Post* special report, February 3, 2006, http://www.washingtonpost.com/wp-dyn/content/linkset/2006/02/03/LI2006020301869.html.

60 "Information Assurance," *National Security Agency*, September 27, 2006, http://www.nsa.gov/ia/ and "Signals Intelligence," National Security Agency, September 27, 2006, http://www.nsa.gov/sigint/.

61 James Risen and Eric Lichtblau, "Bush Lets U.S. Spy on Callers Without Courts," *New York Times*, December 16, 2005, http://www.nytimes.com/2005/12/16/politics/16program.html?ei=5090&en=e32072d786623ac1&ex= 129238920.

62 James Bamford, *Body of Secrets: Anatomy of the Ultra-Secret National Security Agency* (New York: Doubleday, 2001), p. 4.

63 "Frequently Asked Questions," *National Security Agency*, September 28, 2006, http://www.nsa.gov/careers/faqs_1. cfm#ahp_2.

64 "About NSA," National Security Agency/Central Security Service, http://www.nsa.gov/about/about00018.cfm#7.

65 Risen and Lichtblau, *op. cit.*

66 *Ibid.*

67 Jonathan Weisman and Carol Leonnig, "No Compromise on Wiretap Bill," *Washington Post*, September 27, 2006, http://www.washingtonpost.com/wp-dyn/content/article/2006/09/26/AR2006092601272.html.

68 "The President's End Run," *Washington Post*, January 23, 2006, http://www.washingtonpost.com/wp-dyn/content/article/2006/01/22/AR2006012200779.html.

69 "In Focus: Homeland Security," *President's Radio Address*, December 17, 2005, http://www.whitehouse.gov/news/releases/2005/12/20051217.html.

70 "Bush on Domestic Spying," White House news conference, *washingtonpost.com*, January 26, 2006, http://www.washingtonpost.com/wp-dyn/content/video/2006/01/26/VI2006012600914.html.

71 "In Focus: Homeland Security," *op. cit.*

72 Leslie Cauley, "NSA Has Massive Database of Americans' Phone Calls," *USA Today*, May 11, 2006, http://www.usatoday.com/news/washington/2006-05-10-nsa_x.htm.

73 "Court Allows NSA Wiretapping Program To Continue During Appeal," *Associated Press*, October 4, 2006, http://www.fox news.com/story/0,2933,217847,00.html.

74 Siobhan Gorman, "NSA Rejected System that Sifted Phone Data Legally," *Baltimore Sun*, May 18, 2006, http://www.baltimore-sun.com/news/nationworld/bal-te.nsa18may18,1,5386811.story.

75 Niall McKay, "Lawmakers Raise Questions About International Spy Network," *New York Times*, May 27, 1999, http://www.ny-times.com/library/tech/99/05/cyber/articles/27network.html.

76 Patrick S. Poole, "Echelon: America's Secret Global Surveillance Network," http://fly.hiwaay.net/~pspoole/echelon.html.

77 *Ibid.*

78 *Ibid.*

79 *Ibid.*

80 United States Senate, "Supplementary Detailed Staff Reports on Intelligence Activities and the Rights of Americans," *Final Report of the Select Committee to Study Governmental Operations with Respect to Intelligence Activities*, Book III, April 23, 1976, transcribed and published online by Paul Wolf, 2002, http://www.icdc.com/~paulwolf/cointelpro/churchfinalreportI-IIj.htm.

81 National Campaign for Nonviolent Resistance, http://www.iraq-pledge.org/.

82 National Campaign for Nonviolent Resistance, *Nonviolence Guidelines*, http://www.iraqpledge.org/nonviolence_guidlines.htm.

83 Kevin Zeese, "National Security Agency mounted massive spy op on Baltimore peace group, documents show" *Rawstory*, January 10, 2006, http://rawstory.com/news/2005/National_Security_Agency_spied_on_Baltimore_0110.html.

84 *Ibid.*

85 *Ibid.*

86 *Ibid.*

87 Lisa Myers, *et al.*, "Is the Pentagon spying on Americans? Secret database obtained by NBC News tracks 'suspicious' domestic groups," *MSNBC Nightly News*, December 14, 2005, http://www.msnbc.msn.com/id/10454316/.

88 Joel Bleifuss, "FBI, DoD, NSA: All Spying on You," January 28, 2006, *In These Times*, http://www.inthesetimes.com/site/main/article/2474/.

89 Matthew Rothschild, "Rumsfeld Spies on Quakers and Grannies," *Progressive*, December 16, 2005, http://www.progressive.org/mag_mc121605.

90 "Pentagon Caught Spying on U.S. Anti-War and Anti-Nuclear Activists," *Democracy Now*, December 15, 2005, http://www.democracynow.org/article.pl?sid=05/12/15/155219.

91 Department of Defense. DODAntiWarProtestDatabaseTracker.pdf. *MSNBC*, http://msnbcmedia.msn.com/i/msnbc/sections/news/DODAntiWarProtestDatabaseTracker.pdf.

92 Eric Lichtblau, "Documents Reveal Scope of U.S. Database on Antiwar Protests," *New York Times*, October 13, 2006, http://www.commondreams.org/headlines06/1013-01.htm.

93 *Ibid.*

94 James Bamford, "Private Lives: The Agency That Could Be Big Brother," *New York Times*, December 25, 2005, http://www.nytimes.com/2005/12/25/weekinreview/25bamford.html?ex=1293166800&en=3d09922ebe6b2eac&ei=5090.

95 *Brown v. Glines*, 444 U.S. 348, 369 (1980).

96 Benjamin Franklin, Pennsylvania Assembly: Reply to the Governor, November 11, 1755, *The Papers of Benjamin Franklin*, edited by Leonard W. Labaree, (New Haven: Yale University Press, 1963), 6:242.

Chapter Four: From Cradle to Grave

1 Jay Stanley, "The Surveillance-Industrial Complex: How the American Government Is Conscripting Businesses and Individuals in the Construction of a Surveillance Society," August 2004, http://www.aclu.org/FilesPDFs/surveillance_report.pdf.

2 *Ibid.*, p. 92.

3 *Ibid.*, pp. 91–92.

4 Daniel J. Wakin, "The Nation: Identity Crisis; National I.D. Cards: One Size Fits All," *New York Times*, October 7, 2001, http://query.nytimes.com/gst/fullpage.html?res=9E03EFD7143C F934A35753C1A9679C8B63.

5 Simon Davies, "Campaigns of Opposition to ID Card Schemes," *Privacy International*, http://www.privacy.org/pi/issues/idcard/campaigns.html.

6 Jane Black, "Don't Make Privacy the Next Victim of Terror," *Business Week*, October 4, 2001, http://www.businessweek.com/bw-daily/dnflash/oct2001/nf2001104_7412.htm.

7 Robert O'Harrow, *No Place to Hide* (New York: Free Press, 2005) p. 89.

8 Vince Devlin, "Montana ACLU opposes national ID card," *Missoulian*, January 14, 2006, http://www.missoulian.com/articles/2006/01/14/news/local/news05.txt.

9 Ron Paul, "Reject the National ID Card," *LewRockwell.com*, September 7, 2004, http://www.lewrockwell.com/paul/paul202.html.

10 Eliott C. McLaughlin, "Federal ID plan raises privacy concerns," *CNN*, August 16, 2007.

11 "Senate rejects extra $300 million for Real ID," *ZDNet News*, July 27, 2007.

12 Anne Broache, "Homeland Security proposes delayed Real ID rollout," *CNet News*, January 11, 2008, http://www.news.com/8301-10784_3-9848924-7.html.

13 McLaughlin, *op. cit.*

14 Editorial, "Real ID, unrealistic law," *Boston Globe*, March 20, 2007.

15 McLaughlin, *op. cit.*

16 "Senate rejects extra $300 million for Real ID," *op. cit.*

17 *Ibid.*

18 "National ID Cards and REAL ID Act," *Electronic Privacy Information Center*, http://www.epic.org/privacy/id_cards/#state.

19 McLaughlin, *op. cit.*

20 Anita Kumar, "Va. Braces for Driver's License Changes," *Washington Post*, December 17, 2007.

21 Yvonne Abraham, "State says Real ID plan will cost $150m; Predicts agencies will be swamped," *Boston Globe*, May 16, 2007.

22 Anita Ramasastry, "Why the 'Real ID' Act is a real mess," *CNN*, August, 12, 2005.

23 *Ibid.*

24 Thomas Frank, "6 states defy law requiring ID cards," *USA Today*, June 18, 2007.

25 "Real ID: Real Nightmare," *American Civil Liberties Union of Connecticut*, http://www.acluct.org/issues/immigrantsrights/realidrealnightmare.htm.

26 *Ibid.*

27 *Ibid.*

28 Ken Ritter, "Personal information taken in Nevada DMV office break-in," *Las Vegas Sun*, March 11, 2005.

29 *Ibid.*

30 Alice Lipowicz, "A layered approach," *Washington Technology*, August 3, 2007.

31 *Ibid.*

32 *Ibid.*

33 Jerome R. Corsi, "North American Union driver's license created," *World Net Daily*, September 6, 2007, http://www.worldnetdaily.com/news/article.asp?ARTICLE_ID=57502.

34 *Ibid.*

35 Department of Homeland Security, *Notice of Privacy Act System of Records, Comments of the Electronic Privacy Information Center*, http://www.epic.org/privacy/us-visit/comments080405.pdf.

36 Joanne Silberner, "Implanted Chips Provide Access to Medical History," *National Public Radio*, August 15, 2005, http://www.npr.org/templates/story/story.php?storyId=4800061.

[37] Ivan Penn, "Are IV Chips Too Invasive?" *tampabay.com*, July 28, 2007, http://www.sptimes.com/2007/07/28/news_pf/Business/Are_ID_chips_too_inva.shtml.

[38] *Ibid.*

[39] *Ibid.*

[40] *Ibid.*

[41] O'Harrow, *op. cit.*, p. 283.

[42] Nancy Gohring, "Pfizer to use RFID tags on Viagra to prevent fakes," *IDG News Service*, January 9, 2006, http://www.computerworld.com/action/article.do?articleId=107585&command=viewArticleCoverage&continuingCoverageID=1011&intsrc=article_cc_report_side.

[43] Laura M. Holson, "Privacy Lost: These Phones Can Find You," *New York Times*, October 23, 2007.

[44] *Ibid.*

[45] *Ibid.*

[46] *Ibid.*

[47] Jay Stanley, ACLU report, "The Surveillance-Industrial Complex: How the American Government Is Conscripting Businesses and Individuals in the Construction of a Surveillance Society," August 2004. http://www.aclu.org/FilesPDFs/surveillance_report.pdf.

[48] *Ibid.*

[49] *Ibid.*

[50] *Ibid.*

[51] Catherine Komp, "Feds to Fund Controversial School Surveillance," *New Standard News*, November 29, 2005.

[52] *Ibid.*

[53] Chris Walker, "School puts a chip on pupils," *Doncaster Free Press*, October 18, 2007.

[54] Joe Milicia, "School Gunman Had Access Despite Threats," *Associated Press*, October 12, 2007.

[55] Catherine Komp, "Feds to Fund Controversial School Surveillance," *New Standard News*, November 29, 2005.

[56] Annie Cutler, "'Big Brother' in Utah's schools: students under video surveillance," *ABC 4 News*, broadcast October 9, 2007 by ABC-TV.

57 "Fingerprints Pay For School Lunch," *CBS News*, broadcast January 24, 2001, http://www.cbsnews.com/stories/2001/01/24/national/main266789.shtml.

58 "Fingerprint school lunch programs raise concern," www.woio.com/global/story.asp?

59 "Fingerprints Pay for School Lunch Program," www.cbsnews.com/stories/2001/01/24/national/printable266789.shtml.

60 General Accounting Office, "The American Community Survey: Accuracy and Timeliness Issues," September 30, 2002, http://www.gao.gov/new.items/d02956r.pdf.

61 U.S. Census Bureau, "The American Community—Blacks: 2004," American Community Survey Reports, February 2007, p. 24, http://www.census.gov/prod/2007pubs/acs-04.pdf.

62 George Orwell, *1984*, pp. 136–37.

63 "The American Community Survey," U.S. Department of Commerce, accessed on February 25, 2008, http://www.census.gov/acs/www/Downloads/SQuest08.pdf.

64 "Don't Trust the Census," http://www.toad.com/gnu/census.html.

65 "Freedom of Information Documents on the Census: Department of Homeland Security Obtained Data on Arab Americans from Census Bureau," *Electronic Privacy Information Center*, http://www.epic.org/privacy/census/foia/default.html.

66 *Ibid.*

67 "People of Arab Ancestry by ZIP Code Tabulation Area: 2000," *Electronic Privacy Information Center*, http://www.epic.org/privacy/census/foia/tab_1.pdf.

68 "People of Arab Ancestry by ZIP Code Tabulation Area: 2000," *Electronic Privacy Information Center*, http://www.epic.org/privacy/census/foia/tab_2.pdf.

69 Statement by Charles Louis Kincannon, "Apportionment in the Balance," March 1, 2006, http://www.census.gov/Press-Release/www/2006/statement3-1-06.htm.

70 "Top 100," *Defense News*, accessed on February 25, 2008, http://www.defensenews.com/static/features/top100/charts/rank_2005.php?c=FEA&s=T1C.

71 O'Harrow, *op. cit.*, p. 9.

72 *Ibid.*

73 Mark P. Mills, "On My Mind: The Security-Industrial Complex," *Forbes*, November 29, 2004, http://members.forbes.com/forbes/2004/1129/044.html.

74 Gary Stoller, "Homeland security generates multibillion dollar business," *USA Today*, September 10, 2006, http://www.usatoday.com/money/industries/2006-09-10-security-industry_x.htm.

75 Mills, *op. cit.*

76 Stanley, *op. cit.*

77 Mills, *op. cit.*

78 *Ibid.*

79 *Ibid.*

80 O'Harrow, *op. cit.*, p. 9.

81 *Griswold v. Connecticut*, 381 U.S. 479 (1965).

82 *Delaware v. Prouse*, 440 U.S. 648, 663 (1979).

83 David Cole and John W. Whitehead, "I Think We're Being Watched," *Legal Times*, August 27, 2007, www.legaltimes.com.

84 *Hiibel v. Sixth Judicial District Court of Nevada*, 542 U.S. 177 (2004).

85 Ellen Nakashima, "Collecting of Details on Travelers Documented," *Washington Post*, September 22, 2007.

86 *Ibid.*

87 *Ibid.*

88 Mike Littwin, "Give a Wink and a Nod to Fed Center 'Greeter'," *Rocky Mountain News*, December 3, 2005, http://www.rockymountainnews.com/drmn/news_columnists/article/0,1299,DRMN_86_4286190,00.html.

89 Jacob Sullum, "Rocking the Bus: A Colorado Woman Takes a Stand Against Arbitrary ID Checks," *Reason.com*, November 30, 2005, http://www.reason.com/sullum/113005.shtml.

90 Karen Abbott, "Refusal to Present ID Sparks Test of Rights," *Rocky Mountain News*, November 29, 2005, http://www.rockymountainnews.com/drmn/local/article/0,1299,DRMN_15_4274023,00.html.

91 Dennis Roddy, "Roll Over and Beg," *Pittsburgh Post-Gazette*, December 4, 2005, http://www.post-gazette.com/pg/pp/05338/616520.stm.

[92] *Ibid.*

[93] Sullum, *op. cit.*

[94] Karen Abbott, "Fed Center Flap Draws a Busload of Support," *Rocky Mountain News*, December 1, 2005, http://www.rocky-mountainnews.com/drmn/local/article/0,1299,DRMN_15_4279299,00.html.

[95] Doris Colmes, "Ridin' the Bus With Deborah: Flashbacks to Nazi Germany... in Denver," *OpEdNews.com*, November 29, 2005, http://www.opednews.com/articles/opedne_doris_co_051129_rid in_92_92_the_bus_with .htm.

[96] Abbott, "Refusal to Present ID Sparks Test of Rights," *op. cit.*

[97] Maria Luisa Tucker, "Let's See Some I.D," *AlterNet*, December 9, 2005, http://www.alternet.org/story/29268.

[98] *Ibid.*

[99] *Ibid.*

[100] Testimony of Henrietta Samuel, from the transcript of the trial of Adolf Eichmann, Session 36 (May 1961).

[101] Raul Hilberg, *The Destruction of the European Jews* (Teaneck, NJ: Holmes & Meier Publishers, Inc., 1985), pp. 173–80.

[102] "Laws/Effects of Apartheid," *Apartheid in South Africa*, http://home.snu.edu/~dwilliam/f97projects/apartheid/Laws.htm.

[103] http://www.answers.com/topic/pass-laws.

[104] Alison Des Forges, "Leave None to Tell the Story: Genocide in Rwanda," *Human Rights Watch*, April 1, 2004, www.hrw.org/reports/1999/rwanda.

[105] "Rwanda: How the genocide happened," *BBC News*, April 1, 2004, http://news.bbc.co.uk/1/hi/world/africa/1288230.stm; "OAU sets inquiry into Rwanda genocide," *AfricaRecovery*, August 1998, 12:1, p. 4. http://www.un.org/ecosocdev/geninfo/afrec/subjindx/121rwan.htm.

[106] *Prosecutor vs. Jean-Paul Akayesu* (Case No. ICTR-96-4-T), Judgment, September 2, 1998, paragraph 123.

[107] Jim Fussell, Table 3: Governmental population policies facilitated by group classification on ID cards, Group Classification on National ID Cards as a Factor in Genocide and Ethnic Cleansing. Presented to the Seminar Series of the Yale University Genocide

Studies Program, November 15, 2001, http://www.preventgeno-cide.org/prevent/removing-facilitating-factors/IDcards/.

[108] Amelia Gentleman, "ID cards may cut queues but learn lessons of history, warn Europeans," *Guardian*, November 15, 2003.

Chapter Five: Children under Fire

[1] "A Timeline of Recent Worldwide School Shootings," September 10, 2007, http://www.infoplease.com/ipa/A0777958.html.

[2] *Ibid.*

[3] Morris Berman, *Dark Ages America: The Final Phase of Empire* (New York: W.W. Norton and Co., 2006), p. 26.

[4] Urie Bronfenbrenner, *Two Worlds of Childhood: U.S. and U.S.S.R.* (New York: Russell Sage Foundation, 1970), p. 95.

[5] Berman, *op. cit.*, p. 29.

[6] *Ibid.*, p. 26.

[7] Rebecca A. Doyle, "Violence in schools: No easy answers," *University Record*, Jan. 24, 2000, www.umich.edu/9900/Jan24_00/13.htm.

[8] "America's Public Schools: Crisis and Cure," http://www.theolo-gyandeconomics.org/ppolicy/education/school/crisis/ch1.html.

[9] "Indicators of School Crime and Safety: 2006, Indicator 19: Safety and Security Measures Taken by Public Schools," National Center for Education Statistics, http://nces.ed.gov/programs/crime indicators/ind_19.asp.

[10] Greg Toppo, "High-tech school security is on the rise," *USA Today*, October 10, 2006, http://www.usatoday.com/news/edu-cation/2006-10-09-school:security_x.htm.

[11] "Eye Scan Technology Comes to Schools," *Good Morning America*, broadcast January 25, 2006, http://abcnews.go.com/GMA/story?id=1539275.

[12] Maria Sacchetti, "Some see scans for lunch as taste of Big Brother," *Boston Globe*, April 4, 2007, http://www.boston.com/news/edu-cation/k_12/articles/2007/04/04/some_see_scans_for_lunch_as_t aste_of_big_brother/.

[13] Kenneth S. Trump, "School Assessments," http://www.schoolse-curity.org/resources/security-assessment-nassp.html.

14 Russell Skiba and Reece Peterson, "The Dark Side of Zero Tolerance: Can Punishment Lead to Safe Schools?" *Kappan*, January
   1999, http://www.pdkintl.org/kappan/kski9901.htm.

15 John Cloud, "The Columbine Effect," *Time*, December 6, 1999,
   p. 51.

16 *Ibid.*

17 *Zero Tolerance and Alternative Strategies: A Fact Sheet for Educators and Policy Makers*, http://www.naspcenter.org/fact-
   sheets/zt_fs.html.

18 "School strip searches mandated by the House," *World Net Daily*,
   September 23, 2006, www.wnd.com/news/article.asp?ARTI-
   CLE_ID=52125.

19 "Zero Tolerance: Is mandatory punishment in schools unfair?" *CQ
   Researcher*, March 10, 2000, p. 187, www.cq.com.

20 "'Midol suspension' ends: Honor student returns to class," *CNN
   News*, October 3, 1996, http://www.cnn.com/US/9610/03/
   midol.suspension/index.html.

21 "Asthma heroine branded 'drug dealer,'" *BBC News*, May 5, 1998,
   http://news.bbc.co.uk/1/hi/world/americas/87527.stm.

22 "Tracking and Fighting Zero Tolerance," Oct. 27, 2003, *The
   Rutherford Institute*, October 27, 2003, http://www.ruther-
   ford.org/articles_db/legal_features.asp?article_id=71.

23 *Ibid.*

24 Skiba and Peterson, *op. cit.*

25 "Zero Tolerance: Is mandatory punishment in schools unfair?" *op.
   cit.*, p. 190.

26 "Tracking and Fighting Zero Tolerance," *op. cit.*

27 Shannen Coffin, "John Roberts, in His Own Words: Judging him
   by how he judges," *National Review Online*, July 25, 2005,
   http://www.nationalreview.com/coffin/coffin200507250802.asp.

28 "Tracking and Fighting Zero Tolerance," *op. cit.*

29 *Ibid.*

30 John W. Whitehead, "Unpopular Speech and the Debate over the
   Confederate Flag," May 6, 2002, http://www.rutherford.org/ar-
   ticles_db/commentary.asp?record_id=160.

31 Nisha N. Mohammed, "U.S. Supreme Court Refuses to Hear Case of Student Jailed Under Zero Tolerance Policy for Art Sketch," *The Rutherford Institute*, June 6, 2005, http://www.rutherford.org/articles_db/press_release.asp?article_id=561.

32 "Valedictorian unplugged over God comments: She says it was free speech, officials say it was preaching," *Associated Press* posted on *MSNBC*, June 21, 2006, http://www.msnbc.msn.com/id/13461308.

33 "Tracking and Fighting Zero Tolerance," *op. cit.*

34 Centers for Disease Control and Prevention, "Youth Suicide," September 11, 2007, http://www.cdc.gov/ncipc/dvp/Suicide/youth-suicide.htm.

35 Centers for Disease Control and Prevention, "Self-inflicted Injury/Suicide," September 11, 2007, http://www.cdc.gov/nchs/fastats/suicide.htm.

36 American Association of Suicidology, "Youth Suicide Fact Sheet," September 11, 2007, http://www.suicidology.org.

37 Centers for Disease Control, "Youth Suicide," *op. cit.*

38 U.S. Food and Drug Administration, "Antidepressant Use in Children, Adolescents, and Adults," September 11, 2007, http://www.fda.gov/cder/drug/antidepressants/.

39 Centers for Disease Control, "Youth Suicide," *op. cit.*

40 "Suicide Trends Among Youths and Young Adults Aged 10–24 Years," *CDC: Morbidity and Mortality Weekly Report*, September 7, 2007, http://www.cdc.gov/mmwr/.

41 *Ibid.*

42 "Youth Suicide Fact Sheet," *National Youth Violence Prevention Resource Center*, September 11, 2007, http://www.safeyouth.org/scripts/facts/suicide.asp.

43 "Drug Information: M," U.S. Drug Enforcement Administration, http://www.usdoj.gov/dea/concern/m.html.

44 Thomas G. Whittle and Linda Amato, "Education: The Fatal Flaw," *Freedom Magazine*, http://www.freedommag.org/english/vol36i1/page03.htm.

45 "Study shows Ritalin rises in preschoolers," *Associated Press*, October 20, 2006.

[46] Attention Deficit Disorder Help Center, "Ritalin Abuse/ Side Effects," http://www.add-adhd-help-center.com/ritalin_ side_effects.htm.

[47] Todd Zwillich, "House: Don't require Ritalin in school," *United Press International*, November 16, 2005, http://www.citizens-forsocialreform.org/index.php?option=com_content&task=view &id=120&Itemid=1

[48] "Education: The Fatal Flaw," *Freedom Magazine, op. cit.*, p. 6.

[49] President's New Freedom Commission on Mental Health, "Achieving the Promise: Transforming Mental Health Care in America," http://www.mentalhealthcommission.gov/reports/FinalReport/ FullReport.htm.

[50] David Semple, Roger Smyth, Jonathan Burns, Rajan Darjee, Andrew McIntosh, "Child and Adolescent Psychiatry," *Oxford Handbook of Psychiatry*, (New York: Oxford University Press, 2005), http://www.wpic.pitt.edu/education/residency_training/oxford_handbook/zzzChapter14_402.doc.

[51] "TeenScreen: the Lawsuits Begin," *Alliance for Human Research Protection*, June 13, 2005, http://www.ahrp.org/infomail.05/06/13a.php.

[52] "The Key Players: The People Behind the TeenScreen Program," *TeenScreen Truth*, October 8, 2007, http://www.teenscreen-truth.com/teenscreen_key_players.html.

[53] Vera Hassner Sharav, Alliance for Human Research Protection, "Slide 1," Powerpoint presentation given at National Academies of Science Sci-Tech Policy Fellows Seminar, February 22, 2006, www.ahrp.org/children/teenscreen/debateNAS0206.ppt.

[54] "U.S. Preventative Services Task Force: No evidence that screening for suicide reduces suicide," *Alliance for Human Research Protection*, May 21, 2004, http://www.ahrp.org/infomail/04/05/21.php.

[55] "No Child Left Unmedicated," *Phyllis Schlafly Report*, 38:8, March 2005, http://www.eagleforum.org/psr/2005/mar05/psr-mar05.html.

[56] Johanna Neuman, "Acting EPA Chief Withdraws Controversial Pesticide Project," *Los Angeles Times*, April 9, 2005, http://www.ahrp.org/infomail.05/04/09.php.

[57] John Whitehead, "Mengele's Legacy Lives On: Inhumane Experiments on Children in America," *The Rutherford Institute*, April 18, 2005, http://www.rutherford.org/articles_db/commentary.asp?record_id=335.

[58] "MIT, Quaker Oats to settle radiation experiment suit," *CNN Interactive*, December 31, 1997, http://www.cnn.com/US/9712/31/radioactive.oatmeal/.

[59] Alice Cherbonnier, "Nasal Radium Irradiation of Children Has Health Fallout," *Baltimore Chronicle*, October 8, 2007, http://baltimorechronicle.com/rupnose.html.

[60] Carol Rutz, November 2003 lecture at Indiana University, "Experiments on Children," http://www.whale.to/b/willowbrook_state_school_exp.html.

[61] "Child Experiments: D.C. Children's Center in Laurel," October 8, 2007, http://www.whale.to/b/child_exp_q.html.

[62] "Child Experiments: Edmonston-Zagred measles vaccine," October 8, 2007, http://www.whale.to/b/child_exp_q.html.

[63] Liam Scheff, "The House that AIDS Built," *New York Press*, January 2004, http://www.altheal.org/toxicity/house.htm.

[64] "MySpace: Your Kids' Danger?" *CBS Evening News*, broadcast February 6, 2006 by CBS-TV, http://www.cbsnews.com/stories/2006/02/06/eveningnews/main1286130.shtml.

[65] "Millions Suffer in Sex Slavery," *NewsMax.com Wires*, April 24, 2001, http://archive.newsmax.com/archives/articles/2001/4/23/184354.shtml.

[66] "New Report Says Millions of Children are Sexually Exploited," *UNICEF Press Center*, December 12, 2001, http://www.unicef.org/newsline/01pr97.htm.

[67] "The Myth of the Virgin," *Child Exploitation*, October 8, 2007, http://www.childexploitation.org/asia.html.

[68] Martin Brass, "The Modern Scourge of Sex Slavery," *Soldier of Fortune Magazine*, October 8, 2007, http://www.military.com/NewContent/0,13190,SOF_0904_Slavery1,00.html.

[69] *Ibid.*

[70] *Ibid.*

71 Carri Geer, "Mother denies charges of prostituting two daughters," *Las Vegas Review-Journal*, January 10, 1998, http://www.reviewjournal.com/lvrj_home/1998/Jan-10-Sat-1998/news/6745686.html.

72 Jane Hansen, "Special Report: Selling Atlanta's Children," *Atlanta Journal-Constitution*, January 7, 2001, http://www.bestofcox.com/2002/docs/metro/public_01.html.

73 Stuart Aitken, "Schoolyard Shootings: Racism, Sexism, and Moral Panics over Teen Violence," October 8, 2007, http://www.blackwell-synergy.com/doi/abs/10.1111/1467-8330.00200?journalCode=anti.

74 Ron Hutcheson, "Conference on school safety ends with call for focus on character," October 10, 2006, Knight Ridder Washington Bureau (Washington DC).

75 Bronfenbrenner, *op. cit.*, p. 96.

76 *Ibid.*, pp. 96, 97.

77 *Ibid.*, p. 97.

78 *Ibid.*, p. 98.

79 *Ibid.*, p. 99.

80 Bill Dedman, "Journals, poetry scream of violence, despair," *Chicago Sun-Times*, October 15, 2000, http://www.ustreas.gov/usss/ntac/chicago_sun/poeml5.htm.

81 Marcus Kabel, "Boy faces assault charge in Mo. Shooting," *Washington Post*, October 10, 2006, http://www.washingtonpost.com/wp-dyn/content/article/2006/10/10/AR2006101000173.html.

82 United States Secret Service, "Secret Service Safe School Initiative," October 8, 2007, http://www.secretservice.gov/ntac_ssi.shtml.

83 *Ibid.*

84 Bill Dedman, "School Shooters: Secret Service Findings," *Chicago Sun-Times*, October 15, 2000, http://treas.gov/usss/ntac/chicago_sun/find15.htm.

Chapter Six: American Empire

1 Richard Wolf, "A 'fiscal hurricane' on the horizon," *USA Today*, November 14, 2005, http://www.usatoday.com/news/washington/2005-11-14-fiscal-hurricane-cover_x.htm.

[2] Amy Belasco, "The Cost of Iraq, Afghanistan, and Other Global War on Terror Operations Since 9/11," *CRS Report for Congress*, accessed on July 16, 2007, http://www.fas.org/sgp/crs/natsec/RL33110.pdf.

[3] Dan Radmacher, "Could America be the next Rome?" *Roanoke Times*, August 19, 2007, http://www.roanoke.com/editorials/radmacher/wb/wb/xp-128574.

[4] Cullen Murphy, *Are We Rome? The Fall of an Empire and the Fate of America* (New York: Houghton Mifflin, 2007).

[5] Jay Tolson, "Lessons from the Fall," *U.S. News & World Report*, April 29, 2007, http://www.usnews.com/usnews/news/articles/070429/7qa.htm?s_cid=rss:7qa.htm.

[6] Murphy, *op. cit.*, p. 12.

[7] Chalmers Johnson, "Republic or Empire: A National Intelligence Estimate on the United States," *Harper's*, January 2007, p. 63.

[8] Charles J. Dunlap, Jr., "The Origins of the Military Coup of 2012," *Parameters*, Winter 1992–93, pp. 2–20, http://carlisle-www.army.mil/usawc/Parameters/1992/dunlap.htm.

[9] Barton Gellman and Susan Schmidt, "Shadow Government Is at Work in Secret," *Washington Post*, March 1, 2002, http://www.washingtonpost.com/ac2/wp-dyn/A20584-2002Feb28?language=printer.

[10] *Ibid.*

[11] "FEMA History," http://www.fema.gov/about/history.shtm.

[12] Jon Basil Utley, "Preparing for the Terrorist Threat," *Insight on the News*, Vol. 17, January 15, 2001, http://www.freerepublic.com/forum/a3a4493ef14d9.htm.

[13] *Ibid.*

[14] Kurt Nimmo, "Attacks on democratic rights, breaching legal barriers: FEMA and Katrina: REX-84 Revisited," Centre for Research on Globalization, September 11, 2005, http://www.globalresearch.ca/index.php?context=va&aid=929.

[15] *Ibid.*

[16] Ted Gup, "Civil Defense Doomsday Hideaway," *Time*, December 9, 1991, http://www.time.com/time/magazine/article/0,9171,974428,00.html.

[17] "Mount Weather: High Point Special Facility," *Global Security*, http://www.globalsecurity.org/wmd/facility/mt_weather.htm.

[18] John R. Brinkerhoff, "The Posse Comitatus Act and Homeland Security," *Homeland Security Institute*, February 2002, http://www.home-landsecurity.org/journal/Articles/brinkerhoffpossecomitatus.htm.

[19] "U.S. Northern Command," *GlobalSecurity*, http://www.globalsecurity.org/military/agency/dod/northcom.htm.

[20] "Gen. Eberhart's View of the Northern Command," *Online Newshour*, broadcast September 27, 2002 by the Public Broadcasting System (PBS), http://www.pbs.org/newshour/terrorism/ata/eberhart.html.

[21] Peter Byrne, "Battlespace America," *Mother Jones*, May/June 2005, http://www.motherjones.com/news/outfront/2005/05/battlespace_america.html.

[22] *Ibid.*

[23] Gene Healy, "Deployed in the USA?" *CATO Institute*, March 19, 2004, http://www.cato.org/pub_display.php?pub_id=2576.

[24] Mackubin T. Owens, "Soldiers Aren't Cops," *National Review*, August 1, 2002, http://www.nationalreview.com/owens/owens080102.asp.

[25] Chalmers Johnson, *The Sorrows of Empire: Militarism, Secrecy, and the End of the Republic* (New York: Henry Holt and Co., 2004), p. 1.

[26] *Ibid.*

[27] *The Military Balance 2003–2004*, International Institute for Strategic Studies, 2003, referenced at *The Defense Monitor*, 32, no. 5 (November/December 2003): 3 also at http://www.cdi.org/news/defense-monitor/dm.pdf.

[28] Johnson, *The Sorrows of Empire, op. cit.*, p. 4.

[29] *Ibid.*, p. 12.

[30] *Ibid.*

[31] *Ibid.*, p. 5.

[32] John W. Whitehead, "Did George W. Bush Engineer the 9/11 Terrorist Attacks? An Interview with David Ray Griffin," *OldSpeak*, February 6, 2007, http://www.rutherford.org/Oldspeak/Articles/Interviews/oldspeak-Griffin.html.

[33] *Ibid.*

34 Dwight D. Eisenhower, "Farewell Radio and Television Address to the American People," January 17, 1961, *American Presidency Project*, http://www.presidency.ucsb.edu/ws/print.php?pid=12086.

35 Morris Berman, *Dark Ages America: The Final Phase of Empire* (New York: W.W. Norton and Co., 2006), p. 141.

36 *Ibid.*, p. 142.

37 John W. Whitehead, "Lords of War: U.S. Arms Trade," *The Rutherford Institute*, July 17, 2006, http://www.rutherford.org/articles_db/commentary.asp?record_id=418 .

38 Berman, *op. cit.*, p. 143.

39 *Ibid.*, p. 144.

40 Dana Priest, *The Mission* (New York: W.W. Norton and Co., 2003), p. 37.

41 Gore Vidal, *Perpetual War for Perpetual Peace* (New York: Nation Books, 2002), pp. 158–59.

42 Berman, *op. cit.*, p. 145.

43 Guy Dinmore, "US twists civilian arms to fill Fortress Baghdad," *Financial Times*, January 7, 2007, http://www.ft.com/cms/s/0/44bb3006-9e80-11db-ac03-0000779e2340.html.

44 Donald L. Barlett and James B. Steele, "Billions over Baghdad," *Vanity Fair*, October 2007, http://www.vanityfair.com/politics/features/2007/10/iraq_billions200710.

45 Tony Capaccio, "Pentagon Paid $998,798 to Ship Two 19-Cent Washers," *Bloomberg*, August 16, 2007, http://www.bloomberg.com/apps/news?pid=20601070&sid=aY5OQ5xv9HR8.

46 Rupert Cornwell, "Pentagon admits 190,000 weapons missing in Iraq," *The Independent*, August 7, 2007, http://www.independent.co.uk/news/world/americas/pentagon-admits-190000-weapons-missing-in-iraq-460551.html.

47 Lolita C. Baldor, "Army Suicides Highest in 26 Years," *Associated Press*, August 16, 2007, http://www.truthout.org/docs_2006/printer_0816075.shtml.

48 Edward T. Pound, "Saudi Rule Looser Than Pentagon's," *USA Today*, April 24, 2001, http://www.usatoday.com/news/washington/2001-04-24-mcsally.htm.

[49] "Female Pilot Sues Over Muslim Garb," *CBS News*, broadcast January 17, 2002 by CBS-TV, http://www.cbsnews.com/stories/2002/01/17/60minutes/main324757.shtml.

[50] Pound, *op. cit.*

[51] John W. Whitehead, "No Abaya for McSally," *Liberty Magazine* (July–August 2002), http://www.libertymagazine.org/article/articleview/28/1/55/.

[52] *Ibid.*

[53] Michael E. Naparstek, "Grappling with Islam: Redressing a Grievance," *Religion in the News* (Spring 2002, Vol. 5, No. 1), http://www.trincoll.edu/depts/csrpl/RINVol5No1/Martha%20McSally.htm.

[54] Ellen Goodman, "From Burqas to Abayas," *Washington Post*, December 8, 2001, http://www.washingtonpost.com/ac2/wp-dyn?pagename=article&node=&contentId=A11457-2001Dec7&notFound=true.

[55] *Ibid.*

[56] *Ibid.*

[57] Ann Gerhart, "The Air Force Flier in the Ointment," *Washington Post*, January 7, 2002, http://www.washingtonpost.com/ac2/wp-dyn/A605-2002Jan6.

[58] Naparstek, *op. cit.*

[59] Gerhart, *op. cit.*

[60] *Ibid.*

[61] *Ibid.*

[62] John E. Mulligan, "Female Pilot Sues U.S. Alleging Bias," http://multimedia.belointeractive.com/attack/perspective/1205dress.html.

[63] "Female Pilot Sues Over Muslim Garb," *CBS News, op. cit.*

[64] Military Vaccine Agency, "Anthrax," *Anthrax Vaccine Immunization Program*, October 27, 2006, http://www.vaccines.mil/default.aspx?cnt=disease/minidv&dID=21.

[65] Eric Boehlert, "A Shot in the Dark," *Salon.com*, December 10, 2003, http://dir.salon.com/story/news/feature/2003/12/10/anthrax/.

[66] Military Vaccine Agency, "Detailed Safety Review of Anthrax Vaccine Adsorbed," March 6, 2006, http://www.vaccines.mil/documents/854AVASafetyRvw.pdf 85.

[67] Boehlert, *op. cit.*

[68] "Former Marine Claims Illness From Mystery Vaccine," WLWT NBC, broadcast May 8, 2007, http://www.truthout.org/docs_2006/printer_062707M.shtml.

[69] Nisha N. Mohammed, "TRI Sues Donald Rumsfeld and U.S. Military on Behalf of Air Force Sgt. Punished for Speaking Out About Tainted Anthrax Vaccine," *The Rutherford Institute*, November 18, 2004, http://www.rutherford.org/articles_db/press_release.asp?article_id=516.

[70] Joanne Mariner, "The Supreme Court, the Detainees, and the 'War on Terrorism,'" *FindLaw*, July 5, 2004, http://writ.news.findlaw.com/scripts/printer_friendly.pl?page=/mariner/20040705.html.

[71] Joe Kovacs, "The New World Disorder: 'Bush doesn't think America should be an actual place,'" *World Net Daily*, November 19, 2006.

[72] *Ibid.*

[73] "Independent Task Force on North America," *Wikipedia.org*, http://en.wikipedia.org/wiki/Independent_Task_Force_on_North_America#_note-0, accessed on February 26, 2008.

[74] Cliff Kincaid, "North American Union 'Conspiracy' Exposed," *Accuracy in Media*, February 19, 2007, http://www.aim.org/special-report/north-american-union-conspiracy-exposed/.

[75] Jerome Corsi, "North American Union Would Trump U.S. Supreme Court," *Human Events*, June 19, 2006, http://www.humanevents.com/article.php?id=15623.

[76] John W. Whitehead, "The End of America," *The Rutherford Institute*, June 25, 2007, http://www.rutherford.org/articles_db/commentary.asp?record_id=488

[77] Corsi, *op. cit.*

[78] Thomas Jefferson to John Holmes (April 22, 1820), http://www.loc.gov/exhibits/jefferson/159.html.

[79] *Ibid.*

[80] Johnson, "Republic or Empire," *op. cit.*, p. 64.

[81] Priest, *op. cit.*, p. 30.

[82] Tolson, *op. cit.*

Chapter Seven: The Final Frontier

[1] "Annual Immigration to the United States: The Real Numbers," The Migration Policy Institute, May 2007, http://www.migrationpolicy.org/pubs/FS16_USImmigration_051807.pdf.

[2] Ayn Rand, *Atlas Shrugged* (New York: Dutton, 1992), p. 1062.

[3] John Stossel, "The Public Trough Is Bigger Than Ever," *Capitalism Magazine*, May 10, 2007.

[4] "Fact Sheets: The Iraq Quagmire—The Mounting Costs of War and the Case for Bringing Home the Troops," *Stand Up Congress*, September 27, 2007, http://standupcongress.org/content/page.php?cat=2&content_id=20.

[5] Jeremy Pelofsky, "Pallets of US cash sent to Baghdad before handover," *Reuters*, February 6, 2007, http://www.reuters.com/article/latestCrisis/idUSN06312951.

[6] Rajiv Chandrasekaran, "Democrats, Bremer Spar Over Iraq Spending," *Washington Post*, February 7, 2007, http://www.washingtonpost.com/wp-dyn/content/article/2007/02/06/AR2007020601718.html.

[7] Amy Belasco, "The Cost of Iraq, Afghanistan and Other Global War on Terror Operations Since 9/11," *Congressional Research Service*, July 16, 2007, http://www.fas.org/sgp/crs/natsec/RL33110.pdf.

[8] *Ibid.*

[9] Farah Stockman, "US firms suspected of bilking Iraq funds," *Boston Globe*, April 16, 2006, http://www.boston.com/news/world/articles/2006/04/16/us_firms_suspected_of_bilking_iraq_funds/.

[10] "Millions wasted in Iraq reconstruction aid," *Associated Press*, January 31, 2007, http://www.msnbc.msn.com/id/16895294/.

[11] *Ibid.*

[12] *Ibid.*

[13] Philip Shenon, "As New 'Cop on the Beat,' Congressman Starts Patrol," *New York Times*, February 6, 2007, http://www.nytimes.com/2007/02/06/us/politics/06waxman.html?ex=1328418000&en=86728d83 dff30877&ei=5088&partner=rssnyt&emc=rss.

[14] Ron Nixon and Scott Shane, "Contractors Cozy Up to Feds in Explosion of Outsourcing," *New York Times*, February 7, 2007, http://www.envirosagainstwar.org/know/read.php?itemid=5195.

¹⁵ Ron Nixon and Scott Shane, "In Washington, Contractors Take on Biggest Role Ever," *New York Times*, February 4, 2007, http://www.nytimes.com/2007/02/04/washington/04contract.html?ei=5094&en=5a19d7cad91cd66d&hp=&ex=1170651600&adxnnl=1&partner=homepage&adxnnlx=1170641709-52slkvSLEzSSf3IgkI9Z6A.

¹⁶ *Ibid.*

¹⁷ Ronald Smothers, "It's Pork. It's a Pet Project. It's a Christmas Tree," *New York Times* March 5, 2007, http://www.nytimes.com/2007/03/05/nyregion/05xmas.html?n=Toppercent2FReferencepercent2FTimespercent20Topicspercent2FSubjectspercent2FLpercent2FLegislaturespercent20andpercent20Parliaments&pagewanted=print.

¹⁸ *2006 Congressional Pig Book*, Citizens Against Government Waste, http://www.cagw.org/site/PageServer?pagename=reports_pigbook2006.

¹⁹ *See* Martin L. Gross, *The Government Racket: Washington Waste From A to Z* (New York: Avon Books, 1992).

²⁰ Angelo Pesce, "Pork Barrel Spending 2006," *United Citizens of America*, http://www.ucanation.org/porkpercent20report.htm.

²¹ Martin L. Gross, *op. cit.*

²² *Ibid.*

²³ Chris Edwards, "Pork: A Microcosm of the Overspending Problem," *Cato Institute* (August 2005), http://www.cato.org/pubs/tbb/tbb-0508-24.pdf.

²⁴ Matt Taibbi, "Inside the Worst Congress Ever," http://www.rollingstone.com/politics/story/12055360/cover_story_time_to_go_inside_the_worst_congress_ever/print.

²⁵ Jeff Johnson, "Congressional Opponents Lash out at Patriot Act, Ashcroft," *CNS News*, September 25, 2003, http://www.cnsnews.com/ViewNation.asp?Page=percent5CNationpercent5Carchivepercent5C200309percent5CNAT20030925a.html.

²⁶ Peter David Orr, "Congressional Neglect Syndrome," http://peterdavidorr.blogspot.com/2007/05/cns-congressional-neglect-syndrome.html.

²⁷ *Ibid.*

[28] John W. Whitehead, "Should We Re-Elect a Do-Nothing Government?" *The Rutherford Institute,* October 30, 2006, http://www.rutherford.org/articles_db/commentary.asp?record_id=439.

[29] Taibbi, *op. cit.*

[30] Richard Morin, "A Do-Nothing Congress That's Done Too Much of the Wrong Thing," *Pew Research Center,* August 8, 2006, http://pewresearch.org/pubs/45/a-do-nothing-congress-thats-done-too-much-of-the-wrong-thing.

[31] "GOP Failure List: Pork Barrel Spending," *Fiscal Conservatives,* October 1, 2006, http://fiscalconservatives.org/content/blogsection/0/9/.

[32] John Cochran, "'Do-Nothing Congress' Raises Critics' Ire," *ABC News,* broadcast May 12, 2006 by ABC-TV, http://abcnews.go.com/Politics/story?id=1955256&page=1.

[33] *Ibid.*

[34] Neil Tickner, "Campaign Fundraising a Top Priority for New Members of Congress," http://www.newsdesk.umd.edu/archive/release.cfm?year=2000&ArticleID=266.

[35] Kelly Thornton and Onell R. Soto, "Feds Allege Web of Bribery, Debauchery," *Union Tribune,* February 14, 2007.

[36] "Duke Cunningham," *Wikipedia* (accessed on February 22, 2008), http://en.wikipedia.org/wiki/Duke_Cunningham#Scandals_and_corruption.

[37] "Jerry Lewis (politician)," http://en.wikipedia.org/wiki/Jerry_Lewis_(politician)#Controversies.

[38] "Ken Calvert," http://en.wikipedia.org/wiki/Ken_Calvert#Controversies.

[39] "The 22 most corrupt members of Congress (and two to watch)," *Beyond DeLay,* http://www.beyonddelay.org/files/Murthapercent20Profile.pdf.

[40] Jake Tapper, "Dem. Rep. Murtha Accused of Ethics Violation," *ABC News,* May 18, 2007, http://abcnews.go.com/Politics/Story?id=3187575&page=1.

[41] "William J. Jefferson," http://en.wikipedia.org/wiki/William_J._Jefferson#Federal_Indictment.

42 "Gary Miller," http://en.wikipedia.org/wiki/Gary_Miller#Controversies.

43 "Ted Stevens," http://en.wikipedia.org/wiki/Ted_Stevens#Ethical_issues_and_federal_investigations.

44 "Rick Renzi," http://en.wikipedia.org/wiki/Rick_Renzi#Controversies.

45 *See* "Executive Summary: Beyond Delay, The 22 Most Corrupt Members of Congress (and two to watch)," September 18, 2007, http://www.beyonddelay.org/report.

46 "Price Tag Politics," *Lexington Herald-Leader*, October 15, 2006, http://www.kentucky.com/233/story/11052.html.

47 http://en.wikipedia.org/wiki/Alan_Mollohan#Political_Controversies.

48 Howard Kurtz, "Writer Backing Bush Plan had Gotten Federal Contract," *Washington Post* (January 6, 2005).

49 "Greenspan book: GOP swapped principles for power," *CNN.com*, http://www.cnn.com/2007/POLITICS/09/16/greenspan.book/index.html.

50 Susan Milligan, "Back-room dealing a Capitol trend: GOP flexing its majority power," *Boston Globe*, October 3, 2004, http://www.boston.com/news/nation/articles/2004/10/03/back_room_dealing_a_capitol_trend/?page=1.

51 U.S. National Archives and Records Administration, "Signers of the Declaration of Independence,"http://www.archives.gov/national-archives-experience/charters/print_friendly.html?page=declaration_signers_factsheet_content.html&title=NARApercent20|percent20Thepercent20Declarationpercent20ofpercent20Independencepercent3Apercent20Signerspercent20Factsheet.

52 "America's Founding Fathers: Delegates to the Constitutional Convention," *National Archives Experience*, http://www.archives.gov/national-archives-experience/charters/constitution_founding_fathers_overview.html.

53 *Ibid.*

54 *Ibid.*

55 John Locke, *Two Treatises of Government*, edited by Peter Laslett, 3rd edition, 1698, (New York: Cambridge University Press, 1988).

[56] Carl Becker, *The Declaration of Independence: A Study in the History of Political Ideas* (New York: Harcourt, Brace and Co., 1922), p. 57.

[57] *Ibid.*

[58] *Ibid.*

[59] Jeremy Waldron, *The Right to Property* (New York: Oxford University Press, 1990), p. 137.

[60] Locke, *op. cit.*, at 287–88.

[61] Donald L. Doernberg, "'We the People': John Locke, Collective Constitutional Rights, and Standing to Challenge Government Action," 73 *California Law Review*, 52, 59 (1985).

[62] William Blackstone, *Commentaries on the Laws of England* (Callaghan and Co., 1899), p. 127.

[63] Danaya Wright, "Toward a Multi-Cultural Theory of Property Rights," 12 *Journal of Law and Public Policy*, 2, 4 (2000).

[64] Douglas M. Kmiec, "The Original Understanding of the Takings Clause Is Neither Weak Nor Obtuse," 88 *Columbia Law Review*, 1630, 1635 (1988).

[65] "Baron de Montesquieu, Charles-Louis de Secondat," *Standard Encyclopedia of Philosophy*, July 18, 2003, http://plato.stanford.edu/entries/montesquieu/.

[66] *Ibid.*

[67] *See* Paul Merrill Spurlin, *Montesquieu in America: 1760–1801*, vol. 10 (London: Octagon Books, 1969).

[68] Guadalupe T. Luna, "Liberalism and Property Rights," 12 *Journal of Law and Public Policy*, 33, 34 fn. 7 (2000).

[69] F. Forrester Church, *The Separation of Church and State: Writings on a Fundamental Freedom by America's Founders* (Boston: Beacon Press, 2004), p. 11.

[70] *Ibid.*

[71] *Vanhorne's Lessee v. Dorrance*, 2 U.S. 304, 310 (1795).

[72] Margaret Hage Gabbard, "Restoring America's Property Rights," December 21, 2002, http://www.citizenreviewonline.org/Dec_2002/restoring.htm.

[73] Margaret Byfield, "Wayne Hage/US Court of Federal Claims," May 3, 2004, http://www.treasure-signs.com/wayne.html.

74 *Hage v. United States*, USCC91-1470L (1991).

75 "Sagebrush Rebel: Rancher Hage Spoke for Many Westerners," *Colorado Springs Gazette*, June 8, 2006, http://findarticles.com/p/articles/mi_qn4191/is_20060608/ai_n16482822.

76 "Timeline: Hage v. United States, and United States v. Hage and Seaman," *Asheville Tribune*, September 27, 2007, http://www.ashevilletribune.com/archives/timeline.htm.

77 Michael Oberndorf, "Wayne Hage Is ... A Hero for the New West," *Property Rights Research*, March 1, 2003, http://www.propertyrightsresearch.org/wayne_hage_is.htm.

78 "An American Original: An Interview with Wayne Hage," *Liberty Matters Journal*, July 1998, http://www.stewardsoftherange.org/libertymatters/july98/lmj-july98-1.htm.

79 Oberndorf, *op. cit.*

80 Tom Findley, "David & Goliath: When Big Brother decided to hold Wayne Hage and his rights hostage, this articulate, tenacious, driven rancher decided to fight back—and he's winning," *Range Magazine*, September 27, 2007, http://www.rangemagazine.com/archives/stories/summer01/david_goliath.htm.

81 "Sagebrush Rebel," *op. cit.*

82 "Eminent Domain Without Limits?" *Institute for Justice Litigation Backgrounder*, July 2004, http://www.ij.org/private_property/connecticut/con_property_backgrounder.html.

83 Kirstin Downey, "Revitalization Projects Hinge on Eminent Domain Lawsuit," *Washington Post*, May 21, 2005, www.washingtonpost.com.

84 *Kelo v. City of New London*, 125 S.Ct. 2655, 2660 (2005).

85 *Ibid.*, p. 2677.

86 *Ibid.*, p. 2687.

87 Dana Berliner, *Eminent Domain: The Abuse of a Public Power for Private Benefit* (Washington DC: Institute for Justice, April 2003), p. 8. For a detailed report of each state's response, see the Institute for Justice's "Legislative Acts Since *Kelo*" report, available at http://www.castlecoalition.org/pdf/publications/State-Summary-Publication.pdf. *See Also* http://www.castlecoalition.org/legislation/index.html for current statistics and information;

and see the Institute for Justice's Castle Coalition website generally for current information on eminent domain throughout the United States at http://www.castlecoalition.org/.

[88] Dana Berliner, *Opening the Floodgates: Eminent Domain Abuse in the Post-Kelo World* (Washington DC: Institute for Justice), p. 2, http://www.castlecoalition.org/publications/floodgates/index.html. This report documents eminent domain actions or attempts after the *Kelo* decision in most states.

[89] *Ibid.*, p. 6.

[90] *Ibid.*

[91] *Ibid.*, p. 3.

[92] *Ibid.*

[93] "Portion of Eminent Domain Law Unconstitutional, Norwood Taking for Development Overturned," Supreme Court of Ohio, July 26, 2006, http://www.supremecourtofohio.gov/Communications_Office/summaries/2006/0726/050227.asp.

[94] *Ibid.*

[95] Kevin Kemper, "Homeowners win eminent domain fight in Norwood," *Columbus Business First*, July 26, 2006, http://columbus.bizjournals.com/columbus/stories/2006/07/24/daily27.html?jst=b_ln_hl.

[96] Scott Bullock, "A Long Road: Susette Kelo Lost Her Rights, But She Will Keep Her Home," *Liberty & Law* (Institute for Justice, August 2006), http://www.ij.org/publications/liberty/2006/15_4_06_a.html.

[97] *New Jersey Coalition Against the War in the Middle East v. J.M.B. Realty Corp.*, 138 N.J. 326 (1994), cert. denied sub nom *Short Hills Assocs. v. New Jersey Coalition Against the War in the Middle East*, 516 U.S. 812 (1995).

[98] *Robins v. Pruneyard Shopping Center*, 23 Cal. 3d 899 (1979), aff'd sub nom *Pruneyard v. Robins*, 447 U.S. 74 (1980).

[99] Accord *Golden Gateway Center v. Golden Gateway Tenants Assoc.*, 26 Cal. 4th 1013 (2001).

[100] *Bock v. Westminster Mall Co.*, 819 P.2d 55 (Colo. 1991).

[101] *Batchelder v. Allied Stores Int'l, Inc.*, 388 Mass. 83 (1983)

[102] Joel Bakan, *The Corporation: The Pathological Pursuit of Power* (New York: Free Press, 2004), p. 5.

103 *Ibid.*, p. 32.

104 *Ibid.*, p. 34.

105 *Santa Clara County v. Southern Pacific Railroad Co.*, 118 U.S. 394 (1886).

106 Rutherford Birchard Hayes. *Diary and Letters of Rutherford Birchard Hayes: Nineteenth President of the United States*, vol. 4 (Ohio State Archaeological and Historical Society, 1922), p. 374, http://www.ohiohistory.org/onlinedoc/hayes/chapterx1v.html.

107 Bakan, *op. cit.*, p. 8.

108 Sarah Anderson and John Cavanagh, "Top 200: The Rise of Corporate Global Power," Institute for Policy Studies, December 4, 2000. Key findings available at http://www.ips-dc.org/downloads/Top_200.pdf. These findings are based on a comparison of corporate sales and country GDPs.

109 *Ibid.*, p. 1.

Chapter Eight: Igniting the Spark for Justice and the Politics of Hope

1 Carmella B'Hahn, "Be the change you wish to see: An interview with Arun Gandhi," *Reclaiming Children and Youth* [Bloomington] vol. 10, no. 1 (Spring 2001), 6.

2 Jason Salzman, *Making the News: A Guide for Activists and Nonprofits* (New York: Perseus Books Group, 2003), p. 1.

3 *Ibid.*

4 *Ibid.*, p. 7.

5 *Ibid.*, p. 9.

6 *Ibid.*, p. 10.

7 *Ibid.*, p. 14.

8 *Ibid.*, p. 24.

9 *Ibid.*, p. 21.

10 *Ibid.*, p. 25.

11 Frederick Douglass, "If There Is No Struggle, There Is No Progress," 1857 speech, http://www.blackpast.org/?q=1857-frederick-douglass-if-there-no-struggle-there-no-progress.

12 Nat Hentoff, *Living the Bill of Rights: How to Be an Authentic American* (New York: HarperCollins, 1998), pp. 19–25.

[13] *Ibid.*, p. 21.

[14] *NAACP v. Alabama*, 357 U.S. 449 (1958).

[15] Nat Hentoff, *The War on the Bill of Rights and the Gathering Resistance* (New York: Seven Stories Press, 2004), p. 11.

[16] Judith Kohler, "Patriot Act prompting libraries to purge records," *Associated Press*, August 1, 2003, http://www.infoshop.org/alibrarians/public_html/article.php?story.

[17] "Libraries and Liberties," *PBS NewsHour with Jim Lehrer*, June 18, 2003, http://www.pbs.org/newshour/bb/law/jan-june03/library_6-18.html.

[18] Nikki Swartz, "U.S. cities, states fight PATRIOT Act," *Information Management Journal*, September 1, 2003), http://www.allbusiness.com/management/3603865-1.html.

[19] Eldridge Cleaver. *The Columbia World of Quotations*, 1996, http://www.bartleby.com/66/14/12614.html.

[20] "The American Freedom Campaign Agenda," *The American Freedom Campaign*, October 29, 2007, http://www.americanfreedomcampaign.org/index.php?option=com_content&task=view&id=13&Itemid=2.

[21] Naomi Wolf, "Sit Down for the Constitution," *Huffington Post*, October 25, 2007, http://www.huffingtonpost.com/naomi-wolf/sit-down-for-the-constitu_b_69800.html.

[22] *Ibid.*

[23] Naomi Wolf, "American Tears," *Huffington Post*, October 11, 2007, http://www.huffingtonpost.com/naomi-wolf/american-tears_b_68141.html.

[24] Susan Greene, "Women Take a Silent Stand Against Violence," *Denver Post*, September 2, 2003, http://www.commondreams.org/headlines03/0902-09.htm.

[25] *Ibid.*

[26] Anemona Hartocollis, "A Street Performer Crusades for the First Amendment," *New York Times*, September 26, 2007, http://www.nytimes.com/2007/09/26/nyregion/26billy.html?_r=1&oref=slogin.

[27] *Ibid.*

[28] Laura Hauser, "One man's mission to protect the Constitution," *News Review*, March 15, 2007, http://www.newsreview.com/ chico/Content?oid=295438.

[29] *Ibid.*

[30] Barbara Wiedner, "History and Vision," *Grandmothers for Peace*, http://www.grandmothersforpeace.org/info/.

[31] *Ibid.*

[32] *Ibid.*

[33] Joan Wile, "Revolt of the Grandmothers," September 13, 2006, http://www.michaelmoore.com/mustread/print. php?id=730.

[34] Trudy Whitman, "Go, Granny, Go!: Little old ladies from New York City fight to end the war in Iraq," http://www.nyc-plus.com/nyc17/gogrannygo.html.

[35] *Ibid.*

[36] Wiedner, *op. cit.*

[37] Joan Wile, "Why Grandma Went to Jail," *Common Dreams.org*, January 16, 2006, http://www.commondreams.org/views06/ 0116-28.htm.

[38] Ann Shirazi, "Grandmothers Go to Jail for Peace," http://www. grandmothersforpeace.org/directory/chapters/us-ny-new.york. city/times-square.html.

[39] Whitman, *op. cit.*

[40] *Ibid.*

[41] Wiedner, *op. cit.*

[42] Ellen Goodman, "Granny power takes on the Iraq War," *Boston Globe*, May 5, 2006, http://www.boston.com/news/globe/edito-rial_opinion/oped/articles/2006/05/05/granny_power_takes_on_t he_iraq_war/.

[43] *Ibid.*

[44] Bertram Gross, *Friendly Fascism: The New Face of Power in America* (Cambridge, MA: South End Press, 1980), p. 382.

[45] Neil Postman and Steve Powers, *How to Watch TV News* (New York: Penguin, 1992).

[46] *Ibid.*, p. 161.

[47] "Corporate Info: This Is NBC," http://www.nbc.com/nbc/header/ Corporate_Info.shtml.

48 "Top All-Time Donor Profiles," *Center for Responsive Politics*, http://www.opensecrets.org/orgs/list.asp?order=A.

49 "Walt Disney Co," *Center for Responsive Politics*, http://www.opensecrets.org/orgs/summary.asp?ID=D000000128.

50 "About CNN.com," http://www.cnn.com/about/.

51 Postman and Powers, *op. cit.*, p. 163.

52 *Ibid.*, p. 166.

53 James M. Washington, ed., *A Testament of Hope: The Essential Writings and Speeches of Martin Luther King, Jr.* (HarperSanFrancisco, 1991), pp. 290–98.

54 *Ibid.*

55 John W. Whitehead, "When Will They Ever Learn?: An Interview with Pete Seeger," *Oldspeak*, January 4, 2006, http://www.rutherford.org/oldspseak/articles/art/oldspeak-Seeger.html.

56 Paul Rogat Loeb, editor, *The Impossible Will Take A Little While: A Citizen's Guide to Hope in a Time of Fear* (New York: Basic Books, 2004), p. 60.

57 *Ibid.*

58 *Ibid.*, p. 61.

59 Marian Wright Edelman, "Standing Up for Children," in *The Impossible Will Take A Little While, op. cit.*, p. 42.

60 *Ibid.*

61 *Ibid.*, p. 43.

62 *Ibid.*, p. 7.

63 Mary-Wynne Ashford, "Staying the Course," in *The Impossible Will Take A Little While, ibid.*, p. 330.

64 Craig Kielburger, *Free the Children: A Young Man's Personal Crusade Against Child Labor* (New York: HarperCollins, 1998), p. 84.

65 Gross, *op. cit.*, p. 379.

66 *Ibid.*, p. 378.

67 *Edwards v. South Carolina*, 372 U.S. 229 (1963).

68 *Ibid.*, p. 235.

69 *Ibid.*, pp. 230–231.

70 *Ibid.*, p. 236.

71 *Ibid.*, p. 235.

72 Morris Berman, *Dark Ages America: The Final Phase of Empire* (New York: W.W. Norton and Co., 2006), p. 303.

73 George W. Bush, "President Discusses War on Terrorism, Address to the Nation," November 8, 2001, http://www.whitehouse.gov/news/releases/2001/11/.

74 *See* Chris Hedges, *American Fascists: The Christian Right and the War on America* (New York: Free Press, 2006).

75 Laurence W. Britt, "Fascism Anyone?" *Free Inquiry*, vol. 23, no. 2, http://www.secularhumanism.org/library/fi/britt_23_2.htm. *See Also* "Fourteen Defining Characteristics of Fascism," http://www.rense.com/general37/char.htm.

76 *Ibid.*

77 *Ibid.*

78 Naomi Wolf, *The End of America: A Letter of Warning to a Young Patriot* (White River Junction, VT: Chelsea Green, 2007), pp. 13–24.

79 Berman, *op. cit.*, p. 312.

80 Cal Thomas and Bob Beckel, *Common Ground: How to Stop the Partisan War that is Destroying America* (New York: William Morrow, 2007), pp. 205–06.

81 Theresa Vargas, "Va. Police Chief Apologizes for Raid of Homeless Camp," *Washington Post*, July 8, 2006, http://www.washingtonpost.com/wp-dyn/content/article/2006/07/07/AR2006070701470.html?nav=emailpage.

82 *Ibid.*

83 Stephanie McCrummen, "Anti-Crowding Law Repealed," *Washington Post*, January 12, 2006.

84 Arthur M. Schlesinger Jr., *The Cycles of American History* (New York: Houghton Mifflin, 1986), p. 48.

85 Ralph Waldo Emerson, *Nature: Addresses and Lectures* (Riverside Press, 1876), p. 229.

86 Thomas Paine, "The American Crisis," reprinted in *Our Nation's Archive: The History of the United States in Documents*, edited by Erik Bruun and Jay Crosby (New York: Black Dog & Leventhal, 1999), p. 135.

Chapter Nine: No Time for Sunshine Patriots

[1] Nina Baym, ed., *The Norton Anthology of American Literature*, 5th ed. (New York: W. W. Norton & Company, 1998), 1:620.

[2] *Ibid.*

[3] George Brown Tindall and David Emory Shi, *America: A Narrative History*, 5th ed. (New York: W. W. Norton & Company, 1999), 1:214.

[4] Nat Hentoff, *The War on the Bill of Rights—and the Gathering Resistance* (New York: Seven Stories Press, 2004), p. 15.

[5] Pauline Maier, *From Resistance to Revolution: Colonial Radicals and the Development of American Opposition to Britain* (New York: Alfred A. Knopf, 1972), p. 275.

[6] Tindall and Shi, *op. cit.*, p. 225.

[7] Ray Raphael, *A People's History of the American Revolution: How Common People Shaped the Fight for Independence,* New Press People's History series (New York: The New Press, 2001), p. 8.

[8] Erik Bruun and Jay Crosby, eds., *Our Nation's Archive: The History of the United States* (New York: Black Dog & Levanthal, 1999), p. 119.

[9] Tindall and Shi, *op. cit.*, p. 229.

[10] *Ibid.*, p. 230.

[11] Raphael, *op. cit.*, p. 3.

[12] Bruun and Crosby, *op. cit.*, p. 127.

[13] Tindall and Shi, *op. cit.*, pp. 247–48.

[14] *Ibid.*, p. 252.

[15] Bruun and Crosby, *op. cit.*, p. 132.

[16] Charles Royster, *A Revolutionary People at War: The Continental Army and American Character, 1775–1783* (Chapel Hill: University of North Carolina Press, 1979), p. 138.

[17] *Ibid.*, pp. 224–25.

[18] *Ibid.*, p. 31.

[19] Tindall and Shi, *op. cit.*, p. 282.

[20] *Ibid.*, p. 210.

[21] Maier, *op. cit.*, p. 74.

[22] *Ibid.*

23 Tindall and Shi, *op. cit.*, pp. 217–18.

24 Raphael, *op. cit.*, p. 3.

25 Maier, *op. cit.*, p. 274.

26 Raphael, *op. cit.*, p. 185.

27 Jack N. Rakove, *Founding America: Documents from the Revolution to the Bill of Rights* (New York: Barnes & Noble Classics, 2006), p. xi.

28 Tindall and Shi, *op. cit.*, p. 308.

29 Bruun and Crosby, *op. cit.*, p. 167.

30 *Ibid.*, pp. 311–12.

31 Christine Compston and Rachel Filene Seidman, eds., *Our Documents: 100 Milestone Documents from the National Archives* (New York: Oxford University Press, 2003), p. 44.

32 Leonard W. Levy, *Origins of the Bill of Rights* (New Haven: Yale University Press, 1999), p. 14.

33 Robert Harvey, *"A Few Bloody Noses": The Realities and Mythologies of the American Revolution* (New York: The Overlook Press, 2002), p. 454.

34 *Ibid.*

35 Tindall and Shi, *op. cit.*, p. 332.

36 Levy, *op. cit.*, p. 17.

37 Tindall and Shi, *op. cit.*, p. 332.

38 Levy, *op. cit.*, p. 22.

39 *Ibid.*, p. 26.

40 *Ibid.*

41 *Ibid.*, p. 33.

42 *Ibid.*, p. 30.

43 *Ibid.*, p. 33.

44 *Ibid.*

45 *Ibid.*, p. 35.

46 *Ibid.*

47 *Ibid.*, p. 12.

48 Leonard W. Levy, "Paradox Resolved," *Philadelphia Inquirer*, May 12, 1987, quoted in Joseph A. Melusky and Whitman H. Ridgway, comps., *The Bill of Rights: Our Written Legacy* (Nakabarm FL: Krieger Publishing Company, 1993), p. 2.

[49] Bernard Bailyn, *The Ideological Origins of the American Revolution* (Cambridge, MA: Harvard University Press, 1992), p. 119.

[50] Tindall and Shi, *op. cit.*, p. 223.

[51] Raphael, *op. cit.*, p. 2.

[52] Bailyn, *op. cit.*, p. 117.

[53] Levy, *Origins of the Bill of Rights*, *op. cit.*, p. 158.

[54] *Ibid.*, p. 157.

[55] Bailyn, *op. cit.*, p. 108.

[56] Levy, *op. cit.*, pp. 3–4.

[57] *Ibid.*, p. 151.

[58] Pauline Maier, *American Scripture: Making the Declaration of Independence* (New York: Alfred A. Knopf, 1997), pp. 51–53.

[59] Bernard Schwartz, *The Great Rights of Mankind: A History of the American Bill of Rights* (Lanham, MD: Madison House, 1992), p. 1.

[60] Antonin Scalia, *A Matter of Interpretation: Federal Courts and the Law*, University Center for Human Values series, Amy Gutmann, ed. (Princeton, NJ: Princeton University Press, 1997), p. 43.

[61] John F. Kennedy, *Profiles in Courage* (New York: HarperCollins, 2003), p. 224.

[62] H. W. Brands, *The First American: The Life and Times of Benjamin Franklin* (New York: Doubleday, 2000), p. 690.

[63] *Ibid.*, p. 691.

[64] Kennedy, *op. cit.*, p. 225.

Chapter Ten: The Great Rights of Mankind

[1] "Simpsons 'trump' First Amendment," *BBC News*, March 1, 2006, http://news.bbc.co.uk/2/hi/americas/4761294.stm.

[2] "Support for 1st Amendment Slipping," *CBS News* broadcast August 30, 2002 by CBS-TV, http://www.cbsnews.com/stories/2002/08/30/national/main520314.shtml.

[3] Joseph Farah, "The dumbing down continues," *World Net Daily*, December 16, 1999, http://www.wnd.com/news/article.asp?ARTICLE_ID=14874.

4 Allen Weinstein, "Bill of Rights Memories," *Prologue*, Winter 2005, Vol. 37, No. 4 (The National Archives), http://www.archives.gov/publications/prologue/2005/winter/weinstein.html.

5 "The First Amendment in Public Schools," *Freedom Forum*, March 1, 2001, http://www.freedomforum.org/templates/document.asp?documentID=13390.

6 *See* H. W. Brands, *op. cit.* Franklin, under the pseudonym Silence Dogood, considers Cato's Letter No. 15 of February 4, 1720 in the *New England Courant*.

7 Hugo. L. Black, *James Madison Lecture,* New York University Law School, 1960, http://www.criminology.fsu.edu/faculty/gertz/hugoblack.htm.

8 *Sons of Confederate Veterans, Inc. v. Commissioner of the Virginia Department of Motor Vehicles*, 305 F.3d 241, 42 (4th Cir. 2002) (Wilkinson, Chief Judge, concurring in the denial of rehearing en banc).

9 *New York Times v. Sullivan,* 376 U.S. 254, 270 (1964).

10 "Florida College Student Who Was Tasered, Arrested at John Kerry Campus Forum Is Released From Jail," September 18, 2007, http://www.foxnews.com/story/0,2933,297197,00.html.

11 "Feds pay $80,000 over anti-Bush T-shirts, contents of Presidential Advance Manual revealed," August 18, 2007, http://www.americablog.com/2007/08/feds-pay-80000-over-anti-bush-t-shirts.html.

12 Office of Presidential Advance. *Presidential Advance Manual*, October 2002, http://www.aclu.org/pdfs/freespeech/presidential_advance_manual.pdf.

13 Eric M. Weiss, "White House Protester Could Avoid Charges in Deal With Prosecutors," *Washington Post*, June 22, 2006, http://www.washingtonpost.com/wp-dyn/content/article/2006/06/21/AR2006062101640.html.

14 "Capitol Police drop charge against Sheehan, apologize," *Associated Press*, February 1, 2006, http://www.firstamendmentcenter.org/news.aspx?id=16404.

15 "Cajun Town Bans Saggy Pants in Bid to Cover Up 'Private Parts,'" *Associated Press*, June 13, 2007, http://www.foxnews.com/story/0,2933,281932,00.html.

16 Niko Koppel, "Are Your Jeans Sagging? Go Directly to Jail," *New York Times*, August 30, 2007, http://www.nytimes.com/2007/08/30/fashion/30baggy.html.

17 "Reporters who broke Balco story fight prison sentence," *Guardian*, January 11, 2007, http://sport.guardian.co.uk/americansports/story/0,,1987718,00.html.

18 Adam Liptak, "Gonzales Says Prosecutions of Journalists Are Possible," *New York Times*, Mary 22, 2006, http://www.nytimes.com/2006/05/22/washington/22gonzales.html.

19 *U.S. v. Emerson*, 270 F.3d 203, 260 (5th Cir. 2001).

20 Jonathan Elliot, *Debates in the Several State Conventions on the Adoption of the Federal Constitution, vol. 3*, Philadelphia (1836), p. 386. Passage recalls Patrick Henry's comments during the Virginia Convention on the ratification of the Constitution on June 14, 1788.

21 Richard Henry Lee, *Additional Letters from the Federal Farmer* [1788] at 169, http://www.madisonbrigade.com/rh_lee.htm.

22 Elliot, *op. cit.*, at 380 (citing George Mason's comments).

23 *Ibid.*, pp. 425–426.

24 "Right to Keep and Bear Arms," http://www.gmu.edu/departments/economics/wew/quotes/arms.html.

25 Tony Mauro, "Scholar's shift in thinking angers liberals," *USA Today*, August 27, 1999, www.tysknews.com/Depts/2nd_Amend/scholar_angers_liberals.htm.

26 Miguel A. Faria Jr., "2nd Amendment conveys individual rights," *Human Events*, February 4, 2000, http://findarticles.com/p/articles/mi_qa3827/is_200002/ai_n8891396.

27 *U.S. v. Verdugo-Urquidez*, 494 U.S. 259, 265 (1990).

28 Jeremy Scahill and Daniela Crespo, "Blackwater Mercenaries Deploy in New Orleans," September 10, 2005, http://www.truthout.org/docs_2005/091005A.shtml.

29 Henry Peter Brougham, *Historical Sketches of Statesmen Who Flourished in the Time of George III*, vol. 1 (1839), p. 52.

30 Akhil Reed Amar, *The Bill of Rights: Creation and Reconstruction* (New Haven: Yale University Press, 2000), p. 59.

31 "Colonial America: Writs of Assistance," http://www.u-s-history.com/pages/h1205.html.

[32] James Otis, *Against Writs of Assistance* (February 24, 1761), http://www.constitution.org/bor/otis_against_writs.htm.

[33] Thomas Jefferson to John Adams, 1796 *The Writings of Thomas Jefferson*, edited by Paul Leicester Ford, New York, 1892–99, 7:56, http://etext.lib.virginia.edu/jefferson/quotations/jeff0650.htm.

[34] *Semayne's Case*, 5 Co. Rep. 91a, 91b, 77 Eng. Rep. 194, 195 (K.B. 1603).

[35] 468 U.S. 897 (1984).

[36] *United States v. Calandra*, 414 U.S. 338, 343-45 (1974).

[37] Nat Hentoff, *The War on the Bill of Rights and the Gathering Resistance* (New York: Seven Stories Press, 2004), p. 44.

[38] *Hudson v. Michigan*, 547 U.S. 586 (2006).

[39] Section 215 of the USA PATRIOT Act, http://en.wikipedia.org/wiki/USA_PATRIOT_Act (accessed on February 22, 2008).

[40] "Access to 'Non-Content' Communications," Part B of "Surveillance Power: Expanding the Scope of the Government's Surveillance Power," *Civil Liberties Online*, http://www.law.duke.edu/publiclaw/civil/index.php?action=showtopic&topicid=4.

[41] http://www.aclu.org/safefree/nsaspying/31203res20070807.html.

[42] *See, for example*, "Judge rules two provisions of USA Patriot Act unconstitutional," *Seattle Times*, September 26, 2007, http://seattletimes.nwsource.com/html/localnews/2003905730_webpatact26.html; Dan Eggen, "Judge Invalidates Patriot Act Provisions," *Washington Post*, September 7, 2007, http://www.washingtonpost.com/wp-dyn/content/article/2007/09/06/AR2007090601438.html.

[43] John Jay, *A Hint to the Legislature of the State of New York* (1778), reprinted in Philip B. Kurland and Ralph Lerner, eds., *The Founder's Constitution* (Chicago: University of Chicago Press, 1987), 5:312.

[44] Andrew Leipold, *The Heritage Guide to the Constitution* (Washington, DC: The Heritage Foundation, 2005), p. 329.

[45] *Crist v. Bretz*, 437 U.S. 28, 47 (1977).

[46] Bryan A. Garner, *Black's Law Dictionary*, 2nd ed. (St. Paul, MN: Thomson West, 2001), p. 222.

[47] *McNabb v. United States*, 318 U.S. 332, 347 (1943).

[48] Joan Biskupic, "Seizing land for private use OK'd," *USA Today*, June 23, 2005, http://www.usatoday.com/news/washington/2005-06-23-scotus-property_x.htm.

[49] *Rasul v. Bush*, 542 U.S. 466 (2004).

[50] Thomas Jefferson to Thomas Paine, July 11, 1789, *Papers of Thomas Jefferson, Volume XV* (Princeton, NJ: Princeton University Press, 1958), p. 269.

[51] *Gideon v. Wainwright*, 372 U.S. 335 (1972); *Faretta v. California*, 422 U.S. 806 (1975). Despite the procedural safeguards of *Gideon*, the Court has consistently said that a defendant who is competent may choose to exercise his right of self-representation and reject an appointed attorney.

[52] "Many Defendants' Cases Kept Secret," *CBS News*, broadcast March 4, 2006, by CBS-TV, http://www.cbsnews.com/stories/2006/03/04/ap/national/mainD8G4SFRG1.shtml.

[53] Jonathan Turley, "Camps for Citizens: Ashcroft's Hellish Vision," August 14, 2002, http://www.truthout.org/docs_02/08.15B.ashcr.camps.htm.

[54] Peter Dale Scott, "Homeland Security Contracts for Vast New Detention Camps," *New America Media*, February 8, 2006, http://news.pacificnews.org/news/view_article.html?article_id=eed74d9d44c30493706fe03f4c9b3a77.

[55] Paul Joseph Watson, "Halliburton Detention Camp for Political Subversives," *PrisonPlanet.com*, February 1, 2006, http://www.prisonplanet.com/articles/february2006/010206detentioncamps.htm.

[56] Alexander Hamilton, *The Federalist* No. 83, *New York Independent Journal* (July 5, July 9, and July 12, 1788).

[57] Patrick Henry, Speech to the Second Virginia Revolutionary Convention meeting at St. John's Church, Richmond, VA (March 23, 1775), http://www.redhill.org/ph/speeches/liberty.htm.

[58] David F. Forte, *The Heritage Guide to the Constitution* (Washington DC: The Heritage Foundation, 2005), p. 364.

[59] *Harmelin v. Michigan*, 501 U.S. 957, 968 (1991).

[60] *Trop v. Dulles*, 356 U.S. 86, 101 (1958).

[61] 510 U.S. 1141, 1143 (1994).

[62] Death Penalty Information Center, "Methods of Execution," http://www.deathpenaltyinfo.org/article.php?scid=8&did=245.

[63] "Florida governor halts executions," *BBC News*, December 16, 2006, http://news.bbc.co.uk/1/hi/world/americas/6185007.stm.

[64] Linda Greenhouse, "Justices Uphold Lethal Injection in Kentucky Case," *New York Times*, April 17, 2008, http://www.nytimes.com/2008/04/17/washington/17scotus.html?scp=1&sq=baze+v.+rees&st=nyt.

[65] "Death Row Inmates by State," http://www.deathpenaltyinfo.org/article.php?scid=9&did=188#state.

[66] Henry Weinstein, "Judge calls CA lethal-injection procedure 'intolerable,'" *Los Angeles Times*, December 15, 2006, http://www.populistamerica.com/judge_calls_california_s_lethal_injection_procedure__intolerable_.

[67] United States General Accounting Office, Death Penalty Sentencing (February 1990).

[68] James Madison, *The Federalist* No. 46, *New York Packet* (January 29, 1788).

[69] James Madison, *The Federalist* No. 45, *New York Independent Journal* (January 26, 1788).

[70] *Brown v. Board of Education*, 347 U.S. 483 (1954).

[71] Alexander Hamilton, *The Federalist* No. 84 (May 28, 1788).

[72] Thomas Jefferson's Inaugural Address, March 4, 1801, Washington, D.C.

[73] *Brown v. Vasquez*, 952 F.2d 1164, 1166 (9th Cir. 1991), cert. denied, 112 S.Ct. 1778 (1992).

[74] 28 U.S.C. 2254(d)(1).

[75] Scott, *op. cit.*

[76] *Ibid.*

[77] Paul Joseph Watson, *op. cit.*

[78] National Security and Homeland Security Presidential Directive, http://www.whitehouse.gov/news/releases/2007/05/20070509-12.html.

[79] *Hamdi v. Rumsfeld*, 542 U.S. 507 (2004).

[80] 542 U.S. 466 (2004).

[81] 126 S. Ct. 622 (2006).

[82] Linda Greenhouse, "Justices to Answer Detainee Rights Qestion," *New York Times*, December 6, 2007, http://www.nytimes.com/ 2007/12/06/washington/06scotus.html?scp=5&sq=boumediene+v. +bush&st=nyt.

[83] 494 U.S. 259, 275 (1990).

[84] *Ibid.*, p. 265.

[85] *Plyler v. Doe*, 457 U.S. 202 (1982).

[86] 426 U.S. 67 (1976).

Index

About the Author

© Jen Fariello

Constitutional attorney John W. Whitehead's concern for the persecuted and oppressed led him, in 1982, to establish The Rutherford Institute, a nonprofit legal and educational organization whose international headquarters are located in Charlottesville, Virginia. Deeply committed to protecting the constitutional freedoms of every American and the integral human rights of all people, The Rutherford Institute has emerged as a prominent leader in the national dialogue on civil liberties and human rights and a formidable champion of the Constitution.

Whitehead's weekly newspaper commentaries, distributed to daily and weekly newspapers across the country and published on a regular basis, take the pulse of the nation, of what's happening and what's news. Whitehead's articles examining trends and issues have been printed in the *Los Angeles Times, New York Times, Washington Post, Washington Times*, and *USA Today*. Whitehead is also a regular contributor to *The Huffington Post*.

Born in 1946 in Tennessee, John W. Whitehead earned a Bachelor of Arts degree from the University of Arkansas in 1969 and a Juris Doctorate degree from the University of Arkansas School of Law in 1974. He served as an officer in the United States Army from 1969 to 1971. Whitehead and his wife Carol, who have five children and two grandchildren, live in Virginia.